The Heritage of American Catholicism

A TWENTY-EIGHT-VOLUME SERIES DOCUMENTING THE HISTORY
OF AMERICA'S LARGEST RELIGIOUS DENOMINATION

EDITED BY

Timothy Walch

ASSOCIATE EDITOR
U.S. Catholic Historian

A Garland Series

The American Catholic Religious Life

SELECTED HISTORICAL ESSAYS

EDITED WITH AN INTRODUCTION BY
JOSEPH M. WHITE

Garland Publishing, Inc.
New York & London
1988

LIBRARY OF CONGRESS CATALOGING-IN-PUBLICATION DATA

The American Catholic religious life : selected historical essays / edited with an introduction by Joseph M. White.
    p.   cm. — (The Heritage of American Catholicism)
    Includes bibliographies.
    ISBN 0-8240-4082-1 (alk. paper)
    1. Monasticism and religious orders—United States—History.   2. Catholic Church—United States—History.   I. White, Joseph Michael.   II. Series.
BX2505.A44 1988
271'.00973—dc19   88-28618

DESIGN BY MARY BETH BRENNAN

PRINTED ON ACID-FREE, 250-YEAR-LIFE PAPER.
MANUFACTURED IN THE UNITED STATES OF AMERICA

Contents

Acknowledgments

The editor and publisher are grateful to the following for permission to reproduce copyright material in this volume. Any further reproduction is prohibited without the permission of the copyright holder: American Studies Association for material in *Women in American Religion*; Harper & Row for material in *Women and Religion in America;* U. S. Catholic Historical Society for material in *U. S. Catholic Historian*; American Catholic Historical Society for material in their *Records; The Jurist* and the Catholic University of America for material in *The Jurist;* the Catholic University of America Press for material in the *Catholic Historical Review*; American Society of Church History for material in *Church History; Journal of American Ethnic History;* Archdiocese of Boston for material in *Catholic Boston;* University of Notre Dame Press for material in *Corporation Sole; Journal of Church and State.*

Introduction

Until recent decades church historians portrayed the American Catholic experience by writing institutional histories, usually of dioceses, religious orders, and other organizations, and biographies of leading figures, usually bishops. The activities of priests and sisters played a part in these histories, but a specific examination of their roles was not the aim of such studies. The recent trend in historical study has been directed to social history, especially to topics that portray the lives of ordinary people. American Catholic history has followed this trend as scholars produced studies of popular piety, ethnic groups, and education. Since the 1970s, new attention has been directed specifically to priests and sisters, that is, the middle level of Catholic life between the bishops and prominent leaders portrayed in the traditional historiography and the Catholic people addressed more recently. The historians in the present anthology have opened new area of study into the experiences, changing roles, and collective lives of priests and women religious. A limited selection of essays inevitably leaves some issues unexplored, so that a brief historical overview of religious personnel in American Catholic history is a useful introduction to the articles that follow.

From its beginning, the Catholic community in colonial America enjoyed the services of priests. In 1634, the English Catholic founders of Maryland brought priests of the Society of Jesus to what became the United States. These English Jesuits served Catholic settlements that developed in Maryland and Pennsylvania in the seventeenth and eighteenth centuries. After Pope Clement XIV dissolved their religious order in 1773, the former Jesuits (though still priests) continued to minister to the Catholics in the colonies. They formed the nucleus of the diocesan clergy when the diocese of Baltimore was formed in 1789, and one of their number, John Carroll, was appointed the first Catholic bishop in the United States. With his permission, priests of the Society of St. Sulpice, a loosely constituted society of diocesan priests founded in France, came to Baltimore from Paris in 1791 to train diocesan priests. They established what became known as St. Mary's Seminary. The founding of the first diocese and seminary provided the starting point for developing a diocesan clergy. Religious orders of priests also began to make formal establishments by the early nineteenth century. The Dominicans, that is, the Order of Friars Preachers, established an American province in 1805. The Jesuits were reestablished in 1815 and soon engaged in their traditional work in education. Thereafter, members of other male orders came from Europe to take up their orders' particular activity and also to engage in pastoral ministry in a missionary church that depended on foreign-born clergy through most of the nineteenth century.

Through the colonial era Catholics did not experience the services or even the presence of women religious. Carmelite nuns from Belgium established the first convent of women religious in the United States at Port Tobacco, Maryland in 1790. The Carmelites were nuns, that is, they took solemn vows, led a contemplative life of prayer and penance, and remained secluded from the world in their cloister. Following the Carmelites, communities, congregations, and orders of what are variously called sisters, nuns, or women religious began to establish themselves in the early nineteenth century. Each of these terms has a specific canonical meaning but in common parlance they are used interchangeably. Unlike the Carmelite nuns, most communities of women religious are described as "active," that is, they engage in service work such as teaching, orphan care, or nursing. The members of active communities of women religious take simple vows and not the solemn vows that require a rigid adherence to cloister and the obligation of daily recitation of the canonical hours of the Divine Office.

Several active communities of women religious had their original foundation in the United States. The most noted indigenous founder was the convert and widow, Elizabeth Bayley Seton, who established her Sisters of Charity of St. Joseph at Emmitsburg, Maryland in 1809. Other significant communities of American origin arose among the English-stock Catholics of central Kentucky, where three groups were formed: the Sisters of Loretto at the Foot of the Cross in 1812, the Sisters of Charity of Nazareth in 1812, and the Dominican Sisters of St. Catharine in 1822. The Oblate Sisters of Providence, composed of black women, were formed in Baltimore in 1829. As in the cases of individual diocesan priests or of men's religious orders, many orders of sisters from Europe successfully established themselves. For instance, the Sisters of Mercy from Ireland, female branches of the Benedictine, Franciscan, and Dominican orders from German-speaking Europe, branches of Sisters of Notre Dame from Belgium and Bavaria, and Sisters of St. Joseph from France came to the United States to carry on work in education and nursing. The women's orders, whether indigenous or European in origin, are too numerous to mention by name, but by the 1970s some 450 were present in the United States.

For coming to terms with women religious, Elizabeth Kolmer's article discusses their historiography, consisting of histories of individual orders and biographies of founders. She identifies themes for further historical study and prospects of relating women religious to women's historiography. She commends a broad study of the history of women religious, such as Mary Ewens's work on the general status of women religious in the nineteenth century.[1] This synthetic method is an important shift from the fragmented approach of studying histories of individual orders. This development is manifested in Barbara Misner's recent volume on the membership of the first eight permanent orders of women religious in the United States up to 1850.[2] For the present anthology, Ewens brings to life the common problems of women religious in a selection of first-person accounts in which nuns of several orders describe the challenges of nineteenth-century travel and settlement, trials of school teaching, struggles with bishops, conflicts with Protestants, and the favorable regard for Catholicism won because of nursing activities during the Civil War.

Among the following articles, Margaret S. Thompson offers an overview of her projected general history of nuns in the United States to 1918. Her article outlines the main issues of the study: the responses of the varied traditions of women's religious communities to an egalitarian, pluralistic, and mobile culture; the effects of the sisters' works of teaching and nursing in producing religious tolerance for Catholics; and the opportunities that religious communities provided for women to take responsibility for the operation of schools, colleges, hospitals, and asylums. In a separate essay, Thompson takes up the history of the founding of the three black women's orders, the presence of blacks in the early history of several other women's communities, and the experiences of several religious communities engaged in serving blacks.

The study of individual women's communities continues to flourish. The possibilities of one religious order providing a case study for formerly ignored issues is demonstrated in Patricia Byrne's article on the Sisters of St. Joseph. Byrne examines the adaptations that Europeans had to make in the effort to "Americanize." With origins in seventeenth-century France, the Sisters of St. Joseph were traditionally tied to the work of the local church and had a highly decentralized governing structure. These traditions found a number of adaptations in the United States, where Americanization of membership occurred rapidly. The tradition of local development of individual convents was practiced to the extent that many branches of the Sisters of St. Joseph were formed throughout the country. Subject to local bishops, a local centralization developed. Another tradition usually practiced by European sisterhoods was the two-tiered classification of sisters, choir and lay. The choir sisters came from educated and well-to-do backgrounds, did essentially white collar works, followed a more formal schedule of prayers, and participated in governing the community. The lay sisters came from humble backgrounds, were poorly educated, did house and garden work, and did not hold office in their communities. The choir and lay sisters wore garb that differed slightly in color or detail. Byrne finds that the American context did not permit European notions of class to flourish among the Sisters of St. Joseph. The European communities established in the United States had to recruit new members from a Catholic population that did not have middle and upper classes. Among the communities that had them, the double class of sisters soon disappeared.

An assumption running through a number of studies is the importance of relating the study of Catholic sisters to the larger issues in women's historiography. Such an expectation at first seems unrealistic as non-Catholic women did not live in communities as Catholic sisters did. Despite the differences of creed and culture separating American Protestant women from Catholic women religious, of whom many were Europeans, there are common historical themes that can be developed. Joseph Mannard's article on nuns and domesticity points out an area in which the values of Protestant women and Catholic women religious were virtually the same. Comparing social values thereby provides a useful basis for further historical study of the two groups.

The historical study of priests during the antebellum period has not flourished to the same degree as studies of women religious. Priests pose several problems for historical study. Unlike sisters living in communities whose histories can be traced through well-kept institutional records, at least a majority of priests belonged to dioceses where the practice of keeping personnel records had yet to develop during the nineteenth century. Though subject to the supervision of bishops, diocesan priests had a certain degree of personal autonomy and did not live in communities of priests that kept records. Given the demands of active ministry, the priest was unlikely to have a collection of personal papers, and, if he had papers, they were unlikely to survive. Religious orders of men have a historiography consisting of institutional histories and biographies that is similar to women's orders, but studying men's orders, with few exceptions, has not developed in recent years. Unlike the men's communities, the study of women religious has been stirred by a general reconsideration of women's roles in churches and in society.

In the absence of general studies of clergy, the development of a local diocesan clergy can be found in some recent histories of dioceses. To develop a diocesan clergy, bishops adopted several methods in the early nineteenth century. Many dioceses attempted to sustain a local diocesan seminary. These efforts met with limited success, and many seminaries were short-lived, as candidates for the priesthood from the sons of first-generation Catholic immigrants were few. Since few priests in the antebellum era were born, trained, and ordained in the United States, bishops depended on recruiting priests and seminarians from Europe to fill the ranks of the clergy through the era of large-scale Catholic immigration. The antebellum Catholic church was thereby served by a diverse clergy coming from various countries where standards of training varied. European priests migrated for various reasons. Many were highly idealistic and hard-working missionaries; others sought better career opportunities than were available in their native countries; while a few were misfits escaping the demands of European church life. For whatever motivation, many priests moved from diocese to diocese in the quest for suitable positions.

Nineteenth-century bishops faced the challenge of coping with this diverse and rather mobile clergy of uneven quality in the missionary conditions of the time. Robert Trisco's seminal study of the relations of bishops and priests examines the many issues dividing them.[3] Bishops were unwilling to allow the full implementation of canon law pertaining to the rights of priests. For instance, American dioceses did not have cathedral chapters consisting of canons or senior clergy who enjoyed specified rights in diocesan government. There were no parishes in a strict canonical sense with pastors having defined rights such as immovability. Instead, Catholic churches were "missions" to which the local bishop appointed and removed priests at will. This unchecked and seemingly arbitrary power of bishops in the local church did not go unchallenged. A movement for priests' rights was taking shape by the 1860s to defend clergy against bishops' frequent changes of appointment and suspension from clerical faculties. The frequent appeals of aggrieved priests to Roman officials, who often decided in favor of priests, brought the problem to the attention of the highest church officials. To deal with these and other issues facing the American Catholic community, the American bishops convened in their Third Plenary Council of Baltimore in 1884. Though bishops continued to resist pressures from Roman officials for the establishment of cathedral chapters, they agreed to the establishment of diocesan boards of consultors consisting of four to six diocesan priests, half chosen by the priests and half by the bishop. The bishop was bound to consult them in specific areas such as formation of new parishes, appointment of certain diocesan officials, and administration of church property. Consultors also had the right to nominate candidates for the episcopacy.

At their 1884 council, the bishops also attempted to place on a regular footing their troubled relations with religious orders of men and women. Gerald Fogarty explores these issues in an essay on the suppressed decrees relating to religious orders. These problems arose because women's communities often held title to the property of academies, orphanages, and hospitals that they operated from funds raised among Catholics. Likewise, orders of men owned colleges and other institutions, but they also staffed parishes which brought them into close contact with the local bishop's jurisdiction. Questions arose about the rights of the local bishop and Catholics in dealing with orders that held title to religious institutions they developed from funds raised among local Catholics. Bishops and orders had occasional conflicts if the latter attempted to divert property to other uses or sell their property and leave the area.

The tense relationship between priests and bishops during the late nineteenth century provides the context for Robert Emmett Curran's article on a circle of prominent New York priests who formed an *Accademia* that met regularly for intellectual exchange. The demands of parish ministry for diocesan clergy ordinarily did not allow leisure for scholarship, so that such activities were indeed rare for the time. Moreover, the progressive views of *Accademia* members on theological issues and on current social questions set them apart from other clergy and bishops of the time. In another article Curran takes up the case of one *Accademia* member, Edward McGlynn, the most controversial priest of the 1880s. McGlynn's involvement in social reform, partisan politics, Irish nationalism, and opposition to parochial schools brought him into conflict with New York Archbishop Michael A. Corrigan. The range of McGlynn's activities and the intricate case of his suspension from priestly faculties and eventual reinstatement provide a complex story of the outstanding church issues of the time.

In the late nineteenth century the composition of diocesan clergy began to show the effects of generational change. By the end of the century, a full generation had elapsed since the large-scale Catholic immigration at the middle of the century. Large urban Catholic communities with a network of Catholic institutions flourished in major cities of the Northeast and Middle West. Young men who had grown up in these Catholic cultures began to enroll in substantial numbers in new and expanding diocesan seminaries, thereby providing for the "Americanization" of the clergy. James Hitchcock's article on diocesan priests in the archdiocese of St. Louis shows that a stable, native clergy begins to develop after the Civil War, so that local natives form a large bloc of clergy by the end of the nineteenth century. Daniel O'Neill finds a similar pattern in his article on diocesan clergy in the archdiocese of St. Paul. O'Neill extends his study to 1918 to determine the results of Archbishop John Ireland's policies of developing an

American clergy by means of his model seminary system.

In contrast to the rise of an American-born clergy among a population of Catholic immigrants, Stephen Ochs explores the problem of providing priests for the black community as seen through the career of John Henry Dorsey, a black priest and member of the Society of St. Joseph. His society was devoted to ministry among American blacks, yet its leaders were ambivalent about and then opposed to ordaining black men to the priesthood. Dorsey's unfortunate career reveals the ordeal of the black priest even in dealing with white clergy dedicated to Catholic activities for blacks.

The end of the nineteenth century saw the strengthening of Catholic education as the Third Plenary Council of Baltimore decreed the establishment of a national graduate institution, the Catholic University of America, which opened at Washington in 1889 for priests only in its early years. The council sought to improve theological seminaries by decreeing an expanded course of studies. Finally the bishops mandated that each Catholic parish in the country support an elementary school. Realistically, all Catholic parishes were not capable of sustaining a school. However, the decree established the standard of relating church to school and gave impetus to the expansion of the network of parochial schools. The decree had the effect of increasing the demand on the services of women religious as school teachers. As in the case of the clergy, women's communities began to have more American-born members as a full generation had elapsed since the large scale immigration of Catholics at the middle of the century.

Another organizational change was taking place in the Catholic world through the late nineteenth and early twentieth centuries as the status of women's communities was gradually altered. In the past, sisters were tied closely to the supervision of the bishops in many dioceses. The trend toward increasing Roman regulation brought sisters closer to the central authority of the church as communities of women religious obtained constitutions approved by the Holy See. This shift from the status of a so-called diocesan community to one under pontifical jurisdiction gave women's communities a greater independence from the local bishop's control, even if it increased dependence on the Holy See. The relationship of women's communities with local bishops, especially in staffing the growing number of schools and other institutions, became more complex with defined rights on both sides.

Mary J. Oates takes up the issues facing sisters within the changing religious and social environment of Boston between 1870 and 1940. From a Catholic community with a handful of sisters and few schools at the beginning of the period, local church authority began the rapid development of parochial schools early in the century. The growing number of women religious, the larger number of religious communities invited to come into Boston, and the communities' rights and compensation versus the expectations of centralized policies of Catholic school administration constitute the major issues. The archbishop of Boston, Cardinal William H. O'Connell, exerted strong central authority, but had to come to terms with the capabilities and rights of sisters.

Edward Kantowicz offers a similar story for Chicago in the 1920s and 1930s. The centralizing policies of the archbishop of Chicago, Cardinal George Mundelein, in the areas of education had to come to terms with the rights and interests of women's religious communities as they understood them. The particular reference to the cardinal's plans for developing a network of Catholic women's colleges owned by communities of sisters provides an insight into the limits of episcopal authority.

The position of the clergy in the archdiocese of Boston is the subject of Robert E. Sullivan's wide-ranging essay on a social history of Boston priests from the late nineteenth century until the death of Cardinal O'Connell in 1944. A major aspect of his article pertains to the issues related to the rapid increase of priests from the late nineteenth century onward. The number of priests at times grew at a faster rate than the Catholic population, so that admissions policies of the local seminary required periodic adjustments. The relations of the archbishop with his priests reflect some of the ironies of the exercise of episcopal authority for a period once thought to have been marked by an uncritical deference to ecclesiastical superiors.

Through the twentieth century a heightened interest in public affairs was evident among Catholics. This interest was manifested in several ways, such as programs of social reform that the prominent priest John A. Ryan advocated or the very different personalist philosophy of Dorothy Day and the Catholic Worker movement. In the era after World War II, many Catholics associated themselves with the vigorous anti-communism of the time. The Jesuits, who published the opinion journal, *America*, were drawn into a public controversy among Catholics because its Jesuit editor Robert Harnett opposed the tactics of Senator Joseph R. McCarthy in his crusading against domestic communism. Donald Crosby's article on Catholics' and Jesuits' reactions to the stance of *America* reveals a pluralism of Catholic positions on the issue. Another instance of a prominent Jesuit involved in controversial public issues is treated in Vincent Lapomarda's article on the election of the Jesuit Robert Drinan to the United States House of Representatives from Massachusetts in 1970. Drinan's status as a priest provided additional controversy to his position on the Vietnam war. The cases of McGlynn in the late nineteenth century and of Harnett and Drinan in the twentieth century suggest the possibilities for studying priests in public affairs.

The foregoing articles point to some historiographical directions for the study of priests and sisters. Studies of women religious hold promise for future development. Many such works are in progress as women's history commands great interest. Some beginnings have been made in studying the collective experience of diocesan priests despite the problems of pursuing research. However, recent debates about broadening professional ministry in the Catholic community have not stimulated an interest in recovering the history of the male, celibate clergy. Expanding the role of the laity in church life is the current concern that tends to reinforce interest in the religious behavior of ordinary Catholics. Though several articles deal with prominent Jesuits and the relations of bishops with religious orders, including those of men, articles on the collective lives of ordinary priests belonging to religious orders are unavailable for the anthology. Another area in which articles are unavailable and little work is underway is the history of communities of unordained religious men, that is, orders of brothers. Though not as numerous as the women religious, several substantial communities of brothers were engaged in the highly visible work of secondary and higher education. These groups experienced some of the challenges of sisters' communities in dealing with bishops and clergy. The brothers' historical experiences might shed more light on the degree to which sexism was a factor in the sisters' dealings with church authority. Most religious orders of priests also had unordained brothers who normally performed service functions. The issues surrounding their roles in relation to priests have not been examined historically. The promise of future study of women religious and the many lacunae in the study of male church professionals point to the obvious fact that the following articles are a good beginning to an aspect of Catholic life that deserves further study.

Joseph M. White

NOTES

1. Mary Ewens, *The Role of the Nun in Nineteenth Century America* (Salem, New Hampshire: Ayer Company, 1971).

2. Barbara Misner, *"Highly Respectable and Accomplished Ladies:" Catholic Women Religious in America, 1790–1850* (New York: Garland Publishing, Inc., 1988).

3. Robert F. Trisco, *Bishops and Their Priests in the United States, 1789–1918* (New York: Garland Publishing, Inc., 1988).

Sr. Elizabeth Kolmer, A.S.C.

Catholic Women Religious and Women's History

A Survey of the Literature

*A*lthough Catholic sisters have been active on the American scene since the eighteenth century, the story of their life and work remains largely untold. In particular, we know little of their history in relation to that of women in general or to the cycles of feminist thinking and action. On first thought, one might suspect that few such connections existed. Catholic sisters of the nineteenth and much of the twentieth centuries lived in relative seclusion from society at large, their lives centering in the institutions they staffed and managed. In addition, the women's movement until recent times was almost exclusively Protestant and middle-class. Nevertheless significant opportunities exist for serious researchers in this untouched area of social history.

This essay will evaluate the existing literature on the history of Catholic nuns, identify bibliographical aids, and indicate the archival and other sources available for investigation of the history of women religious. First I will survey scholarly works on American religious history in general, histories of individual congregations and biographies of their foundresses, and unpublished dissertations on the role of sisters. Second, I will comment on materials available for the study of the relationship of Catholic sisters and their congregations to the women's movement of the 1960s and 1970s. In conclusion I will offer some recommendations for future study.

*G*eneral histories of religion in America say little if anything about Catholic sisters or sisterhoods. Sydney Ahlstrom's wide-ranging *Religious*

History of the American People mentions the work of women's orders and their contributions to Catholic education in America, citing very briefly the Ursulines, the Carmelites, and Elizabeth Seton and her Sisters of Charity. In the second edition of his *Religion in America*, Winthrop Hudson also mentions Seton and gives passing recognition to the "sacrificial devotion of the members of numerous sisterhoods" who became the backbone of parochial education in America. Otherwise Hudson gives space only to radical stances taken by some religious organizations of women in the 1960s vis-à-vis the authority of the Church.[1]

Lack of space might account for the brevity of coverage in the general religious histories, but publications centering on the Catholic Church in the United States similarly neglect women religious. John Gilmary Shea, the classic early historian of the American Church, touched upon the sisters in each of his four volumes, but mostly in passing reference to their work in the schools and other Catholic institutions. More recently, Thomas T. McAvoy wrote a *History of the Catholic Church in the United States* almost without mentioning the sisters, let alone their work in such an important Church institution as the parochial school. John Tracy Ellis in his short *American Catholicism* also gives them very little attention. While Theodore Roemer discusses the sisters' place in the history of the Church, his interpretation is limited and the book has other weaknesses.[2] Where these and others do discuss women, they treat the sisters by individual orders and in descriptive terms emphasizing their works. Only when recounting their service as nurses in the Civil War do these authors consider women in orders as a single sociohistorical group.

The researcher will find two bibliographies more helpful: Ellis' *Guide to American Catholic History* and Edward R. Vollmar's *The Catholic Church in America*.[3] Ellis' noteworthy second chapter describes manuscript repositories and his sixth chapter discusses some of the histories of the foundation of women's communities. Critics generally consider the Vollmar work (1956) the most complete bibliography on the Catholic Church in the United States; the second edition includes unpublished

[1] Sidney E. Ahlstrom, *A Religious History of the American People* (New Haven: Yale Univ. Press, 1972), chap. 32. Winthrop S. Hudson, *Religion in America*, 2d ed. (New York: Scribner's, 1973), 249–50, 420–21.

[2] John Gilmary Shea, *History of the Catholic Church in the United States* (New York: John G. Shea, 1886–1892). Thomas T. McAvoy, C.S.C., *A History of the Catholic Church in the United States* (Notre Dame: Univ. of Notre Dame Press, 1969). John Tracy Ellis, *American Catholicism* (Chicago: Univ. of Chicago Press, 1956). Theodore Roemer, O.F.M. Cap., *The Catholic Church in the United States* (St. Louis: B. Herder, 1950), 156, 192ff, 216ff, 235ff, 253, 258, 284, 339, 354.

[3] John Tracy Ellis, *Guide to American Catholic History* (Milwaukee: Bruce, 1959). Edward R. Vollmar, S.J., *The Catholic Church in America: An Historical Bibliography*, 2d ed. (New York: Scarecrow, 1963).

masters' theses and doctoral dissertations written at Catholic colleges and universities. Vollmar's entries are alphabetical, but the book contains an excellent topical index, as well as a 40-page historiographical essay. "A Selected Bibliography of the Religious Orders and Congregations of Women," by Joseph B. Code, published in the *Catholic Historical Review* (1937), lists the source material then available on orders of religious women founded in the United States before 1850. Though limited in its usefulness today, the article represents an early effort to assist in the study of religious women and their work.[4]

Most of the periodical literature published on the history of women religious has appeared in the Catholic press. One can readily locate these articles through the *Catholic Periodical Index.* Their concern has been either with the sisters' devotional lives or with the history of women's orders or provinces within the larger congregations. Essays in the scholarly journals, the *Catholic Historical Review,* published by the American Catholic Historical Association, and the *Records of the American Catholic Historical Society of Philadelphia* have the same limitations as the longer historical studies: they have not considered nuns from the viewpoint of their common identity or their relationship with other groups of women.

A large number of the some 450 orders of American sisters listed in the *Official Catholic Directory* for 1976 have provided a biography of their foundress or a history of their congregation. Many of these works have been privately printed, and are available primarily to members of the particular congregation or can be found in libraries of Catholic institutions. In quality they run the gamut from scholarly studies to popular episodic sketches. Most have drawn upon letters and papers relating to the congregation, but these are often used to poor advantage, either because of the writer's deficiencies or because of gaps in the congregation's archives. Often the book will not even list these sources.[5]

A few selected titles will suffice as a sample. Excellent both in scholarship and style is *The Society of the Sacred Heart in North America* by Louise Callan (1937). *With Lamps Burning* by Mary Grace McDonald

3

[4] Joseph B. Code, "A Selected Bibliography of the Religious Orders and Congregations of Women Founded Within the Present Boundaries of the United States (1727–1850)," *The Catholic Historical Review,* 23 (Oct. 1937), 331–51. An extended form of this bibliography is found in *CHR,* 26 (July 1940), 222–45.

[5] Titles of many of these works can be found in Vollmar's bibliography and Ewens' dissertation noted below. Ewens estimates that 45 percent of the books she examined (59 titles) were of scholarly value, with generous use of primary sources and good documentation; another 8 percent (11 titles) were diaries, letters, or journals; 20 percent (26 titles) used primary sources, but without documentation; and 27 percent made no use of scholarly technique.

(1957), a history of the Benedictines in Minnesota, and *Not With Silver or Gold* (1945), an account by the Dayton Precious Blood Sisters of their foundation in Ohio, are also works of distinction. In *We Came North* (1961), Julia Gilmore draws upon congregation archives, local newspapers, and personal interviews to recount the history of the Sisters of Charity of Leavenworth, Kansas.[6] Veronica McEntee's *The Sisters of Mercy of Harrisburg, 1869–1939*, gives evidence that there are ample resources in the houses of the Mercy Sisters, though the book is undocumented, as is *Mother Caroline and the School Sisters of Notre Dame in North America*. Other histories are written in a more popular style, among them Covelle Newcomb's *Running Waters* and *Builders by the Sea* by S. M. Johnston. One final example is Angela Hurley's *On Good Ground*, semipopular in style and written primarily from secondary works and newspaper sources.[7]

Biographies of such outstanding women as Elizabeth Seton and Philippine Duchesne are readily available. In addition, the pages of the histories mentioned above are full of other strong, fearless women who faced great odds and dangers in founding their convents and institutions. Poverty, the threat of starvation, overdemanding bishops, and hostile neighbors were some of their trials. Among the many "nameless" women in our pioneer history we should not forget the sisters who built not only schools but hospitals, foundling homes, and shelters for the sick and poor which served as the chief charitable resources of many nineteenth-century American communities.

Did the nineteenth- or early twentieth-century nun identify with the problems of women outside the cloister, or with secular women's movements of the time? Perhaps not. Her sequestered existence would make this unlikely, and in any case many congregations of that time were still in the building phase, struggling to establish themselves. In this effort they seem to have worked alone. We do not know if they recognized a need for bettering the position of women in society whether inside or outside convent walls; certainly there is little evidence that they looked to an or-

---

[6] Louise Callan, R.S.C.J., *The Society of the Sacred Heart in North America* (New York: Longmans, Green, 1937); Mary Grace McDonald, O.S.B., *With Lamps Burning* (St. Joseph, Minn.: St. Benedict's Priory Press, 1957); Dayton Precious Blood Sisters, *Not with Silver or Gold* (Dayton: Sisters of the Precious Blood, 1945); Julia Gilmore, S.C.L., *We Came North* (St. Meinrad: Abbey Press, 1961).

[7] Mary Veronica McEntee, R.S.M., *The Sisters of Mercy of Harrisburg, 1869–1939* (Philadelphia: Dolphin Press, 1939); School Sisters of Notre Dame, *Mother Caroline and the School Sisters of Notre Dame in North America* (St. Louis: Woodward and Tiernan, 1928), 2 vols.; Covelle Newcomb, *Running Waters* (New York: Dodd, Mead, 1947); S. M. Johnston, *Builders By the Sea: History of the Ursuline Sisters of Galveston, Texas* (New York: Exposition, 1971); Angela Hurley, *On Good Ground: History of the Sisters of St. Joseph* (Minneapolis: Univ. of Minnesota Press, 1951).

ganized women's movement for inspiration or aid in dealing with their own problems. If they refused to accept a bishop's categorization of them as weak, inexperienced, and ineffective, they worked, so far as we know, on a practical level as individuals or individual congregations to prove him wrong, rather than looking for intellectual or moral support in the broader society. It would be an interesting undertaking to determine whether a feeling of solidarity existed among the sisters earlier than the mid-twentieth century with contemporary secular women and, if so, with which classes of women they identified.

The availability of source material on this topic is an important consideration. The headquarters of most congregations have some archival material, but little of it has been catalogued. Furthermore, there has been no guide indicating how much and what kind of material is to be found in any given religious house such as that to the Canadian religious archives published by the Canadian Religious Conference, or Abbé Charles Molette's guide to religious women's archives in France.[8] Some of these needs, however, are soon to be met.

The Leadership Conference of Women Religious has initiated a program to promote the preservation and organization of the records of sisterhoods in the United States. As a first step, the Conference in 1977 and 1978 held six workshops in basic archival training for designated members of religious orders. Directed by Evangeline Thomas, C.S.J., the workshops were funded by the National Historical Publications and Records Commission. The Conference has now embarked upon a survey of some 650 convent archives in the United States, under a grant from the National Endowment for the Humanities. They expect to complete the survey by late 1980, and publish a *Guide to Source Materials in Repositories of Women Religious in the United States.* The *Guide* is designed as a research tool for scholars not only in women's history but also in related fields in the humanities and social sciences.

Meanwhile, a researcher would have to contact individual congregations for information. One can find the most readily available list of these houses in the annual *Official Catholic Directory.* A few other volumes might be helpful. Although certainly dated, *Religious Orders of Women in the United States* (1930) provides a brief historical and institutional account of many congregations. More up to date but less complete in information are Thomas P. McCarthy's *Guide to Catholic Sisterhoods in the*

5

---

[8] Canadian Religious Conference, *Abridged Guide to the Archives of Religious Communities of Canada* (Ottawa, Canada); Molette, *Guide des sources de l'histoire des congregations feminines francaises de vie active* (Paris: Editions de Paris, 1974).

United States (1952) and Joan Lexau's *Convent Life: Roman Catholic Religious Orders for Women in North America* (1964).[9]

Of great value and directly related to the topic of this essay is Mary Ewens' "The Role of the Nun in Nineteenth Century America," an American Studies dissertation from the University of Minnesota.[10] Ewens concludes that sisters were generally regarded with hostility in the early part of the nineteenth century, largely because the Protestant public's concept of them had come from European literature which portrayed a distorted image. Following the public's first hand experience with sister nurses in the Civil War, however, the nuns became highly regarded for their commitment to Christian living and humane concerns.[11] By the end of the century, they had moved to a stronger position in the sense that realistic questions were being asked about their cloistral practices and their adaptation to American society. Throughout her study Ewens examines the image of the nun in the serious literature of the times and compares it with the actual lives and work of the sisters. The bibliography contains a wealth of material about sisters in the profession of nursing and in popular and serious literature, as well as works of a broader scope on the Catholic Church in America. One section lists biographies and histories of individual religious congregations.

Limited material can be found in other dissertations in history, education, and sociology. Those in history are largely studies of the foundations of specific orders, although there is one on the Sisters of Mercy as nurses in the Crimean War.[12] Those in the second group deal with the education of sisters, the education of children by sisters, or the educational contributions of individual orders. The sociology dissertations have a special interest since they approach a religious situation from a different perspective, as part of a larger social structure. Some of the themes treated in these studies are the religious community as a social system; power, status, and institutionalization in the occupational milieu of the Catholic

[9] Elinor T. Dehey, *Religious Orders of Women in the United States* (Hammond, Ind.: W. B. Conkey, 1930); Thomas P. McCarthy, *Guide to the Catholic Sisterhoods in the United States* (Washington, D. C.: Catholic Univ. of America Press, 1952); Joan Lexau, *Convent Life: Roman Catholic Religious Orders for Women in North America* (New York: Dial, 1964).

[10] Mary Ewens, O.P., "The Role of the Nun in Nineteenth Century America: Variations on the International Theme" (1971), published by Arno Press in 1978.

[11] For example, when a statue of Abraham Lincoln was erected at Oak Ridge Cemetery in Springfield, Ill., President Grant, who himself was being honored by the citizens of Illinois on the same occasion, insisted that two nuns unveil the statue, in acknowledgment of the country's debt to sisters for their wartime services to the wounded. The story can be found in Sister Thomas Aquinas Winterbauer, O.P., *Lest We Forget . . .* (Chicago: Adams Press, 1973).

[12] Mary Gilgannon, R.S.M., "The Sisters of Mercy As Crimean War Nurses" (Diss. Univ. of Notre Dame, 1962).

sister; the process of socialization in a religious community; and the integration of dual professional roles in sisters.[13]

The historian who seeks to record and interpret the effects of the women's movement in recent Catholic religious history will face several difficulties. So far there has been little written on the subject, and the literature that does exist tends to have a wider perspective. Sisters of today do not see themselves as set apart from other religious women, or even from other women generally. In the sixties and the seventies, in contrast to the past, there has been a pronounced expression by many Catholic sisters of feelings of solidarity with women in all walks of life, professional or otherwise, as well as with religious women of all faiths. Yet the impact of the feminist movement, in varying degrees, has been a common experience for the Catholic sisters in this country, 130,000 in number according to the 1978 *Official Catholic Directory* and constituting a more or less homogeneous group.

The inquiring student might begin with Sarah Bentley Doely's book entitled *Women's Liberation and the Church* (1970).[14] This deals with the question of women and religion on an interdenominational level, and from several different aspects. One essay discusses Catholic sisters, choosing as an example the Immaculate Heart Sisters of California, who wished to determine their own destiny in terms of lifestyle and apostolic work. When their male superiors in the Church disapproved of their plans, the group renounced their canonical status in the church and formed a lay association. Many sisters today are struggling for and gaining greater self-determination, but most strive to remain within the traditional structures of the religious congregation and Church authority. Study of these developments in the lives of women religious has hardly begun.

The subject of sisters and the women's movement is treated, but only briefly, in several books published in the late 1960s, such as Elsie Culver's *Women in the World of Religion*, *Women in Modern Life* by William Bier,

7

---

[13] Mary George O'Toole, *Sisters of Mercy of Maine—A Religious Community as a Social System* (Washington, D. C.: Catholic Univ. of America Press, 1964); Rosalma G. Wedhe, "The Occupational Milieu of the Catholic Sister" (Diss. St. John's Univ., 1966); Blake Hill, "Women and Religion: A Study of Socialization in a Community of Catholic Sisters" (Diss. Univ. of Kentucky, 1967); Mary Brigid Fitzpatrick, "The Sister Social Worker: An Integration of Two Professional Roles" (Diss. Univ. of Notre Dame, 1962).

[14] Sarah Bentley Doely, *Women's Liberation and the Church* (New York: Association Press, 1970).

and *Women of the Church* by Mary Lawrence McKenna.[15] Culver makes a case for the importance of the sister's role when she says that "within these orders women have an unusually good opportunity to develop special talents for religion, administration, the arts and professions, though they may not have the temporal power some did in earlier ages" (221). *Women in Modern Life*, dealing with women in general, discusses sisters only in connection with a survey of priests' attitudes toward them and another survey of attitudes of young girls toward sisters (55–96). McKenna, too, concentrates on the general topic of women in the Church, only briefly discussing the role of sisters. She concludes that active religious today perform real functions but no longer belong to the Church's hierarchic structure, only to her "life and holiness." She sees the present position of women in the Church as less than it was in the primitive Church, although the status of women in society at large has supposedly been bettered. "What is lacking today is the status of ecclesiastical order, and the attendent sense of having a definite place and function in the Church's official structure" (147).

Two other books represent the 1960s in still another way. *The New Nuns* and *New Works for New Nuns*[16] were written at the height of the renewal in the Catholic Church, when sisters were asking what they should be doing to meet the needs of present-day society. The informal essays in *New Works* discuss the ways of reaching those who need help—in education, social justice, or any other form. *The New Nuns* (1967) consists of essays gleaned from the "Sisters' Forum" of the *National Catholic Reporter*, which surveyed the sisters' life as it was a decade ago and their growing involvement in new areas of work. Both are now dated, but they do reflect the development of thought that women religious went through to come to renewal in the Church and greater participation in society. A final publication to mention is *The Role of Women in Society and in the Church* (1975), the work of the Canadian Religious Conference. Basically this is an extended annotated bibliography on several themes dealing with women; some twelve pages are devoted to the life of sisters.

Probably the most valuable source of material regarding nuns and the women's movement is the periodical literature of the recent past. Increasingly, magazines devoted to sisters are featuring articles that deal specifi-

[15] Elsie T. Culver, *Women in the World of Religion* (Garden City: Doubleday, 1967); William Bier, S.J., *Women in Modern Life* (New York: Fordham Univ. Press, 1968); Mary Lawrence McKenna, S.C.M.M., *Women of the Church: Role and Renewal* (New York, 1967).

[16] Mary Charles Muckenhirn, O.S.C., *The New Nuns* (New York: New American Library, 1967); Mary Peter Traxler, S.S.N.D., *New Works for New Nuns* (Saint Louis: B. Herder, 1968).

cally with the movement in one form or another. *Sisters Today*, a popular journal devoted chiefly to their religious lives, occasionally publishes personal reflections, such as Evelyn Mattern's "Woman—Holy and Free," or informative pieces like Angelita Fenker's "Sisters Uniting," which explains the function of the organization of that name, formed in 1974 as a forum for exchange of information.[17]

Review for Religious deals with feminist issues more frequently, and while its articles do not always relate specifically to religious women the implications are clear enough. Judith Vollbrecht's "The Role of Women in Social Change"[18] is of special interest for its anthropological approach to American social structure. She suggests a more radical living of the vows professed, through which the sister might be a voice that bespeaks values not totally accepted by her society. An article with a contrasting point of view is Rose Marie Larkin's article on "Religious Women and the Meaning of the Feminine" in *Communio*.[19] Larkin believes that radical feminism has obscured the true feminine and that faith is the most important element in its restoration. Surrender and the veil symbolize the essence of womanhood, the secret wisdom which the woman is to use through compassion, love, and sharing and in this way fulfill her vocation. Larkin's very nineteenth-century definition could have little appeal for today's feminists, religious or nonreligious. The literature on sisters and the women's movement does not usually take such a conservative position, except for some of the articles on the issue of the ordination of women in the Catholic Church.

Another periodical that deserves mention is *Benedictines*, which presents articles on Benedictine history and spirituality, as well as reporting on recent efforts of these sisters to redirect their lives and work. A look through the index discovers no articles on nuns and the women's movement, yet the periodical itself attests to women's independence. That these women have published a magazine of high quality for 30 years with almost no support from the male sections of the Church indicates some degree of liberation. The *Church Woman* is another kind of magazine, published by Church Women United, an international ecumenical group

9

---

[17] Evelyn Mattern, I.H.M., "Women—Holy and Free," *Sisters Today*, 47 (May 1976), 553–57; Angelita Fenker, "Sisters Uniting," *ST*, 45 (Apr. 1974), 465–73.

[18] Judith Vollbrecht, R.S.C.J., "The Role of Women in Social Change," *Review for Religious*, 35 (Mar. 1976), 265–71. One also finds in the periodical press bibliographies more or less complete; the same issue of *Review for Religious* prints a list of 30 books and 100 periodicals dealing with "every phase of womanhood." Though less than exhaustive in any of these areas, it gives some idea of what is available, particularly in the popular Catholic press, and could be a starting point for some types of research.

[19] Rose Marie Larkin, "Religious Women and the Meaning of the Feminine," *Communio, An International Catholic Review*, 3 (Spring 1976), 67–89.

of women united in faith who work to effect better participation of women in society through social action. Their 1971 pamphlet by Joan O'Brien entitled *Goal in Common* deals with the relation between Church Women United and Roman Catholic sisters. The magazine publishes many articles on social justice, and discusses aspects of the women's movement in all churches.

Newer periodicals are *Probe* and *Origins*, both started in the early 1970s. *Origins* is published by the National Catholic News Service (Washington, D. C.), and though it deals with a larger spectrum of religious considerations, articles by sisters on the women's movement are included from time to time—for instance, "The Role of Women in the Church" (July 3, 1975) by Margaret Farley, and Margaret Brennan's "Women's Liberation/Men's Liberation" (July 17, 1975). Lora Quinonez addresses herself to "The Women's Movement and Women Religious," (November 21, 1974). In her view the feminist movement and the renewal of life for Catholic sisters reflect some of the same concerns: for personal maturity, new ministries in the Church, and a new vision of celibacy. She says in conclusion: "I see affinities between our search and that of other women—a desire to experience ourselves and to be experienced as persons, not as symbols or mythic figures. . . ." *Probe* is the official magazine of the National Assembly of Women Religious (NAWR). This too deals largely with the social concerns of sisters in their work, but also from time to time publishes articles on feminism as it affects their lives.

Almost any of the general Catholic magazines carries articles on women's issues, women in the Church, and sisters in particular. These vary in depth and scholarship, the differences more often than not determined by the type of readership. One of the best has been the December 1975 issue of *Theological Studies*, devoted to women and religion. Though this is not confined to women religious, it presents some excellent scholarly essays by some of today's most prominent Catholic sisters. Particularly valuable is the bibliographical article on "Women and Religion: A Survey of Significant Literature, 1965–1974" by Anne E. Patrick, which includes books on historical analysis and works on selected issues such as canon law, ministry, and ordination, as well as some publications on constructive efforts and radical challenges. This is an insightful essay which makes a real contribution toward further research.[20]

Any discussion of sisters and the women's movement must include the issue of women's ordination, the debate over proposals that they be admitted into the traditionally male role of priest. Literature on this issue

---

[20] Anne E. Patrick, S.N.J.M., "Women and Religion: A Survey of Significant Literature, 1965–1974," *Theological Studies*, 36 (Dec. 1975), 737–65.

has been so abundant in the past few years that it is impossible to do justice even to part of it in this essay. At the conference on the ordination of women held in Detroit in November 1975, some of the speakers were among the most distinguished sisters in the country, who have written much on the issue of women in the Church. The meeting made available an eight-page bibliography, compiled by Donna Westly, of works since 1965 on the ordination of women. Related to this is the bibliography on women and ministry published in *Origins* in May 1972. The work of this initial conference was continued through an organized group, the Women's Ordination Conference, which held a second meeting in November 1978. Some 2,000 women and men attended from forty-three states and thirteen foreign countries. Following the conference a delegation of women proceeded to Washington, D. C. to attempt the beginnings of dialogue with the Bishops at their annual meeting. Since December 1976, WOC has sponsored a *Newsletter* which keeps interested parties abreast of developments, alerts them to needs for action, and informs them of happenings elsewhere. The objective of WOC is not simply the ordination of women in the traditional priest role. Rather it seeks to "explore how priesthood should and could be transformed in the twentieth century and how the ministry-style of women will help bring that about" (*Newsletter*, June 1978). Anyone interested in this aspect of sisters and the women's movement should contact this group, whose headquarters are in Rochester, New York.[21]

11

Finally we call attention to a production of a very different type, "Women of Promise," by Kay Schwerzler and Joyce Fey. This is a slide presentation available through the Leadership Conference of Women Religious which deals with sisters and the women's movement. It celebrates the great figures such as Frances Xavier Cabrini, Philippine Duchesne, and Elizabeth Seton, as well as the many nameless sisters who risked their lives caring for the sick and homeless and who "invented, administered, planned . . . who did 'men's' work without waiting to be permitted." The style of this presentation is visual and poetic; its scholarly base is inconspicuous. Most of the research was done in the Church History collection at the University of Notre Dame, a source which no researcher should overlook.[22]

---

[21] Women's Ordination Conference, 34 Monica Street, Rochester, N. Y. 14619.

[22] Because of the number and quality of manuscript collections housed in its University Archives, Notre Dame ranks second in importance to Baltimore as a research center for American Catholic history. The collection includes the early papers of the Archdioceses of Cincinnati, Detroit, Indianapolis, and New Orleans, as well as the personal papers of a number of leading Catholic laymen, and is well indexed and calendared. See Ellis, *Guide*, for descriptions of other depositories in the United States, 7–12.

Anyone seriously considering research in the areas discussed in this essay should contact some of the key organizations of sisters. Two are especially prominent. The Leadership Conference of Women Religious (LCWR) with headquarters in Washington, D. C. represents mostly those sisters who hold administrative positions in their congregations. More of a grass roots organization of the rank and file is the National Assembly of Women Religious, publishers of *Probe*. From its headquarters in Chicago, NAWR attempts to mobilize sisters for service to their Church and nation. Many of the religious active in these organizations are among the most competent and knowledgeable women leaders in the country and would be helpful to the researcher. Other organizations that could be contacted are the Black Sisters Conference, whose publication is *Signs of Soul*, and the National Coalition of American Nuns.[23]

Anyone interested in studying women and religion should find a rich mine in the American Catholic sisters, a group large and homogeneous enough to permit research to be carried on with some facility and valid conclusions to be drawn. It is well to remember in dealing with religious women of any faith that, if indeed they are interested in the women's movement, they also have another motivating force, namely their religious commitment. Also, in the natural order, their lives are probably less immediately dominated by men, although they too ultimately are subjected to some of the same discrimination suffered by other women. The following are some suggested areas for research.

1) One of the first that could be explored is the pioneer or founding experience. Just as colonial women performed many tasks and carried on businesses from sheer force of necessity, so did Catholic religious women in setting up their congregations and institutions. Most of these foundations were made in the nineteenth century, yet these women were apparently oblivious to concepts of "the Victorian lady" and "the cult of domesticity." With or without the support of men of the Church, they did what needed to be done. As mentioned above, many of these stories are separately recorded but the Catholic woman religious as a type has not been studied. The question might well be asked how free were these women to determine their own existence and policy. Staffing hospitals, schools, colleges, asylums for children, and other kinds of institutions gave them a certain degree of autonomy; still we know that they often encountered difficulties in their relationships with Church authorities.

[23] Further information (addresses, officers, etc.) is available in the current issue of *The Catholic Almanac*.

2) Certainly an extension of Mary Ewens' work would be of value—to ascertain attitudes towards sisters in the twentieth century through experience and interviews with sisters and through the serious and popular literature of the times.

3) If the Roman Catholic girl always had the choice of a career in religion, does this explain why Catholic women were not attracted to the women's movement, especially in the nineteenth century? In a day when women were expected to marry, the life of the sister possibly constituted an appealing, respectable alternative. We know that, in the mid-twentieth century, many of the college presidents who were women were Catholic sisters. This seems to indicate that sisters enjoyed a freedom of movement, self-determination if you will, that other women did not have at that time.

13

4) Looking back a bit, and outside the confines of the United States, one might test McKenna's thesis that because the sister lacks an ecclesiastical order in the Church the status of women now is probably lower than it was in the early Church. Did religious life for women evolve in order to give those interested in working in the Church some kind of "status," but a status which at the same time removed them from such an official position as deaconess? In developing societies women frequently have roles that are later denied them when the society becomes more complex. Did this happen in the early Church, that once the primitive period passed and Church structure became more complex, the official position of deaconess was abandoned and women were relegated, so to speak, to the "life and holiness of the Church" (McKenna, 147)? Or in other words, were they given some "status" as sisters but, lacking an ecclesiastical order, no power of determining policy or making decisions?

5) It would also be interesting to ascertain what forces in the 1960s really brought about the change in the lives of sisters. Vatican II and the women's movement converged at some point, yet one wonders just how the motivating forces worked for individual sisters.[24] Accompanying this inquiry should be an assessment of attitudes towards feminism, not only the leaders' attitudes, but also those of the rank and file.

These topics and others could make a significant contribution not only to the religious history of the United States but to our knowledge of women and their roles in American society. The source material is available and abundant, a ready field for the interested researcher.

[24] This question is partially pursued in the Fitzpatrick dissertation noted above, in which she concludes that the role of the religious takes first place in the hierarchy of role obligations. Conflict is solved by making decisions in favor of the religious role. If an integration of the two is achieved, she says (as in this case, social work), a redefinition of the role of religion to include the occupational role is necessary.

The Leadership of Nuns in Immigrant Catholicism

MARY EWENS O. P.*

Roman Catholic nuns or "sisters," as they are popularly called, exerted an important influence on the Catholic Church in America in the nineteenth century. Catholicism in that period faced the challenge of preserving and fostering its faith among millions of immigrant members, and of establishing her credibility in an alien and often hostile society. If adequate means could be found to measure the relative importance of personal influences, it might well be shown that sisters' efforts were far more effective than those of bishops or priests in the Church's attempts to meet these challenges. It was they who established schools in cities and remote settlements to instruct the young in the tenets of their faith, who succored the needy, who brought the consolations of religion to soldiers in military hospitals, who changed public attitudes toward the Church from hostility to respect. Their numbers grew from under forty to more than forty thousand during the nineteenth century. (Document 1.) They outnumbered male church workers in the last half of the century in almost every diocese for which we have records, and there were almost four times as many nuns as priests by the century's close.[1]

Sisters performed many charitable works, but their chief preoccupation was with teaching. They staffed several kinds of schools: elementary ones, academies, free and pay schools, night schools, industrial, parochial, private, and public ones. There were 3,811 parochial schools by 1900, most of them run by sisters, and 663 girls' academies (but only 102 Catholic academies for boys). Sisters taught their students, mostly girls, the rudiments of their religion, prepared them to receive the sacraments, and gave them a solid grounding in Christian living and a sense of responsibility for the maintenance of a Christian atmosphere in the

*MARY EWENS, O.P., is Professor of American Studies at Rosary College in River Forest, Illinois. She received her Ph.D. from the University of Minnesota, writing on the adaptation of Catholic women's religious orders to the United States. Her study has been published by the University of Notre Dame Press.

homes they would one day run and for the religious instruction of their children.

Schools like those established in the Indiana woods by Mother Theodore Guerin and Mother Angela Gillespie were found in many remote frontier outposts and were attended by Protestants as well as Catholics because of their reputation for learning and piety. Many young women brought up to believe the anti-Catholic propaganda of the times learned in these schools to respect and even love the sisters and later helped to change the attitudes of their Protestant families and friends towards the Catholic Church. Sisters' schools won friends for the Catholic Church wherever they were established, and were a potent force in lessening the virulence of anti-Catholic sentiment.

Nowhere was the Church's charity towards others more readily apparent than in the nursing done by sisters in private homes, almshouses, and hospitals. The scanty statistics available to us indicate that sisters administered at least 265 hospitals in America during the century.[2] They also did heroic work during the cholera and yellow fever epidemics that ravaged the country periodically and in every American war of the nineteenth century.

15

It was particularly through their nursing in military hospitals of both the North and the South during the Civil War that sisters brought about a dramatic change in public attitudes towards Catholicism. In the military hospitals in which they nursed, thousands of men who had never before come into contact with sisters or Catholics had a chance to observe them firsthand. Accounts of sisters' military nursing are full of testimony to the changed attitude towards things Catholic that resulted from this work. Reports of their work in both the Civil and the Spanish-American wars make it clear that they had an important spiritual ministry. They prepared men to receive the sacraments, helped them to face death, encouraged lapsed Catholics to return to the Church, and instructed patients in the beliefs of the Catholic faith. They did not interfere with the beliefs of non-Catholics, but responded to requests for information and often did the actual baptizing when a soldier so desired it.

The priest came, often from a nearby town, to say mass and administer the sacraments to those who had been prepared for them by the sisters. When we consider that there were only eighty-four official Catholic chaplains in the Civil War, but 640 sister-nurses serving in the military hospitals, we get a clearer picture of just who it was who represented the Catholic Church to the soldiers and hospital personnel in that war. Nor was the situation any different in the Spanish-American War, in which were thirteen Catholic chaplains but 282 sister-nurses. Surgeons, doctors, officers, and patients were all impressed by the devotion of the sisters to the sick, their willingness to nurse patients with deadly contagious diseases whom no one else would approach, their honesty and genuine virtue in the most trying circumstances, their concern for others rather than themselves.

In addition to their major works of teaching and nursing, sisters ran day-care centers, infant and maternity homes, homes for the aged, mental institutions, settlement houses, residences for working women, and homes for delinquent girls and unwed mothers. In the convents there was ample scope for the talents of any woman, and the opportunity for travel and adventure as well. (Document 8.) Large numbers of young women were attracted to this life. Indeed, there were complaints in some places that the convents were removing too many of the marriageable girls from the countryside.

Many nuns responded to a call to leave their families, friends, and homelands to spread the Gospel message on foreign shores. They came to America as foreign missionaries. Ninety-one of the 119 communities of sisters established in America in the nineteenth century had European or Canadian origins. The letters and journals of these women who came to America as immigrants are full of the lively details of their travels: the long Atlantic journey by sailing ship (on which they encountered pirates, gales, seasickness, sand bars, and thirst); the problem with luggage, dishonest porters, and customs officials; the journey across America by canal boat, ferry, stagecoach, open wagon, and railroad; the travel up the Mississippi by steamboat, overland to the Southwest, around South America to San Francisco. Their observant comments on all that they saw—buildings, manners and customs, climate, geography, foods, and especially people—are full of wit. (Document 2.) Immigrant sisters sympathized with their own countrymen in America. German sisters complained about the predominance of Irish bishops, and French ones disdained the Americans as cold, calculating boors.

A European class consciousness was not only a part of their world view; it was also built into the structure of their religious life. Many communities had two classes of members, choir sisters (who possessed some degree of education and chanted the Divine Office, the official prayer of the Church) and lay sisters (who had less education, were often from the lower classes, and performed the manual labor). Often there was a distinction in color or detail in the habits worn by the two groups. Americans found this lack of equality shocking, and European sisters were highly suspicious of American democracy.

As the targets for the attacks of two groups of bigots, sisters encountered a great deal of hostility and persecution in nineteenth century America.[3] Their foreign language, customs, and methods roused the ire of nativists, and their religion and manner of life were denounced by the anti-Catholic forces in American society. Often the membership of the two groups overlapped. Several events of the first half of the century roused the anti-Catholic feeling that had always been latent in American Protestantism, among these events the storm of resentment that greeted the passage of the Catholic Emancipation Act in Britain in 1829 and a meeting of all American Catholic bishops that was held in Baltimore in the same year. In the hostility towards Catholicism that swept the country in waves in the 1820s, 1850s, and 1890s, sisters were prime targets for abuse because their distinctive costume and their retired lives set them apart. Indeed, sisters soon learned that it was dangerous to wear their religious garb on the streets as they went about their work of mercy. Many adopted contemporary dress.

In the 1830s and 1850s, the country was flooded with pamphlets, books, and newspapers that purported to reveal what "really" happened behind convent walls. The tales of secret tunnels, rape, seduction, infanticide, prison cells, and absurd penances that appeared in print were reinforced by the sermons of ministers who enlarged upon the "Catholic threat." Prominence was given to lectures delivered by ex-nuns and ex-priests. The revelations of "escaped nuns" attracted large audiences. The most famous of them all, the prototype of those who came after her, was Maria Monk, a girl who had suffered brain damage in childhood. After her escape from a Montreal asylum for wayward girls, she came to New York with tales of her alleged experiences in a convent. Ministers were not slow to turn her stories to profitable use. Reverend J. J. Slocum, with the advice of Reverend George Bourne and Theodore Dwight, undertook the task of writing her story for publication, calling the book that appeared in 1836 *Awful Disclosures of the Hotel Dieu Nunnery of Montreal.* This book and its sequels roused a storm of controversy, with charges and countercharges, delegations to the Montreal convent, and so forth. Miss Monk's public appearances helped to sell the book. Over three hundred thousand copies were sold prior to the Civil War, and it has remained in print into the 1970s.

17

It is no wonder that people who believed these tales insulted nuns on the streets, organized mobs to attack convent property, tried to undermine sisters' schools, and proposed convent inspection laws with the intention of freeing nuns from their prisons. As anti-Catholic sentiment grew, attacks on sisters and convents became more serious. Bigots focused attention on the convent as a symbol of the evils of Catholicism. Mount St. Benedict, the flourishing Ursuline academy in Charlestown, Massachusetts, was destroyed by a mob in 1834. (Document 6.) This incident was denounced by sensible people everywhere, but it established a precedent for attacks on convents that was followed later in Baltimore, Frederick, St. Louis, Galveston, and elsewhere. In the mid-1850s, when the activist Know-Nothing Party enjoyed success in state and national elections, bills aimed at the inspection of convents were introduced in the legislatures of several states. Sisters in Roxbury, Massachusetts, and elsewhere suffered the indignity of being visited unexpectedly by a dozen or more unruly men. It was only after large numbers of Americans actually saw sisters in action, nursing in the Civil War, that the attitude toward Catholicism began to change. (Document 7.)

Many communities of sisters who were denounced as foreigners, minions of the pope, prisoners, etc. may have unwittingly provoked some of this abuse themselves by the European customs that were a part of their lives. As they came to understand the American milieu and the needs of the American Church, they saw that adaptations had to be made, if religious life were to be lived successfully in their adopted country. The Church's canon law regulations, which formed the framework for the constitutions that governed communities of nuns, dated back to the thirteenth century. They reflected the medieval view of women as childish, emotional, "misbegotten males" who were incapable of controlling their own lives. These rules were formulated in an age when young women were sometimes consigned by their families to convents against their will and had to be carefully supervised lest they seek to escape or indulge in behavior not suitable for a nun.

18
Such regulations, intended to preserve the virtue of cloistered nuns who devoted themselves to prayer and penance and never stepped outside their convent walls, were unsuitable in nineteenth century America. Here sisters served others through active works of charity. The American culture stressed the freedom of every individual. But the constitution of each religious order reflected the culture of the time and place in which it had been written. A serious problem for communities with European roots (and for American sisterhoods that imitated European ones) was the question of whether their constitutions could be adapted to American ways and still retain what was essential for an authentic religious life. European superiors often insisted on exact adherence to the constitutions as the *sine qua non* of eternal salvation.

Sisters who saw the needs of the American Church, and heard their bishops' pleas for adaptation and flexibility, pondered the best solution to their dilemma. Often it was found in a complete break with the European motherhouse. As the century progressed, Rome established the practice of giving its approval to new constitutions. This freed the sisters, to a certain extent, from the jurisdiction of the local bishop. Many superiors spent long years in their attempts to achieve this independent status for their communities.[4]

The careful study of constitutions was essential because they were a religious community's bill of rights, which clearly stated privileges and obligations on all sides. Constitutions could not be changed by the action of a single individual, even a bishop, so they were a protection against the occasional bishop who sought to interfere in a community's internal affairs. In the few instances in which bishops tried to overstep the limits of their authority, as in the dispute between Bishop Hailandiere and the Sisters of Providence, sisters were within their rights in refusing to transgress their constitutions. (Document 4.)

Instances of such high-handedness on the part of bishops were not common in the nineteenth century, though they loomed large in the communities in which they occurred. The instances in which bishops worked to the detriment of a community are far outweighed by those in which they were helpful. Usually a bishop who invited a community to his diocese was delighted to have such capable workers and gave them every support and encouragement. Though the bishop was responsible for all church activities in his diocese, he usually left the sisters to run their own internal affairs. Often he appointed an ecclesiastical superior as his delegate in matters that concerned the community. In practice, the ecclesiastical superior usually became a close friend, advisor, spiritual director, and defender of the community, especially of its leaders. The histories of most communities recount the names of many priests and bishops whose advice and help have been invaluable to them.

In the disputes which did sometimes arise between religious communities and bishops in this period, the disagreement was often over a difference of opinion regarding policy rather than male-female polarities. Disputes were usually negotiated or arbitrated. The sisters were equals, not subordinates, in the discussions. Perhaps the primary cause for disagreement was the question of the adaptation of European customs to the needs of the American Church. American bishops who were concerned with satisfying the needs of large numbers of immigrants became irritated with sisterhoods whose rules forbade contact with male students and orphans, choir work, employment at schools at a distance from the convent, or adaptation to American teaching practices.

Constitutions which had been adequate for a community under the jurisdiction of the bishop of a European diocese were not sufficient when that group established convents all over America. Sometimes the lines of demarcation between the authority of the bishop, the ecclesiastical superiors, and the sisters' superiors were not clearly drawn. Bishops especially resented the control of personnel in schools, hospitals, orphanages, and similar settings by motherhouse superiors. It was precisely because they were independent that such superiors were resented. Indeed, they often had more church workers under their jurisdiction than did the bishop in whose diocese they lived. It was natural that many bishops should come to prefer diocesan communities that would be responsible to them rather than to some bishop or sister superior in another diocese.

There was often no clear-cut right or wrong answer in disagreements over policy, and there were sisters and male clerics on either side. Thus when the administrators and ecclesiastical superior of the Sisters of Charity of Emmitsburg decided to seek affiliation with the French Daughters of Charity, they thought they were doing what was best for their community. Their sisters in New York and Cincinnati, however, in conjunction with their bishops, deplored the move as a betrayal of the ideals of their foundress, Elizabeth Seton, and seceded from the parent group. This alternative of forming a new community when there were ideological differences was fairly common. Sometimes it was basically a clash of personalities that led one group to back a particular leader and form a separate community. Sometimes priests or bishops stepped in when they sincerely felt that it was important for a community's well-being that changes be made.

19

Bishops and priests came to have a healthy respect for the power of sisters, and with good reason. The sisters were important influences in the Catholic community and ran most of the Church's charitable institutions. In disagreements sisters fought for their rights and usually won. Then too, they could and did vote with their feet, or threatened to, when the occasion warranted it. There was always another bishop, just over diocesan borders, who needed the services the sisters provided. Communities like that of the Sisters of the Holy Cross and the Dominicans, which included both male and female branches, often went through various stages in their relationship with male members of the group, as one or the other seemed to be in control. There were benefits and disadvantages on both sides, so no generalizations can be made. Thus we see the Dominican sisters seeking affiliation with the male branch of the order and Holy Cross priests. (Document 5.)

An interesting aspect of the relationship of nineteenth century American nuns with men is the number of friendships that flourished between sisters and priests. The long distances from home and lack of communication must have encouraged support and friendship among sympathetic souls. Thus we see, for example, Mother Philippine Duchesne confiding to Fathers Barat and Varin in France, Mother Pia Backes counting on Father May, Mother Guerin turning to Bishop Bouvier for advice, Sister St. Francis Xavier unburdening her soul to Father (later Bishop) Augustine Martin, and Mother Theresa Gerhardinger writing long intimate letters to Father Siegert.[5] (Document 3.) In many ways, these relationships are impressive as models of mutual respect between equals.

In many aspects of their lives, nuns in nineteenth century America enjoyed opportunities open to few other women of their time: involvement in meaningful work, access to administrative positions, freedom from the responsibilities of marriage and motherhood, opportunities to live in sisterhood, and egalitarian friendships. Perhaps it was this freedom from the restrictive roles usually ascribed to women that enabled them to exert such a powerful influence on the American Church. Though barred from the priesthood, they exercised a sacramental and educational ministry that was essential for Catholicism's continued existence. They administered its charitable institutions, conducted its religious instruction, prepared its members for the sacraments, were exemplars of its holiness, and won a grudging acceptance and even respect for Catholicism from other Americans. We can only speculate on what the fate of the Church would have been, had they not been willing to labor so valiantly for its survival.

Sister Blandina Segale's pioneering work in the American Southwest is recorded in her letters to her sister Justina during the last decades of the nineteenth century. [From Sister Blandina Segale, *At the End of the Santa Fe Trail* (Milwaukee: Bruce, 1948). Used by permission of Crowell, Collier and Macmillan.]

Mother Elizabeth Bayley Seton was the first American saint and foundress (in 1809) of the Sisters of Charity, the first American women's religious order. [Courtesy the Archivist, St. Joseph's Central House, Emmitsburg, Maryland.]

22

Catholic nuns won acceptance into American life in no small measure because of their devoted nursing during the Civil War. This photo shows the staff and nurses outside the Satterlee Military Hospital near Gettysburg, Pennsylvania, during the war. [Courtesy the Archivist, St. Joseph's Central House, Emmitsburg, Maryland.]

These four members of the America Congregation, an Indian sisterhood, nursed during the Spanish-American War at Camp Onward,
Savannah, Georgia. They are shown with their chaplain, the Reverend Francis Craft. The four sisters are, left to right, Sister Josephine
Two Bears, Sister Ella Clarke, Sister Bridget Pleets, and Sister Anthony Bordeaux. Sister Bordeaux died in Cuba and was given a military
funeral. Sister Bridget Pleets treasured to the end of her life the
apron on which dying soldiers had written their names and addresses
so that she could write to their relatives. [Courtesy the Milford (Pennsylvania) Historical Society.]

Photographs from an article by Lida Rose McCabe entitled "The Everyday Life
of a Sister of Charity" (below and on the following pages) show the sisters not only
performing the corporal works of mercy but also teaching immigrant women
work skills. [From *Cosmopolitan* magazine 23 (1897), pp. 289–96. Photo courtesy
the Newberry Library, Chicago, Illinois.]

25

Documents: The Leadership of Nuns in Immigrant Catholicism

Document 1: The First Indigenous American Women's Order

Mother Elizabeth Bayley Seton was a widow with five children when she founded the Sisters of Charity in 1809. In this letter approving the community's constitution, Archbishop John Carroll, the first American Catholic bishop, touched on several important themes. He wanted the sisters to control their own internal affairs, to be free from ties with male communities (the Sulpicians, in this case), and to have a way of life adapted to American conditions.[6]

Baltimore Sept. 11th. 1811

To Elizabeth Seton

Hond. & dear Madam. Shall I confess that I am deeply humbled at being called on to give a final sanction to a rule of conduct & plan of religious government, by which it is intended to promote and preserve amongst many beloved spouses of Jesus Christ, a spirit of solid & sublime religious perfection? . . . it affords me great pleasure to learn that all the material points on which a difference of opinion was thought to exist have been given up by Messrs de Sulpice in their last deliberations. If they had not, I do not think that I should have approved the Constitutions, as modified in the copy thereof which has been before me. Mr. Dubois has not exhibited the rules of detail & particular duties of the Sisters, but they being matters of which yourselves & your Rev. Superior will be the best judges, I commit you & them with the utmost confidence to the guidance of the Divine Spirit. I am exceedingly anxious that every allowance shall be made not only to the sisters generally, but to each one in particular, which can serve to give quiet to their conscience, provided that this be done without endangering the harmony of the Community & therefore it must become a matter of regulation. I am rejoiced likewise to know that the idea of any other connexion than that of charity, is abandoned between the daughters of St. Joseph's & the society of St. Sulpice; I mean that their interests, administration & government are not to be the same, or at least under the same control. This removes many inconveniences for you & for Messrs of St. Sulpice. No one of the body but your immediate Superior residing near you will have any share in the government or concerns of the Sisters, except (on very rare & uncommon occasions) the Superior of the Seminary of Balte, but not his society. This however is to be understood so as not to exclude the essential superintendance & control of Archbp over every Community in his Diocese. Your own particularly situation required special consideration on account of your dear children. It seemed to me that only general principles for your & your family's case should be now established, grounded on justice & gratitude & that any special considerations should be deferred to the period when the circumstances may require them. At present too many persons would be consulted

27

& amongst them some who are incompetent to judge; and even they who are most competent might find their most equitable provisions rendered useless by the changes produced in a few years. Mr. Dubois has been very explicit in communicating, I believe, whatever it was proper for me to know; on my side it has been my endeavor when I read the Constitution to consult in the first place the individual happiness of your dear Sisters & consequently your own; 2ndly, to render their plan of life useful to religion & the public; 3dly, to confine the administration of your own affairs & the internal & domestic government as much as possible to your own institutions once adopted & within your own walls. Your Superior or Confessor need be informed or consulted in matters where the Mother & her Council need his advice. I shall congratulate you & your beloved Sisters, when the Constitution is adopted. It will be like freeing you from a state in which it was difficult to walk straight, as you had no certain way in which to proceed. In the mean time assure yourself & them of my utmost solicitude for your advancement in the service & favor of God, of my reliance on your prayers; of your prosperity in the important duty of education which will & must long be your principal, & will always be your partial employment. A century at least will pass before the exigencies & habits of this Country will require & hardly admit of the charitable exercises towards the sick sufficient to employ any number of the [illegible] sisters out of our largest cities; and therefore they must consider the business of education as a laborious, charitable & permanent object of their religious duty. Mention me in terms of singular affection to your dear, sons & daughters. . . . The Baltimore girls in your school form a special object of my affection, though I cannot name half of them. Your account of Miss Wiseman has added much to my high estimation of her. Julianna & Maria White, Mary Anne Jenkins, Ann Cox & Ann Nelson occur this moment to my memory, yet I omit some equally dear to me. Mr. Harper thinks of sending up his daughter. I have not seen her since her return home. Adieu. Mr. Js Barry still in Washn. as is our ever honored friend. I am with esteem & respect Honord & dr. Madam Yr. sevt in Xt.

> J. Abp. of Balt
> C SJCH

Document 2: Travel and Settlement

Mother Theodore Guerin led a small band of Sisters of Providence from their motherhouse near Lemans, France, to the woods of Indiana in 1840 to establish the American foundation of her community. Her travel journal and letter to Canon Lottin, rector of the Cathedral in Lemans, gives us a vivid impression of how the strange American society looked to an aristocratic Frenchwoman.[7]

It would be difficult to describe what passed in my soul when I felt the vessel beginning to move and I realized that I was no longer in France. It seemed as if my soul were being torn from my body. Finally we left the harbor. Fort Francis First was the last object we beheld. It too disappeared, for we were already on the ocean.

We watched the sails being unfurled one after the other; we saw them swelled by the wind, hurrying us away from our beloved France. I shall not undertake to describe what was going on aboard the ship. Sad, and leaning against the cordage, I was contemplating the shore of my country, which was flying away with inconceivable rapidity and becoming smaller and smaller at every moment. All was commotion and noise on deck, but, absorbed in painful reflections, we neither saw nor heard anything. We again offered up to Heaven the sacrifice of all that we loved, and we thought of those who were weeping for us.

29

O my dear friends! O my Country! How much it costs to give you up! And you, my sister, the only one left of my family, I did not see before my departure but you were not forgotten, nor will you ever be, nor will he who has been such a father to me [Monsieur de la Bertaudiere, benefactor at Soulaines].

While I was thus preoccupied, my poor companions were weeping also; nearly all had bid adieu to a tender father or beloved mother. How their hearts were bleeding at that time! . . .

At New York

"At last, we have arrived," we said to one another, "the perils of the sea are passed!" We threw ourselves on our knees, and with hearts full of gratitude we offered our thanks to God for all the benefits He had bestowed upon us. We prayed to Him also for our future; we could not but feel some anxiety about it. The ship ceased to move. What joy for the Americans! They were going to see again those that were dear to them. They were expected. The telegraph, in announcing the arrival of the *Cincinnati*, had caused many a heart to throb; but not one was anxious about us, not one was throbbing for us. "Behold," we said, "houses, but not our dear Providence home. Behold people, but not our Sisters. We shall not meet with friendly faces, with devoted hearts, in this foreign land. Here we shall be looked upon with contempt, perhaps with hatred; at most, we shall meet only pity."

While these painful reflections were oppressing our hearts, the Custom House officers came to visit the ship. They were very friendly but no one was so kind as the good doctor of whom I have already written, and who came now bringing refreshments to us. In our circumstances his kindness did more good to our hearts than to our stomachs. I am happy to give you the name of this gentleman—Doctor Sidney A. Doane. Later he told the people it would bring a blessing to any one who would render us the least service. Do pray for him, for he is a Protestant. Without him, what would have become of us in New York? It was he who informed the Bishop of our arrival, because the deputy of Monseigneur de la Hailandiere the Bishop of Vincennes had not yet arrived in the city. It was he who spoke to us the first consoling words we heard in the New World, so new to us. "Soon," he said, "you will be surrounded by numerous friends who will be happy to see you. The Bishop of New York will be much pleased to make your acquaintance. You will find in his Vicar General, Father Varela, a real father. He is a Spanish priest who speaks French, and an excellent man whose life is spent in doing good."

30

Doctor Doane presented us with some beautiful peaches which he himself had gathered, and the other good things he had brought. His words, and his manner of acting—a stranger, a non-Catholic, and an American—surprised us so much that we were almost mute. I could stammer out only a few words of thanks. . . .

I wrote you also about the Church, St. Peter's, Barclay Street, of its elegance, of its being as light as if it had been made of crystal, of the dazzling whiteness of its walls, of the pews which were of solid mahogany, of its galleries with four rows of seats placed in tiers, which give it the appearance of a theatre. The speaker seemed to be talented, though we really understood nothing of his sermon. His audience listened attentively. The Mass and Vespers were sung to music which, however, did not particularly please me. I had a great deal more devotion in our poor barn at Soulaines, notwithstanding the lack of harmony there. The church was filled with men, there were at least as many men as women, and all comported themselves perfectly well. We did not see one woman who did not have on a bonnet. Here the shepherdess wear bonnets and even the milkmaids while milking their cows. The milk is carried around in quite a stylish conveyance drawn by two horses at such a rate that one might think it were the president's carriage rolling along. The men who distribute the milk from door to door are dressed up as if for a wedding. It is impossible to have any idea of the extravagance of the Americans without having witnessed it.

The houses have an elegant appearance, especially those in the country. The city of New York is beautiful, but of a beauty severe and sombre—quite depressing. The houses are mostly red brick, extremely high. The streets are over thirty feet wide, with fine brick sidewalks, above which are suspended awnings to shade the numerous stores. At certain distances there are crossings paved with a stone that looks very much like our slate stone. The Americans never cross a street but at these places, which are at right angles. The other streets are badly paved. There are here, as at Paris, many fine carriages, especially a new style which is unusually elegant.

There are separate sections in the city for different kinds of business; for example: for the sailors, for the soldiers, for the wholesale merchants, etc., etc. In the latter, and in the navy quarter, no women are to be seen; not from fear of being insulted, however, for women are much respected here, more so than in Europe. To be wanting in respect towards them would be a shameful thing, and would brand the guilty one with an indelible mark. We saw no public buildings other than the City Hall and the Post Office which, however, offered nothing remarkable. The Catholic churches are small and badly built, even the cathedral.

In Philadelphia

During our stay in the city the good Bishop gave us constant marks of friendliness. He came frequently to see us and received us always with admirable benevolence. As soon as our arrival was known in the city, a crowd of French people came to visit us. Our costume was admired by all. And indeed ours is much superior to that of our good Sisters, who are dressed in black serge and wore a little lustring cap not worth two sous. They have also a sort of bonnet made of pasteboard covering with lustring; and, truly, holy poverty loses nothing here. . . .

Baltimore

Frederick is rather small and built on a level. A carriage sent by the Sisters was waiting to take us to their house, as they also had been notified of our coming by the Bishop of Philadelphia. We were graciously received by Mother Rose, former Superior General of the Sisters of Charity. This good ex-Mother is a model religious, filled with the virtues of her state, especially humility and charity. All the Community regret her, but she is delighted to be relieved of the burden of the superiorship. She told us all about the beginning of her institute, which had very trying times. These good Americans had, in fact, to undergo inconceivable privations; but Heaven blessed their sacrifices, for they have now a Community that does great good. It is destined especially for the instruction of the poor and chiefly of orphans: however they have a fine Academy. They teach the various sciences scarcely known in our French schools, but they excel in music, which is an indispensable thing in this country, even for the poor. No piano, no pupils! Such is the spirit of this country—Music and Steam! At Frederick, of the five Sisters three teach piano and guitar. These Sisters have an excellent religious spirit; tender piety, great charity, regularity,—in fine, all the virtues of the true Religious. I am happy to render them this testimony.

At last we had arrived at Vincennes! Vincennes!! The conveyance stopped. We were taken to the Sisters of Charity, who live near the episcopal residence, and who had been requested by the Bishop to

31

take care of us until his return. After partaking of some food and putting on again our religious dress, we begged to be taken to the cathedral. Ciel! What a Cathedral! Our barn at Soulaines is better ornamented and more neatly kept. I could not resist this last shock and wept bitterly, which relieved me somewhat. I could not possibly examine this poor church on that day—the following day I did so with more calm. . . .

The Journey's End

I cannot tell you what passed within me during the next half hour. I do not know myself, but I was so deeply moved that I could not utter a word. We continued to advance into the thick woods till suddenly Father Buteux stopped the carriage and said, "Come down, Sisters, we have arrived." What was our astonishment to find ourselves still in the midst of the forest, no village, not even a house in sight. Our guide having given orders to the driver, led us down into a ravine, whence we beheld through the trees on the other side a frame house with a stable and some sheds. "There," he said, "is the house where the postulants have a room, and where you will lodge until your house is ready." . . .

The day after our arrival we went to look at our new house, now building. Like the castles of the knights of old, it is so deeply hidden in the woods that you cannot see it until you come up to it. Do not conclude, however, that it is built on the model of Father Buteux's. No, indeed. It is a pretty two-story brick house, fifty feet wide by twenty-six feet deep. There are five large openings in front. The first stone was laid August seventeenth and it is already roofed. Today they began plastering, but there are yet neither doors nor windows; all is being done, little by little. As to our garden and yard, we have all the woods. And the wilderness is our only cloister, for our house is like an oak tree planted therein.

Here is the list of our movables: twelve folding beds, an old bureau, a small cupboard or buffet—bois blanc—for the dishes and bread, a dozen wooden chairs and a table for the kitchen. Our dining-room table belongs to the farmer. As to the kitchen it is only a stove placed outside. We have pots, pans, etc., also a soup tureen, two dozen plates, two dozen spoons and forks, and one dozen knives. Besides these we have the trunks and boxes in which we brought our belongings from France. Some unbleached muslin was bought for sheets. This, then, is what we have for the foundation of a house, which the Bishop foresees will one day be a flourishing institution. No doubt; but we shall have to suffer much. Many things are wanting us, yet we dare not complain. Shall we not be, and are we not already, in our own little nook? Besides, did we not come here to suffer—we who were so well provided for in France?

32

Early Experiences

I am not sure whether I told you of the insupportable pride of the Americans. However, I shall give you a little incident which happened yesterday, and which came very near putting me in the bad graces of everybody. Well, yesterday we had our washing done, the first of this kind, probably, ever done here. I shall not relate all the trouble we had to organize things, to get a tub, etc. I leave that for you to imagine. But I shall tell you that we had employed a young woman, an orphan, wretchedly poor and miserably clad, to help us wash. I attempted to show her what to do. At first she refused to take any direction, but, by coaxing, I secured the favor of showing her.

When dinner time came, there was my washerwoman sitting down at the table with us. I was so indiscreet as to say it would be better for her not to take dinner with the Community. I wish you could have seen the change in the countenances of our American postulants! I had to compromise by telling the girl she might eat with the reader at the second table. The mere name of "servant" makes them revolt, and they throw down whatever they have in their hands and start off at once. You cannot hire either a man or a girl for more than a month at a time.

It is astonishing that this remote solitude has been chosen for a novitiate and especially for an academy. All appearances are against it. I have given my opinion frankly to the Bishop, to Father Buteux, and, in fine, to all who have any interest in the success of our work. All have given reasons that are not entirely satisfactory; yet I dare not disregard them. The spirit of this country is so different from ours that one ought to be acquainted with it before condemning those who know more about it than we do; so I await the issue before passing judgment in a positive manner. If we cannot do any good here, you know our agreement, we will return to our own country.

Dear France? Though far away, it is nevertheless who, like a good mother, sends help to this poor diocese.

Mother Guerin's account is continued in a letter on May 25, 1841 to Canon Lottin.

We have at present ten postulants, exclusive of those we have dismissed and some others who have offered themselves but whom we cannot accept on account of our poverty. In this country no dowry is given to girls even at marriage. They come with a silk dress, a fine hat, and a tiny trunk.... The education of our candidates corresponds with their poor exterior. In religion they are ignorant of the first essentials, and I am now beginning to teach them a little catechism, often with an interpreter. They ask me questions as learned as that of St. Paul the Simple, who asked of his father Anthony whether our Lord lived before the Prophets. They tell me that the Son of God is a thousand years younger than the Eternal Father, and the Holy Spirit still younger. I should never finish if I gave you details of the absurdities which they retail. Can it be otherwise when these poor children have seen a priest only once or twice a year? And is it not surprising that God inspires in persons who know Him so little the desire of consecrating their lives to His service, and submitting themselves to strangers, this latter a virtue which costs so much to the pride of Americans, who long only for liberty and independence? There is great fervor among those good children. Uncertain though we may be of the success of our boarding school, such is not the case with our Novitiate. If we had thirty Sisters all formed and ready to go on mission, they could all be placed within a year and would accomplish an infinite amount of good in their poor Indiana, which has needs so great, so pressing, and so acutely realized. The Protestants are as eager as the Catholics in asking for Sisters, although motivated by self-interest and business, which are the two great wheels by which all America goes forward. God who knows how to draw good from evil will doubtless cause these inclinations to tend to His Glory.

34

In truth, how much good there is to do here, and how great and sublime the mission confided to us! But one must be a saint to fulfill it, and I own to you, Father, that I understand better each day how far I am from the perfection of my state and from the qualities necessary for the important duty which is mine. . . .

This thought makes me tremble, and I have written to our venerated Mother begging her to send us someone who has indeed the spirit of God and especially profound humility, great piety, and an earnest spirit of sacrifice. With these, one could perform miracles here. . . . I conjure you, Father, in the name of Jesus, in the name of the countless souls which we could win here, to induce our good Mother to send us the two Sisters for whom I am asking with so much earnestness, one to replace, or at least to assist me, a musician for our boarding school, and Irma to teach drawing. With this help I have assured her that we shall succeed, and without it, we shall fail. Only after studying the circumstances with the most scrupulous care do I repeat this. You have been our father and our friend. Be our advocate now, and if you accept, our suit is won.

The Bishop of Vincennes seems to take the keenest interest in our establishment and has given me during my illness very great proofs of devotedness. His exterior, however, is of icy coldness, and our chaplain, who is the same northern temperature, asked me lately to write to our Mother that he was an ill-conditioned bear. They are, nevertheless, men of a sanctity terrifying for my cowardice. If my illness seems to last too long, Monseigneur will probably send me back to France. In that case, I shall go to my little room in the Rue des

Portes, to my dear friends, but in that as in all else, my desire is to wish for nothing. . . .

If Sisters come to us, it is essential for them to write to the Bishop of New York before leaving the ship. He will send for them and have them accompanied to Mme. Parmentier's house where the tenderest attentions will be showered upon them, and their persons and their belongings will be in perfect safety. I recommend these dear Sisters especially to you. They will not need a passport except perhaps to go to Havre, and in that case a single one will suffice. I am awaiting a long letter from you, and what joy shall I have in receiving it! Have you my address? Terre Haute, Indiana, is sufficient.

Document 3: Letters to a Priest-counsellor: The Trials of School-teaching in America

Mother Theresa Gerhardinger, foundress of the School Sisters of Notre Dame, came from her motherhouse in Munich to open dozens of convents in America and other countries in her lifetime. She traveled with a pioneer band of sisters to America in 1847 and remained several months to study conditions there. During this period she wrote long letters to Father Mathias Siegert, the ecclesiastical superior of her congregation in Munich, with whom she shared her fears and hopes and appealed for counsel. Her letters are full of shrewd observations on American manners.[8]

35

J.M!

Baltimore, December 22, 1847

To Reverend Mathias Siegert

Dear Reverend Father

We have sent you more than twelve letters, and still have no news from you since July 17. This is doubly painful for us, since we are concerned about you, and we miss your advice in our trouble. . . .

We can write in all sincerity that we are concerned day and night about you, and all we have left behind, and in general about the young and sorely tried work of God. Let us hope our presentiments are unfounded. We would gladly bear your pain if we could. . . .

Difficult as it is for us to do, we are forced to beg to be supplied with money, until this work of God has developed sufficiently to allow us to pay it back. In our earlier letters we asked you, Reverend Father, to procure for us, through the mediation of the Most Reverend Archbishop and the Reverend court chaplain Mueller, a check for 18,000–20,000 florins, because our motherhouse, whose financial burdens and capabilities we so well know, is not in a position to help.

We are to pay to the Reverend Redemptorists at least 60,000 dollars (15,000 florins) soon, since it is very necessary to pay them promptly. They themselves are burdened with many debts. There are also alterations to be made, and many necessary articles to be bought during the coming spring. We have not yet sufficient income to procure the necessities of life. Perhaps it will be several years before this is possible.

We can count on nothing now but the small tuition, not even enough to hire the secular personnel we need; we must depend on candidates. The money brought with us from the loved motherhouse in Munich will soon be completely spent. Since we do not consider it prudent to make known our poverty, we trust entirely in the almighty and merciful God, and ask help from you. It is with a heavy heart that we do this, because we have heard from immigrants that scarcity of goods and even famine is prevalent in our beloved Fatherland. If this should be the case, there is no hope of our receiving money from Germany. . . .

Of course, the hardships and dangers of the journey, and the unhealthy climate here can be not endured without injury except by a few. There is an abundance of the best of food here, but the prices are exorbitant, so that a religious community like ours will experience difficulties if the community does not possess investments, or a large farm which can be worked by our own members. The Benedictine Fathers and the Christian Brothers from Alsace intend to do this at St. Mary's. We could never undertake it profitably; in fact it would be impossible here as well as there.

The Carmelite sisters here, who do not own a farm and are not provided with capital, experience great difficulties. They are obliged to teach school for their livelihood. The same is true of the colored sisters, who can not improve their situation. In fact, they were in danger of dispersing, but some priests helped them by increasing the number of school children, and entrusting more children of the poor to them for education. This is the harsh fate of religious societies that are not provided with capital which bears a large annual interest; 6% is the lowest interest rate.

Convents which are not in want of the necessary means of support are able to live according to their Rule with no disturbance or hindrance. Should circumstances force you and our entire Congregation to come here, Reverend Father, the Lord has already provided accommodations, as I have said. We trust we will have sufficient work in a few years with the children in cities close by: Pittsburgh, Philadelphia, New York and Buffalo. Of course, until these places become available, the sisters would have to live on their means; therefore, it would be advisable to save every penny and article of clothing and bring it along. How delighted we would be to see you, and all our sisters here with us!

It is impossible to learn to know America from the writings and

36

oral accounts of others; one must live here and experience it. Things
are different from the ideas prevalent in Europe. One can not possibly write about it.

Much consideration must be given to the dispensations from Holy
Rule which will become necessary for America, and which must be
obtained from·Rome. Here again, I cannot write about it. We are
concerned about this, and are very anxious about it. It requires much
prayer. We beg you and our dear companion sisters to remain faithful
in prayer, faith, hope and love for Jesus, Mary, and the dear children. . . .

In our earlier letters we asked our order for three or four house
sisters. Now that we have been in Baltimore for three months, we
know that in this case, too, things have developed entirely differently
from what we originally planned. In case not every one comes, send
us only teachers. I would like to remind you that these should be
healthy, strong, robust and courageous; each must be capable of
filling the post of superior, and must be a competent teacher in the
elementary school and the Industrial Arts department. The requirements for German are not as rigid here as in Munich. Great prudence
is needed to manage the children and their parents successfully, and
only a keen insight and strong will can meet and conquer the various
difficulties that arise in the school room and outside it. Without these
qualities it is not apparently possible to hold one's own in a German-
American school. Neither are mannish, rough sisters acceptable.
They would be a torment to themselves, to the children, to their
parents and the priests, and they could accomplish nothing, bringing
shame and disgrace upon the order.

We cannot use sisters and young ladies who desire only to live a
quiet, retired conventual life, those who cannot be employed in
school; unless they bring with them considerable funds which bear a
yearly interest of at least 200 dollars. This is considered the lowest
amount annually needed for the support and needs of an individual.
Several young ladies have already applied for domestic service; this
will save us traveling expenses for sisters from Bavaria. Besides, these
people are accustomed to the climate and are familiar with the habits
and customs. They know the temperment of the people, and speak
English. Therefore, for the present we have no need of sisters to do
cooking, gardening, painting, gilding, shoemaking and cobbling,
bookbinding or secretarial work. Neither do we require a hired man
or extern, for we could not support them and we can hire people here
for these services. Crescentia Schrupp, if she changes for the better,
could cook in German style for us, since she would be aided by a sister
in charge of the kitchen. A lady whom we brought from St. Mary's
is gardener, and does this for a small compensation. She also tends
animals, and does other work around the house. Such a lay person

is of more use to us in this country than a house sister would be, because she can also deal with people, which the sisters could not do. The method of painting and gilding employed here is quite different from the one used at home, because of the different materials used.

Should necessity arise, Crescentia Schrupp, who has learned something of these two trades from painter Petzer, could take care of them in the manner in which they are done here. Sister Magdalene is able to attend to the shoes we wear in the house. Leather shoes will have to be provided by a shoemaker in any case. Under the present circumstances there is no need for book binding, since the Redemptorists have all the needed school books on hand, and intend to have our grammar printed. Perhaps the sister proposed for the bookbindery could be of use here, since we shall need copybooks for the private school. However, we hesitate somewhat, because of Sister Emmerana's health, work habits, self-conceit, and hearty appetite. A dollar a day would scarcely suffice to support her. She could be employed with delicate craftwork in pasting and basket weaving, and thereby earn her livelihood. Perhaps she can still learn something along these lines. Small wax figures of the Infant Jesus might also find a market here.

French is not needed, as English is the national language. Probably all our teaching sisters should learn it. The schools are half German, half English. For this reason it would have been good if our motherhouse might have been established in an entirely German Catholic city, as St. Mary's is. Perhaps in five or six years this may become possible. We are deeply concerned about these half English-speaking, half-German schools, since we are afraid that the English language, English customs, and English attitudes might also enter our convent. May God preserve us from this!

We have accepted three school candidates, 20 years old. With God's help we will succeed with them. An eleven-year-old pupil joined them, but we shall have to see what God's plans are in her regard. This coming Sunday four more young ladies are coming. All of them, however, are without financial means; only our eleven-year-old boarder pays.

It is advisable for the sisters who come to reduce the amount of luggage as much as possible. We recommend they not take more than they are able to carry and watch it personally. . . .

Difficult tasks are awaiting these dear children, even if they come invested with the habit. It is possible that one or other will experience what happened to our novice Colette when she was sent to Pfaffenhofen. We wish those sisters who make profession might be entirely prepared or even better, that they make profession before coming, so that they would need only renew their vows here. We want to avoid dealing with the Archbishop until we can present our Rule to him as

approved by Bishop Reisach. Without a letter from our Archbishop
in Munich there is no thought of approaching the Ordinary here. It
would be good if the letter were brief, and would explain that until
now we have lived according to the Rule of Notre Dame, have been
received and made profession in it, and that we beg for permission
to continue thus until the required dispensations in the Rule have
been obtained from Rome, and that the Archbishop of Munich will
inform him as soon as they have been granted. . . .

About four weeks ago our church and little convent were threatened with burning, and we were closely guarded for a week. The Lord
will be our protector. We wonder, too, how many trials have befallen
you and the Congregation during our absence. We suspect sickness
and death, and our worries about all of you are increased by your
silence. Perhaps our houses cannot help each other any more. . . .

Here are some experiences we have had in our three schools which
might prove helpful in sending personnel. Schools will not become
large, for there are too many of them, and attendance is voluntary,
which is bad. Children attend one school today, another tomorrow,
just as they please. If they are corrected they do not come back;
learning they often consider recreation. All they want to do is eat
cookies, taffy and molasses candy, a cheap sweet. This causes us much
trouble. If we forbid it they threaten not to come to school any more.
At the slightest punishment the parents say, "In this country one may
not treat children so severely; they, too, must be given freedom."
They do not listen to any one, and even strike their parents if they
do not give in to them. They laugh and jeer at priests. They ask boldly,
"Can I go down stairs? I want to go home now." They will not write
one letter of the alphabet at home. "I go to school for that," is their
answer. Homework cannot be introduced here; the parents do not
want it either. Therefore, everything must be studied with them in
school. They do not manifest the slightest eagerness to learn German.
English, however, they want to learn to read and write. They hate
German. All one hears is English. If they want to insult each other
they say, "You German!"

They comprehend little or nothing if one tries to convey ideas to
them, because they do not know enough German to understand what
we mean. They will never learn spelling, for they neither speak German correctly, or do they understand it. Because of the English they
inevitably write ch for g and other similar errors. It is difficult to give
them grades or keep school records; today one or other leaves, and
four to six weeks absence is not uncommon. They show little or no
interest in needlework. What is most to their liking is jumping, running, dancing, tagging, singing and fighting. They are like wild animals, and try out all their naughtiness in school.

Children sit in the school benches with legs crossed, backs leaning

39

and arms folded like men at the theater in our country. They even speak to priests in this position, and the latter must put up with it in order not to displease the parents. It is difficult to make them come to holy Mass on Sundays and holy days. As soon as it becomes a bit warm they use fans, want a drink constantly, and do not want to study. If it is cold, only a few come to school; these do not take off their wraps, but write with their mittens on. This is how pampered and spoiled even German children are in America. If they do not know something they answer boldly, "Teacher did not know it either when she was little."

They mumble all kinds of abusive language in English. One of the reasons the children do not want to study is the fact that their minds are filled with concern for boys. They write little notes to each other, exchange gifts, etc. They consider this all right, and parents laugh about it if told. In the lavatories they behave indecently, do not close the door, talk, laugh and sing while there. This is common in America, even with adults. Clothing, too, is immodest. All wear pants; the girls' dresses are low-cut and short, only to the knee. The smallest girls appear like women and acrobats. Naturally they do not want to hear about prayer. Teaching school is difficult and we implore the dear Lord fervently for his grace. . . .

When we tell parents they ought punish their children for their own good they say in the children's presence, "I can not punish my own flesh and blood." A mother who came to call for her child whom we had detained for disobedience said, "It is already twelve o'clock; come, Mary, and eat something." She wept because the child had not had anything to eat for so long. A father said, "My child is handsome and talks sensibly; I can not strike him; it would hurt me too much."

Stealing is a daily occurrence in school. Some one even took the pen from my desk. Another child stole an earring from a classmate which I found on her. Like confirmed thieves they know how to hide what they have taken. One hears horrible things about their parents from the children. "My father, the scoundrel, was shot. I am glad." Or, "I wish my mother were hanged, and my father forced to go begging," said a girl, angry because she did not get her will.

At St. James school we will employ only two persons, one sister and a candidate, who will teach in English. It is not possible for the sisters to live there, and we shall continue to drive to school. The missions here can hardly develop as the branch houses in Bavaria did.

Dear Reverend Father, pardon my poor writing and many mistakes; it is late at night, and I am sleepy. Time does not permit me to read over this letter. A thousand greetings to all the sisters, boarders, and school children. . . .

Write to us. We can not describe the depth of our loneliness and the desires of our hearts. If God had not borne with us, what would have become of us, and what will become of us? If I could only speak with you, Father, for an hour, and with the most Reverend Archbishop as well. . . .

I feel urged to take care of everything which needs to be completed; to put all things in order, but my hands are tied without both of you. This fact would make my death doubly difficult.

I feel less capable of being a superior here than in Europe, and I must take steps to resign: otherwise I shall spoil everything. Sisters Caroline and Seraphina have a calling for America; their views are opposite mine, and I am sure the Lord will assist them when they are in a position of authority.

I must tear myself away from writing, but again beg you to write us. I can not adequately express my anxiety for the order and for you.

41

Document 4: Struggles with Bishops

The constitutions of religious orders were designed to set forth clearly the rights and obligations of sisters, ecclesiastical superiors, and bishops to each other. In spite of this, nuns sometimes had to struggle against the efforts of bishops to usurp undue power over them. Mother Guerin and the Sisters of Providence in Indiana were placed in this position when Bishop de la Hailandiere of Vincennes repeatedly interfered in their internal affairs, reassigning sisters to different convents, closing and opening missions without consulting them, intercepting their mail, refusing them the sacraments, and forcing them to accept candidates they regarded as unsuitable. Finally, after exercising much patience, Mother Guerin gave the bishop an ultimatum, threatening to move the sisters to the diocese of Detroit. This forced Bishop de la Hailandiere to accede to their conditions rather than lose the services of the sisters.[9]

Letter Circular

St. Mary-of-the-Woods, March 8, 1846

Very dear Sisters,

It is a joy to me to be able myself to tell you that, thanks to your fervent prayers, Our Lord still permits me to live and to suffer with you. We will thank Him together, and to prove our gratitude we will repeat to Him from the depth of our hearts that we will belong to Him more perfectly than ever. And this we will more particularly prove to Him by the tender charity that unites us; for it is by this that we shall preserve the spirit of God amongst us, and that we can rely on His assistance—assistance of which we have no greater need than ever before; as, my dear daughters, the moment has come when we must leave the distressing state in which we have been for so long a time.

During the first days of my illness we received a letter from the Bishop whom you know about [the Bishop of Detroit]. He offered, together with his fatherly protection, to approve our Rules and Constitutions for his diocese, and he entreated our Father [Corbe] to come with us to continue to be our Superior. But this is all he can do for us at the present time.

I also received on the 27th of January, a letter of ten pages from the Bishop of Vincennes. It is full of accusations and reproaches which are personal, three-fourths of which are palpably untrue. I am obliged to communicate this to you, for in a little corner your names are written; as is also that of Father Corbe, who read only two pages of it and then threw it aside with the greatest indignation.

Notwithstanding, we think here that before taking the final step it would be more according to the spirit of God to renew again our petitions to His Lordship, the Bishop of Vincennes, without mention of the past. In view of this we are sending you the letter that we are addressing to him, in order that you may sign it, if, as we do not doubt, you share our opinion in the matter. . . .

Your devoted
Sister St. Theodore
Sup'r Gen'l

You know, my dear Sisters, you are not obliged to sign the letter I am sending, if it is contrary to your views. You also know that in signing it you engage yourselves to remain in the diocese of Vincennes, if the Bishop grants us what we ask, and of leaving soon if he does not grant it. Reflect well and act according to your lights and intentions. Write to me as soon as you will have taken your determination. You understand that this letter is for you alone.

Always yours in our Lord,
Sr. St. T.

To the Right Reverend Cel. de la Hailandiere, Bishop of Vincennes

Saint Mary-of-the-Woods, March 8, 1846

My Lord:

It has not been possible to reply sooner to your letter of January 25; even today we can speak of only one item of that letter. We are confronting circumstances too grave to be deterred by personal considerations.

You say that we are mistaken in thinking that your refusal to reply to our letter of the month of August is equivalent to a refusal to those things we asked of you. If such is the case, we take the liberty to renew, once more, those same requests.

The first is, as you know, that you give in writing, with your signature and under your episcopal seal, permission to dwell in your diocese according to the Rules and Constitutions which we brought from France, in order that we may have the assurance of being al-

42

lowed to follow them as perfectly as is possible for a body not yet organized. The second is that you give us the deed of the property of Saint Mary's so that we may begin to build. Your Lordship knows that we have never asked aught but these things in order to establish ourselves in Indiana as a Congregation subject to you. Many times you have said, and even written, that you intended to grant us these things, but that we had put obstacles. These obstacles are now all removed—all the Sisters of Providence can now hold property legally; therefore, we dare hope that you will not delay to give us this last proof of your good will, which, in putting an end to a state so painful for all, will open to our view a brighter future and afford us the occasion to prove to you by our gratitude and submission how it has pained us to be, in a way, compelled to afflict your heart.

43

However, faithful to the spirit of candor which we have always followed, we must say that, after all that has occurred since our first request, your silence, or any reply which would not be the Acts we ask for, could not but be regarded by us, this time, as a formal refusal; in which case we would consider ourselves obliged to take a definitive resolution, and that with very little delay.

The fate of our Congregation is yet in your hands. We shall pray with even greater fervor than in the past that God may inspire you to act in the manner that will procure Him more glory and unite us more closely to Him. In these sentiments we remain, with the most profound respect, my Lord.

Of Your Lordship
> The very humble and obedient servants,
> SISTER ST. VINCENT   SISTER MARY JOSEPH
> SISTER ST. FRANCIS XAVIER   SISTER MARY CECILIA
> SISTER MARY LIGUORI   SISTER ST. THEODORE

Document 5: Securing the Freedom of the Order to Work in America

In the European Dominican tradition, nuns of the "second order" were strictly cloistered, while "third order" nuns were allowed to live a more active life in the world. Many orders sought direct approval of their constitution from the Vatican, because in becoming a papal or exempt congregation, they were independent of the control of the local bishop. In this letter Mother Hyacintha, administrator of the Dominican community in Racine, Wisconsin, explains to Mother Pia, superior of the Dominican community in San Jose, California, the reasons for seeking third order status and Vatican approval.[10]

Racine, December 31, 1889

Dear good Reverend Mother Pia:
Your inquiry regarding affiliation necessitates a long explanation.

Our Convent became affiliated with the Dominican Order as early as
1877 as a convent of the Third Order through J. Sanvita, at that time
master general. More than this cannot be claimed by the Sisters of our
Order who are engaged in the schools, especially if they have charge
of institutions and orphanages. The Second Order cannot dispense
with the strict canonical enclosure. This enclosure forbids under pen-
alty of excommunication travel under any pretext whatsoever. All
visits, moreover, from externs are forbidden; and only a limited number of members may be received. Under these circumstances what
would we be able to do and how could we obtain our livelihood? For
a long time we were confused about the conditions and, like many
other Dominican Communities in this country, considered ourselves
Sisters of the Second Order. Our confessor, who for many years was
professor of Canon Law, called our attention to this mistaken view of
ours, and pointed out that we were not members of the Second Order
and could not hope ever to be such, because we would never be able
to observe strict enclosure. He told us, moreover, that if we desired
to be members of the Dominican Order, we would have to be affiliated
with the Order; that is, that our Convent must be recognized as
Dominican by the Master General. . . .

44

His answer clearly indicated that we could only become Dominicans by becoming affiliated with the Third Order and that bishops
and priests did not have the power of admitting members into the
Third Order unless they were especially empowered to do so. We had
no choice but to follow the advice of our Confessor and to accept the
offer made by the master general. Since then we have the assurance
of really belonging to the Order and of really being Dominicans. We
have a quiet conscience and are happy. Don't hesitate to follow our
example. Remember that the privileges and the spiritual advantages
of the Third Order are scarcely less than those of the Second Order.
Besides as members of the Third Order we have the privilege of
following our good judgment in the circumstances that arise. Simple
affiliation in the Third Order does not satisfy us, however. We strive
after higher things. We want the approval of our Congregation by
Rome. If a Congregation is not recognized by Rome, it is simply an
episcopal association and depends in every respect upon the bishop
of the diocese, who has full charge of the Sisters, and who can act at
will in their regard. It is, moreover, of greatest importance to have a
Rule designed for our special circumstances and approved by the
Holy See. Our Father Confessor went to Rome last year in the interests of the convent. . . . The strict fast and abstinence of the Order was
declared incompatible with the duties of Sisters engaged in teaching.
Our Reverend Confessor is engaged at present in writing a Rule for
our Community in accordance with directions he received in Rome.
It will consist for the most part of the ordinary regulations, but it

will be arranged to conform with the Third Order requirements. It will, therefore, contain little that is new to us, and, on the whole, will require only what we have been observing up to the present. . . . The Reverend Confessor hopes to complete the task within a few months. It will then be printed and sent to Rome for approval. It will probably be several years before the approbation is given, as Rome is very deliberate in matters of this kind. . . .

The matter is so important for all of us. No doubt I have surprised you by the contents of this letter, but I hope that I have convinced you of the necessity of affiliating with Rome, for we can get help from no one else—neither bishop nor priest. If we do our part, God will supply what is missing.

45

With heartfelt greetings,
Mother Mary Hyacintha, O.S.D.

Document 6: Conflicts with American Protestant Bigotry

When Catholic sisters first began to be seen in America in the first half of the nineteenth century, they were greeted with hostility and suspicion. Rumors of evil practices and women held by force in convents were circulated, and Protestant ministers argued against Catholicism from their pulpits, directing their attacks particularly against nuns. Nuns were frequently insulted or pelted in the streets. Occasionally riots broke out, and mobs pillaged and burned the convents.

One of the most famous of such cases was the burning of the Ursuline convent in Charlestown, Massachusetts, on August 11, 1834. This incident was inspired by misinformation circulated by Rebecca Reed, who had been dismissed from Mount St. Benedict as unsuited to religious life after a six-month novitiate. (She later wrote the first of the anticonvent books, Six Months in a Convent, *published in 1835.) A second nun, Elizabeth Harrison, had left briefly because of a breakdown caused by overwork, but then had petitioned to reenter. It was falsely rumored that she was being held by force. The mob looted the buildings and desecrated the chapel, even digging up the bodies of the sisters in the cemetery, before burning the convent and academy. In the following account from the transcript of the trial, Sister Mary Edmund St. George, the Ursuline superior, describes the scene followed by two other nuns, including Miss Harrison.*[11]

From the Boston Transcript—Trial of the Convent Rioters.

The trial of the convent rioters commenced yesterday, at East Cambridge. . . .

The district attorney, after opening the case, called as the first witness Mary Ann Ursula Moffat, otherwise called Mary Edmond St. George, the Lady Superior of the Ursuline Community. . . . She gave the following testimony, as reported by the Atlas:

I am the superior of the Ursuline Community in this state. I had the entire jurisdiction of the institution at Charlestown. Have held my present rank ten years. There was a school in our establishment, of which I was director. On the Thursday preceding the day on which the outrage was committed, I was told that the convent would be pulled down, and on the Saturday following several papers were sent to the institution concerning the "mysterious lady." On Sunday one of the selectmen of Charlestown called upon, and told me the convent would be destroyed if the "mysterious lady" could not be seen. By the "mysterious lady" I understood him to mean Miss Harrison.

On Monday the selectmen, five in number, came and were shown over the whole establishment. They remained three hours, and searched the building from the cellar to the highest apartment, looking in every box—even the paint boxes; also into all the drawers and closets. Two of the sisters went with me; one of these was the "mysterious lady," Miss Harrison. I do not know whether the out-buildings were examined. The selectmen went away at about six in the afternoon, and at a little after nine, I heard a great noise on the Medford Road, and distinguished the words—"Down with the convent!" I sent to tell the community that I thought we were in danger.

There were fifty pupils, from the age of six to eighteen years, and ten sisters in the establishment at this time. Two of the latter were novices. One of the sisters has died since. . . . After I had alarmed the inmates of our house, I went into a room on the second story, opened the window, and asked the people outside what they wanted. I told them they were disturbing the peaceful slumbers of the pupils, some of whom were the children of their most respectable fellow citizens. They then asked to see "the nun that had run away," and I sent up to fetch her, but found her lying insensible in the arms of four of the sisters. She had fainted with fright. I returned to the window and told the people that this was the case. She was incapable of showing herself to them that night, but if they would come the next day, they should receive every satisfaction.

I also told the mob that the selectmen had examined our institution and were satisfied; but if they [the mob] were not satisfied, they might come on the following day and investigate for themselves; I said the report of the selectmen would appear in the Morning Post. They replied, that all I said was false; that they had one of the selectmen with them, and that he had opened the gate for them. They asked if we were prepared to meet them. I did not wish them to know that our male domestics had left us. The mob shortly after this went away, saying they would not return til Thursday, when they would pull down the convent.

Before they went, they had fired a gun from under a willow tree near the house. I told them at the time they were making a noise, shouting and screaming, that my sister was ill of a consumption, and that the state of alarm they had thrown her into would cause her death. They replied, "So much the better." My sister is since dead. When they were gone, I thought there was no longer any cause for apprehension, and told the pupils and sisters to retire to their dormitories. They had no sooner done so, than the men returned and began to break the fence to make a bonfire.

At this time Mr. Runey, the selectman, came up with another person and told me he did not think he could quell the mob, but if I and the pupils would throw ourselves on his protection, he would do the best he could for us. I told Mr. Runey, if he wished to show himself friendly to us, to go and tell the people to desist from breaking the fences. He said he would go and do all in his power to prevent them. About five or six minutes after this I heard renewed shouts of "Down with the convent," and I then told the pupils and sisters it would be best for them to get to the summer-house, but before the former had time to leave their dormitories, the mob commenced breaking the doors and windows.

47

I went to each of the dormitories afterwards to see if all the pupils had escaped. I called at every door and found that they were all gone. I then went down to my own room, in which was a drawer containing valuables, but when I opened the door I saw the mob had already entered. I turned to go away, and saw twenty or thirty men in the same passage with me; they were about ten or twenty feet from me. I then went to the summer-house, where I found about forty of the pupils, some in their fright having climbed over the fence and gone to Mr. Cutter's; I sent the remainder after them, and went myself to Mr. Adam's whither all the pupils were eventually brought.

I never recovered any of the property of the institution, excepting a few articles of very small value. . . .

Mary Ann Barber, otherwise Sister Benedict Joseph, was next called. This lady is very beautiful. She gave her testimony with great clearness and self-possession, and her manner and language were those of a highly educated and accomplished female: I have been more than eight years in the Ursuline Community. I was in the convent on the night of the 11th Aug. Was awakened from sleep by the superior, who told me to dress quickly and arouse the community. I did so, and went afterwards to a window, from which I saw the mob, and heard them using abusive language towards the superior. They called her "a figure head, and said she was made of brass." The remainder of the witness's testimony was similar to that of the lady who preceded her, and which had been already before our readers. She identified a work-box and cross, as forming part of the property taken from the convent.

Miss Elizabeth Harrison (otherwise Mary St. John, the individual who left the convent) examined: I have been a member of the Ursuline Community for thirteen years. I was a teacher of music in the establishment. I did not leave the convent in consequence of any difficulty with the Lady Superior. The cause of my leaving was mental derangement. Had any one told me I should have done what I did, I should have thought it impossible. Everything was done in the institution to contribute to my happiness and that of the other inmates. I had never before felt any desire to leave the convent. I gave 14 lessons per day, and of 35, 40, and 45 minutes each. The witness further stated that her recollection of what took place after she left the community was very indistinct; she was bereft of reason.

48

Mr. Farley was proceeding to put other questions, when she suddenly covered her face with her handkerchief and burst into tears. Mr. F. under these circumstances, and considering what had been said respecting the witness's state of health, expressed his willingness to refrain from further interrogations. Miss Harrison was then suffered to retire from the court, which she did under the escort of the Russian consul.

In a somewhat more humorous style, Sister St. Francis Xavier of Saint Mary-of-the-Woods, Indiana, writes back to her family in France of the anti-Catholic hostility and superstitions of the Americans as well as of newfound friends.[18]

This good news [of the conversion of a hardened sinner] will console you a little for the burning of the house of the Sisters of Charity at Fredericktown. The incendiaries, before enkindling the fire, disabled the fire engines so that the progress of the fire could not be arrested. The house was burned to the ground. We may, perhaps, have to endure a similar misfortune. A few days ago we received an anonymous letter warning us to be on our guard. For two or three nights our workmen have watched, armed with guns. Some men were found hiding in our fields, but God permitted one of our neighbors to see them. We trust that the Blessed Virgin, who has always been a mother to us, will continue to protect our poor community.

I have already told you that our mission at Madison is greatly exposed to the persecutions of the enemies of Catholicity. Not long since, our Sisters wrote that the Presbyterian minister assembled his congregation in the church, and then, transported by the *Spirit,* disclosed all the infamies perpetrated by priests and nuns since the beginning of the Church! He ended his harangue by hurling anathemas against the parents who sent their children to Catholic schools, and he predicted that they would not escape the divine vengeance. "When we go to Mass," wrote one of our Sisters at this time, "the little rogues of boys, seeing us with our pupils, run after us, screaming,"

'Sheep, sheep, sheep!' They also pelt us with snowballs (but that does not hurt us), and sometimes even with eggs and stones."

The persecutions that our Sisters have been suffering at Madison are somewhat abated. Their most formidable adversary, however [Mr. Curtis], called together three hundred ministers last month, in order to devise in council some means of doing away with the *nuns*. But God laughs at the designs of men. Their ridiculous assembly inspired only contempt, and since that time the people are more favorably disposed toward our holy religion.

There is here an apostate monk from Italy, who goes from city to city giving lectures on the progress and danger of Catholicity. He was lately at Cincinnati, and I read a portion of his sixth discourse from which I quote: "When the demon wished to introduce evil into the world he made use of woman to corrupt man; now, to introduce Catholicism in America, he makes use of the nuns, true Eves, with their sweet and engaging manners, their knowledge, and their attractions. The Jesuits are dangerous, but the nuns are their agents, and are still more to be feared. Guard against sending your children to their schools, and even against placing among them servants trained by the Sisters, for they will instill their bad principles into the hearts of your children. The evil is greater than you think; and I know better than you that Catholicism is daily increasing," etc.

49

We do indeed remove the prejudices of our pupils. The parents have to choose between the inferiority of the other schools and what they call the *superstition* of ours; but, as many prefer having their children well instructed, they send them to us. Our boarding school is the best in Indiana, and would be considered very good even in France. We have about eighty pupils and several others are expected. I have never met young girls better taught than our first pupils. Mr. Pinatel, an old naval officer, was astonished at their knowledge of mathematics and astronomy. As these subjects and drawing were the ones to which he had principally devoted himself, this part of the examination pleased him best. The children especially excel, however, in Christian doctrine and in sacred and ecclesiastical history. They were highly commended, and with good reason, for the skill they show with the needle, particularly in plain sewing.

Every kind of absurdity and calumny finds acceptance with some of the people here. They were even so foolish as to believe that our chaplain had horns. One mischievous little woman, now a Catholic, told the villagers that if each of them would give her twenty-five cents, she would beg Father Corbe to take off his hat and let them see the horns. Not seeing them on his head the people wanted to look in his hat, supposing he had left them there.

A solicitous friend wrote as follows to an old lady who had her daughter in our school at Terre Haute: "Dear Madam: Although I have not the honor of your acquaintance, the interest I take in your daughter prompts me to tell you that, if you leave her with the nuns, she will be lost. Twenty years from now she will remember the detestable principles she has imbibed there; and if she does not become a Catholic, she will at least defend the Sisters all her life and on all occasions."

The good lady replied that she was old enough to judge for herself and wise enough to know how to bring up her own children; that not only would she leave her daughter with the good Sisters, but that she herself, when her dear husband should be no more, would offer herself to the Sisters, not to teach in the boarding school, but to serve them in their houses, an office she would consider an honor. We have the strangest imaginable applications for admission. Some, like this lady, still have their dear husbands, and are not even baptized; others ask to be received for a year only, in the absence of their husbands; others would like to be Sisters, but have not yet decided to become Catholics, and so on.

Document 7: The Sisters as Nurses: Turning the Tide of Bigotry

At a time when nursing was still considered a daring profession for a woman, Catholic nuns offered their services to all in the most dangerous circumstances, such as the yellow fever epidemics in the 1850s in Charleston, North Carolina. In the following account, a Sister of Mercy of Charleston describes their work in that city during the epidemics.[13]

The first yellow fever I remember was the terrible epidemic of 1852. There was a new hospital just built, called the "Roper Hospital." The Rev. Dr. Lynch, then in charge, Bishop Reynolds being absent and requested not to return (on account of the danger), opened it as a relief hospital. Here the Sisters worked day and night with Dr. Lynch and Dr. Corcoran. . . . Numbers of valuable lives were saved, and many who had neglected their religion for years were prepared for happy deaths; whilst others at the sight of their danger made their peace with God. . . .

When Bishop Reynolds arrived, he found his flock almost decimated, and a large number of orphans to be provided for. The Sisters had been obliged to contract a considerable debt, which the city of Charleston generously assumed as its own and paid.

In 1854, 1856, and, I think, 1858, the city received visits from the same dread disease. During these years the Sisters had no hospital, but went about from street to street, through lanes and alleys, wherever the sick might be found, carrying baskets filled with the necessaries of life and medicine, as these were needed. They worked heroically, all through the periods of disease, and all classes of citizens recognized the debt of gratitude due to these noble women. Some, such as Sister Mary Joseph, and Sister Mary Peter, fresh from Ireland and full of vigor in body and soul, were as little alive to human respect as they were to danger, and I remember on one occasion during the wet season, it was quite laughable to see them wade through the mire, with large boots, their habits and cloaks tied up, and lugging along their baskets, which seemed twice as large as themselves, that they might bring relief to the sick in the poor quarter of the town. When the troubles were over, our Sisters quickly returned to their school-rooms and seemed to have forgotten, what no one had seen them could ever could ever forget, that they had but a short time before been active amid the dark scenes of death from yellow fever haunting an entire community. It was not strange then that the people of Charleston should have been greatly attached to these nuns, and honored the little black bonnet. In truth the ladies of South Carolina called to a religious life think no dress so respectable as that of the Sisters of Mercy. In later years, whenever the epidemic broke out, the Sisters were supplied with vehicles in order that they might carry out their mission to the sick with greater facility and despatch. At times no one was seen in the streets but the doctors, the priests, and the Sisters on their rounds, and no sound was heard but the rumble of carts that were carrying off the dead. Coffins were often heaped one upon the other. About this time a society was formed among the first Protestant gentlemen of the district for the relief of the yellow fever sufferers, called the "Howard Society." The members worked heartily with the Sisters in their way, and frequently alms were distributed from the society through the Sisters. Natives of the region or those who were acclimated were not subject to the fever, except the children. Hence it was possible to hire good nurses; but they required to be well paid and well looked after. The Sisters managed to bring many of these nurses under their direction, and whilst the Howard Society usually paid for the lay service, the influence of the Sisters could not be paid for nor equalled by any hired service. Indeed the nuns so impressed the people by their efficiency and unselfish charity that they were not infrequently called to the sick before priest or doctor would be consulted. Finally, an hour had to be fixed after which people could not call the Sisters out of the convent. The door or gate was then to be locked, and no further calls to be answered. This was a great relief, as our poor Sisters were almost exhausted.

Although Catholics were a small percentage of the American population at that time, one-fifth of the nurses during the Civil War were Catholic nuns. Ninety-one Sisters of Charity, under the direction of Sister Gonzaga Grace, nursed at Satterlee Military Hospital near Gettysberg. In this account by Sister Gonzaga, the affection and esteem of the soldiers for the sisters is described.[14]

51

Cases of small-pox had occurred in the hospital from time to time, but the patients were removed as soon as possible to the Small-pox Hospital, which was several miles from the city. The poor fellows were more distressed on account of their being sent away from the Sisters to be nursed than they were on account of the disease. It was heart-rending when the ambulance came to hear the poor fellows begging to be left, even if they had to be entirely alone, provided the Sisters would be near them to have the Sacraments administered in the hour of danger. We offered our services several times to attend these poor sick, but were told that the Government had sent them away to avoid contagion. At last, however, the Surgeon in Charge obtained permission to keep the small-pox patients in the camp some distance from the Hospital. The tents were made very comfortable, with good large stoves to heat them, and "flys" (double covers) over the tops. The next thing was to have the Sisters in readiness, in case their services were required. Every one was generous enough to offer herself for the duty, but it was thought more prudent to accept one who had had the disease. As soon as the soldiers learned that a Sister had been assigned to the camp, they said: "Well, if I get the small-pox now, I don't care, because one of our Sisters will take care of me." From November, 1864, until May, 1865, we had upward of ninety cases—of whom nine or ten died. Two had the Black Small-pox. They were baptized before they died. We had, I may say, entire charge of the poor sufferers, as the physician who attended them seldom paid them a visit, but allowed us to do anything we thought proper for them. The patients were very little marked, and much benefited by drinking freely of tea made from Saracenia Purpura, or Pitcher Plant. When the weather permitted, I visited those poor fellows almost every day. Like little · children, at these times they expected some little treat of oranges, cakes, jellies, apples and such things, which we always had for them. They often said it was the Sisters who cured them and not the doctors, for they believed they were afraid of the disease. Our small-pox patients appeared to think that the Sisters were not like other human beings, or they would not attend such loathsome contagious diseases, which every one else shunned. One day I was advising an application to a man's face for poison—he would not see one of the doctors, because, he said, the doctor did him no good—and I told him this remedy had cured a Sister who was poisoned. The man looked at me in perfect astonishment. "A Sister!" he exclaimed. I answered "Yes." "Why!" said he, "I didn't know the Sisters ever got anything like that." I told him "To be sure they did. They are liable to take disease as well as any one else." "To be sure *not!*" he said. "For the boys often say they must be different from other people, for they do for us what no other person would do. They are not afraid of fevers, small-pox or anything else." The physicians acknowledged that they would have lost many more patients had it not been for the Sisters' watchful care.

In Ward R, there was a patient named John Smith. He was a month in the ward, and suffered very much. Morally speaking, he was a good man, and very patient and respectful. He had never been baptized, and did not know that it was necessary to salvation. As Sister saw that he was ignorant on that point, she explained it to him. He dreaded death, and could not think it was so near. He was conscious until the last. During the last three days of his life he seemed to be in deep thought. Sister said but little of death to him; she saw it was in vain. An hour before his death, she was passing near his bed, when he called her, and said in a tone of despair, "Oh, Sister, I am going to die!" Sister asked him if he was sorry for not having been baptized? He answered, "Oh, yes!" Sister told him it was not yet too late. He appeared overjoyed at hearing this, and she asked who he wished should baptize him? He answered, "A Catholic priest." Sister replied: "There is no Catholic priest here, and there is no time to send for one, but in a case like yours, the Catholic Church permits anyone to administer Baptism." He said at once: "Sister, baptize me. I want to be a child of God." He repeated some prayers after Sister in a very fervent manner. She asked him: "If you recover, do you intend to be a faithful Catholic?" He replied: "Oh, yes." He recited the Hail Mary with her, and in five minutes after he was baptized, he died in great peace.

53

In the same ward, another patient, an Indian named James Graham, who had been brought up where God was not known, was altogether ignorant of Him and His goodness. Sister told him of his danger, and of the little hope there was of his recovery, and of the necessity there was of preparing for a happy death. As well as he knew how, the poor man tried most fervently to prepare himself. He appeared never to have had any care, and the little we showed him won him so much that he thought nothing was right except what Sister did. He asked to be baptized in the Church that Sister thought was the right one and in no other. She gave him some instructions and left him a few days to consider them. He wore a medal of the Blessed Virgin, and would kiss it, and say: "My sweet Mother, I will soon see you in heaven!" A Protestant minister came to see him, and Sister asked him if this was the one he would choose to have baptize him. He asked: "Is this the one you would bring?" She told him "No," and he said: "Well, bring the right one." The priest had not yet arrived and he was sinking rapidly, so Sister baptized him as he earnestly desired, praying at the same time that God would have mercy on his soul. He died about two hours after, in peace.

From our taking charge of the Hospital, June the 9th, 1862, until we left it on August 3rd, 1865, ninety-one Sisters had been on duty there. The war being over in April, 1865, the Government only desired our services after that until the convalescents could obtain their discharge. The physicians, however, requested us to remain until all the sick were removed to the Soldiers' Home, or returned to their own homes. I am happy to be able to state that during our whole sojourn at Satterlee Hospital, there never was an unpleasant word between the physicians or officers and the Sisters. The eve of our departure, the Executive Officer said to me: "Sister, allow me to ask you a question. Has there ever been any misunderstanding or dissatisfaction between the officers and the Sisters since you came to this Hospital?" I answered: "None at all." "Well," he said, "I will tell you why I asked. The other evening we were at a party. The conversation turned on the Sisters in the Hospitals, and I said there had never been a falling-out between us at Satterlee—that we were all on the same good terms as on the first day we met. Some of the City Hospital doctors said they did not believe that forty women could live together without disputing, much less that they could be among such a number of men without it."

The number of Baptisms we have on record is fifty-seven. The number of communicants could not be ascertained, as some approached the Holy Table every Sunday. . . .

Document 8: Nuns on the Frontier: Sister Blandina's Adventures in the Southwest

Sister Blandina Segale, a Cincinnati Sister of Charity, was a remarkable woman who traveled alone to Colorado in 1878 at the age of twenty-two and spent eighteen years working in Colorado and New Mexico. During this period she put up a school and a hospital without prior resources, ended the lynch law in New Mexico, tamed Billy the Kid, built the tallest building in the territory, and proved herself more than the equal of the forces of greed and violence that surrounded her. She described these adventures in a personal journal written to her sister Justina, also a sister of Charity.[15]

Ending the Lynch Law in Trinidad, Colorado

One of my oldest pupils came to ask to have his sister excused from school. He looked so deathly pale that I inquired, "What has happened?" He answered, "Haven't you heard?"

"Nothing that should make you look as you do."

"Sister, dad shot a man! He's in jail. A mob has gathered and placed men about forty feet apart from the jail to Mr. McCaferty's room. The instant he breathes his last, the signal of his death will be given, and the mob will go to the jail and drag dad out and hang him."

"Have you thought of anything that might save him?" I asked.

"Nothing, Sister; nothing can be done."

"Is there no hope that the wounded man may recover?"

"No hope whatever; the gun was loaded with tin shot."

"John, go to the jail and ask your father if he will take a chance
at not being hanged by a mob."

"What do you propose doing, Sister?"

"First to visit the wounded man and ask if he will receive your
father and forgive him, with the understanding that the full force of
the law be carried out."

"Sister, the mob would tear him to pieces before he was ten feet
from the jail."

"I believe he will not be touched if I accompany him," I said.

"I'm afraid he will not have the courage to do as you propose."

"That is the only thing I can see that will save him from the mob
law. Ask your father to decide. This is Friday. I'll visit the sick man
after school this afternoon. Let me know if he will consent to go with
me to the sick man's room."

Immediately after school, with a companion, I went to see the
wounded man. Sister Fidelis had preceded me. She was writing a
letter to his mother bidding her good-bye until they would meet
where the Judge was just, and their tears would be dried forever.

I looked at the young man, a fine specimen of honesty and manli-
ness. My heart ached for the mother who expected frequent word
from her son, then to receive such news! To be shot unjustly, to die
in a strange land, among strangers, so young!

As soon as Sister Fidelis and companion took leave of the sick man,
the subject of the present visit was broached. The young man was
consistent. He said, "I forgive him, as I hope to be forgiven, but I want
the law to take its course."

Fully agreeing with him, he was asked: "Will you tell Mr. _____
this if he comes to beg your pardon?"

"Yes, Sister," he answered.

Friday evening the prisoner's son came to say his father was very
much afraid to attempt to walk to Mr. McCaferty's room, but if Sister
would walk with him, he would take the chance of having the court
pronounce sentence on him.

Early Saturday morning we presented ourselves to the Sheriff in
his office.

"Good morning, Sister!" was the Sheriff's pleasant greeting.

"Good morning, Mr. Sheriff. Needless to ask if you know what is
taking place in our two principal streets."

"You mean the men ready to lynch the prisoner who so unjustly
shot the young Irishman?"

"Yes. What are you going to do to prevent the lynching?"

"Do! What has any sheriff here ever been able to do to prevent a
mob from carrying out its intent?"

"Be the first sheriff to make the attempt!"

"How, Sister?" Standing to his full height—he must be six feet

55

four—he reminded me of a person with plenty of reserve strength, and on the qui vive to use a portion of it.

"The prisoner was asked if he would be willing to walk between the sheriff and Sister to the victim's sick bed and ask his pardon." The sheriff interrupted:—"Sister, have you ever seen the working of a mob?"

"A few, Mr. Sheriff."

"And would you take the chance of having the prisoner snatched from between us and hanged to the nearest cottonwood?"

"In my opinion, there is nothing to fear." He straightened himself and looked at me, shrugged his shoulders and said, "If you are not afraid, neither am I."

We—the sheriff, my companion and myself—started to walk to the jail. All along the main street and leading to the jail were men at about a distance of a rod apart. These were the men who were to signal Mr. McCaferty's death by three taps of our school bell, in order that the mob might proceed to the jail, take the prisoner and hang him. Our group arrived at the jail, where we encountered the greatest discouragement. The prisoner saw us coming. When we got near enough to speak to him, he was trembling like an aspen. We saw his courage had failed him. We paused while we assured him he was safe in going with us.

He hesitated, then said: "I'll go with you." All along the road we kept silence, and no one spoke to us. When we got within a block of the sick man's room, we saw a crowd of men outside his door. It was at this juncture that my fears for the prisoner began. Intent upon saving our protégé from mob law, we hastened to the sick man's door. The crowd made way. Intense fear took possession of me. "Will the prisoner be jerked away when he attempts to enter his victim's room?"

The Sheriff and I remained at the foot of the few steps which led into the room. Meanwhile, I quietly said to the prisoner: "Go in," which he did, myself and companion following. The sheriff remained outside. The door was left wide open that those standing outside might hear the conversation taking place within.

The culprit stood before his victim with bowed head. Fearing a prolonged silence, I addressed the prisoner: "Have you nothing to say?"

He looked at the man in bed and said: "My boy, I did not know what I was doing. Forgive me."

The sick man removed the blanket which covered his tin-shot leg, revealing a sight to unnerve the stoutest heart. The whole leg was mortified and swollen out of proportion, showing where the poisonous tin had lodged and the mortification creeping toward the heart.

"See what you have done!" said the wounded man.

"I'm sorry, my boy, forgive me."

"I forgive you, as I hope to be forgiven, but the law must take its course."

I added, "Yes, the law must take its course—not mob law." Those outside the door with craned necks distinctly heard the conversation.

We returned to the jail where the prisoner was to remain until the Circuit Court convened.

Encounters with Billy the Kid

My scattered notes on "Billy the Kid's Gang" are condensed, and some day you will be thrilled by their perusal.

The Trinidad Enterprise—the only paper published here—in its last issue gave an exciting description of how a member of "Bill's Gang" painted red the town of Cimarron by mounting his stallion and holding two six-shooters aloft while shouting his commands, which everyone obeyed, not knowing when the trigger on either weapon would be lowered. This event has been the town talk, excluding every other subject, for the past week.

Yesterday one of the Vigilant Committee came to where I was on our grounds—acting as umpire for a future ball game—and said: "Sister, please come to the front yard. I want you to see one of 'Billy's gang,' the one who caused such fright in Cimarron week before last." My informant passed the news to the Nine and their admirers, so that it became my duty to go with the pupils, not knowing what might take place.

When we reached the front yard, the object of our curiosity was still many rods from us. The air here is very rarefied, and we all are eagle-eyed in this atmosphere. We stood in our front yard, everyone trying to look indifferent, while Billy's accomplice headed toward us.

He was mounted on a spirited stallion of unusually large proportions, and was dressed as the *Toreadores* (Bull-Fighters) dress in old Mexico. The figure passed from our sight. I tried to forget it, but it was not to be. Our Vigilant Club, at all times, is on the alert to be of service. William Adamson, a member of the Club, came excitedly, to say—"We have work on hand!"

"What kind of work?" I asked.

"You remember the man who frightened the people in Cimarron, and who passed our schoolhouse some weeks ago?"

"Yes, William."

"Well, he and Happy Jack, his partner, got into a quarrel, and each got the drop on the other. They kept eyeing and following each other for three days, eating at the same table, weapon in right hand, conveying food to their mouth with left hand.

"The tragedy took place when they were eating dinner. Each thought the other off guard, both fired simultaneously. Happy Jack was shot through the breast. He was put in a dugout 3 × 6 ft.

57

Schneider received a bullet in his thigh, and has been brought into Trinidad, thrown into an unused adobe hut, and left there to die. He has a very poor chance of living."

"Well, William, we shall do all we can for him. Where did this all take place?"

"At Dick Wootton's tollgate—the dividing line between Colorado and New Mexico."

At the noon hour we carried nourishing food, water, castile soup and linens to the sick and neglected man. After placing on a table what we had brought, my two companions, William Adamson and Laura Menger, withdrew. I walked towards the bed and, looking at the sick man, I exclaimed, "I see that nothing but a bullet through your brain will finish you!"

I saw a quivering smile pass over his face, and his tiger eyes gleamed. My words seemed heartless. I had gone to make up for the inhuman treatment given by others, and instead, I had added to the inhumanity by my words.

After a few days of retrospection, I concluded it was not I who had spoken, but Fear, so psychologists say.

At our first visit I offered to dress the wound, but to my great relief the desperado said, "I am glad to get the nourishment and the where-with to dress my wound, but I shall attend to it myself." Then he said: "What shall I call you?"

"Sister," I answered.

"Well, Sister, I am very glad you came to see me. Will you come again?"

"Yes, two and three times a day. Good-bye."

We continued these visits for about two months, then one day the sick man asked: "Sister, why is it you never speak to me about your religion or anything else?"

I looked and smiled.

He continued: "I want to tell you something. I allude to the first day you came. Had you spoken to me of repentance, honesty, morals, or anything pertaining to religion, I would have ordered you out. 'I see that nothing but a bullet through your brain will finish you.' Sister, you have no idea what strength and courage those words put into me. I said to myself, 'No shamming here, but the right stuff.'"

Dear Sister Justina, imagine what a load was lifted, to know for a certainty I had not added pain to the downtrodden culprit.

Another month passed by and the patient was visibly losing strength. I managed to get his mother's address. She lives in California.

After a week we resumed our visits. At the noon call our patient was quite hilarious. I surmised something unusual had taken place. He lost no time in telling me that Billy and the "gang" are to be here,

58

Saturday at 2 P.M., and I am going to tell you why they are coming.

"Do you know the four physicians who live here in Trinidad?"

"I know three of them," I answered.

"Well, the 'gang' is going to scalp the four of them" (and his tiger eyes gleamed with satisfaction) "because not one of them would extract the bullet from my thigh."

Can you imagine, Sister Justina, the feeling that came over me? One of the gentlemen is our Convent physician!

I looked at the sick man for a few seconds, then said: "Do you believe that with this knowledge I'm going to keep still?"

"What are you going to do about it?"

"Meet your gang at 2 P.M. next Saturday."

He laughed as heartily as a sick man could laugh and said, "Why, Sister, Billy and the gang will be pleased to meet you. I've told them about you."

I cannot give you any idea of the anxiety of the days previous to the coming ordeal of meeting the gang.

Saturday, 2 P.M., came, and I went to meet Billy and his gang. When I got to the patient's room, the men were around his bed. The introduction was given. I can only remember, "Billy, our Captain, and Chism."

The leader, Billy, his steel-blue eyes, peach complexion, is young, one would take him to be seventeen—innocent-looking, save for the corners of his eyes, which tell a set purpose, good or bad. Mr. Chism, of course this is not his real name—has a most bashful appearance. I judge he has sisters. The others, all fine looking young men. My glance took this description in while "Billy" was saying: "We are all glad to see you, Sister, and I want to say, it would give me pleasure to be able to do you any favor."

I answered, "Yes, there is a favor you can grant me." He reached his hand toward me with the words: "The favor is granted."

I took the hand, saying: "I understand you have come to scalp our Trinidad physicians, which act I ask you to cancel." Billy looked down at the sick man who remarked: "She is game."

What he meant by that I am yet at a loss to understand. Billy then said: "I granted the favor before I knew what it was, and it stands. Not only that, Sister, but at any time my pals and I can serve you, you will find us ready."

I thanked him and left the room.

Building the Tallest Building in New Mexico

April, 1878

The question of building is assuming large proportions. I smile, knowing the financial condition of the convent treasury. . . .

59

Sister Augustine called me to her office and very suavely broached the subject of building. In part she said, "Most Rev. Archbishop Lamy thinks one great need in the Territory is a Trade School for girls. Now, Sister, will you undertake to build it?"

"How much money have we with which to begin building?"

"Nothing, Sister. Do as you did in Trinidad. I was told you had not a cent when you started to build your adobe schoolhouse, and you finished it without debts."

"Ah! Sister, that was only an insignificant matter compared to what a Trade School should be."

"Well, Sister, keep the size of the building within the boundary of your judgment."

"And the money within the same boundary?"

She smiled and continued, "Use your originality as you did elsewhere, and with God's blessing you will get through."

I immediately thought of the young artist, Mr. Projectus Mouly, son of Antoine, whose feelings made him shrink from meeting his friends.

Mr. Mouly has come to the Convent. I saw at once he was strangely touched that I should send for him. I told him my plans for building an Industrial School. The plans are out of all proportions to any building here, and far away from the imagination of the present population of Santa Fe.

I must confess, I have a strong repugnance to building; not on account of the hardships the work will entail, but because some things are not clear to me. At an interview with His Grace, he said: "One great need of the territory is a Trade School. Go at it with my full blessing." Here is the interview with the Rector of the Cathedral, Rev. Augustine Truchard. He thinks the object of the training school is most laudable and greatly needed.

"How much money have you to begin with, Sister?"

"Not a cent, Father."

"And you want to build a three-story house in a country where there is not a planingmill, not a brickyard, nor a quarry of your own, nor limekilns, and, worst of all, not a cent on hand!" Yet you want to begin to dig the foundation Monday morning. Do you know what some of us will say of you?"

"I can surmise, but if you will do what I ask of you I'm not afraid to begin work Monday morning."

"Let me hear, Sister, what you wish me to do."

"Simply to announce at the next Sunday Masses that the Sisters of Charity wish to build a house where girls in need can be trained in industries by which they can make a livelihood. Please say that our present wish is that a number of peons be paid by those disposed to do so, and sent to our front grounds to work on Monday and continue daily until the foundations are laid, each man to bring pick and shovel."

"Well, Sister, I will make the announcement, but I do not believe the men will come."

Monday, June 3, 1878

Seven o'clock. Twelve men with picks and shovels came to work. I registered the names and became timekeeper.

June 17, 1878

Two weeks ago we started work on the foundations for an Industrial School. Part of the land excavated makes a natural foundation, so we are ready for masonry work.

I had another interview with the Rector of the Cathedral. When he saw me he said: "Now, Sister, what do you want?" The answer was, "Wagons, mules, drivers."

"And how do you propose getting them?

"If you please, in the same way we got men, picks, and shovels."

"Well, Sister, I shall announce your second plea at all the Masses tomorrow."

Meanwhile, a quarry had been opened and the men who were not needed to work on foundations were quarrying stone. After the second announcement in the church so many men and wagons were sent to us that they were in one another's way. A Mr. Antonio Ortiz y Salazar, who has taken an active interest in our plan of building without money, said to me:

"Sister, when you dismiss these men and wagons, I shall send you a regular team on one condition that when the mules need shoeing and the wagon needs repairs you send them to Mr. Paul's blacksmith shop and charge to me."

"Thank you, Sir!" I said gratefully. You will note, Sister Justina, that by this arrangement we will have a steady team to depend on.

We have given a contract to a native who will employ his own men to cut the trees and handsaw the lumber to the dimensions required. The nearest place trees are available for lumber is twenty-three miles from Santa Fe.

We have started our own brickyard, 250,000 bricks will be burnt at the first firing. We have eight gentlemen pledged to send workingmen to wait on the bricklayers.

The intersecting interior walls are to be of adobe laid in mortar. This will make the school cool in summer, and warm in winter. The work is to settle for months before the bricks and adobe walls are interlocked.

We have neither gas nor water-works here, but we are going to install pipes for both commodities in case we ever "wake up." This place is not a "Sleepy Hollow" only "Sunshine Asleep."

61

July 26, 1878

The bricks are all piled ready to use.

I sold the span of horses and wagon for $200, paid the owner of the horses $150, and gave $40 to the poor family who had no use for the wagon, and thereby gained $10. This will help pay for lime.

We have made no financial appeal to the people of Santa Fe, yet they have shown themselves most liberal. Seldom do I go to the plaza to order supplies, but I return with much more money than I started out with. God provides when one does his best.

I must tell you, dear Sister Justina, that the erection of this building has brought out many ludicrous opinions. Some asked; "How can a building sixty feet high, and a cupola on top of that, stand? The first big wind will blow it down." Others said that if the inside adobes were not laid with mud, the first rainy weather would melt the building. These critics thought the roof would be mud-covered.

We started our own brickyard, opened our own quarry, had our lime burnt to order, and had our lumber hand-sawed by our natives. After this had been done, a sawmill was started at Glorieta and planing-mill was opened in Las Vegas. There was a sawmill sixty miles this side of Trinidad, but having to rely on teams to haul the lumber, it was better economy to do as we did. Can you picture what work this entailed?

February 12, 1880

Here is the latest criticism on the Industrial School Building. Some ladies who are not troubled for want of money took this view: "If those Sisters who had no cash to build succeeded in putting up the finest building in the Territory, why cannot we, who have money, build our own homes?" It would take pages to note all that has been said about the structure.

Discovering Foremothers:
Sisters, Society, and the American Catholic Experience[1]

63

Margaret Susan Thompson

In 1808, Elizabeth Bayley Seton left New York City on the initial leg of a journey that would lead her to Emmitsburg, Maryland, where she would found the first community of active Catholic sisters within the boundaries of the United States.[2] Exactly a century later, in *Sapienti Consilio,* Pope Pius X declared that the United States was no longer to be regarded as

---

1. This essay is adapted from a prospectus that was written in April 1984 for submission to potential publishers of the book it described. *The Yoke of Grace: American Nuns and Social Change, 1808–1917* is scheduled to be completed in 1988 and to be published by Oxford University Press. The author is grateful to Dr. Robert K. Merton, of Columbia University and the Russell Sage Foundation (where both she and he were scholars in residence in 1984), and to Charles O'Connell, F.S.C., of Manhattan College, for comments on the initial draft.

2. This was not the first community of women religious (as nuns and sisters collectively are described), or even the first active one, within what then was U.S. territory. Nine French Ursuline Nuns arrived in New Orleans in 1727 and, shortly thereafter, opened a school. A monastery of Discalced Carmelites (contemplatives) was established at Port Tobacco, Maryland, in 1790; at one point they, too, ran a school. A few years later, three French Poor Clares settled in Washington and, dispensed from their rule of strict enclosure, attempted to run a school, too; by 1804, however, this foundation failed and its two surviving members returned to Europe. But three "pious ladies" who had begun working with them in 1799 continued on the site and with the school, lived as religious, and eventually were professed as Visitation Nuns in 1816. The Ursulines, Carmelites, and Visitandines all are still extant. And there is yet another claimant to being "first": the Sisters of Loretto at the Foot of the Cross, organized in Kentucky in 1812. Although their origins postdate those of Mother Seton's group, the Lorettines boast of being the first entirely indigenous American community, since the Emmitsburg sisters followed a rule based on that of the French Daughters of Charity. (In 1850, the branch of American Charities that remained headquartered in Maryland affiliated formally with the French congregation.) In contrast, the Loretto rule was written here, albeit mainly by a Belgian-born and trained priest.

273

"mission territory." During the intervening years, meanwhile, literally hundreds of sisterhoods were established, including indigenous American institutes, branches of the major European orders, missions from independent Old World or Canadian congregations and, eventually, autonomous offshoots from earlier establishments.[3] And the women religious who comprised these groups—numbering several thousands in over 250 active communities—had become vital components of the American Church, essential to its social and spiritual vitality, and among the most visible witnesses to its burgeoning presence in the nation's life.[4]

The story of that experience is the subject of my current research: the personalities, endeavors, struggles, and accomplishments of those pioneering women, from the birth of Mother Seton's Sisters of Charity through 1917, when a new code of canon law led to greater standardization among such communities and when their previous individual distinctiveness and flexibility began noticeably to lessen.[5] The result will be a book, *The Yoke of Grace: American Nuns and Social Change*, now scheduled for publication sometime in 1989. In both substantive and chronological scope, it represents the most extensive cross-community study to date, and draws heavily upon materials in congregational archives, many of them never before made public. This essay shall summarize what I plan to do and, equally important, *why* I want to do it. For detailing the story of sisters is far from an exercise in historical trivia, it illuminates not only the developing contours of the U.S. Catholic Church, but also those of the nation generally.

Three principal questions focus most of my research. First, how did religious life change in response to the relatively egalitarian, pluralistic, mobile, and rapidly expanding environment of nineteenth-century America? Here, I am interested both in adaptations of organization and

---

3. Prior to 1983, designations such as "order," "congregation," "institute," "society," and "community" had precise and distinct canonically legal meanings—as did the titles of "religious," "nun," and "sister." In this study, however, the terms will be used interchangeably (except when their technical significance is intended and explicitly noted), as they are in most of the primary and secondary literature, in past and present common usage, and in the 1983 revised Code of Canon Law.

4. The most recent chronology of American communities, in *Women Religious History Sources: A Guide to Repositories in the United States*, edited by Evangeline Thomas, C.S.J. (New York, 1983, 169–180), lists a total of 275 foundations—256 of them active—prior to 1908 that persist in some form today; some have since merged, while those that did not survive, such as the Washington Poor Clares mentioned earlier, are omitted. There are other gaps, as well. The Dominican Sisters, Servants of Relief for Incurable Cancer (founded in 1899 by Rose Hawthorne Lathrop), the Cincinnati Sisters of Mercy (founded in 1858), and the Sisters of the Holy Ghost and Mary Immaculate (founded in 1893)—all still extant and to be studied here—are among those not included, probably due to the communities' own failures to report their holdings to the volume's editor.

5. By 1917, again according to *Women Religious History Sources*, there were at least 307 still-surviving American foundations, 281 of them active.

Rule and in the taking on of new types of ministries, or active works. Second, what were the contributions of active sisters, both to the evolution of the American Church and to American society? Much of my concern here centers on the involvement of religious with native minorities, especially Blacks and Indians, and with immigrants, for whom they provided invaluable assistance during the process of secular assimilation as they helped to maintain the Church's "relevance" in what might otherwise have seemed an alien or even hostile setting. In relation to this, I will also deal with the effects on religious tolerance that sisters exercised through their work, such as nursing during wars and epidemics, and through admission of non-Catholics to their institutions. Finally, what opportunities (apart from the obvious spiritual ones) did religious life offer to women, *as women*, particularly the poor and immigrants? For, despite their stereotypic image as naive or strictly otherworldly creatures, sisters as a group were among the best educated and most accomplished of late nineteenth- and early twentieth-century women—and nearly the only women who bore responsibility for administering large-scale operations such as schools and colleges, hospitals, asylums, and the like.[6] Thus, nuns should be of interest to modern feminists and students of women's history. Of course, I do not intend to imply here that nineteenth-century Catholic sisters were conscious or self-identified feminists, since the vast majority clearly were not. But I would suggest that both their way of life and their occupations denote them as appropriate and edifying subjects for feminist analysis.

I intend throughout to illuminate subsidiary, but nonetheless interesting, facets of nineteenth-century religious life. For example, I shall examine the two antebellum Southern communities of Black sisters (Baltimore's Oblates of Providence and New Orleans' Sisters of the Holy Family) as well as early, if abortive, efforts (such as that by Kentucky's Sisters of Loretto) to form integrated institutes. The plan calls as well for comparative analyses of indigenous and transplanted communities, of ethnically homogeneous groups with more diverse ones, of congregations in different geographic areas, and of various branches within large orders. It also calls for detailed investigations of the relationships between women religious and male authorities within the Church, ranging from spiritual directors and parish priests, through ordinaries, to clerics in the Curia (who came into the picture increasingly as institutes sought pontifical status). And I want to tell the stories of significant or representative individuals, from

65

---

6. Incidentally, because most of these institutions—and many congregations, as well—operated under official charters, nuns deserve to be recognized as comprising America's first sizeable cohort of female corporate executives!

66

Mother Elizabeth Ann Seton

foundresses and superiors to the little-known, whose diaries and reminiscences abound in many archives.

In the end, the analysis will combine particulars and synthesis. Thus, I am devoting special attention to communities that, because of their missions, membership, or motivation, are distinctly American—groups such as the Sisters of Loretto, Oblates of Providence, Sisters of the Blessed Sacrament, and Maryknoll. But I will also draw general conclusions about women religious in the United States, conclusions that apply across the spectrum of congregations. This requires primary research in the archives of at least four dozen institutes chosen to provide, so far as possible, a representative sample of the active sisterhoods that existed here before 1917.[7] (A tentative list of communities is given in Appendix A.) Beyond that, I am reading widely in the religious and secular press, in published histories and biographies, in dissertations and theses, in diocesan records and printed collections of documents, and in pertinent scholarship on the nineteenth-century Church, immigration, and other collateral topics. For I am profoundly aware that, in pursuing work of this broad scope, I must rely considerably upon the earlier efforts of other scholars, especially

7. A Rockefeller Foundation Humanities Fellowship has enabled me to take a leave from teaching for the 1985-86 year, during which I expect to complete most of the archival research.

when it comes to matters that are tangential, but relevant, to fundamental foci and objectives.

It is fortunate, of course, that so much material exists and that so much research has already been done—much of it since 1965, when religious were urged, in *Perfectae Caritatis,* to explore their founders' experiences and charisms as part of their efforts at renewal. Moreover, as the 1983 publication of Evangeline Thomas's *Women Religious History Sources* indicates, archives are better organized and more accessible to outsiders than ever before. Yet as Elizabeth Kolmer noted in a 1980 essay on "Catholic Women Religious and Women's History," with the exception of Mary Ewens's 1971 dissertation and Barbara Misner's more focused 1980 one, little historiography deals with the collective experience of American sisters.[8] A major motive for this book is to change that condition, so far as that can be done in a single volume.

67

Catholic sisters are probably the most thoroughly documentable women in the world and, almost certainly, in the nineteenth-century United States. For one thing, every congregation is required by canon law to maintain an archive and to file regular reports with appropriate diocesan and Roman Church authorities. The majority of repositories hold data on individual nuns, which normally include their applications for admission or records of their entrance, formation, and profession. They may also contain birth dates and places, places of baptism and confirmation, and information on education and family background; nearly all have complete necrologies, and most take note of departures and dismissals from the ranks. Other typical records include lists of sisters' assignments and their locations; rosters of officers and elections; correspondence with the hierarchy and with sister communities; chronicles of various foundations and ministries; and financial statements and account books. Many also contain members' diaries, unpublished memoirs and, increasingly, oral history interviews; photographs, clippings and scrapbooks; materials pertaining to the evolution of constitutions and customaries; applications for pontifical status and the organization of federations (or, conversely, intracommunity provinces); in-house congregational periodicals and circular letters; minutes and decisions of General Chapters and Councils; privately published commemorations of foundation anniversaries and similar cele-

---

8. Citation for Thomas is given above. Elizabeth Kolmer, "Catholic Women Religious and Women's History: A Survey of the Literature," in *Women in American Religion,* edited by Janet Wilson James (Philadelphia, 1980), 127–139; Mary Ewens, *The Role of the Nun in Nineteenth-Century America* (New York, 1978); Barbara Misner, "A Comparative Social Study of the Members and Apostolates of the First Eight Permanent Communities of Women Religious Within the Original Boundaries of the United States, 1790–1850," (Ph.D., diss., Catholic University of America, 1980).

brations of particular interest to the institute; and sundry other materials of potential value to historians.[9]

Pertinent primary sources, of course, are not confined to community archives. Information on sisters abounds in Church records, both in dioceses and in Rome—particularly, so far as the latter is concerned, in the files of what now is known as the Congregation for Religious and Secular Institutes and, since the United States was mission territory until 1908, the Congregation for the Evangelization of Peoples (formerly, Propagation of the Faith). The Cushwa Center for the Study of American Catholicism at the University of Notre Dame houses many useful collections—and an almost complete set of diocesan newspapers (available on microfilm through interlibrary loan); additional materials can be found at other Catholic universities throughout the country.[10] The archives of certain men's orders, particularly those associated with (and/or with authority over) female communities—the Dominicans, Benedictines, Carmelites, Franciscans, etc.—ought not to be ignored; at the very least, I plan to look at those of specific men's congregations, such as the Dominicans and the Holy Cross Fathers, that had extensive interactions with one or more of the groups of women on which I shall focus.[11] There also are papers for many individual clerics, especially those who were instrumental in the founding of women's communities or who eventually served as bishops. Worthy of special note is the collection on Black Catholicism and mission efforts of the Josephites (St. Joseph's Society of the Sacred Heart), a congregation of priests and brothers founded specifically for work among Blacks. Finally, certain government records are relevant, especially to the efforts of sisters in education, nursing (including that during epidemics and wars), various areas of social welfare, with minorities, and in the United States territories (including, for the period I am covering, Alaska, Hawaii, and much of the continental West). While it will not be possible, of course, for me to use all these materials, I do intend to investigate as many and as large a variety as time and other resources will permit.

Published and other nonarchival material is voluminous, too. I already have a file of nearly 500 books, articles and graduate theses, consisting of

---

9. These generalizations, and the discussion that follows, are based on my work to date in the archives of over two dozen congregations; they are supplemented and confirmed by the descriptions of holdings in Thomas's *Women Religious History Sources,* and by conversations and correspondence with archivists for communities I plan to visit in the future.

10. Thanks to a grant I received from the Cushwa Center in 1984, I was able to spend a month there, exploring its holdings.

11. Many religious priests in orders that did not have their own female branches—e.g., the Jesuits and Redemptorists (among whom there was no active branch of women)—served as co-founders, spiritual directors, or clerical "superiors" to women's communities.

Mother M. Angela Gillespie

congregations' histories; local, diocesan, and state-level histories of Catholicism; general discussions of the American Church; analyses of particular professions that sisters pursued in their ministries; diaries, collected correspondence, biographies and autobiographies (of founders, other sisters, relevant clerics, etc.); and studies of certain locales, ethnic groups, and other topics that include substantial references to women religious. Furthermore, practically every diocese has had a newspaper; these, as well as many other Catholic publications intended for general readers—and, of course, the secular press—contain numerous stories about the contemporary experiences of nuns. Clearly, more material exists than any individual could ever exhaust. And more is being generated all the time.

Despite its extensiveness, however, the primary sources on sisters have been subjected to only limited serious scholarship, and both they and the secondary literature reveal remarkably large and significant limitations and gaps. Several factors account for this. So far as archives are concerned, although congregations have long been required to have them (as clauses in some of even the earliest constitutions reveal), few until recently had either trained personnel or the motivation to maintain them in ways that insured completeness or facilitated use by researchers. Their supervision typically was relegated to institutes' Secretaries General, who bore a broad range of responsibilities and who, either by choice or by default, frequently gave this one low priority.[12] Similarly, although most communities called for their local missions to keep chronicles, few enforced this rule consistently; the result is annals that are often sporadic, sometimes nonexistent, and all too frequently confined to superficialities or statistical summaries.[13]

Without professionals to oversee congregations' archives, and without the facilities to preserve them securely, many collections have suffered form poor maintenance and to this day some remain incomplete or disorganized. Several sisterhoods are only now beginning to establish formal archival departments, but a number have relegated their supervision to retired sisters with no previous experience in such matters, to members with other fulltime assignments who are expected to pursue this one as a sideline, or to officers whose primary qualification is their organizational ability rather than their sense of history. At least one small order, with a shortage of personnel, has not been able to replace an archivist who went blind nearly a decade ago.

An additional complication is that documents often were lost or misplaced when groups moved into new facilities; others were destroyed by fires or natural disasters. Almost everything belonging to the Galveston (now Houston), Texas, Sisters of Charity of the Incarnate Word, for instance, was lost when their motherhouse was obliterated by the "great storm" of 1900; after the New Orleans Dominicans took possession of a new convent, they simply could not find many items, and the assumption is that they ended up in the trash. Moreover, there is no denying that materials were at times destroyed deliberately, particularly if they were deemed potentially embarrassing or damaging to an order's—or a cleric's—

12. Clauses in several congregations' constitutions that I have seen mandated such responsibility; that research is supplemented by interviews with a number of current archivists, most notably Sister M. Emmanuel, S.H.G., now archivist—and former Secretary General—of the Sisters of the Holy Spirit and Mary Immaculate, San Antonio, Texas (5 February 1986).

13. At worst, one finds page after page like the following: "For the year 1873-74, St. Hieronymus Parish School in East Yahoo, Missouri, the Rev. Father Antonius McCardigle as pastor, was the call of Holy Obedience for Sister M. Aloysius, Superior, and Sisters M. Agatha, M. Mechtilde, M. Gertrude, and M. Innocentia. Enrollment consisted of 227 students, of whom 186 were Catholic. The year brought 29 pupils to the Inestimable Joy of receiving their Eucharistic Lord in Most Holy Communion for the first time; eight others, with their parents' consent, were admitted through the Portals of Truth in Holy Baptism. (Through prayer, the Sisters hope to bring these poor parents, too, out of the bonds of ignorance and unfaith.) In April, the Sacrament of Confirmation was administered to 18 by Rt. Revd. Bishop Claude David LePuce, which occasion provided the Sisters with the privilege of hearing a highly-edifying conference on the Necessity for Mortification of the Senses from the learned lips of His Lordship. . . ." At best, one finds candid, detailed, and even witty accounts of sometimes atrocious living conditions, collisions with obstinate clergy, harassment by nativist townspeople, and a variety of other revealing anecdotes. Unfortunately, the former flowery sort is far more likely to predominate.

reputation. After twenty years in office, Mother St. Andrew Feltin, foundress of San Antonio's Sisters of Divine Providence, was deposed by an autocratic bishop whom she had offended; today, practically nothing of her papers is extant, because that same bishop ordered that they be removed from the community's records. The Houston Dominicans began as an offshoot of the sisterhood at St. Mary-of-the-Spring, Ohio, apparently because there was a split in the older group following a controversial election. But relevant pages from the Ohio order's General Council minutes, which might document this absolutely, have been torn from the manuscript record. And virtually all traces of a late nineteenth-century Mother General of the Mount St. Vincent, New York, Sisters of Charity were deliberately excised from that congregation's holdings by a mid-twentieth century successor. The earlier superior was an Afro-American who "passed" as white, a fact which the later official clearly wanted to keep as obscure as possible.

71

Even more damaging phenomena that I have discovered (of which the Sisters of Charity case mentioned above is a very minor instance) are cases of outright distortions of certain congregations' histories, by persons either within or outside their ranks, who—through omission or other elusive practices that may or may not have involved destruction of documents—effectively altered the most fundamental dimensions of their pasts. This may have been done so long ago that, after a time, no living members of the groups are aware of the alterations. Here, three examples are illustrative.

(1) It makes a great difference to one's understanding of the history of the Sisters, Servants of the Immaculate Heart of Mary, and of the troubled life of its foundress, Teresa Maxis Duchemin, if one is aware that she was not Caucasian, but rather a light-skinned Afro-American. For a century after the group was established, however, this fact was kept hidden—and, even now, one independent branch of the order is attempting to perpetuate the old racial illusion.

(2) Standard accounts assert that the Sisters of St. Mary of Oregon, a diocesan teaching institute, was founded by Archbishop Gross in 1886; in fact, the sisters are holding an official celebration of their centennial this year. But as a soon-to-be-published account by Wilfred Schoenberg, S.J., will reveal—and as the community's members now know from long-ignored materials that have been in their possession all along—its roots are traceable to the 1840s, to a rather bizarre splintering of Ohio's Congregation of the Precious Blood, led by one schizmatic priest and his faithful

Mother M. Teresa

72

followers. The earliest nuns were their unknowing dupes, and it is not surprising that some would come to see this as cause for embarrassment; the fact remains that, until a year or two ago, the "official" story was accepted as accurate.

(3) It was not until after Vatican II that the group known for nearly the entire span of its existence as the Sisters of St. Joseph of Newark recaptured from oblivion both its original name—the Sisters of St. Joseph of Peace—and its foundress, Sister Francis Clare (Margaret Anna) Cusack. Cusack, one of the most accomplished and controversial women of her time—the famed "Nun of Kenmare" who, as a Poor Clare, wrote dozens of historical treatises and political tracts and who was the only nineteenth-century sister I have found who actually used the word "feminist"—eventually became so embittered by ongoing fights with a recalcitrant hierarchy in Britain, Ireland, and the United States that she felt forced not only to leave her community, but also the Catholic Church. By official edict of her order's bishop-superior in England, the group was retitled, he was designated as its founder, the habit was altered, and members were forbidden to mention her name or her connection with the society. Only in 1970 was all of this formally repaired; mean-

while, a century after Cusack's departure, archivists and historians among the Sisters of St. Joseph of Peace are finding it difficult to identify and re-collect all the documents relevant to their past.

Complications like these naturally mean that primary sources relating to sisters vary considerably in comprehensiveness and reliability. The quality of much of the historical writing has suffered accordingly. But additional factors have also been at play. Before Vatican II, for instance, both custom and Church law demanded rigid separation between religious and seculars—and even between members of a particular institute and other religious. Thus it was forbidden for outsiders (other than appropriate hierarchs) even to see copies of Rules, constitutions, and customs-books (indeed, aspirants to an order usually were kept in the dark about them until they were admitted to the novitiate); archives, meanwhile, almost always were kept within areas of enclosure (cloister), to which outsiders, including scholars of course, were denied access. So whatever research there was, was done almost exclusively by sisters, frequently amateurs, often in their limited "spare time" and rather haphazardly.

An unpublished paper by Barbara Misner points to other reasons for the restricted scope and quality of such literature. In particular, she notes that, for the most part, its objectives were limited—and explicitly not analytic. Early accounts by nuns were intended simply as factual "annals," or they were "characterized chiefly by a desire to edify and inspire, and there is often more hagiography than apologetics. (One might suspect there were vocation directors behind the projects.)"[14] And since publications by non-members were heavily dependent on such sources, their emphases and tone inevitably were perpetuated.

Despite these impediments, however, there is a surprisingly massive body of generally reliable, if not always imaginative, historiography that has been accumulating for quite some time: the legacy of a sizeable cadre of sister-scholars who began to appear around the turn of the twentieth

---

14. Barbara Misner, "Historiography of Women's Religious Communities in the 19th Century," unpublished paper prepared for a Conference about Perspectives on American Catholicism, University of Notre Dame, 1982; quotation is from p. 2. A notable example of the flowery prose, hagiography, and inaccuracies of interpretation (and sometimes fact) that ensued is Elinor Tong Dehey, *Religious Orders of Women in the United States—Catholic—Accounts of their Origin, Works, and Most Important Institutions, Interwoven with Histories of Many Famous Foundresses,* revised edition (Hammond, Ind., 1930). This 908-page volume, however, is nonetheless invaluable as a chronologically accurate source of unparalleled completeness as to the dates and circumstances of foundations up to the time of its publication; it also is excellent in tracing the spread of larger orders, the establishment of missions and provinces, and in identifying the dioceses in which particular institutes were active.

century. Their existence was initially attributable largely to internally inconsistent Church policies that on the one hand directed nuns to obtain professional training comparable to that of their secular counterparts, and that on the other prohibited their admission to nearly all Catholic institutions of higher learning, which were operated by and for men. Thus, sisters were impelled to open their own colleges (if only to train their own members), and to send prospective professors for graduate degrees (generally to state universities, until Catholic ones reluctantly opened their doors to women) in order to secure the necessary credentials.[15] Since most congregations could not afford to spare such talented individuals for more than a couple of years of full-time study, if that, most had to write their theses while "on the job," usually at an academy or college connected with the Motherhouse. The result is a plethora of research derived from the archives located there, which collectively comprises a body of work that proves tremendously useful to anyone trying to understand the experience of nineteenth- and early twentieth-century women religious. The principal limitation of this literature is, as has already been noted, that almost all of it is community-specific. Until now, only Barbara Misner and Mary Ewens have attempted to put the available pieces together—to explain religious life in general terms, terms that transcend congregational lines.

Related historiographic fields, meanwhile, contain dramatic voids when it comes to their treatment of nuns. Sisters, like all women—and because they *are* women—have largely been ignored by both Church and secular historians, nearly all of whom have been male. Until very recently, standard Catholic histories were "institutional" in orientation: focusing mainly upon the hierarchy, and certainly upon the clergy. Sisters, therefore, who are *not* clergy, are rarely mentioned, even though they have always outnumbered priests in this country and have been in more varied and closer contact with nonreligious. Even the establishment of nuns' communities (when such references exist at all) is usually credited to the efforts of clerics. Other scholarship, meanwhile, has not only been produced mostly by men, but by Anglo-Saxon Protestants who have either ignored the Church or manifested anti-Catholic biases. Until about fifty years ago, then, whatever meager notice nuns received from them tended to be subject to nativist distortion. Most of that prejudice, fortunately, has been excised in recent years, as has some of the exclusion of women from both the practice and focus of research.

Nonetheless, the exclusion of sisters from studies not focused directly

Mother M. Katharine Drexel

on them, or on the Church, persists almost unabated. It would be hard to
conceive of analyses of social welfare work, for instance, that did not
devote considerable attention to Jane Addams and other women settlement workers. Yet even feminist accounts of this tend to ignore the fact
that virtually all the efforts of Addams and her peers were preceded (often
by several decades) by similar ones on the part of nuns. Few Americans
realize, either, that sisters were the first in this country to provide training
and education for the deaf or that, long before Prudence Crandall was
pilloried for trying to open a school for Blacks in Connecticut, sisters were
making similar efforts in places like Baltimore, Louisville, and Charleston.
Nuns operated the only hospitals, orphanages, and even schools in some
locales; in such cases, these were normally open to all, regardless of faith
(and often despite opposition to that openness from the hierarchy). And,
based on a decidedly unscientific poll of historians of women, Afro-
Americans, and the South, I have yet to find one who was aware before
hearing it from me that two communities of Black sisters existed in the
slave states before 1845.

Increasingly, therefore, I have come to realize that the study of sisters
in nineteenth-century America is hardly a parochial exercise. Rather, it
has the potential to fill a number of gaps in our historical understanding; it

provides dramatic evidence indeed of the extent to which women's history is "real" history, and of the wide-ranging distortions that can ensue when even a single group of women is ignored. In other words, while a principal contribution of *The Yoke of Grace* will be its overview of nuns generally in the United States (in contrast to the community-specific approach, undertaken mainly by insiders, that has predominated up to now), its informational and analytic implications should affect a number of research fields, some outside the discipline of history, and including a few that might seem surprising or unexpected.

Some potential audiences are obvious. Among historians and readers of history, I expect this work to appeal to those interested in Catholicism— and religion generally, in women, in the histories of relevant professions (especially teaching, nursing, and social work), in immigration and ethnicity, in the westward movement (since nuns were frequently pioneers in that migration), and in the overall social history of nineteenth- and early twentieth-century America. It also ought to reach those concerned with the social missions of religious groups, various sectors of sociology, organizational behavior and theory, students of social change, and a broad spectrum of feminists and others interested in the lives and experiences of women.

I would hope, however, that what I have to say would be of interest to more than even this considerable number of groups. Consider, for example, military history. Its experts have long appreciated that, prior to the twentieth century, most wartime casualties ensued from disease and infection, rather than immediately on the battlefield. Thus, medical care in times of conflict is an important area of inquiry—and the most sizeable group of nurses during all wars fought by the United States prior to World War I consisted of nuns. Among other things, nuns were professionally experienced and without family responsibilities, and their training inured them to sacrifice and bound them by obedience. They were freer than other women to travel with the troops and to devote extended periods of time to their care. Their convents—especially those located in the border states and near battle sites during the Civil War—were frequently transformed into military hospitals for so long as they were required. Considerable contemporary evidence demonstrates that sisters' care saved the lives of countless soldiers; it also suggests strongly that nuns' ministrations served significantly to dispel anti-Catholicism among those who benefitted from and observed their efforts. Military history, therefore, is just one tangential field that should feel the effects of *The Yoke of Grace*. In similar ways—because of sisters' ministries and the clienteles they served—so, among others, should Afro-American and Native American Studies.

Nonetheless, I suspect that, intentionally or not, my topic and approach

Mother Praxedes Carty

may prove most exciting to feminists. Sisters, after all, were (and are) women who did not marry, who pursued professional careers, who founded, financed and ran complex institutions, and who lived in community with other women—as family, colleagues, and friends. Religious life was unquestionably an attractive alternative to marriage and childbearing for many nineteenth-century women—and especially for the poor, mainly immigrant, women for whom the traditional way of life was likely to bring continued poverty, too many and too frequent pregnancies (with the concomitant dangers of miscarriage and high infant mortality), low-paying and menial employment outside the home, little chance for education, and so on. Nuns, in contrast, were respected (at least within the Catholic community)—and, as we have seen, understandably so—and, despite their vows of poverty, generally enjoyed at least as high a standard of living as those they served.[16] Moreover, despite their very real subordina-

---

16. Here, and elsewhere, I do not ignore or minimize the spiritual dimensions of religious life, although I do not intend to deal in great detail with theology, ritual, or beliefs. I do, however, expect it to be taken as given that spiritual depth and commitment were essential to the lives of sisters. Indeed, only strong faith can explain the persistence, serenity, and strength with which some of the crises these sisters faced were endured and overcome.

Mother Mary Joseph Rogers

tion to men within the Church, sisters (individually and collectively) exercised greater control over their lives than any other sizeable group of female contemporaries in this country. Even within the Church, their charisms, mutual support, and services rendered them more power and autonomy than organization charts, canon law, and superficial appearance might suggest.

Consider, for example, that dozens of American congregations successfully sought pontifical status during the decades just before and after 1900. The reasons to do so were many. Not the least was a desire to lessen the authority that idiosyncratic and autocratic bishops were otherwise able to wield over them. For this status to be achieved, however, a religious community had to satisfy several requirements, including the securing of endorsements from every bishop in whose diocese their members were located—from the very men, in other words, from whose control the sisters were trying to free themselves. One of the most important and interesting stories I have to tell is of the ways and the frequency with which these seemingly impossible suits were won. It reveals that these women possessed remarkable shrewdness and political savvy, that congregations learned from and cooperated with one another (the sainted Mother Cabrini, whose connections in Rome were unparalleled, was well known for the skill with which she advised other Superiors General to proceed)—and that, even today, women can learn much from their nineteenth-century religious foremothers about how to work within male-dominated institutions and processes.

Indeed, many secular feminists in the 1980s are coming to appreciate that many of today's religious sisters are not only their allies, they are in many cases more determined, committed to—and experienced in—the struggle for women's equality than their counterparts "in the world." Within the past few years, the media have been filled with intentionally eye-catching and dramatic stories about the so-called "new nuns": wearing secular clothes instead of habits; coming out of the cloister and onto the frontlines of battles for peace, civil rights, and economic and social justice; falling as martyrs in the revolutionary struggles of Third World nations; lobbying and holding political office, despite threatened and actual sanctions from Rome; suing their bishops in civil court—and winning; pressing for their own ordination; forming noncanonical communities to free themselves from the domination of clerics; and challenging the Church's teaching on such matters as birth control, women's rights, and abortion. Clearly these images are not universally apropos, but they are quite different from those conveyed on the big screen by Audrey Hepburn, Loretta Young, and Ingrid Bergman—and on the small one by Sally Fields! So both media commentators and members of the public express great surprise at the striking contrast such women present to the "good sisters" of yesteryear: swathed in yards of serge, hidden in their cloisters, outwardly deferential in their dealings with clerics, and naive, timid and probably incompetent when it came to confronting issues of the everyday secular world.

It is my contention—here and in *The Yoke of Grace*—that the apparent inconsistency between old and new is based largely upon a lack of understanding about what sisters in the past were really like. We can understand how it is that today's nuns are more aware of the solid ground on which they stand than are most of the rest of us. In the years since Vatican II, they have been engaged—by direct order of the Pope!—in exploring their own histories, and most particularly their founders' charisms and visions, so that they might "renew" themselves to function both more effectively *and more traditionally* (that is, in the traditions of their founders) within the modern context. What this exploration revealed, to a great extent, is a past filled with strong, dedicated, charismatic, courageous and often controversial women. Founders of religious communities, after all, are innovators, and even revolutionaries, almost by definition; they decide to start new groups because existing ones are inappropriate or inadequate to what they believe needs to be done. In the long run, some of them end up being canonized. But in the short run, many had to overcome enormous obstacles in the course of their efforts; some suffered harassment, censure, persecution, exile, imprisonment, and even martyrdom. A few were repudiated during their own lifetimes, even by some of their own sisters; we

79

have seen already what happened to Margaret Anna Cusack and Theresa Maxis Duchemin.

Individuals like Cusack and Duchemin were atypical, to be sure, although not unique. Far more common were women like Catherine McAuley, founder of the Sisters of Mercy, who loathed the idea of becoming a nun and did so by strength of will only because she was persuaded that in no other way could a woman in nineteenth-century Ireland acceptably meet the challenges she saw around her; or Mary Ward, the seventeenth-century Englishwoman who founded the Institute of the Blessed Virgin Mary—a society she envisioned as a female counterpart to the Jesuits: without habits, convents, or fealty to local bishops, who was imprisoned by one Pope and who walked hundreds of miles to Rome to win the patronage of another and whose descendants did not win approval of their Rule for 150 years or permission to acknowledge her as their founder until the 1800s; or Katharine Drexel, an American who used the millions of dollars left to her use by her banker father (a partner of J. P. Morgan) to found and fund the works of a community dedicated solely to "Indians and Colored People" and who, because her father authorized that only she receive the income from his estate and only for the duration of her natural life, managed to survive until the age of 97 so as to get as much of that income as possible.

In short, the "renewal" that sisters have undergone since the Second Vatican Council—a renewal that produced the so-called "new nuns" that many, both within and outside the Catholic Church, have found so unsettling—is actually more nearly a "restoration." Although its surface manifestations may be most apparent in changes of clothes, it has to do with issues far more crucial than habits of dress. It consists, rather, of matters of spirit, responsive and responsible living, risk-taking, challenges to hierarchy, and true sisterhood that is symbolized, but not created, by the taking of vows. Through my study of American nuns during the formative years of religious life in this country, I hope to provide a better understanding of the traditions—of substance, style and, most important, spirit—that provided the bedrock on which the current restoration is based. For that, in 1808 as much as in 1986, is what "the yoke of grace" has always been about.

80

Philemon's Dilemma:
Nuns and the Black Community
in Nineteenth-Century America:
Some Findings

By Margaret Susan Thompson*

[The Epistle to Philemon recounts the Christian conversion of a slave, whom Paul then persuaded to return to his
master. The master, in turn, was urged to treat him "no
longer as a slave but as more than a slave, a beloved
brother . . . since now you will know him both as a man
and in the Lord." (v. 16)]
"The delicate tone of this letter reflects, against the legal
fact of slavery at the time, the incipient Christian insight
into its injustice. Paul does not attack the institution, for
the small Christian communities were in no position to
raise such an issue. . . . [Yet] that Onesimus the slave was
'brother' to Philemon, his legal master, was a revolutionary idea in the context of the time."
 — intro to *Philemon,* New American Bible.

While the Colored Missions are grateful to many religious
communities for coming into the field of the Colored
Harvest, even at the eleventh hour, . . . The sad fact is that
barely [a handful of] communities of nuns are still carrying
the larger burden . . . . There is no edification in organizations with ready resources of personnel and finances point-
ing to one or two missions or schools for Negroes and
justifying themselves with a sense of duty well done. . . .
The glory of the "old-timers" lies in the fact that they bent
their necks to the yoke in a day when it was something
more than foolhardy to espouse his cause.
 — John T. Gillard, SSJ (1941)[1]

Twenty years ago when Sister Margaret Ellen Traxler, a
School Sister of Notre Dame, asked her superior's permission to participate in the voters' rights march in Selma,
Alabama, the answer was: "Go ahead. But stay in the back
and don't get into any trouble." Traxler went ahead, but
she didn't stay in the back. . . .
 — *Ms.* Magazine (1985)[2]

*Margaret Susan Thompson is Associate Professor of History at Syracuse University.
The above paper is based on one read at the 1985 meeting of the Organization of
American Historians, Minneapolis, Minnesota. A Rockefeller Humanities Fellowship
grant and a grant from the Syracuse University Faculty Research Fund assisted her in
the preparation of the article.

Few Americans would dispute that civil rights was one of the most pressing national concerns of the 1960s. It was also one of the most heavily-covered stories on network television news; almost nightly, particularly during the summers of 1963-65, viewers were offered scenes of sit-ins, marches, prayer meetings, and demonstrations — as well has horrifying glimpses of racist catcalling, police-instigated brutality, and the battered bodies of casualties to the cause of democracy. But for Roman Catholic viewers especially, another sort of image may have seemed at least as striking as these: that of (mostly white) collar-clad priests and — even more incongruously — habited nuns, on the front lines striving for racial justice. These were hardly the "good sisters" of pious literature and Hollywood fantasy, or the sternly rigid, or naive, or simply vacuous "brides of Christ" who supposedly confined their out-of-convent sojourns to St. Stanislaus Church, Precious Blood Parish School, Macy's at Christmastime, and the Bijou for a special showing of "Going My Way."

Given the ecclesially-fostered images (and, to a large extent, reality) of religious life from 1917 to the time of Vatican II — what Mary Ewens has called "the Great Repression" — public astonishment over such apparently pathbreaking sisters is scarcely to be wondered at.[3] Indeed, not a few of those who actually participated in the civil rights movement were themselves unaware that their activity had historical precedent.[4] But as this paper will demonstrate, nuns in the 1960s were far from the first nuns to have involved themselves with the interests of the black community, or the first to have been subject to harassment (including legal sanctions) and opprobrium for having done so. This is not to say, of course, that their behavior was commonplace or typical (nor was that of their foremothers); neither sisters nor U.S. Catholicism generally deserves credit for broad-based, deep, and consistent commitment to the interests of Afro-Americans. For the most part, as shall be seen, the relationship between the Church and blacks is best characterized by words like sporadic, ambivalent, tentative and paternalistic. Nonetheless, from the days of Mother Seton on, individual and small groups of nuns have steadily worked, often in the face of both public and clerical resistance, to ameliorate the oppressive lives of blacks in slavery and freedom. The purpose of the present study is to present preliminary findings and to form the basis of further detailed studies of the nineteenth centry American nun.

To summarize over a century's story in this format is virtually impossible. Much of what is herein contained, therefore, must be understood merely to scratch the surface. Generalizations and examples inevitably must substitute for thoroughness and detail. Still, the effort has been made to discern and present both the most prominent and most common varieties of nuns' nineteenth century black apostolate; none of the essential arguments or conclusions would be altered by what has been omitted.

During the early nineteenth century, both slavery and Catholicism were found mainly in the southern United States. Thus, interaction between women religious and Afro-Americans was inevitable and, in fact, probably dates from the arrival of Ursulines in then- French New Orleans, forty-nine years before the Declaration of Independence and seventy-six years before the Louisiana Purchase. It took various forms, although that between owner and bondsperson may have been dominant initially. For of the first eight congregations within the nation's borders, at least five are on record as direct participants in the peculiar institution. Lorettines, Carmelites, Dominicans, Sisters of Charity of Nazareth, and the Religious of the Sacred Heart all admitted candidates who brought slaves as part of the required dowry, and would-be Visitandines in the District of Columbia may have done so, as well.[5] This was not, even at the outset, the only form of racial contact, of course. Elizabeth Seton (d. 1821) is said to have taught black children in the vicinity of Emmitsburg, Maryland, and the band of her sisters whom she sent to New York initially admitted Negroes to their orphanage. The Sisters of St. Joseph of Carondelet's first mission away from their motherhouse (est. 1836) was a school for free black girls in St. Louis. Moreover, the impulse that gave birth in 1829 to the Sisters of Our Lady of Mercy of Charleston, S.C., was in large measure Bishop John England's desire to "do something" for persons of color within his diocese (although the school that resulted was forced to close in less than a decade when the state legislature forbade education of blacks.)[6]

Instances like these, of isolated and frequently short-lived individual or community ministry to Afro-Americans, are scattered throughout American Catholic history and persist almost to the present day.[7] In quantitative terms they touched the lives of few persons, white or black, and had little effect upon the collective experience of either sisters or the minority race. In qualitative terms, meanwhile, the impact of such tokenism was probably more negative than positive: alternately raising and then (when missions were halted, often abruptly) dashing the expectations of blacks, and enabling a generally uninvolved church and its orders to excuse themselves from charges of timidity and inaction.[8] Thus, tokenism, despite its admitted frequency throughout the 1800s, cannot be seen as evidence of strong Catholic concern for the needs of Afro-Americans. Rather, it serves as explicit demonstration of the hesitancy and ambivalence that characterized the bulk of the Church's nineteenth-century efforts to work among blacks.

Indeed, that ambivalence continues to assert itself in ways that distort a number of congregations' understanding and accounts of their own pasts (not to mention the complications they pose for attempts at historical inquiry!) Four incidents from the writer's own research experience are illustrative. More than mere anecdotes, they illuminate vestiges of a basic attitude that prevailed within most of nineteenth-century Catholicism.

First; the only full-length history of the Mount St. Vincent Sisters of Charity describes Mother Mary Rosina Wightman (1825-94) as "this most hidden of the community's Mothers General," identifying her only as a descendant "of an old English Puritan family," born in Charleston, S.C., "a Southerner to her fingertips, with all the gracious charm embodied in the traditions of the deep South," and remembered by her sisters mainly for devotion to the Sacred Heart. What it does not say — indeed, what it strives mightily to obscure — is that Mother Rosina was legally black. It is this, in fact, that accounts for her "elusiveness. . . which [has] not yielded thus far to painstaking research;" one of her successors, embarrassed when she learned of Wightman's race, destroyed everything in the archives that pertained to her — except a prayer book and rosary.[9]

Second, during the 1870s, the Religious of the Sacred Heart opened a "colored school." Published biographies and annals about the period refer to this mission openly, and even with a measure of pride. What they do not say, however, is that, a quarter of a century earlier, two of the founders of the Sisters of the Holy Family — a black community in New Orleans to be returned to later — were admitted to a white Sacred Heart academy (St. Michael's) in order to make their novitiate. No mention of this appeared in anything published under RSCJ auspices until 1983; prior to that, the only source of this information was a 1976 pamphlet, privately-issued (and not widely available) by the Holy Family sisters to commemorate the bicentennial.[10]

Third; a 1930 compendium of *Religious Orders of Women in the U.S.* contains an article on a group known as the Sisters of the Sacred Heart of Jesus (of St. Jacut), which made a foundation in San Antonio, Texas, in 1903. The piece is accompanied by a group photograph in which at least one (perhaps as many as four) of the women is unmistakably black. The community's published history, in French, is silent on the matter. Curious, the writer telephoned the Texas Provinciate. A nun who identified herself as the first American to enter the order (in 1919) denied absolutely that they had ever had a black member; when told about the photograph, she said she was not familiar with the book in which it appeared, and persisted in her denial.[11]

Fourth; the most fascinating story of all, however — and one which space constraints prevent telling fully here — is that of Teresa Maxis Duchemin, one of the four founders of the black Oblate Sisters of Providence in 1829, and later foundress of the Michigan and two Pennsylvania communities of (white) sisters of the Immaculate Heart of Mary. Her racial identity, insofar as the IHMs were concerned, remained hidden (as did her tenure with the Oblates) until 1945, when the matter was made public in an article in *America*; three years later, it figured briefly in a centennial history of the congregation. Since then, the Michigan and Scranton groups have acknowledged the race of their founder, and a recent biography by a member of the latter covers it thoroughly and with pride. Philadelphia, however, remains insistently silent (and even had the offending number of *America* removed from the college archives.) One of its sisters, who has persisted for six years in her effort to research Mother Teresa's life has been barred from her own order's archives. Another is currently in the process of transferring to the branch in Michigan.[12]

Such incidents, considered collectively, demonstrate one dimension of "Philemon's dilemma": that is, the dilemma inherent in a church that preached the equality of all persons before God at the same time that it could or would not offer direct or serious challenge to earthly realities that stood clearly in defiance of its precepts. In many respects, of course, nineteenth-century Catholicism's reluctance to defy the racial status quo — slavery until 1865, then segregation afterward — was perfectly understandable. Catholicism was, first of all, a minority denomination, especially in the South where most blacks were to be found. And the nativism that plagued it elsewhere is too well known to need recounting here.[13] There was some legitimacy, then, in Catholic claims that its position in the United States was too precarious to afford it the luxury of aggressively promoting the interests of a group even more beleaguered that itself, especially since so few members of that beleaguered group were Catholic. Second, outside of a few large cities, the nineteenth-century Church lacked sufficient priests, sisters, and brothers to serve even its own communicants, most of whom espoused racial attitudes similar to their other white neighbors'. They were, therefore, unlikely to criticize clerics and religious orders for not devoting more of their limited energies and resources to meeting the needs (or even saving the souls) of Afro-Americans.

Under the circumstances of personnel shortages, nativism, an almost entirely non-Catholic racial minority and a large and largely impoverished membership with problems of its own, it is less surprising that the nineteenth-century Church devoted so little to ministering

85

among blacks than that at least some Catholics devoted so much. Among those who demonstrated that commitment, a disproportionate number were members of an already overextended and overworked sector of the body of believers — nuns.

Over 225 communities of active sisters were at work in the United States by 1900.[14] It is virtually impossible to determine how many engaged at least peripherally or sporadically in the black apostolate. In some communities, a handful among several hundred members may have devoted themselves to Afro-Americans; unless they later served as major superiors, however, it is unlikely that a detailed account of their efforts will have survived, even in community annals. Consider, for example, the case of Sister M. Herlinde Sick, for 25 years an apparently unextraordinary member of the School Sisters of Notre Dame. She never held office; her name does not appear in the published histories. Her 150-word obituary is the most extensive biography of her in the SSND archives, and it notes merely that "she labored with untiring zeal for many years in the Negro school in Quincy, Illinois." She did more than that; she *founded* the black school and then took charge of it and, insofar as she could, struggled to ensure its survival (in today's terms, she "designed her own ministry.") Almost surely, she was inspired to do so by her experience as teacher of the first black pupil in the Quincy parochial system: an unusually bright youth to whom she gave private tutoring in her spare time and whom she (almost singly) encouraged in his aspirations for a long time after his graduation. Years later, Augustine Tolton came back to Quincy after studying in Rome as the first "full-blooded" Afro-American Catholic priest, and as pastor of the church founded in conjunction with (but subsequent to) Sister Herlinde's school.[15] It should not be suggested that this woman was typical but it is equally improbable that she was unique.

Still, the bulk of work among blacks occurred within permanent ministries that were maintained in the race's exclusive interest. Many of these were segregated schools, run by congregations otherwise devoted to whites. One of these, the Belle Prairie (later Little Falls), Minnesota, Franciscans may have been the first white order knowingly to have admitted an Afro-American to its ranks, which it did in the early 1880s.[16] In addition, both the Good Shepherd nuns and Little Sisters of the Poor ran Negro homes similar to those they had for Caucasians, the former for "wayward girls" and the latter for the elderly.[17] But the most, and certainly the most sustained, ministry tended to be done under the auspices of communities who committed themselves solely or predominantly to Afro-Americans. That explicit purpose made such groups, of which the writer has been able to discover only seven (including one that never got off the ground), qualitatively as well as quantitatively distinct from the others. For this reason, they deserve special consideration here. Each, of course, was in some ways unique. Nevertheless, despite what may at first appear to be great differences among them, they exhibit enough in common to suggest at least four factors that almost always were instrumental in determining long-term success or failure in the black apostolate.

That which was first chronologically was also an example of failure: the abortive attempt by Rev. Charles Nerinckx to establish a black branch of the Sisters of Loretto, which he had co-founded in Kentucky in 1812. Five candidates were admitted in 1824, intended to be professed to work solely among members of their own race. Within months of the start of their novitiate, Nerinckx was forced out of his position as the Lorettines' spiritual director, allegedly for the strictness of the community's rule. In any event, the Afro-American novices were immediately sent home by the priest who replaced him, and the experiment was never again resumed.[18]

Five years later, however, in 1829, another black community was founded and, after severe trials, this one survived: the Oblate Sisters of Providence, located in Baltimore, Maryland. Two decades earlier Baltimore had become the refuge for hundreds of Catholics fleeing Santo Domingo. Many of them were black, free, and possessed independent means. Two young women from that group began a school to teach black children catechism and reading; they, along with a black Cuban and American-born Teresa Maxis Duchemin (one of their students), would become the first four Oblates. For a time, the order prospered. Subsidized by the financial resources of the Superior (Mary Lange), their school grew and new ones were started, and several additional candidates entered. But a series of misfortunes — too-rapid expansion, complicated by the successive loss of direction by Sulpician, Redemptorist, and Jesuit priests, almost brought about the congregation's ruin. Several members (including Duchemin and another sister who joined her in founding the IHMs) left. For a time, the Oblates lacked a confessor and even access to the sacraments, and were forced to take in laundry and sewing to pay for food and rent. Only after the group was placed under diocesan direction, over fifty years after its beginning, did its survival become assured.[19]

The third community, organized in 1842, was also black: the Sisters of the Holy Family of New Orleans. Like the Oblates, its first members were also free Afro-Americans of independent means who came from the largest and oldest concentration of black Catholics in the United States. Again, the congregation's original ministry, care of orphans and the indigent homeless, evolved from the work its

87

founders began as laywomen. But the New Orleans' order enjoyed a number of advantages that the Oblates had not had. They had diocesan encouragement from the outset, more extensive financial grounding, and greater support from a bigger and more affluent black Catholic community. Thus, despite some hostility from Louisiana whites, they were never in danger of being destroyed. Rather, their efforts (in spiritual, if not monetary, terms) were prosperous from the outset.[20]

No additional black orders emerged during the nineteenth century, although the first white foundation dedicated primarily to work among Afro-Americans was established in 1866. These were the Sisters of St. Joseph of St. Augustine, Florida, brought over from Le Puy, France by Bishop Augustin Verot, to minister to the recently freed slaves. Verot had been one of slavery's most ardent ecclesial defenders until just a year earlier; once it was abolished, he became Catholicism's most aggressive American advocate for ministry to the minority race. Unfortunately for the interests of Afro-Americans, though, the Bishop died in 1876. Within three years, the Josephites he had invited to his diocese expressly to run Negro schools were teaching nearly twice as many whites as blacks, a ratio that only widened in subsequent decades.[21]

Great constancy was evidenced by the next community which, like those in Florida, were products of the Old World: the members of the British Mill Hill Missioners who, some time after their settlement in Baltimore in 1881, became the independent congregation of Baltimore Fanciscans. Apart from that, their history was markedly different, not only from that of the Sisters of St. Joseph, but from those of their Afro-American predecessors and their Caucasian successors. These were not women of means. Moreover, they never wavered from their commitment to work exclusively in behalf of blacks (the only white community to do so.) But they did enjoy a singular advantage which greatly facilitated their ministry. Their arrival was preceded a decade earlier by a band of Mill Hill priests, who also intended to labor solely among blacks and who later provided the nucleus for the American Josephite Fathers, who are still dedicated to the Afro-American apostolate. Virtually all the Franciscan nuns' nineteenth-century missions were under the auspices of these priests, which provided them with a degree of ecclesial legitimacy and security in what otherwise might have been a controversial field of action. Beyond this, it should not be forgotten that these sisters were neither the first nor the only nuns serving among Baltimore's blacks; almost surely they benefited from groundwork laid by fifty years of effort by the Oblates![22]

The only nineteenth-century black-oriented congregation to be instituted outside the former slave states was founded just outside Philadelphia in 1891. It has also been the most prolific in missions and ministries, and probably the most well known among American Catholics — not because of its location, of course, but because its founder, Katharine Drexel, was one of the wealthiest women in American (her father was a partner of J. P. Morgan) and a source of fascination now for nearly a century. Both of Katharine Drexel's parents were active in numerous charities and philanthropies; when still quite young, she herself became interested in work among Native Americans and blacks. During an audience with Leo XIII, the impulse was planted to found her own missionary congregation. The result was the Sisters of the Blessed Sacrament for Indians and Colored People. Thanks to Katharine Drexel's resources, they founded dozens of schools at all levels (including Xavier University, New Orleans, the only black [now integrated] Catholic college in the United States), technical institutes, social welfare centers, and other missions. Today there are more black sisters in this group than in any other predominantly white order, although it remained segregated for quite awhile — mainly because the founder did not want to undermine the potential strength of Afro-American communities. For this reason, too, she was reluctant to send Sisters of the Blessed Sacrament to places were black nuns were already active, and thus many of her earliest black missions were in the urban North.[23]

Only a year after Katharine Drexel's order began, a somewhat less wealthy, if comfortable, Texas widow named Margaret Mary Healy-Murphy was organizing a group of her own. Margaret Mary Healy-Murphy was unique among founders herein mentioned as she was the only former slaveowner. Ironically, income from the ranch on which slaves had labored would later help to subsidize her Negro missions. Never comfortable with the peculiar institution, Margaret Mary Healy-Murphy began to do missionary work among blacks in and around her home, which work expanded after the Civil War. Shortly after her husband's death in 1884, she attempted to open a school for blacks in Temple, Texas. It failed, and she moved to San Antonio, which appeared to offer more potential for such efforts. There, Healy-Murphy subsidized construction of St. Peter Claver Mission in 1888 which, four years later, became the first arena of labor for the newly-established Sisters of the Holy Ghost and Mary Immaculate. Although the founder's financial resources would eventually run out, they were indispensable in sustaining her early endeavors and in aiding her to resist the efforts of some religious priests (the Oblates of the Immaculate Heart) from wresting control of St. Peter's from her. Today,

89

the Holy Ghost sisters work among both Afro- and Hispanic-Americans in Texas and the American Southwest.[24]

Based upon these admittedly cursory descriptions, what sorts of conclusions are justifiable? First, working among blacks was undeniably controversial, even for black sisters. But in resisting opposition and maintaining a group's commitment, money could contribute mightily. The four most active communities, the Oblates, and Sisters of the Holy Family, Blessed Sacrament, and Holy Ghost, were all founded by women of at least some financial means, enabling them to initate works that inspired little if any public or ecclesial support. We need only contrast the early years of the two black orders, during which both were relatively successful, with subsequent decades of trial for the Oblates, whose very survival was threatened, in no small degree because of depleted resources. Similarly, Mother Margaret Mary, SHG, was able to defend her mission against the threat of takeover by the OMIs because she could impress upon the local bishop that *she* had built the church and school — and that no mere pastor could assume control over it (and over her!) Katharine Drexel, of course, was able virtually to write her own ticket; the few persons (private citizens usually, not clergy) who tried to impede her efforts found her too formidable, in both acumen and means, to be dissuaded from her objectives.

Second, sustained commitment to help Afro-Americans was not something to be imposed by outside authority; it had to come from the sisters themselves.[25] The four most active orders all grew out of their founders' prior involvement in direct ministry to the black community and (except for Katharine Drexel, whose previous role had been primarily philanthropic) their first "religious" missions were merely continuations of works begun as laywomen. These experiences may be compared with that of the Florida Josephites, who were organized for their apostolate by a bishop, and who lacked the same motivation to maintain their devotion after his death.

Third, ecclesial authorities, especially ordinaries, wielded tremenous power over sisters' lives, and could be decisive in the success or failure of missions, and even entire communities.[26] The Josephite case is instructive here, as is that of the Franciscans, but no examples convey the role that clerics could play more forcefully than those of the Oblates and the attempt by Fr. Nerinckx to start a black branch of the Lorettines. The latter failed, it will be recalled, because a hostile bishop transferred Fr. Nerinckx out of his diocese. The Baltimore group survived only after half a century of uncertainty, during which they were unable alone to combat successive metropolitans' efforts to disband them. Only the patronage (however short-lived) of members of several male religious orders, whose assistance allowed the archdiocese to absolve itself of direct responsibility for the nuns, prevented the Oblates' dissolution. It was not until after 1877, when the more sympathetic Archbishop (later Cardinal) Gibbons was installed, that all questions as to the congregation's permanence were resolved.

The fourth and final generalization offered is perhaps the most important. But it is also the most complicated, elusive, and difficult to document concretely — based, as it must be as this stage of the research, on nuance, implication, and the indirect evidence of what is *not* said in the documentary accounts of these communities. Still, the conviction remains that, until after World War II, nuns could work among Afro-Americans only if they did not challenge the fundamental status quo, particularly segregation.

It would be refreshing to be able to declare that sisters operated in this fashion reluctantly or under duress. There is no data to support this; on the contrary, even histories written within the past decade or two contain no overt signs of nineenth-century integrationist impulses, of explicit attempts to promote equal rights, or even of much interest in raising the sights of black students or others in the nuns' care beyond the limited number of career options that American society had determined were appropriate to the minority race. One cannot, of course, read these women's minds; among members of the black congregations, especially, one suspects there must have been some who harbored feelings of frustration and anger over the plight of Afro-Americans and the limitations of Catholicism's commitment to do anything about it. But no matter how strong such sentiments might have been, there was very little concretely they could do. This was, after all, the nineteenth century — and, after all, the Catholic Church. Nuns were not supposed to "speak out" — ever; they were subject to an ecclesial authority with power to put them out of business, and to whom they had vowed obedience. And if sisters did, even 100 years ago, sometimes dare to defy the hierarchy, those engaged in the black apostolate seemingly were sufficiently aware and astute to realize that this was not a matter over which to do so. Working among Afro-Americans was risky enough by itself, without complicating its execution by attempting to challenge Church (and societal) norms.

There is, on the other hand, no reason to assume that the majority of sisters *wanted* to challenge the status quo. It would be unfairly ahistorical to expect them to have espoused what we today accept as appropriate attitudes toward interracial justice but which were held by virtually no one in the nineteenth century. Nuns and clerics were per-

91

sons of *their* time, products of an environment in which racism was almost universal.

Having said that, however, it is necessary to go a step further and to recognize in mission work among Afro-Americans something that went beyond the realm of mere consensual and historically under-standable racism. This was the posture of noblesse oblige that characterized the efforts of every congregation the writer studied, in-cluding the Oblates and Sisters of the Holy Family. To some extent, this posture was a function of class. Both the black and white nuns came from backgrounds far more privileged than those of nearly all American Negroes in the 1800s. Moreover, contemporary church and secular philosophies were not intended to (nor did they) foster desires to stand "in solidarity with" the poor, or to exhibit a "preferential op-tion" for them. Rather, religious annals convey impressions of "ladies bountiful," out to bestow the benefits of their charity upon a lesser and benighted people.

Class elitism helps to explain why such sentiments prevailed even within the Afro-American orders — but only, as has been said, to some extent. It derived as well from what can only be described as Catholicism's sense of *spiritual* superiority. Blacks were not just of a "lesser" race, and poor; if not Catholic they were *unsaved*: a category that included, according to accepted theology, non-Catholic Chris-tians as well as the completely unchurched. Unless this matter of ec-clesial triumphalism is appreciated it would be easy to underestimate the complexity of motivation behind the ministry to Afro-Americans and to miss an important, if subtle, dimension that underlay what the writer perceives as Philemon's dilemma — but which the writer also suspects most nineteenth-century Catholics did not perceive at all.

The fundamental premise under which nineteenth-century Catholic missionary work proceeded was that its foremost objective was to save souls — first through baptism, and then through prevention of "leakage" from the ranks of the baptised, or reclamation of the "fallen away."[27] This had two major consequences for work among blacks. One was that, as the number of identifiably Catholic immigrants swelled during the post-Civil War decades, the top priority of the American hierarchy became ministry to them, which inevitably meant less commitment of scarce resources to other efforts, including the Afro-American missions. It also meant that, in whatever was done with any group, including blacks, success was measured largely in terms of baptisms, first communions, confirmations, church atten-dance, and the like.[28] Objectives like quality secular education, for ex-ample, clearly took a back seat to soul-winning — as did anything that pertained solely to the temporal, such as reordering social and economic institutions and structures. Baptism brought equality before God; in light of that, what did earthly inequality matter? The saved could look forward to an eternity of equality in heaven. Within such a theology, which regarded the kingdom of God as celestial and separate from the here-and-now, Philemon's dilemma was, of course, hardly a dilemma at all.

The nineteenth-century record, when it came to Afro-American soul-winning, was almost uninterruptedly dismal, for reasons too extensive and complicated to enumerate here.[29] Given that, an earlier point must be reiterated in conclusion. As limited as Catholicism's commitment was to black people, its persistence at all in light of the scarcity of church resources, American racial prejudice, and its lack of ecclesially-defined success, was actually rather respectable. And those black and white sisters who performed the dominant share of those missionary labors must be regarded as risk-takers and pioneers: women who deliberately took on a ministry that was neither easy nor popular, whose initiatives in education, health care and other areas did ameliorate the deprivations suffered by thousands within the minority race. However tentatively or unconsciously, they were laying foundations that would enable at least some Afro-Americans to assume greater control of their own destinies. Moreover, they did it with little help from the establishment.

93

To criticize nineteenth-century nuns for not rising above the constraints of Philemon's dilemma would be to blame those who were themselves products — and victims — of secular and religious systems that blinded virtually all contemporary Catholics, and Americans generally, to the very facts that there *was* a dilemma. Subsequent generations, however — these same women's spiritual daughters — would not be similarly blinded. And as they proceeded, in the wake of Vatican II, to explore their own roots as part of the process of Church-mandated renewal, they could claim the pioneering impulse that motivated their foremothers: legitimately restoring, reshaping, and building upon it in the context of their own times.[30] In this manner, that pioneering impulse would take on new life and new forms. These women would address the contradictions inherent in Philemon's dilemma that were inaccessible to those who went before, — not as a repudiation of their legacy, but at least partly as a consequence of it.*

*The following persons provided assistance in obtaining information and insights for this paper: Diane Edward Shea, IHM; Mary Jo Maher, IHM; Margaret Gannon, IHM; Margaret Ellen Traxler, SSND, Mary Caroline Jakubowski, SSND, Sister Emmanuel, SHG, Mary Assumpta Ahles, OSF, and participants in the Syracuse University Women's Studies Faculty Seminar. I alone, of course, am responsible for the resulting essay.

FOOTNOTES

1. John T. Gillard, SSH, *Colored Catholics in the United States* (Baltimore, 1941), pp. 256-57.

2. Carol Kleiman, "Sister Margaret Traxler and the Vatican 24," *MS.*, April 1985, p. 124.

3. Mary Ewens, "Removing the Veil: The Liberated American Nun in the 19th Century," Working Paper No 3 (Spring 1978), Cushwa Center for the Study of American Catholicism, Univ. of Notre Dame, p. 23.

4. Conversations with participants, including Margaret Ellen Traxler, SSND (see account of Sr. Herlinde Sick, SSND, below), and Meme Woolever, a former member of the Hartford, Conn., Sisters of Mercy, whose members ran a black school in St. Augustine, Florida, in the mid-1860's (Michael V. Gannon, *Rebel Bishop: The Life and Era of Augustin Verot* [Milwaukee, 1964], p. 130).

5. Mary Ewens states that seven of the first eight communities owned slaves; *The Role of the Nun in Nineteenth Century America* (New York, 1978), p. 68; see also histories of respective communities and Frances Jerome Woods, "Congregations of Religious Women in the Old South," in *Catholics in the Old South: Essays on Church and Culture,* ed. Randall M. Miller and Jon L. Wakelyn (Macon, Ga., 1983), pp. 99-123.

6. Sources in n. 5; in addition, Joseph B. Code, "Negro Sisterhoods in the United States: A Record of Fellowship and Love," *America,* 8 Jan. 1938, p. 318; Mary Lucinda Savage, *The Congregation of Saint Joseph of Carondelet* (St. Louis, 1923), p. 63; Elinor Tong Dehey, *Religious Orders of Women in the United States,* rev. ed. (Hammond, Ind., 1930), pp. 183-84.

7. The qualification of "almost" is based upon the complete integration of virtually all Catholic institutions and ministries today, and the consequent unlikelihood of the sorts of initiatives that occurred in the nineteenth century.

8. Two books by John T. Gillard expand on this: *Colored Catholics,* especially ch. 3-4; and *The Catholic Church and the American Negro* (Baltimore, 1929), passim.

9. Marie de Lourdes Walsh, *The Sisters of Charity of New York, 1809-1959,* 3 vols. (New York, 1960); I: 225-27; conversations with several members of the congregation, including Phyllis Price, Karen Helfenstein, and Eileen McGrory.

10. No references in Louise Callan, *The Society of the Sacred Heart in North America* (New York, 1937); or Margaret Williams, *Second Sowing: The Life of Mary Aloysia Hardey* (New York, 1942.) The author was not able to obtain a copy of Margaret Williams; *The Society of the Sacred Heart: History of a Spirit, 1800-1975* (London, 1978), the 1983 reference is in Evengeline Thomas, ed., *Women Religious History Sources: A Guide to Repositories in the United States* (New York, 1983), p. 41. The pamphlet referred to is Audrey Marie Detiege, *Henriette Delille, Free Women of Color* (New Orleans, 1976), p. 43.

11. Dehey, *Religious Orders of Women,* pp. 752-53; conversation with Sister Rose of Lima, SSCJ, 11 March 1985; A. Guyot, *The Congregation of the Sisters of the Sacred Heart* (Vannes, France, 1921).

12. Joseph B. Code, "Mother Theresa Maxis Duchemin, *America,* 22 Dec. 1945, pp. 317-20; Rosalita Kelly, *No Greater Service: The History of the Congregation of the Sisters, Servants of the Immaculate Heart of Mary, Monroe, Michigan, 1845-1945* (Detroit, 1948), Part I, passim; see also Immaculata Gillespie, *Mother M. Teresa Maxis Duchemin* (New York, 1945); [anon.] *Thou, Lord, Art My Hope: The Life of Mother M. Theresa* (Lancaster, 1961); Maria Alma, *Sisters, Servants of the Immaculate Heart of Mary* (Lancaster, Pa., 1934.) The recent biography is "Mother Teresa Maxis Duchemin, I.H.M.: Let Your Heart Be Bold," by Margaret Gannon (unpublished mimeograph.) Conversations that enlightened the author as to the situation within the Philadelphia IHMs must, understandably, remain anonymous here.

13. Ray Allen Billington, *The Protestant Crusade, 1800-1860: A Study of the Origins of American Nativism* (New York, 1938); John Higham, *Strangers in the Land: Patterns of American Nativism, 1860-1925* (New Brunswick, N.J., 1955.)

14. Count based on "Table of U.S. Founding Dates," in *Women Religious History Sources,* pp. 169-175; it is a low estimate, as the author has already encountered a number of congregations that were not included in this compedium.

15. The writer encountered Sr. Herlinde in Caroline Hemesath, *From Slave to Priest: A Biography of the Rev. Augustine Tolton (1854-1897), First Afro-American Priest of the United States* (Chicago, 1973), passim; obituary provided in letter to the writer from Mary Caroline Jakubowski, SSND, Provincial Leader of the SSND,

Milwaukee Province, 14 March 1985. Tolton was preceded by the remarkable Healy brothers, offspring of a mulatto mother and Irish father; one became a bishop, another a Jesuit and President of Georgetown University, and the third a theological consultant at the First Vatican Council; Albert S. Foley, *God's Men of Color: The Colored Catholic Priests of the United States, 1854-1954* (New York, 1955), ch. 1-3. Materials in the Milwaukee, St. Louis and Rome, Italy, SSND archives indicate that the American Vicar of the Congregation, Mother M. Caroline Friess, was supportive of Sister Herlinde's desire to work with blacks; nearly all her assignments after her initial effort in Quincy were with that group. (The author's thanks to Sister Mary Margaret Johanning, SSND, Superior General, for having these materials collected and sent; materials in the Milwaukee archives, mainly in the randomly collected papers of Mother Caroline, were seen by the author during research in Nov. 1985.)

16. The author is grateful to Mary J. Oates for calling this to her attention; telephone conversation, 1 April 1985; confirmed by telephone conversation with Mary Assumpta Ahles, OSF (author of *In the Shadow of His Wings* [St. Paul, Minn., 1977], a history of the Little Falls Franciscans), 1 April 1985. The woman in question was Frederica Law (Sister M. Benedict), who died in 1883 while still a novice. She was admitted as a lay sister, but even that apparently required a special dispensation from Cardinal Monaco La Valetta (Vicar to the Pope.) Nonetheless, this Congregation's constitution contained a specific clause forbidding discrimination based on race in the admission of candidates; for example, an announcement in its popularly circulated periodical, *Annals of Our Lady of the Angels* (Vol. 23, 1898, p. 178), declares that Pope Leo XIII had granted a special benediction to its desire to admit black sisters, and continued: "We cordially invite the correspondence of such aspirants to the Religious life, the Habit, Profession and Privileges of which, in our Institute, are the same for all, without any distinctions between race or nationality . . ." in materials in the Archives of the Little Falls, Minn. Franciscans.

17. Gillard, *Catholic Church and the Negro*, pp. 162-64, 201-203, 206; and *Colored Catholics*, pp. 216-17, 227-28, 235.

18. Ewens, *Role of the Nun*, p. 55; Gillard, *Catholic Church and the Negro*, pp. 135-36; Paul Camillus Maes, *Life of Rev. Charles Nerinckx* (Cincinnati, 1880.)

19. Code, "Negro Sisterhoods;" Grace H. Sherwood, *The Oblates' Hundred and One Years* (New York, 1931), Part I, passim.

20. Detiege, *Henriette Delille;* Mary Francis Borgia Hart, *Violets in the Kings Garden: A History of the Sisters of the Holy Family* (New Orleans, 1976), passim.

21. Gannon, *Rebel Bishop*, esp. pp. 128-42; Jane Quinn, *The Story of a Nun: Jeannie Gordon Brown* [SSJ] (St. Augustine, Florida, 1978), esp. pp. 72 ff. Although outside the timespan of this paper, it is interesting to mention the case of Sister Mary Thomasine Hehir, SSJ, who was arrested in 1918 under a Florida statute that prohibited whites from teaching blacks. She resisted, and the verdict in her case resulted in a landmark decision that such laws did not apply to private ventures, such as Catholic schools; thus, this community did retain limited commitment to education of blacks. Quinn, *Brown*, pp. 205-11.

22. A history of this community has not been located; an inquiry to its motherhouse revealed that none seems to exist. Data are from Dehey, *Religious Orders of Women*, pp. 467-69; *Women Religious History Sources*, pp. 45-46; National Sisters Vocation Conference, *Guide to Religious Communities for Women* (Chicago, 1983), p. 124; and survey of missions of the sisters and the Josephite Fathers in the late nineteenth and early twentieth century in *Official Catholic Directories*.

23. Consuela Marie Duffy, *Katharine Drexel: A Biography* (Cornwall Heights, Pa., 1965), passim.

24. Mary Immaculata Turley, *Mother Margaret Mary Healy-Murphy, A Biography* (San Antonio, 1969); incident on attempted takeover of St. Peter Claver Mission is on pp. 84-87, 90-93. The community is now known as the Sisters of the Holy Spirit and Mary Immaculate; its original St. Peter Claver Mission is now the Healy-Murphy Center, a publicly-subsidized high school for problem learners, community center, and a clinic; despite public auspices, it is still run by the sisters (Visit to the Healy-Murphy Center, 5 Feb. 1986.)

25. This argument was first advanced by Michael J. McNalley, "A Minority of a Minority: The Witness of Black Women Religious in the Antebellum South," *Review for Religious*, 40 (1981), p. 267, but he applied it only to black sisters; the writer discovered that it applied to white communities, as well.

26. This obviously was true in all areas, not simply in the black ministry. Mary Ewens analyzes this extensively throughout her *Role of the Nun;* it shall be a major

theme of the author's forthcoming book-length study of nineteenth-century American nuns. For a factual account of bishops' hegemony, see Benjamin F. Farrell, *The Rights and Duties of the Local Ordinary Regarding Congregations of Women Religious of Pontifical Approval* (Washington, D.C., 1941); and Hector Papi, *The Government of Religious Communities: A Commentary of Three Chapters of the Code of Canon Law* (New York, 1919); both these works are based upon the 1917 code of canon law. Prior to that, however, bishops' authority was even more extensive.

27. Both of Gillard's books, *Catholic Church and the Negro* and *Colored Catholics*, discuss this extensively in respect to the black missions; the former volume even contains about seven chapters in which matters such as "leakage" are analyzed explicitly (see Part Six.)

28. Again, this is implicit throughout Gillard's work, and is analyzed in Gannon, *Rebel Bishop,* esp. chap. 5. Moreover, it is striking that community histories (e.g., those by Sherwood and Turley) contain extensive lists of sisters' black students who were baptised, received first communion, were confirmed, etc. — but contained no similar lists of graduates from the schools. These attitudes are implicit throughout the two principal pastorals of the American bishops in the nineteenth century, from the 2nd and 3rd Councils of Baltimore (1866, 1884, both of which contain explicit references to missions among blacks; the latter, however, articulates the higher priority to be given to work among Catholic immigrants): Hugh J. Nolan, ed., *Pastoral Letters of the American Hierarchy, 1792-1970,* (Huntington, Ind., 1971), pp. 143-86.

29. Again, the two Gillard volumes discuss this extensively.

30. For the official Catholic Church impetus to renewal, see *Perfectae Caritatis: The Decree on the Adaptation and Renewal of the Religious Life* (published variously; issued 1965.) Renewal actually began before this; see Elizabeth Kolmer, *Religious Women in the United States: A Survey of the Influential Literature from 1950 to 1973* (Wilmington, Del., 1984), esp. the analytic chap. 1. On responses to renewal, see Ann Patrick Ware, ed., *Midwives of the Future: American Sisters Tell Their Story,* (Kansas City, 1984.)

Sisters of St. Joseph:
The Americanization of a French Tradition

Patricia Byrne, C.S.J.

On 25 March 1836 the first Sisters of St. Joseph ever to leave France arrived in the nine-year-old diocese of St. Louis. Those six women brought with them the rich heritage of a nearly 200-year tradition that had roots in the renewal of the Catholic Church in France during the seventeenth century. Like other immigrant groups, the sisters found that success in the new world depended upon adjustment to changed conditions. Challenged by the necessity of cultural assimilation, they were able to draw upon the legacy of their particular history in France in order to form a style of religious life that worked remarkably well for them as a way of being Catholic and American. The history of the Congregations of St. Joseph in the United States can be viewed as the Americanization of that French tradition.[1] This study explores several elements in the nineteenth-century experience of Sisters of St. Joseph which highlight the interaction of French background and American milieu. The data is taken primarily from six of the United States congregations established before 1870: Carondelet (1836), Philadelphia (1847), Wheeling (1853), Brooklyn (1856), St. Augustine (1866), and Ebensburg, Pennsylvania (1869).

---

1. Twenty-five congregations of St. Joseph now in the United States can be traced to six foundations made from motherhouses in France: Carondelet, 1836 (Lyons); New Orleans, 1855 (Bourg); St. Augustine, 1866 (Le Puy); Lee, Massachusetts, 1885 (Chambéry); Fall River, Massachusetts, 1902 (Le Puy); and Jackman, Maine, 1906 (Lyons). Only the latter and the Chambéry foundation remain provinces of the original congregations. Margaret Quinn, C.S.J., and Patricia Manning, C.S.J., "Federation of the Sisters of St. Joseph in the United States of America and Canada: Historical Development of the Congregations" (Brentwood, New York: By the authors, 1985).

98

Patricia Byrne, C.S.J.

French Origins

The Congregation of St. Joseph came to America on one of several waves of expatriated French Catholicism which affected the Catholic Church in the United States during its formative years. The nineteenth-century French influence on the American Church was the result of the contemporary religious revival in France, activist in color and missionary in scope, exemplified in the organization of the Society of the Propagation of the Faith at Lyons in 1822.[2] The Society was to play an important part in the foundation of the Sisters of St. Joseph in the United States.

The origins of the Sisters of St. Joseph considerably antedate their coming to America, going back to the middle of the seventeenth century. A fruit of the immense spiritual and organizational energies of the Counter-Reformation in France, the Congregation of St. Joseph was in the vanguard of the modern movement of women's congregations which, in spite of ecclesiastical law, were directed specifically toward the service of the

---

2. *Dictionnaire de spiritualité ascètique et mystique, doctrine et histoire,* s.v. "France: 8, De la Révolution au début du 20ᵉ siècle," by André Rayex, and S. Delacroix et al., *Les missions contemporains (1800–1957),* vol. 3 of *Histoire universelle des missions catholiques,* ed. S. Delacroix (Paris, 1958), 20–71.

neighbor and therefore did not observe canonical cloister.[3] The precise date of the foundation of the Sisters of St. Joseph is unknown. It was an evolutionary event, connected with the labors of the Jesuit priest Jean-Pierre Médaille in the mountainous and poverty-stricken areas of south central France.[4] Between 1646 and 1651, six women took over the administration of the hospital-orphanage in the rue de Montferrand in Le Puy and became Sisters of St. Joseph. They obtained ecclesiastical approbation from Henry de Maupas, bishop of Le Puy, 10 March 1651. There were at the same time other foundations in the diocese of Le Puy—the earliest recorded being that of Dunières, where Anne Deschaux, a woman of the parish, began a community of St. Joseph on 29 September 1649.[5]

Father Médaille envisioned "this new way of life" as at once deeply spiritual and eminently practical. He defined its purpose in terms of the perfect love of God and neighbor: "Our selfless congregation . . . tends to achieve [the] total double union of ourselves and the dear neighbor with God, and of ourselves and all others, whoever they may be, of all others among themselves and with us, but totally in Jesus and in God his Father." In order to make this ideal tangible within the social order of the day, the Sisters of St. Joseph were to practice "all the spiritual and corporal works of mercy of which woman is capable."[6] Not restricted to any specific work, they were free to respond to the needs of a situation—a fact that was to have great importance for their history in America.

During the century and a half of their existence before the French Revolution, foundations of Sisters of St. Joseph spread rapidly in the Massif Central and some surrounding areas to the south and east. At no

99

---

3. The Council of Trent and subsequent papal legislation had required cloister and solemn vows for all women religious. Sess. 25, 3–4 December 1563, decree *De Regularibus et Monialibus*, in *Concilium Tridentinum: Diariorium, Actorum, Epistularum, Tractatuum*, ed. Societas Goerresiana, 13 vols. (Freiburg, St. Louis, 1901–1938), 9(1924): 1077–1085; and Pius V, constitution *Circa Pastoralis*, 29 May 1566, in *Codicis Iuris Canonici Fontes*, 1:112, cited in James R. Cain, "Cloister and the Apostolate of Religious Women," *Review for Religious* 27(1968):272.

4. *Dictionnaire de spiritualité*, s.v. "Médaille, Jean-Pierre," by Marius Nepper, S.J.

5. Compte rendu par Estienne Treveys des recettes et dépenses acceptées par lui pour la maison des filhes orfelines de St. Joseph de la rue Montferrand du Puy, April 1646–March 1648, 8 A 1, Archives of the Sisters of St. Joseph of Le Puy (hereafter cited as ACSJLP); Lettres de provision données par Monseigneur Henry de Maupas du Tour evesque du Puy en faveur des Filhes de la congregation de St. Joseph du Puy touchant leur establissement 10 mars 1651, 12 H 1, Filles de St. Joseph-Hôpital de Montferrand, Departmental Archives of the Haute-Loire, Le Puy; and Constitution de dot soy faite par soeur Anne Deschaux superieure de la congregation des filles de St. Joseph, 10 February 1662, Dunières papers, ACSJLP.

6. *Règlements*, no. 5; *Lettre eucharistique*, no. 29; and *Constitutions primitives*, no. 49, in Soeurs de Saint Joseph, eds., *Textes primitifs* (Clermont-Ferrand, 1981), 105, 8, 23. Translations by the Intercongregational Research Team, Federation of the Sisters of St. Joseph, U.S.A.

time before the Revolution did they have a centralized organization. Each house was independent, and one may speak in a true sense of parish communities. Although the bishop was the ultimate authority in regard to each community, the curé often acted as the local ecclesiastical superior. Community records show that he gave the habit, received vows, confirmed elections, and sometimes kept the books.[7]

Membership was drawn largely from the parish, and communities tended to be small, numbering perhaps six or seven.[8] Surviving acts of association show that Sisters of St. Joseph were most often daughters of laborers or farmers with small holdings, but there were considerable differences from house to house. Only in the larger towns, and late in the eighteenth century, did their dowries exceed those typical for women of the lower classes.[9] The sisters supplemented their meager income through cottage industry, usually lace- or ribbon-making.[10]

Sisters of St. Joseph did what was needed in the parish: they operated primitive grade schools, catechized the women, took care of the sick and orphans in small local "hospitals," visited homes of the needy, and were sacristans for the parish church. Listing the useful activities of the Sisters of St. Joseph there in 1761, the citizens of Job concluded: "Since there is no one other than the *filles associées* . . . to instruct and train the young girls, it is very important that this community exist as being very advantageous for the said parish."[11] Their sentiments are echoed in the judgment of the social historian, Gabriel Le Bras, who asserted that without the

---

7. Acte d'association, 1660, Boisset Papers, ACSJLP; Profession de Marie Limousin, 8 March 1734, Registre, Aurec papers, ACSJLP; Registre, Bas papers, ACSJLP; Acte d'association de Claudine Antoinette Montaland, 25 May 1744, C-2, Aubépin papers, Archives of the Sisters of St. Joseph of Lyons (hereafter cited as ACSJL); and Registre, C-12, Izieu papers, ACSJL.

8. Due to the extensive destruction during the Revolution, French congregational sources do not permit a statistical analysis; these figures represent an impression formed by examining papers of the pre-Revolutionary communities contained in the motherhouses at Le Puy, Lyons, and Clermont-Ferrand.

9. Dowries from 300 to 500 *livres* are typical of acts of association found in many of the houses represented in ACSJL and ACSJLP; some larger city houses show dowries of 1,000 *livres* or more. Registre des délibérations des actes des administrateurs de la maison du Refuge, 18 August 1758, H 7, le Bon Pasteur, Departmental Archives of the Puy-de-Dôme, Clermont-Ferrand; and acte d'ingrès de Catherine Jouve, 2 August 1769, Craponne Papers, ACSJLP. See F. Gouit, *Une congrégation salésienne: Les Soeurs de Saint-Joseph du Puy-en-Velay* (Le Puy, 1930), 138; and Olwen H. Hufton, *The Poor of 18th Century France (1750–1789),* (Oxford, 1974), 28.

10. Most pre-Revolutionary documents identify the Sisters of St. Joseph as "filles dentellières" or "filles rubanières," as in Petition addresse a M Verardier, con[seill]er du Roy, president en l'Ellection de St. Etienne, 13 April, 1719, C-30, Saint-Genest-Malifaux papers, ACSJL.

11. Deliberation of the inhabitants of Job in favor of *lettres patentes* for the Sisters of St. Joseph, 1761, "12-Débuts des soeurs de Saint-Joseph à Job, près d'Ambert (1742–1761)," in Roger Sève, Jean Perrel, and Jean Chapelle, eds, *L'enseignement sous l'Ancien Régime en Auvergne, Bourbonnais et Velay* (Clermont-Ferrand, 1977), 28–29, my translation.

The city of Le Puy-en-Velay, France, where the Sisters of St. Joseph were founded

sisters there was often no one in a village to provide this kind of social assistance, the parish being the sole source of such service.[12] In addition to parish work, sisters also staffed institutions—including general hospitals, *hôtels-Dieu,* a few detention homes for *filles repenties* such as the Refuge du Bon Pasteur in Clermont, and some schools which, in the scheme of Louis XIV, served for the indoctrination of recently "converted" young Protestants.[13]

In its pre-Revolutionary development, the Congregation of St. Joseph was characterized by membership drawn from people of the most ordinary means and education. No personal letters of Sisters of St. Joseph before the Revolution survive; the only evidence of literacy is from convent registers and legal documents, which demonstrate merely the ability to execute a signature. These reveal that, like four-fifths of the French population at the end of the seventeenth century, many Sisters of St. Joseph were illiterate.[14]

12. *L'église et le village* (Paris, 1976), 149–52.

13. Notes of A. Achard, Tence and Saint-Paulien papers, ACSJLP; Lettres patentes, 1754, Privas papers, Archives of the Sisters of St. Joseph of Viviers, Aubenas; and *Dictionnaire d'histoire de l'Eglise de France,* s.v. "France: 4, Les 17ᵉ et 18ᵉ siècles," by André Latreille, col. 88.

14. Pierre Goubert, *The Ancien Régime: French Society 1600–1750,* trans. Irene Cox (New York, 1973; 1974), 262, citing Maggiolo, *Etat récapitulatif et comparatif...,* published by the Ministère de l'Instruction publique, n.p., n.d., Bibliothèque Nationale, 4° Lf 242–196.

Without benefit of privilege or education, through their activities in parishes, rudimentary hospitals and schools, congregations like the Sisters of St. Joseph achieved the direct participation of women in the pastoral care of the Church. Significant for this study is their integral role among the common people in the society of the *ancien régime*, and the history of intense localization, the strong identification of communities with the local Church, which seemed to become a habit, and was to re-emerge in the American scene.

The aftermath of the French Revolution found the Sisters of St. Joseph with a handful of martyrs, many quiet heroines, a few apostates, and the majority who tried to survive the storm without compromising themselves.[15] In many parishes where they had been before the Revolution, a few of the old guard struggled to reorganize their community life, and were joined by new recruits. Under the Napoleonic system these communities found themselves at first independent of each other, and later, for the sake of utility, pressed into a centralized organization under diocesan mother-houses.[16]

Cardinal Joseph Fesch, uncle of Napoleon and archbishop of Lyons, is credited with authorizing the re-establishment of the Sisters of St. Joseph in his archdiocese in 1807 at Saint-Etienne. To be more exact: there were many separate communities of St. Joseph being founded or refounded in the diocese of Lyons after the Revolution. Under the administration of Fesch and his vicar-general, Claude Cholleton, former pastor at Saint-Etienne and spiritual director for a group known as the *Filles Noires*, the latter were transformed into Sisters of St. Joseph. They were an unofficial community of pious women, some of them ex-nuns, who had been practicing an ascetic life at Saint-Etienne for about six years, waiting for the day when they could become cloistered. Contemplatives, however, were despised by Napoleon, and the needs of the vast archdiocese demanded, above all, workers. In order to change the direction of the *Filles Noires* into an active vein, in 1807 Mother St. Jean Fontbonne, former superior of the Sisters of St. Joseph at Monistrol, came to Saint-Etienne. Im-

---

15. Four, possibly five, Sisters of St. Joseph were executed during the Terror: Marie-Anne Garnier and Jeanne-Marie Aubert at Le Puy, 17 June 1794; Antoinette Vincent, Marie-Anne Sénovert, and Madeleine Dumoulin at Privas (Ardèche), 5 August 1794. (Although tradition has identified Jeanne-Marie Aubert as a Sister of St. Joseph, there is no documentation to prove it.)

Like their eccentric bishop, Charles Lafont de Savines, fourteen of the sixteen sisters at the hospital of Aubenas in the diocese of Viviers took the constitutional oath. Extraits des Archives de l'Hôpital d'Aubenas, CS V 10, 135, Archives of the Sisters of St. Joseph of Viviers, Aubenas.

16. Roger Aubert, *The Church between Revolution and Restoration*, trans. Peter Becker, vol. 7 of *The History of the Church*, ed. Hubert Jedin and John Dolan (New York, 1981), 66–67; and Paul Nourisson, *Histoire légale des congrégations religieuses en France depuis 1789*, 2 vols. (Paris, 1928), 1:82–83, 100–103.

103

Sister Febronie Fontbonne   **Sister Delphine Fontbonne**

prisoned during the Terror, and reputedly slated for execution, she had been spared by the fall of Robespierre.[17] After a year's novitiate under Mother St. Jean, seventeen of the *Filles Noires* received the habit as Sisters of St. Joseph on 14 July 1808, and the nucleus of the Lyons Congregation took shape. By 1816, Mother St. Jean had moved from Saint-Etienne to the episcopal city of Lyons, and in 1829 a centralized novitiate was established there for all the houses of the Sisters of St. Joseph in the diocese.[18]

---

17. The history of Mother St. Jean Fontbonne is problematic, making it difficult to sort legend from fact. Her correspondence was reportedly destroyed in a fire while in the possession of her first biographer, whose account of her life is undocumented and strictly hagiographic: J. Rivaux, *Vie de la Révérende Mère Saint Jean née Fontbonne* (Grenoble, 1885), trans. and ed. by [M. Assissium Mc Evoy, S.S.J.], under the title of *Life of Mother St. John Fontbonne: Foundress and First Superior-General of the Congregation of the Sisters of St. Joseph in Lyons* (New York, 1887). A second biography, which makes corrections and significant additions to Rivaux's material while borrowing much of it is [Marie-Stéphanie Hervier, C.S.J.], *Simple et grande: Mère Saint-Jean Fontbonne, fondatrice de la congrégation de Saint-Joseph de Lyon, restauratrice de l'Institut* (Paris-Bruges, 1929), trans. and ed. by A Sister of St. Joseph of Brentwood, New York [M. Leonilla Cleary], under the title of *Mother Saint John Fontbonne: Foundress of the Congregation of the Sisters of St. Joseph of Lyons* (New York, 1936). See [Hervier], *La congrégation de Saint-Joseph de Lyon,* Les ordres religieux (Paris, 1927), 44–45.

18. Prise d'habit 14 juillet 1808, Registre "Profession," unclassified papers, ACSJL; and Ordonnance sur le Noviciat des Soeurs de St. Joseph, Jean-Paul Gaston de Pins, Archêveque d'Amasie, Administrateur Apostolique du Diocèse de Lyon et Vienne, 23 December 1828, 1 0 III, Mère Saint-Jean papers, ACSJL.

In the post-Napoleonic era, the Sisters of St. Joseph retained the parish orientation and the variety of occupations which they had had before the Revolution.[19] The motherhouse structure added the dimension of mobility and a larger pool of personnel, which made possible greater specialization in works and expansion through deployment of sisters who had received uniform religious training in the central novitiate. The stage was set for a missionary venture.

Foundations of an American Identity

The American foundation of the Sisters of St. Joseph in 1836 resulted from a conjunction of circumstances, and there were quite a few fingers in the pie. There was the city of Lyons, during the thirties a center for American connections in Europe, due to the location there of the headquarters for the Society of the Propagation of the Faith. There was a countess, Félicité de Duras, the pious and philanthropic wife of the Count de la Rochejaquelein. She, like many Catholics of her day, was a reader of the *Annales* of the Society of the Propagation of the Faith.[20] The Mission of Missouri was a regular feature in the *Annales,* with letters from priests in the field, including a number from Joseph Rosati, the Bishop of St. Louis, with vivid descriptions of life in America, as well as appeals for missionaries and funds.[21] Mme de la Rochejaquelein, determined to do something for the foreign missions, decided to finance a group of Sisters of St. Joseph for America. She enlisted Fr. Claude Cholleton, ecclesiastical superior of the Sisters of St. Joseph in Lyons and European agent for Rosati, to convince the latter that what he needed on the Missouri frontier were Sisters of St. Joseph.

The countess had a definite project in mind. "I would send six Sisters of St. Joseph to North America," she wrote to Rosati, "with a view to their converting the savages, instructing the little ones, and educating and converting the children of Protestants."[22] The dual emphasis on savages and

104

---

19. Etat des maisons des soeurs de St-Joseph existant dans le Diocèse de Lyon, 10 April 1812, V 262, Cultes, Departmental Archives of the Rhône, Lyons.

20. *Annales de la Propagation de la Foi* (Paris, 1822–   ). For their impact on French Catholics in the nineteenth century, see Edward J. Hickey, *The Society for the Propagation of the Faith: Its Foundation, Organization, Success (1822–1922),* The Catholic University of America Studies in American Church History, no. 3 (Washington, 1922; reprint, New York, 1974), 140–142, 169–172.

21. Mgr. Rosati, evêque de Saint-Louis et administrateur de Nouvelle Orléans à M l'abbé P., 3 août 1828, *Annales de la Propagation de la Foi* 28 (May 1929): 545–571; idem à M Cholleton, vicaire général, St. Louis, 8 mai 1832, *Annales* 36 (April 1834): 101–102.

22. Félicité de Duras to Bishop Rosati, Chambéry, 10 June 1835, copy and trans., Archives of the Sisters of St. Joseph of Carondelet, St. Louis (hereafter cited as ACSJC); original, Archives of the Archdiocese of St. Louis (hereafter cited as AASL).

sectarians reflected the reports which filled the *Annales* at the time. The countess' visions of an evangelizing enterprise were rooted in her confidence in the ability of the Sisters of St. Joseph to adjust in America, which she rightly associated with the flexibility of their rule,[23] and the diversity of their occupations:

They give themselves to all the works of mercy, they take charge of free schools or boarding schools, hospitals, asylums for foundlings or for the aged: they may look after prisoners; attend on the poor and the sick in their houses; take care of the infected—they are ready for anything.[24]

Mme de la Rochejaquelein described what she had seen in France, but her perception of the sisters as a pious and versatile labor force was to prove a constant in their history in America.

105

The American experience of the Sisters of St. Joseph begins in 1836, when the first six came to St. Louis, accompanied by a priest. Two more were to follow in 1837. With the exception of one sister sent in 1860, these eight were the extent of the French personnel to be supplied from the motherhouse at Lyons.[25] The original band were all between the ages of twenty-one and thirty-one; five had been professed in France and three came to America as novices. One was a lay sister.[26] There were connections of family and bonds of friendship among the group. Two were blood sisters—Febronie and Delphine Fontbonne—nieces of Mother St. Jean in Lyons; the priest who came with them was their brother, Jacques Fontbonne. Although they did not realize it at the time, these pioneering sisters were no longer able to look to Europe for support; they would have to make their own way in a new world.

When the sisters arrived in 1836, their Frenchness determined their role in the St. Louis diocese. They began work in two settlements with French-Canadian and Creole populations: at Cahokia, on the Illinois

---

23. "It will fructify there all the more because in this Order a foundation according to rule is not so restricted as in some other Orders; it accommodates itself to times and circumstances." *Ibid.*

24. *Ibid.* The same theme appears in a letter of Jean-Paul Gaston de Pins, Administrator of the Archdiocese of Lyons to Bishop Rosati, 1 January 1836: "They will be excellent catechists, good nurses for the sick, perfect sacristans, zealous teachers." Copy and trans., K–A–23, ACSJC; original, AASL.

25. Sisters Fébronie Fontbonne, Delphine Fontbonne, Marguerite-Félicité Bouté, Marie-Fébronie Chappelon, St. Protais Déboille, Philomène Vilaine, and Father Jacques Fontbonne arrived in 1836; Sisters Célestine Pommerel and St. Jean Fournier, 4 September 1837, and Sister Marie de la Sainte-Croix Bennelin in 1860. Dolorita Marie Dougherty, C.S.J. et al., *Sisters of St. Joseph of Carondelet* (St. Louis, 1966), 421–422. (In the text, the pioneers' names appear in their anglicized forms.)

26. In a report of Bishop Rosati, Philomene Vilaine is listed at the end of the community, after the single novice as "Soror Conversa-Philomena (Marie Vilain) emisit vota die 3 Januari 1838." Excerpt from Status diocesis 1838, copy, ACSJC; original, AASL.

bank of the Mississippi, and a place with the unpromising epithet of *Vide poche* a few miles south of St. Louis—better known today as Carondelet. In her old age, Sister St. Protais Déboille recalled in still-broken English that the people of Cahokia had venerated the sisters as women "come from the same mother as them, the Catholic France, to have care of their sick, their poor, their children . . . they think of them as their mother."[27]

The French language was to be an advantage in promoting the sisters' schools. One of the first boarders at the enlarged log cabin in Carondelet, popularly known as "Madame Celestine's School," explained that her mother sent her there because "she was anxious of my acquiring a French education in all the purity of the language."[28] In 1839, the institution at Carondelet was a French convent school with a large dose of Missouri frontier—in winter the sisters' duties included shaking snow from the boarders' beds in the middle of the night. By 1841, however, there was a three-story brick building, and the French character of St. Joseph's Academy attracted daughters of Southern planters until the Civil War.[29] French was also a drawing card for the select schools, established in conjunction with a free school as a means of support until the parochial system was established later in the century. In 1858, recently arrived in Oswego, New York, the Sisters of St. Joseph placed an ad in the September 6 edition of the *Palladium Times:*

New Advertisements: Select School and Private Lessons. The Sisters of St. Joseph, having taken the direction of St. Mary's School, will also open, on the 13th inst., a Select School for Young Ladies, in their house, No. 68 West Sixth Street, where they will teach all the branches generally taught in the best Academies. They will also give private lessons in French, Music, Embroidery, Painting, etc., to young ladies who may desire. For terms apply to SISTER STANISLAUS Sup'r.[30]

It was the presence, in the Oswego community, of Sister Hyacinth Blanc, a missionary from Moûtiers, which enabled them to offer French in addition to their basic curriculum. Although their French background provided

---

27. Memoirs of Sister St. Protais Déboille, n.d., D–M–7a, ACSJC.

28. Memoirs of Eliza Mc Kenny Brouillet, D–M–5b,c, ACSJC. Apart from a number of letters to Bishop Rosati, there is little documentation for the initial period at Carondelet. Many details are known only from later recollections, many recorded at the request of Sister Monica Corrigan around 1890 and preserved in ACSJC; also a long letter containing notes on the American foundations which had been requested by the Lyons superior: Soeur St. Jean née Fournier à la Sup^r G^{le} des Soeurs St Joseph de Lyon [1873], ACSJL (reproduced with English trans. in Marie Kostka Logue, S.S.J., *Sisters of St. Joseph of Philadelphia: A Century of Growth and Development 1847–1947* [Westminster, MD, 1950], 326–353).

29. Brouillet and Déboille memoirs; and Mary Lucida Savage, C.S.J., *The Congregation of Saint Joseph of Carondelet: A Brief Account of Its Origin and Its Work in the United States, 1650–1922* (St. Louis, 1923), 59.

30. Cited in Dougherty et al., 218.

107

Sister Febronie Chapellon   **Sister Marguerite-Felicite Boute**

them an entree in the diocese of St. Louis, the Americanization of the Sisters of St. Joseph began almost immediately, through the introduction of American membership in the congregation and interaction with the wider civic and ecclesiastical communities.

The first American woman joined the community at Carondelet in October 1837, just one year and a half after the United States foundation. She was Anne Eliza Dillon, who had met the Sisters of St. Joseph as a boarder at the convent school of the Sacred Heart in St. Louis, where two of the St. Joseph Sisters had come for English lessons in the summer of 1836. She was to provide an American element within the community from the dawn of its history in this country; life under the rigorous French regime entailed compatible conflict. In March 1838, the new Sister Mary Joseph wrote to Bishop Rosati protesting the severity of Sister Delphine's governance and the hardships which threatened her health:

The superior requires me to do work, for which I have not strength sufficient. My health is not very good and at times I have severe pains in my breast and side. Mother is forever scolding me, she says as a novice I ought to be employed in the kitchen and that it is an honor for me to teach.[31]

---

31. Sister Mary Francis Joseph Dillon to Bishop Rosati, Carondelet, 22 March 1838, copy, ACSJC; original, AASL.

108

Sister St. Protais Déboille   *Mother Celestine Pommerel*

In truth, the sisters could hardly do without her teaching at that time, since she was the only one in the community who spoke fluent English.[32] When Sister Mary Joseph Dillon died of her pains at twenty-two years of age, 30 October 1842, she was replaced as English teacher in the Academy by Sister Mary Rose Marsteller, an American novice who was a native of Alexandria, Virginia.[33]

The incipient process of Americanization was promoted when the sisters became involved with civic structures through the services they offered. Two of them, Sisters Celestine Pommerel and St. John Fournier, had been trained for a year in France in methods for teaching the deaf-mute. This skill earned a government subsidy from the State of Missouri for the "asylum" at Carondelet—in reality a conglomeration of deaf-mutes, boarders, orphans and sisters who managed to pursue their goals elbow-to-elbow.[34] The sisters also functioned for a time as public school teachers,

---

32. "Nous n'avons mis aucune conversion ni aucun baptème parce que nous sommes encore dans l'impossibilité d'instruire des américaines." Sister Febronie Fontbonne to Bishop Rosati, Cahokia, February 1838, copy, ACSJC; original, AASL. Eliza McKenny Brouillet recorded that during her years as a boarder at Carondelet (1839–45) none of the French sisters could speak English well, Sister St. John Fournier being the most conversant. Brouillet Memoirs.

33. Savage, 61.

34. *Missouri Session Laws,* 8 February 1839, 334 cited in Dougherty et al., 67, and "Cahier de fondation-1838," C–M–1a, ACSJC.

The Déboille and Brouillet memoirs relate that before the brick structure of 1841, everyone shared the same dining and recreation rooms—pupils, mutes and orphans at two tables and sisters at a third. These rooms served by turn as dormitory, classroom, parlor and chapel, with beds stored in a loft during the day.

109

First students at Mt. Gallitzin Academy, Ebensburg, Pa., 1869

being paid by the Corporation of Carondelet for the education of girls of the town.[35] Although these arrangements with the government were not permanent, they provided incentive to learn English and provoked inter-action with the American milieu.

The sisters in St. Louis were also reaching beyond their French context by teaching only nationality groups in the diocese. In 1845 they opened

---

35. Minutes of the Board of Trustees, 23 April 1839, cited in Savage, 53. Mother St. John Fournier related, "We had all the children of the village in our school. The city paid us every year in land." Logue, 328–329.

their first mission in the city of St. Louis, a school for Black children on Third and Poplar Streets. There they taught free Blacks a general curriculum, but were restricted to catechetical instruction for the slaves of Catholic families. Under pressure of racial prejudice, city officials urged Bishop Kenrick to abandon the project, and the school was closed the following year.[36] Also in 1845, the sisters opened a school in St. Vincent de Paul parish, which at that time was composed of German- or English-speaking members, the latter chiefly Irish immigrants.[37]

In 1846, in a significant and ironic twist of events, the French Sisters of St. Joseph took over the boys' orphan asylum in St. Louis which had been abandoned by the American Sisters of Charity. The latter had been obliged to withdraw from this institution when they affiliated with the French Daughters of Charity whose rule forbade the care of male orphans. The same procedure was to be repeated the following year in Philadelphia, extending the works of the Sisters of St. Joseph beyond the limits of the St. Louis diocese.[38] Although there was no clear precedent for the care of boys by the Sisters of St. Joseph in France, there was nothing explicitly against it in their rules, and they did in fact take charge of boys in this country whenever it was necessary. This was to be an important factor in the history of their expansion in the United States, for bishops were anxious to have sisters for male orphanages, and pastors often preferred a community who could teach boys in the parochial school, since a parish could ill afford separate institutions for boys and girls.[39] The decision to take on unprecedented works and to move into new areas gave the Sisters of St. Joseph greater visibility in the Catholic Church in America and enlarged their ranks with additional members.

Despite the hardships aggravated by their poverty and the somewhat Jansenist leanings of a rigorous French piety, the Sisters of St. Joseph

---

36. Extract from the Records of St. Louis Diocese, entry signed by Edmund Saulnier, Book 1, A.D. 1845, K–A–8, ACSJC; Letter of Mother St. John Fournier in Logue, 330–332; and Dougherty et al., 123–124.

37. Peter Richard Kenrick to Archbishop Milde of Vienna, St. Louis, 10 December 1844, *Berichte der Leopoldinen Stiftung,* 18:6–14, original in English; retranslated from the German in John Rothensteiner, *History of the Archdiocese of St. Louis: In Its Various Stages of Development from A.D. 1673 to A.D. 1928,* 2 vols. (St. Louis, 1928), 1:822.

38. Logue, 28; and Savage, 66.

39. A letter of Mother Clement Lannen to Rev. John W. Shanahan, 29 May 1889, reveals that objections to the sisters' teaching boys above twelve or thirteen years came not from them, but from Archbishop Ryan. M–29–1–4, 3.441, Archives of the Sisters of St. Joseph of Philadelphia (hereafter cited as ACSJP). Further correspondence shows that pastors managed to get around the episcopal objections: John W. Shanahan to Mother Clement Lannen, Philadelphia, 26 December 1889; idem, 25 September 1849; and William A. Duffy to Mother Clement Lannen, Pottstown, Pa., 8 August 1889, M–29–1–3, 3.390; M–29–1–4, 3.451–52, ACSJP.

continued to attract American candidates.[40] By 1845 the number of sisters in the community who could not speak French necessitated the translation of the constitutions into English. The profession of novices was delayed until the completion of this translation, an indication of the importance of an English document for the life of the community at this time.[41] The English *Constitutions of the Congregation of the Sisters of St. Joseph* printed in 1847 signifies not only a shifting pattern of membership in the community, but an implicit decision to become American, since in fact the French language and culture had not been imposed on novices as a condition for being a Sister of St. Joseph. By the end of their first decade in this country, the Sisters of St. Joseph had an English rule, a growing American membership, and a ministry which included a variety of ethnic groups. The foundations were in place for the emergence of a community with a properly American identity.

111

Separation from France

The single most important element in the rapid Americanization of the Sisters of St. Joseph was the independence of American communities from the motherhouse in France. Although congregational histories explain the separation of the French and American congregations as a result of mutual agreement, archival sources are curiously silent on this matter.[42]

The decade between 1847 and 1857 was a time of tremendous expansion for the Sisters of St. Joseph, with foundations in the dioceses of Philadelphia, St. Paul, Toronto, Hamilton, Wheeling, Buffalo, Brooklyn, and Albany. This growth necessitated the definition of lines of authority, and brought into focus the question: Who is the superior? Since the constitutions of Sisters of St. Joseph at the time provided for both a sister

---

40. By the beginning of 1845, five American-born women, plus one each from Ireland and Germany had entered the community. Register of Professions, ACSJC.

41. Sister Aloysius Fitzsimmons (received 1839, professed 1845) reported that during the five years while "Bishop Barron of Savannah" [Edward Barron] was translating the rule, she had to wait to make vows. Memoirs, 1879; and Register of Professions, ACSJC. The English version was published under the title of *Constitutions of the Sisters of St. Joseph* (St. Louis, 1847). Page iv reads: "translated from the French edition of Lyons, 1827," referring to *Constitutions pour la petite congrégation des Soeurs de saint Joseph,* Nouvelle édition (Lyons, 1827), which is essentially the same as the first edition printed at Vienne, 1693.

42. Dougherty et al., 363; Logue, 173; Savage, 108; and M. Evangeline Thomas, C.S.J., *Footprints on the Frontier: A History of the Sisters of Saint Joseph, Concordia, Kansas* (Westminster, MD, 1948), 59–60, all suggest some kind of formal separation from France, but neither the archives at Lyons nor at Carondelet yield any correspondence between the congregations regarding separation. Savage, 108, cites correspondence from Father S. Auguste Paris, C.M., to Mother Celestine as early as 1856 which indicates that a form of government centralized at Carondelet was already under consideration.

Sister Petronilla Stibolitski and her nephew, Johnstown, Pa., 1881

superior and a male ecclesiastical superior, the question had to be answered in terms of each.

The ecclesiastical superior—the bishop or some priest designated by him—exercised extensive powers over the life of a community: the constitutions gave him the right to impose corrections, confirm elections, and even to appoint or remove the sister superior.[43] The legal unity of a congregation of more than one house depended on the bishop rather than on the sister superior. Canonically, this meant that when the sisters left Lyons and came under the jurisdiction of the bishop of St. Louis, they were in fact a separate community.[44] The juridical situation notwithstanding, the Sisters of St. Joseph remained connected with France in mind and heart for some time. In 1848, Sister St. John Fournier, became superior in Philadelphia, puzzled as to why there had been no new recruits from Lyons for the American missions; in Lyons, congregational communiqués continued to report the deaths of sisters "in our community at Carrondelet (America)."[45] The conscious realization that the sisters in America had

---

43. Part 1, chap. 6, *Constitutions* (1847), 9–11.

44. Such a separation is implied in a letter of Father Claude Cholleton to Sister Delphine Fontbonne, Lyons, 4 April 1837: "Sister St. John is yet a novice. When she appears to you sufficiently proven and well disposed, you shall ask Monseigneur Rosati . . . to be kind enough to receive the vows himself. . . . You will follow the same procedure in the future for the admission of subjects who by the divine goodness will be confided to your maternal care." Copy and trans., K–A–7, ACSJC; original, AASL.

The Lyons constitutions were not revised to provide for a sister as superior general until 1858. *Constitutions pour la petite congrégation des Soeurs de Saint-Joseph établies dans le Diocèse de Lyon,* Deuxième édition (Lyons, 1858).

45. Francis Patrick Kenrick to Peter Richard Kenrick, Philadelphia, 15 December 1848, in *The Kenrick-Frenaye Correspondence: Letters Chiefly of Francis Patrick Kenrick and Antony Frenaye 1830–1862,* trans. and ed. Francis E. Tourscher (Lancaster, Pa. 1920), 289.

in fact become an independent foundation with distinct authority structures, membership, and cultural identity developed only gradually, and in relation to the role played by the sister superior vis-à-vis the bishops.

The original French constitutions did not define the role of a sister as Superior General; no sister exercised authority beyond her particular house. This was the practice adopted in America at the beginning. Each of the two houses, Cahokia and Carondelet, had a sister superior; each received novices.[46] Neither house had precedence over the other, the bishop being superior over both. At the beginning of 1845, however, when they started to open other missions in the St. Louis diocese, the Sisters of St. Joseph had only one house in this country: Cahokia had been flooded out the previous June and Sister Febronie Fontbonne, the superior there, returned to France.[47]

113

Thus, precisely at the moment when expansion began, there was only one sister superior—Celestine Pommerel at Carondelet; of necessity it was she who made assignments to the new houses. Sister Celestine was a charismatic leader, much respected and loved by the sisters, and she continued in this role, appointing superiors and assigning personnel, when foundations were made in dioceses outside St. Louis. She was acting as a virtual superior general, without constitutionally possessing such authority.[48] Following the untimely death of Sister Celestine at forty-four years of age, 7 June 1857, a movement to regularize the situation resulted in a provisional constitution drafted in 1860, which called for a provincial structure of government with the motherhouse at Carondelet, and granted extensive powers to the archbishop of St. Louis over houses in other dioceses.[49]

Most of the bishops who already had congregations in their dioceses vigorously opposed the centralization. John Timon of Buffalo went to Philadelphia and spoke against it at the sisters' annual retreat in 1863, as

---

46. Archival sources indicate that Sister Febronie Fontbonne opened a novitiate at Cahokia, where Sister Antoinette Kincaid received the habit 6 March 1842. MS notes, K–A–15, ACSJC. The date of the establishment of the novitiate at Carondelet is given as 1844 in *Constitutions* (1847), iv.

47. She and Sister Marie-Febronie Chapellon, her close friend, returned to France in October of 1844. They both lived at Chagny, where Febronie Fontbonne was superior until her death, 10 April 1881; Marie-Febronie Chapellon died there 3 January 1890. Dougherty et al., 60–61.

48. *Rules and Constitutions of the Sisters of St. Joseph,* Approved of and adopted by, the Most Reverend the Archbishop of St. Louis, for the Diocess [*sic*] of St. Louis (Carondelet, MO, 1860), 291, explains that the sisters have "regarded the Mother Superioress of that house [Carondelet] as being virtually our Superioress-General."

49. The section of the *Constitutions* of 1860 (part 1, chap. 7, 24–25), which made the Archbishop of St. Louis in effect superior general over all houses, in whatever diocese, was changed by Rome as prejudicial to the jurisdiction of other bishops. Observations of Cardinal Quaglia on the constitutions, 1863, K–K–11, ACSJC.

did Bishop Loughlin at the community elections in Flushing, New York.[50] A paper drafted by Bishop James F. Wood of Philadelphia, replete with citations from Roman documents, identifies the neuralgic point:

> The general principle is that the rights of an Ordinary cannot be encroached by his equal. . . . And this is the danger perpetually recurring. Where a Bishop pretends to jurisdiction over religious Communities in another diocese, even where they subject themselves freely and willingly to the exercise of such authority.[51] [*sic*]

It was in part a power struggle among bishops, and Thomas L. Grace, O.P., of St. Paul, at odds with the plan for centralization endorsed by his metropolitan, Peter Richard Kenrick of St. Louis, earned himself a reprimand from the Propaganda Fide for interfering with the constitutions of sisters.[52]

The end result was the formation of independent diocesan congregations in Philadelphia, Toronto, Hamilton, Wheeling, Buffalo, and Brooklyn, while Albany and St. Paul became provinces of Carondelet. Some of the women who had entered at Carondelet returned there when the various communities chose independent status; others deplored the change and repudiated the "new" rule:

> Six of our religious were weak enough to let themselves be seduced by the attraction of a false liberty and have left our congregation in the course of the last two years. Thanks to Divine Mercy two have already recognized their error and have re-entered the straight road of dependence.[53]

Such was the view from Carondelet. In Wheeling, where the small community was jeopardized by the exodus of sisters to Carondelet, the writer of the annals lamented, "All that had been done before was undone by the action of the Carondelet House."[54]

The events occasioned by centralization demonstrate the proprietary attitude of bishops toward the communities, and the considerable effects of their insistence on indigenous diocesan congregations in the process of

114

---

50. "At Retreat Bishop Timon spoke of St. Louis' seeking approval. He is against it." First Council Book 16 January 1863, C–B–1, ACSJP; and Annals, 24 August 1863, 1:17, Archives of the Sisters of St. Joseph of Brentwood, New York (hereafter cited as ACSJB).

51. "Jurisdiction of Bishops over Religious Communities Outside of Their Diocese," [post 1864], ACSJP.

52. Propaganda Fide to Thomas L. Grace, bishop of St. Paul, 26 April 1866, Lettere, vol. 357, fol. 379 v; and Peter R. Kenrick, Archbishop of St. Louis, to PF, 13 January 1864, Scritture riferite nei Congressi, America Centrale, 1866–1867, vol. 21, fols. 73 r, 74 v, Archives of the Congregation for the Propagation of the Faith, Rome.

53. Mother St. John Facemaz to Cardinal Quaglia [1869], K–B–25, ACSJC.

54. Record of profession, 6 August 1861 [probably written in 1864 by Sister de Chantal Keating], Annals. Archives of the Sisters of St. Joseph of Wheeling (hereafter cited as ACSJW).

Americanization. This dynamic would be epitomized at the turn of the century in St. Augustine, when the ailing bishop, John Moore, enforced separation of the Sisters of St. Joseph, who had been in Florida since 1866, from the Le Puy motherhouse. His letter to the superior in France explains his frame of mind:

> I believe I see a necessity to have only Sisters who are entirely diocesan, Sisters who obey the Bishop of the Diocese. . . . I repeat, I want Sisters who obey me like their Bishop; and who are not in any manner subject to orders of a Superior in another distant country.[55]

As in Florida at a later date, the bishops' maneuvers in the 1860s punctuate how important the contributions made by sisters were in the face of exploding needs in the young dioceses, which were desperately short of personnel, and had already begun to feel the impact of immigration. The episode indeed points out the sisters' own identification in many cases with the local setting, since they too played a part, and their motives were influenced by psychological and sociological realities. Most telling of all, by 1860, twenty-four years after their arrival in the United States, there was no longer any question of formal dependence on France for these Sisters of St. Joseph. The matter at hand was strictly the clarification of lines between several flourishing American congregations.

115

Cultural Tensions

By 1860 the Congregations of St. Joseph had become American-based communities, with a numerical dominance of American members. In at least two of the largest congregations, however, sisters still looked to their French component for leadership. Mother St. John Fournier, one of the pioneers, was the superior in Philadelphia until her death, 15 October 1875. At Carondelet, a new influx of missionaries from the congregation of Moûtiers, in Savoy, continued to supply novice mistresses, provincial superiors, and a superior general, Sister St. John Facemaz, who served in that capacity from 1857 until her resignation in 1872.[56]

At the death of Sister Celestine Pommerel in 1857, the community elected an American, Sister Seraphine Coughlin, a native of New York

---

55. John Moore to Reverend Mother [Pélagie Boyer], St. Augustine, Florida, 31 January 1900, copy, Archives of the Sisters of St. Joseph of St. Augustine; original, ACSJLP; trans. Mary Albert Lussier, S.S.J., St. Augustine.

56. Between 1854 and 1887 the Sisters of St. Joseph of Moûtiers sent thirty-nine missionaries to the United States who were incorporated into the Carondelet congregation. Dougherty et al., 113, 223, 424–425.

who had entered the novitiate at Carondelet in 1846.[57] When she declined the office, begging inability and poor health, Archbishop Kenrick of St. Louis acted on his authority as ecclesiastical superior to appoint Sister St. John Facemaz, who had come from Moûtiers just three years previously. His announcement hardly met unanimous approval. According to the report of a contemporary, "The sisters screamed, threw themselves on the floor, etc., etc.—. The Archbishop left immediately, even ran from the chapel and would not hear or see anyone."[58] Perhaps this scene in the Carondelet chapel demonstrated the reaction of an increasingly American (if undisciplined) community to what they feared would be a severely Gallic rule.

116

The French sisters were a minority in the growing congregations. As early as the 1850s and throughout the century, the greatest number of candidates were Americans, followed by a large element of Irish-born women, with a smaller but significant group of Germans, and a sprinkling of other nationalities.[59] Ethnic patterns in congregations reflected the Catholic populations of areas where the sisters worked. By the fourth quarter of the nineteenth century, for many communities derived from Carondelet, the French character of the congregations would have been hearsay.

Yet the French women had proved indomitable forerunners, and they carried Sisters of St. Joseph to nearly every frontier of American Catholicism. At the end of the Civil War, when Augustin Verot sought educators for the freed Blacks in his episcopal jurisdiction, he obtained Sisters of St. Joseph from his native Le Puy:

I want you to understand clearly and thoroughly, that it is for the Negroes, and for them almost exclusively that I am having the sisters of your Order come to my Diocese. I have five to six hundred thousand Negroes without education and without religion and without baptism for whom I wish to do something.[60]

The labors of the French sisters contributed toward making Georgia and Florida the scene of the only organized effort on the part of the Catholic Church for the education of Blacks during the Reconstruction period.[61] The seven Sisters of St. Joseph, whose adventurous trek across the desert

57. Savage, 89.

58. Memoirs of Sister Febronia Boyer, n.d., D–M–5a, ACSJC.

59. Registers of Profession, ACSJC and ACSJP.

60. Augustin Verot to Madame la Supérieure et très-chère en N. S. [Léocadie Broc], Savannah, 21 February 1866, my translation; also *idem*, Brest, 25 August 1865; and *idem*, Atlanta, Georgia, 18 September 1865, copies, Archives of the Sisters of St. Joseph of St. Augustine; originals, ACSJLP.

61. Michael V. Gannon, *Rebel Bishop: The Life and Era of Augustin Verot* (Milwaukee, 1964), 138; see 131–144.

A lay sister, St. Augustine, Florida, 1887

117

from San Diego to Tucson in 1870 was dramatized in a *Playhouse 90* production starring Helen Hayes, included five missionaries from Moûtiers.[62] One of the original volunteers from Lyons, Sister St. Protais Déboille, spent the last twenty years of her long life among the Chippewa at St. Francis Xavier Mission in Baraga, Michigan, where she was buried in 1892.[63]

Significant as the works with native American or Black populations were, they formed a scant part of the whole. Most Sisters of St. Joseph found themselves among the urban Catholics of the United States. There they shared the poverty of an immigrant church. Like other women of their day, sisters stretched their income by plying the needle. At Carondelet, the pioneers sewed powder sacks which sold for one cent; the Flushing account books show receipts for sewing scapulars and "habits" (shrouds). The St. Augustine sisters survived by making the beautiful bobbin-lace for which Le Puy is still famous: "We would have starved," they reported starkly, "but for the sale of our lace."[64] Sisters also took on menial tasks

---

62. [Corrigan] Taggert, Sister Monica, "Diary of the Journey of the Sisters of St. Joseph to Tucson, Ariz. 1870," *St. Louis Catholic Historical Review* 2 (April-July 1920): 101–113. Sister Monica, born Annie Taggert, was the widow of John Corrigan. St. Claire Coyne, C.S.J., "The Los Angeles Province," in Dougherty *et al.*, 289–294.

63. Dougherty *et al.*, 134. During the nineteenth century the Sisters of St. Joseph of Carondelet staffed missions among native Americans in Michigan, Wisconsin, Minnesota, Arizona, and California.

64. Déboille memoirs; sample entries from 1858 to March 1860, Expenses and Receipts. ACSJB; *Living Waters,* a commemoration of the centennial of the Sisters of St. Joseph (St. Augustine, 1966); and Sister Louise Antonia to Worthy and good Reverend Mother, Ybor City, Florida, 12 February 1900, copy and trans. Archives of the Sisters of St. Joseph of St. Augustine, original, ACSJLP.

in church institutions. While they humbly contributed to providing basic necessities of civilized life for clerics and scholars, at least one sister understood the social ramifications of these roles. In a notarized statement dated 14 March 1900, Sister de Chantal Keating testified regarding property rights of the Wheeling congregation which were being disputed by a diocesan priest:

None of us would have felt we were receiving more than our due had the deed been presented to use for a dollar in the time of Bishop Whelan: he knew the amount of slavish work that was performed by the Sisters in the College where such a number of Boarders and Seminarians were cared for in health and sickness: the washing and mending for them and the Cathedral, etc., and all this where there were so few conveniences.[65]

118

"Slavish work" was the price paid by many sisters to secure a niche in the society, both ecclesiastical and civil, of the United States of America.

Integral as they were to the great system-building of nineteenth-century Catholicism, sisters were an oddity to the larger population. Until the Civil War, Sisters of St. Joseph wore lay clothing for travel; the Brooklyn community disguised their veils with a sunbonnet even in their own yard. In 1875, the first sisters in New Castle, Pennsylvania were met with a vulgar display of bigotry.[66] Their participation in the Civil War won a qualified acceptance for Catholics as a bona fide part of American society, and heightened their own sense of identity as citizens. In February of 1864, the United States government rented space in Wheeling Hospital and hired the Sisters of St. Joseph who staffed it to care for the wounded soldiers. When Washington failed to pay, the superior took action. "Despairing of justice without a personal application," she wrote in the community annals, "Sr. de Chantal left Wheeling today [6 February 1865] for Washington City accompanied by an Orphan child, an insane soldier & guard, also received Govt. transportation." [*sic*] There she made the rounds of the War Department, and within two weeks had word that all arrears would be paid.[67]

Many women, lay and religious alike, who served in camps and on the battlefield were not trained nurses. They worked primarily as cooks and ward managers. Dr. Henry H. Smith, Surgeon-General of Pennsylvania,

---

65. St. John's home [Brooklyn], 14 March 1900, [signed] Mother M. de Chantal Keating, ACSJW.

66. The Philadelphia archives contain a record of Mother St. John Fournier's going to the Chapter in St. Louis in 1860 "dressed in secular attire." Council Book 1, C–B–1, ACSJP; Mary Ignatius Meany, C.S.J. *By Railway or Rainbow: A History of the Sisters of St. Joseph of Brentwood* (Brentwood, NY, 1964), 46–47; and Adele Whaley, S.S.J., *Salute to the Pioneers: Pages in the Early History of the Sisters of St. Joseph of Baden, Pennsylvania* (Pittsburgh, 1952), 29.

67. Annals, 26 February 1864–18 February 1865, ACSJW; and Rose Anita Kelly, S.S.J., *Song of the Hills: The Story of the Sisters of St. Joseph of Wheeling* (Wheeling, 1962), 213–222.

was insistent in his letter to the Philadelphia superior regarding sisters for Camp Curtin, new Harrisburg: "Good cooks & house keepers rather than nurses are required. Sister Philomene and two lay sisters would make an excellent party."[68] Letters of one of the ten Sisters of St. Joseph of Carondelet who served in the Spanish American War reveal (in addition to unadorned generosity, good humor, and common sense) the simplicity of her education: "Yesterday nine of us was sworning [*sic*] in to serve Uncle Sam which we will loyally I hope." Their tour of duty took them to Camp Hamilton, Kentucky, Americus, Georgia, and Matanza Bay, Cuba.[69]

Despite the sisters' intimate involvement in the most convulsive events of the century in American history, they showed an extraordinary reserve in discussing them afterward. "[They] resumed their former duties as if they had never left them," wrote an admiring sister in Philadelphia. "Seldom did they allude to their war experiences . . . nor did they ever record their story."[70] Their reticence was likely inspired by a desire to avoid "singularity"—a considerable transgression of convent manners. It also reflected the "world within a world" ethos which permeated Roman Catholicism, and particularly convent life. Although immersed in the concerns of education, social work and health care for nineteenth-century Americans, within their own houses sisters had a separate culture, which operated according to its own dictates. A curiously Catholic variety of civil religion appears in an 1894 decree permitting the sisters to observe national holidays as feasts "of the II. class."[71] (A second class observance meant, unlike other days, that talking was allowed at dinner and supper, and for most of the evening). The comic element in this juxtaposition does not hide the fact that Sisters of St. Joseph in the United States never enjoyed the same kind of complete integration with the prevailing culture which had been second nature for them in their "mother . . . the Catholic France."

The American identity of the Sisters of St. Joseph did not emerge in perfect harmony with the spirit of the older tradition. There were tensions

119

68. To Madame St. John, Surgeon-General's Office, State of Pennsylvania, 22 January 1862. In a letter of 14 April 1862, Dr. Smith reiterates the need for "*hardy . . . or strong* Sisters." *Idem*, Fortress Monroe, 21 April 1862 alludes to "friendly competition with a party of females directed by Miss Dix." M–27–1–4, 1.71, 74, 79, ACSJP; see Logue, 119–134.

69. Sr. Ligouri [McNamara] to Mother Agatha Guthrie, Camp Hamilton [Kentucky], 5 October 1898, D–M–4a, ACSJC; and Dougherty et al., 128–129.

70. "Brief account," MS, n.a., n.d., M–27–1–1, ACSJP.

71. Decrees of the General Chapter 1894, 2–1, S17, ACSJP; the same is found in "Regulations of the Sisters of St. Joseph, c. 1915, Archives of the Sisters of St. Joseph of Baden, Pennsylvania.

caused, on the one hand, by the general conflict in the Roman Catholic Church in this country between the republican, democratic spirit of its American context and the inherited European forms;[72] on the other by the specific differences of French and American cultures.

Sisters of St. Joseph had to balance French custom and American sensibilities in their religious life. Their spirituality had been formed in Europe, and they preserved the Gallican idiom in practices such as kissing the floor, praying *les bras en croix,* and using penitential instruments like the discipline. Aware of their abrasiveness to Americans, sisters confined such things strictly to the privacy of the convent. Even there, however, old world etiquette sometimes proved uncomfortably at odds with the American way. On 30 December 1884, the day of her re-election as superior general of the Philadelphia congregation, Mother Mary John Kieran noted in her diary, "I asked to be dispensed with the Srs. kissing the hand as they had before. He [Archbishop Ryan] allowed it to be dispensed with. That was a relief."[73]

Conflict between an authoritarian regime and a strong spirit of independence was not the preserve of Americans. Some of the more notable nonconformists among the nineteenth-century Sisters of St. Joseph were Irish, or daughters of Irish immigrants. Outstanding among them was Anna Fogerty, a native of County Louth. Professed in 1854 at St. Louis as Sister Mary Blanche, she transferred to the Wheeling community in 1869, "desirous of returning to the old Rule"—in other words, objecting to a central government. She had further objections to ecclesiastical centralization, for on 19 May 1871, she "left the Com'ty dispensed from her vows, and at the same time left the Church, obstinately refusing to accept the dogma of Papal Infallibility."[74]

The period after 1875 in the history of the congregations is marked by a certain stabilization among the older ones, and at the same time by a restlessness that went in search of new frontiers. The eight permanent foundations which were made after 1880 are related to the enterprising activity of two women, both first generation Irish born in New York, whose separate and arduous peregrinations covered this country from East to West. They were Sisters Stanislaus Leary and Mary Herman (alias Margaret Mary) Lacey. Mostly, they were on the run in conflicts

120

---

72. James Hennesey, S.J., "American History and the Theological Enterprise," *Proceedings of the Catholic Theological Society of America* 26 (1977): 94–95.

73. Diary of Mother Mary John Kieran, vol. 1 (1873–1885), M–28–1–6⁺, ACSJP.

74. Register of Professions, ACSJC; and Annals, 4 February 1869, 19 May 1871, ACSJW [where she is identified as Anne Gogerty].

121

A choir sister, St. Augustine, Florida, 1887

with bishops or major superiors.[75] The history of these and other mavericks in the congregations deserves to be written for it shows how the diocesan structure of communities indirectly promoted extension, since one could seek escape from an oppressive regime by removing to another jurisdiction. It also represents the French tradition in perhaps its most American pose.

If qualities of individualism, activism, aggressiveness and adventure can be considered typically American, then the American spirit had more than a few exponents within a scheme of convent life which called for hiddenness, obedience, and docility. Few were as outspoken as Sister Assissium Shockley, superior of the Albany province from 1866 to 1869. She took great pride in the fact that her forebears on both sides dated to the Revolution. Worthy of her ancestry, Sister Assissium put a quite American appreciation of progress to work in building the provincial

---

75. Sister Stanislaus Leary, first postulant at Canandaigua, New York, and subsequently superior of the Rochester congregation, founded the congregations of Concordia, Kansas (1883) [whence Wichita (1888)], and La Grange, Illinois (1899) [whence Orange, California (1912)]. Thomas, 81–98, 198.

Sister Lacey was originally Sister Mary Herman of the Albany province of Carondelet. As Sister Margaret Mary, she established the congregations of Watertown, New York (1880), and Kalamazoo, Michigan (1889), aiding that of Tipton, Indiana (1888). She returned to Carondelet in 1890, and died a member of that congregation in California. Emily Joseph Daly, C.S.J., "Part Four: The Albany Province," in Dougherty *et al,* 226–229.

house and novitiate at Troy, New York. Her enthusiasm for the up-to-date set her at odds with the higher authorities at Carondelet: "The bone of contention," reported Sister Assissium, "seems to have been the introduction of modern improvements.... Even the wise Jesuits could not quiet their scruples on this point." Her troubles may have been at bottom a cultural conflict—of the five members of the general council at that time, two were French and one German.[76]

Along with her sense of national pride and her broad-minded approach to modernity, Sister Assissium simply enjoyed being the boss. Having returned to Carondelet in 1869 on the very day her term as provincial expired, she was informed of the fact and told to resume her ordinary rank in the community. Forty years later she still remembered that she had accepted her demotion with dignity: "I thanked them," she wrote, "and did as I was told without showing the least mark of emotion, which I had every reason to feel."[77] It is possible that only the immense conservative strength of the Roman Catholic Church was able to temper the enterprising pragmatism native to these American women, in some cases by giving them work to do worthy of their energies. At least in the role of superior, one had plenty of opportunity for the baptized exercise of the "American" virtues.

The Lay Sister Issue

The conflict of a democratic spirit with European notions of a stratified society came to a painful focus among the Sisters of St. Joseph over the issue of lay sisters, and the history of law sisters in the American congregations serves as a prime example of how pressures from the new sociocultural context served to change the received French tradition. In France by the nineteenth century, there were two classes of membership, the choir sisters, who wore a veil and guimpe and carried on the white collar occupations of the community such as teaching and administration, while lay sisters, usually women with minimal education and dowery, wore a bonnet and paid their way by doing housework.[78] Lay sisters had no voice in community elections and occupied the lowest rank, after the choir novices.[79]

---

76. Memoirs of Sister Assissium Shockley, 1912, D–M–9c, ACSJC; and Dougherty et al., 366.
77. Shockley memoirs.
78. *Kenrick-Frenaye Correspondence,* 289.
79. *Constitutions* (1860), 28. The Carondelet customs book of 1868, 33–34, reads: "Postulants and novices are required to pay $100.00 for their board during the probationary & Novitiate term, plus another $100.00 dowry. Lay sisters need bring only the $100.00 dowry." ACSJC. See p. 26 for the difficulties caused by dowry in the American setting.

122

The system of class distinction meant trouble for the sisters from their beginnings in the United States. Although one of the original group, Sister Philomene Vilaine, was a lay sister, they adopted a uniform habit at the suggestion of Bishop Rosati who advised them to avoid any outward marks of inequality.[80] Lay sisters nevertheless continued to do the menial work in communities, in which they enjoyed responsibility without privilege. According to Father Edmond Saulnier, voluble pastor at Carondelet and self-appointed monitor of the community there, they were treated "like Negro women."[81]

Distinctive garb for lay sisters was reintroduced around 1853, partly as a result of Mother St. John Fournier's concern to bring the American practice in line with the French.[82] She believed the American innovation to be a cause of the unwillingness of the superiors in France to send more subjects. The role of the bonnetted sisters is concisely summarized in a letter of Mother St. John to Bishop Bayley of Newark in 1872. "When we open a mission," she explained, "we generally send a lay sister so as not to be troubled with servant girls."[83]

123

What seemed quite compatible to a French mentality never sat well in the American milieu. Miss Eliza Gilligan, accepted as a choir postulant in Wheeling (apparently because her brothers had agreed to pay $500 for her education), "Left of her own accord August 9th 1868 unfit for the Choir, & unwilling to embrace the Lay rank." Another member of the Wheeling community, Sister Mary Magdalen (Julia) Quill, an Irish immigrant, was professed as a lay sister, 28 December 1868. In 1870, her superiors had her rank changed to choir, citing "evidence of capacity sufficient to bear us out in believing that the change is for the glory of God and the advantage of the Com'ty." Eight years later she was elected superior general of the Wheeling congregation.[84]

There is ample testimony to a rising tide of dissatisfaction with class distinction in the communities as the century progressed. Mother Mary John Kieran's diary reveals that it ran high on the day of her election as superior of the Philadelphia congregation in 1875. "All the professed sisters and novices voted," she observed; "All the lay sisters were in very bad humor all day."[85] As a Redemptorist, William H. Gross, bishop of

---

80. *Kenrick-Frenaye Correspondence*, 189. See n. 36, above.
81. Edmund Saulnier to Joseph Rosati, Carondelet, 29 November 1837, copy and trans., ACSJC; original, AASL.
82. Boyer memoirs; and *Kenrick-Frenaye Correspondence*, 289.
83. Mother St. John Fournier to James Roosevelt Bayley, Chestnut Hill, 15 June 1872, M-27-2-5, 1.42, ACSJP.
84. Annals, ACSJW.
85. Diary, vol. 1, 21 October 1875, M-28-1-6⁺, ACSJP.

Savannah (1873–1885), had first-hand experience of community life, and forbade the reception of lay sisters. When his successor reinstated the practice, the American superior of the Sisters of St. Joseph there thought she would have to appeal to France for a lay sister, and in 1888 expressed her anxiety to Le Puy: "You know our first Lay Sister . . . became insane on the subject of her habit and they all hate the cap." Conflict over the incompatibility of the *converses* with American mores plagued the Le Puy foundations in Florida and Georgia from their beginnings. As a missionary in Savannah had reported triumphantly to France in January of 1868, "We finally succeeded in giving the lay habit to one of our postulants; this was a real *coup d'état;* no one wants to be a 'lay sister.' " Mother Helene Gidon, commenting to the European superiors on the same event, put her finger on the heart of the dilemma: "It was feared we should be criticized; we are in a country which esteems equality so much."[86]

Mother St. George Bradley (an Irish-born woman of independent mind who had left Carondelet following centralization), solved the problem in her own way. The Sisters of St. Joseph of Cleveland, established by her in 1872, never had lay sisters.[87] In fact, indigenous American sisterhoods such as the Sisters of Loretto did not, as a rule, form a separate servant class within their communities.[88] (Some antebellum congregations in the South did, however, follow the American tradition and had slaves.) For the Sisters of St. Joseph, cut off from their European roots, a separate class within the community grew more and more problematic. Part of the difficulty involved public image, in cases where lay sisters were needed for teaching and catechetical works, but the variations in their dress advertized them as servants.[89] By 1898 the sisters at Ebensburg, where a Jacksonian air breathed from the beginning, decided in one stroke to suppress the lay habit and limit the term of the mother superior.[90]

---

86. Sister St. John [Kennedy] to Rev. Mother de Sales [Pays], St. Joseph's Convent, Washington, Ga., 19 September 1888; *idem,* 13 December 1888; Sister Josephine Déléage to Mère Agathe, Savannah, [January], 1868; and Sister Helene Gidon to Ma bonne et excellente Mère [Léocadie Broc], Savannah, 9 January 1868. Copies, Archives of the Sisters of St. Joseph of St. Augustine; originals, ACSJLP, translation by Sister Mary Albert Lussier.

87. Sister Dorothy Glosser, Archivist, Sisters of St. Joseph of Cleveland, to author, June 1985. References to Mother St. George [Mary Bradley, received at Carondelet as Sister Georgiana; Provincial at St. Paul (1865–68) as Mother George] and the sisters who joined her in Cleveland are found in the Register of Professions; and MS notes, D–M–6c, ACSJC.

88. Correspondence of the author with archivists of Sisters of Loretto; Sisters of Charity of Nazareth; Sisters of Mercy of Charleston; Dominican Sisters of St. Catherine, Kentucky; and Sisters, Servants of the Immaculate Heart of Mary.

89. John Ireland, MS, 1908, K–K–43, ACSJC.

90. "Questions regarding the change of habit," 26 July 1898, [signed] Rev. John Boyle, Ecclesiastical Superior; Rev. John Boyle to Mother Joseph Burke, Johnstown, Pa., 12 August 1898, and *idem,* 29 August 1898, Archives of the Sisters of St. Joseph of Baden.

Nurses at Camp Hamilton, Kentucky, 1898

The Ebensburg decision created ripples in other congregations. From Philadelphia the superior went to Washington in December of 1899 to consult the Apostolic Delegate on community matters, including "the threatened change in lay Sisters' dress."[91] The same ferment was at work in other congregations, and the clergy were involved. From St. Paul, Archbishop John Ireland sent a letter in his own hand to the General Chapter assembled at Carondelet, proclaiming the unequal status of lay sisters simply un-American:

the spirit and customs, prevailing in the United States are much contrary to such distinctions in dress and appearance, and the enjoyment of rights and privileges, as indicate social classification. Whatever the arguments for distinctions of this kind may have existed in other times or may exist in other countries, such argument is scarcely to be found in the United States.[92]

The sisters themselves concurred with Archbishop Ireland's judgment on lay status as "antiquated and practically meaningless," for it was suppressed by the Carondelet Congregation in 1908. Although a distinctive dress was abandoned by the other congregations at nearly the same time,

---

91. "Answers on Constitutions," notes by Sister M. Assissium McEvoy, 25, S–9–1, ACSJP.
92. Ireland MS.

it was not until later in the century that lay sisters were completely inte-grated in all congregations through the assumption of rank and vote.[93] The issue of lay sisters remained sensitive long after the practice was dead, a kind of skeleton in the closet—in reality a sin against the American way of life.

I have suggested the Americanization of a French tradition as an interpretive framework for the history of the Sisters of St. Joseph in the United States during the nineteenth century. How to assess that process of adaptation? How well did the sisters really adjust to the American way of life? To what extent did they remain true to their French origins?

Adaptation in America was a function, at least in part, of what the sisters did *not* bring with them from France. The lack of persistence of French culture or language among the American Sisters of St. Joseph must be accounted for by their early separation from France, but also by the social composition of the congregations. Neither the French sisters nor the Americans who joined them in this country were drawn from the upper classes. In 1869, requesting release from the obligation of demand-ing a dowery, Mother St. John Facemaz explained the American situation to an official in Rome: "Generally, there are many vocations for the religious life, but they are especially from the class which is less wealthy, since wealth is principally in the hands of Protestants in this country."[94] The poor are generally not so invested in preserving a cultural tradition as those who have reaped the benefits of a given social system. Like the Irish immigrants who flooded their ranks during the last century, the French Sisters of St. Joseph were more ready for social adaptation in America than other groups who with their European cultural connections had something to lose.[95]

What the Sisters of St. Joseph had brought from France was a con-gregational heritage of remarkable openness and flexibility that enabled them in many ways to be at home in the American context. The long history in France had provided a model for adaptation to the exigencies of the local situation. Their spirituality, at least in its authentic interpretation, provided a coherent identity for women involved intimately with people through all kinds of service. The French tradition supported the readiness of sisters in this country to become involved in every dimension of parish life and to take on an enormous variety of institutional endeavors. They even fulfilled the dreams of the Countess de la Rochejaquelein by working with Indians. Protestants, however, were another story.

---

93. Dougherty et al., 369.
94. To Cardinal Quaglia, K–B–2, ACSJC.
95. Dennis Clark, *The Irish in Philadelphia: Ten Generations of Urban Experience* (Philadelphia, 1973), 26.

The essentially Protestant cast of American society in the nineteenth century spelled the limitation of genuine accommodation of the Sisters of St. Joseph to life in the United States. Like many other sisters, they suffered nativist hostility. At the end of the century, in 1895, they were barred by a special act of the Pennsylvania legislature from teaching in the public schools because of their distinctly religious garb.[96] The lack of fit in the American society was due, not to the fact that the Sisters of St. Joseph were French, but that they were Roman Catholic. In some ways the sisters epitomized the separateness of the Catholic Church in the United States.

The real assimilation of Sisters of St. Joseph in this country was not so much to the American way of life as to the American Catholic Church. The Sisters of St. Joseph became American in the sense that the Catholic Church became American—that is, ambivalently.[97] Within the ecclesiastical enclave, however, the fit was hand in glove. Like the larger church, the sisters' membership and professional orientations were shaped by the press of immigration; they, like their Catholic matrix, formed a masterpiece of institutionalization which was, for the most part, urban and separatist.

127

The role of the bishop in the American church, often that of benevolent tyrant, was the most influential factor in shaping the place of sisters within the American Catholic culture. The bishop considered the Sisters of St. Joseph as "agencies that he might summon to his aid." Their flexibility of organization and diversity of works allowed them to respond readily, and they became identified in the United States as a group on whom the bishops could rely for effective and loyal assistance.[98] There is no denying the price which was paid by sisters for a place in this paternalistic system in terms of subservience and real limitation in forming their own policies. They learned, however, to use this controlling relationship with the bishop to advantage. In congregations which were for the most part diocesan, Sisters of St. Joseph became deeply involved with the life of the locality. Although they formed, to be sure, an exotic part of the congregation, Sisters of St. Joseph attended the parish church. And the church which they knew conferred upon them a certain dignity and prestige. The numbers who joined their communities attest to the attractiveness of the Sisters of St. Joseph as a way of life for young Catholic women.

---

96. Act 282, 27 June 1895, *Pennsylvania State Reports,* 164:657, cited in Whaley, 33–34.

97. James Hennesey, S.J., *American Catholics: A History of the Roman Catholic Community in the United States* (New York, 1981), 4.

98. John Ireland, *Sermon on the Occasion of the Fiftieth Anniversary of the Sisters of St. Joseph in St. Paul, Minn. (August 20, 1902)* (New York, n.d.); and John J. Wright, *The Sisters of St. Joseph: A Sermon Preached at a Solemn Pontifical Mass in Saint Paul's Cathedral, Worcester, Commemorating the Three Hundredth Anniversary of the Sisters of St. Joseph, Saturday, October 21, 1950* (Worcester, MA, n.d.).

By 1900 there were twenty-one independent American Congregations of St. Joseph, as well as four in Canada. The history of these groups forms a pattern consistent with the French origins in their being closely woven into the fabric of the local church, identified with the common people they served, and "ready for anything."[99] It is a paradox that distance and detachment from the French structures enabled the Sisters of St. Joseph, in the conditions of nineteenth-century America, to remain faithful to the original French inspiration of service to the neighbor through whatever they could do as women in a given time and place.

128

---

99. Félicité de Duras to Bishop Rosati.

Maternity . . . of the Spirit:
Nuns and Domesticity in
Antebellum America*

Joseph G. Mannard

"In America the independence of woman is irrevocably lost in the bonds of matrimony." Thus wrote Alexis de Tocqueville in his famous description of the restricted position of married women in the American ideology of domesticity. "If an unmarried woman is less constrained there than elsewhere," he continued:

a wife is subjected to stricter obligations. The former makes her father's house an abode of freedom and of pleasure; the latter lives in the home of her husband as if it were a cloister. . . . Thus in the United States the inexorable opinion of the public carefully circumscribes woman within the narrow circle of domestic interests and duties and forbids her to step beyond it.[1]

Tocqueville's comparison of the home to a cloister suggests a parallel between the lives of American wives and mothers and Roman Catholic nuns. Ironically, at the time he wrote, religious sisters were establishing numerous convents, schools, and charitable institutions in America,

---

*Presented at the Cushwa Center Conference on American Catholicism, October 4, 1985.

1. Alexis de Tocqueville, *Democracy in America*, 2 vols., ed. Phillips Bradley, trans. Henry Reeve (New York, 1945), II, 212. In 1840, the year Tocqueville's second volume appeared in the United States, there existed in the country a total of twenty-eight Catholic "female religious institutions," whose members directed and staffed nearly all of the forty-seven female academies and seventy-six charitable institutions of Catholic affiliation. By 1860, the number of convents had mushroomed to 160, the number of female academies to 202, and the number of charitable institutions to 183. Figures are taken from *The Metropolitan Catholic Almanac and Laity's Directory* (Baltimore, 1840, 1860). Hereafter referred to as the *Catholic Almanac*.

thereby proving apparent exceptions to his assertion that public opinion would not tolerate female divergence from domestic norms. Taking a cue from Tocqueville, this paper analyzes the relationship of women religious to the antebellum ideology of domesticity by examining the views of Protestant critics, Catholic defenders, and nuns themselves. Did the convent vocation primarily conform to or conflict with dominant cultural beliefs and assumptions about woman's nature and proper place? Did the work of women religious tend to challenge or reinforce the domestic doctrine of separate male and female spheres? What attitudes toward domesticity did nuns try to instill in the females under their care and instruction? Answers to such questions suggest much about the opportunities and limitations of the convent, and religion generally, as an avenue to women's fuller participation in nineteenth-century society.[2]

Carmelite nuns founded the first community of women religious in the United States in Port Tobacco, Maryland in 1790. It was not until the Jacksonian era, however, that the presence of convents generated great public outcry. Anti-convent sentiments emerged as part of the revived spirit of anti-Catholicism in the 1830s. Anti-Catholic nativism was reflected in hostility to the rising tide of immigrants from Ireland and Germany, in the popularity of publications like the Rev. Lyman Beecher's *A Plea for the West* (1835) and Samuel F. B. Morse's *Foreign Conspiracy against the Liberties of the United States* (1835)—both of which alleged the existence of Catholic plots to capture the American Republic for the Pope—and, most notoriously, in the burning of the Ursuline Convent in Charlestown, Massachusetts by a Protestant mob in August 1834.[3]

The growth of convents in American society profoundly alarmed many Protestants, not simply because nuns were Catholic and often foreign-born, but also because their vocation seemed in various ways to challenge the "cult of true womanhood" and the ideal of "Republican motherhood." By renouncing marriage and motherhood for themselves, by allegedly proselytizing Protestant children and attempting to enlist Protestant daughters into their ranks, nuns appeared to endanger the essential links

130

---

2. This paper uses the word "nun" in its popular sense to describe any woman religious, whether contemplative or active, who takes holy vows, whether solemn or simple.

3. An Ursuline Convent was founded in New Orleans in 1727, when that city was still a French possession. It became the fourth convent in the United States in 1803, following the American purchase of the Louisiana Territory from France. Sr. Mary Ewens, OP, *The Role of the Nun in the Nineteenth Century: Variations on an International Theme* (New York, 1978), 22, 33. Ray A. Billington, *The Protestant Crusade, 1800–1860: A Study in the Origins of Nativism* (New York, 1938), 119–129; though dated, Billington's book remains the best survey of anti-Catholic nativism before the Civil War.

Joseph Mannard

between family, church, and state enunciated in the ideology of domesticity.[4]

Originating in the Northeast among middle-class Protestants at the end of the eighteenth century, the ideology of domesticity crystallized in the 1830s and 1840s as advances in printing made possible its wide dissemination in ministers' sermons and women's magazines and advice literature. Domesticity emphasized the central role of the nuclear family in transmitting cultural values and maintaining social order, and especially stressed the significant contribution of woman as the chief agent in this process. Woman as wife and mother represented a beacon of stability, a preserver of tradition, in a society undergoing unprecedented industrial development, urban growth, and geographical expansion. While a man was to be preoccupied with the public sphere of business and politics, a woman's responsibilities lay fundamentally within the family circle where

---

4. On "true womanhood," see Barbara Welter, "The Cult of True Womanhood: 1820–1860," *American Quarterly* 18 (Summer 1966): 151–174. On "Republican motherhood," see Linda Kerber, *Women of the Republic: Intellect and Ideology in Revolutionary America* (Chapel Hill, NC, 1980), chapter 9. The ideology of domesticity reflected and shaped social, economic, and demographic transformations begun in the late eighteenth century that increasingly moved men's workplace outside the home and shifted women from being primarily producers in a family economy to being consumers in a market economy. The discussion of the origins and tenets of domesticity presented in this paper has been drawn principally from Nancy F. Cott, *The Bonds of Womanhood: "Woman's Sphere" in New England, 1780–1835* (New Haven, 1977); Mary P. Ryan, *The Empire of the Mother: American Writing about Domesticity, 1830–1860* (New York, 1982); and Kathryn Kish Sklar, *Catharine Beecher: A Study in American Domesticity* (New Haven, CT, 1973).

her main duties included instructing her children in religion, morality, and patriotism. Limiting in theory, domesticity could prove flexible in practice. The female sphere sometimes expanded outside the home in order that women might better protect those values peculiarly entrusted to them.

Some Protestants, then, saw nuns as veiled threats to American domesticity as they defined it. Convent opponents did not always agree among themselves as to the nature of this threat, because male and female convent critics tended to focus on those points most in conflict with their respective gender interests. Males made up the chief leadership and membership of the "convent reformers"—supporters of legislation for state inspection and regulation of nunneries. First voicing demands for convent reform in the early 1830s, these male writers, ministers, and editors expressed a common set of concerns but lacked the formal organization that characterized the antislavery and temperance crusades. It was not until the emergence of the anti-Catholic, anti-foreign American, or Know-Nothing, Party in the 1850s that convent reformers found the mechanism to put their demands into action. Anti-convent petition campaigns in Massachusetts and Maryland resulted in the legislatures of those states appointing "Nunnery Committees" to examine the issue. This temporary success for convent reform backfired, however, when these investigations failed to substantiate reformers' claims that women were being held in convents against their will.[5]

Females provided the principal spokespersons and the majority of what could be "convent competitors"—advocates of Protestant-financed female seminaries and teachers to compete with convent schools. In the mid-1840s and early 1850s, convent competitors successfully formed female education societies to effect their goals. Although convent competitors and reformers shared a mutual suspicion of the subversive nature of Catholic female academies, women most commonly directed their energies to providing an alternative to the convent menace, while men were likely to be more disturbed by the fear that nunneries were "priests' prisons for women."[6]

While expressing concern for the plight of females in convents, male reformers denounced the vocation of the nun as a form of social deviance

---

5. Ray A. Billington, *The Protestant Crusade, 1800–1860,* 414; John R. Mulkern, "Scandal Behind the Convent Walls: The Know-Nothing Nunnery Committee of 1855" *Historical Journal of Massachusetts* 11 (January 1983): 22–34; *Journal of the Proceedings of the House of Delegates of the State of Maryland* (Annapolis, 1856), 641–643; Sr. M. St. Patrick McConnville, *Political Nativism in the State of Maryland, 1830–1860* (Washington, DC, 1928), 108–111; Jean Baker, *Ambivalent Americans: The Know-Nothing Party in America* (Baltimore, 1977), 88–99.

6. Polly Welts Kaufman, *Women Teachers on the Frontier* (New Haven, CT, 1984). Andrew B. Cross, *Priests' Prisons for Women* (Baltimore, 1854).

directly at odds with a woman's sacred roles of wife and mother within the home. Reformers attacked the celibacy of women religious as flouting the laws of God and Nature. The publisher's introduction to the American edition of Scipio de Ricci's classic exposé *Female Convents: Secrets of Nunneries Disclosed* warned that celibacy was "unnatural . . . unjust and ruinous." He concluded that "nunneries and the conventual way of life, are altogether contradictory to the Divine appointments respecting the order of nature, and the constitution of mankind and human society."[7]

The maverick Catholic James Gordon Bennett also questioned the purpose of nunneries in a modern republic. Bennett, editor of the *New York Herald,* condemned celibacy publicly in his newspaper, charging that insanity resulted from its practice. "The natural position of a woman is to marry—have a family—and be surrounded by blooming children," he wrote. "To be shut up in a convent, and restricted from the happiness of a husband, is enough to drive any woman out of her senses." Bennett concluded that convents were antithetical to the American way of life and proposed their abolition throughout the land.[8]

In their arguments against celibacy, reformers also revealed their own sexual anxieties. The thought of females living without traditional male guidance stimulated the imaginations of reformers. Scurrilous works such as Maria Monk's best-selling *Awful Disclosures of the Hotel Dieu Nunnery of Montreal* (1836) decried celibacy as a deliberate sham that permitted debauched priests to violate helpless females. "The popish doctrine of celibacy—the unreserved obedience due to bishops and priests from all nuns and females in all the holy orders, opens the way for the corruptions that would be expected," concluded Rev. Robert J. Breckinridge and Rev. Andrew B. Cross in their journal, the *Baltimore Literary and Religious Magazine.* "Unmarried men have the charge of unmarried women, and hear them confess in these secret abodes. Need more be said?" asked Rev. Edward Beecher.[9]

Reformers also believed that the well-being of the community depended upon American women assuming responsibilities in their proper domain—the home. Anti-convent petitions to the Maryland legislature in 1856 charged that nunneries were detrimental to the "positive welfare of society" because they "cut off so many from their social duty and a sphere

133

---

7. Scipio de Ricci, *Female Convents: Secrets of Nunneries Disclosed* (New York, 1834), x–xi.

8. *New York Herald,* August 22–23, 1839.

9. Cross, *Priests Prisons for Women; Pope or President? Startling Disclosures of Romanism as Revealed by Its Own Writers* (New York, 1850; facsim. ed. New York, 1977), 88–122; *Baltimore Literary and Religious Magazine* 2 (September 1836): 359; Edward Beecher, *The Papal Conspiracy Exposed* (Boston, 1855), 418.

134

Mother Catherine McAuley

of usefulness." Another anti-convent writer admonished that "no woman can be justified for abandoning all the obligations which she owes to society." According to the American and Foreign Christian Union, any woman who entered a nunnery forsook her duties "to the family, and to society."[10]

Not only abjuring marriage and motherhood for themselves, women religious reportedly directed many of their female students into taking the veil, thus creating a self-perpetuating system in direct opposition to the domestic roles of true womanhood. Lewis H. J. Tonna neatly expressed this fear in his *Nuns and Nunneries,* a work originally published in England but widely circulated in the United States in the early 1850s. "At an early age when the heart is especially open to those impressions which may be called romantic or sentimental," warned Tonna, ". . . [a girl] is beset with continued commendations of the heavenly state of a nun. The duties of a wife, the cares of a mother, are denounced as dangerous, and interfering with the soul's health."[11]

Reformers' objections to the convent vocation reflected underlying concerns about maintaining the patriarchal authority of fathers and

---

10. *Frederick Examiner* (MD), February 13, 1856; Ricci, *Female Convents,* xiv; American and Foreign Christian Union, *Eighth Annual Report,* 29.

11. Lewis H. J. Tonna, *Nuns and Nunneries* (London, 1852), 17. Convent reform became a trans-Atlantic issue in the 1850s, with much sharing of information between Great Britain and the United States. See Walter S. Arnstein, *Protestant versus Catholic in Mid-Victorian England: Mr. Newdegate and the Nuns* (Columbia, MO, 1982).

husbands. Upholding a highly restrictive standard of domesticity, reformers focused on how nuns rejected the forms of domesticity—marriage, motherhood, and home. In contrast, the mainly female convent competitors stressed how Catholic sisters threatened to usurp the principal functions of domesticity—the care, education, and religious training of children—and, thereby, replace American mothers as the moral and cultural arbiters of the nation. In their view, nuns imperilled what historian Mary P. Ryan has labelled "the Empire of the Mother" in antebellum society. Much as native-American craftsmen looked upon Irish laborers as undercutting their social status and economic security, Protestant women who formed female education societies identified nuns as their chief rivals in a struggle to shape the cultural identity of the United States.[12]

Echoing Lyman Beecher's warnings of a Papal conspiracy to win the West for Catholicism, important female theorists of domesticity such as Sarah J. Hale and Catharine Beecher—Lyman's daughter—sounded the alarm about the dangerous growth of convent schools, especially on the frontier. Hale, editor of the Boston-based *American Ladies Magazine,* dedicated her publication to the cause of convent competition with a vow and a warning. "Female education and its results shall be the ruling theme of our Magazine," she wrote in 1834. "Female education must be provided for—otherwise convents will increase and Catholicism become permanently rooted in our country." Abigail G. Whittelsey expressed similar concerns in her journal, *The Mother's Magazine,* published in Utica, New York. The cover of the May, 1835 issue listed the number of Catholic schools and nunneries then existing in the United States. In the adjoining article Whittelsey warned her readers that Catholic sisters attempted to convert Protestant daughters who attended their schools. As one letter to the editor explained, "When these young ladies become mothers, they will educate their children for the special service of the Pope of Rome, and their Catholic sons will become our rulers, and our nation a nation of *Roman Catholics.*"[13]

135

---

12. Ryan, *The Empire of the Mother,* 18. Ryan contends that mothers in the home commanded a critical social position, providing "the vital integrative tissue for an emerging middle class." See also, Mary P. Ryan, *Cradle of the Middle Class: The Family in Oneida County, New York, 1780–1865* (Cambridge, 1980).

13. *The American Ladies' Magazine* 7 (December 1834): 564. Though concerned about the growing influence of convent schools, Hale bore no personal animosity towards the sisters who taught in them. She considered the Mother Superior of the Ursuline Convent in Charlestown to be a friend and publicly condemned the burning of that institution as an outrage upon all women; *The American Ladies' Magazine* 7 (September 1834): 419. *The Mother's Magazine* 3 (May 1835): 76–77. Fears similar to those expressed by Whittelsey are found in *General View of the Principles and Designs of the Mount Holyoke Female Seminary* (n.p., 1837), 8–10; and *Roman Catholic Female Schools: A Letter of an American Mother to an American Mother* No. 360 (New York, n.d.).

136

Above, *"Maria Monk" and child, a "scandal" that threatened Catholics in 1836; at right, one of the flood of "Nativist" pamphlets that agitated against immigrants and Catholics in the 1840s; below, cartoon from 1844 in which Archbishop Hughes of New York is attacked by editor James Gordon Bennett, and defended by unruly Irishmen.*

The panic of 1837 and subsequent economic depression delayed these women's hopes for Protestant female education for several years. In the mid-1840s, through the impact of her book *The Duty of American Women to their Country* and lecture tours to major Northern cities, Catharine Beecher elicited broad support from Protestant clergymen and local churchwomen for her projects to provide female education and women teachers to the frontier. As a result of her efforts, Beecher encouraged the formation of the Ladies' Society for the Promotion of Education at the West (LSPEW), in 1846; and directly founded the Board of National Popular Education (BNPE), in 1848; and the American Woman's Education Association (AWEA), in 1852.[14]

The annual reports of these societies regularly invoked the specter of convent academies in order to solicit funds for their work. Indeed, the LSPEW declared its twin purpose was "to furnish teachers of every grade" and thereby "to prevent the necessity of patronizing papal seminaries." These organizations fundamentally believed in women's indispensable role in advancing American institutions and argued for an expansive notion of the female sphere. "Politicians may plan and legislate," contended the 1847 report of the LSPEW, "and the ministers of religion may labor and pray for the extension and perpetuity of our free, civil, and religious institutions, but without the cooperation of *educated women* in the nursery and schoolroom, they will prove a failure." Catholic sisters, however, threatened to unravel this delicately spun web of family, church, and state, by undermining the value and influence of Republican motherhood, and creating a new generation of "Romish mothers." As the AWEA ruefully noted in 1854, "Nine-tenths of their schools are for females, showing that they mean to make the *mothers* who will make the nation." These educational associations justified teaching by women as an extension of the maternal duty to mold the character of the young, but they believed that nuns subverted the true purpose of that instruction—transmission of Protestant and republican values.[15]

For convent competitors like Beecher and Hale, the idea of female education was central to their theory of domesticity, which sought to elevate the position of American women by using the home as the base of female influence in society. Because their version of domesticity was inextricably linked to Protestantism and republicanism, convent competitors

137

---

14. Catharine Beecher, *Educational Reminiscences and Suggestions* (New York, 1874), 84, 105–115, 153–154.

15. Ladies Society for the Promotion of Education in the West, *First Annual Report* (Boston, 1847), 21, 31; American Woman's Educational Association, *Second Annual Report* (New York, 1854), 20. See also, Ladies Society, *Third Annual Report* (1849), 21–29; Board of National Popular Education, *Third Annual Report* (Cleveland, 1850), 37–40.

138

AWFUL DISCLOSURES,

BY

MARIA MONK,

OF THE

HOTEL DIEU NUNNERY OF MONTREAL,

REVISED, WITH AN

APPENDIX,

CONTAINING,

PART I. RECEPTION OF THE FIRST EDITIONS.
PART II. SEQUEL OF HER NARRATIVE.
PART III. REVIEW OF THE CASE.

ALSO, A SUPPLEMENT,

GIVING MORE PARTICULARS OF THE NUNNERY AND GROUNDS.

———————

ILLUSTRATED BY A PLAN OF THE NUNNERY, &c.

———————

NEW-YORK:
PUBLISHED BY MARIA MONK,
AND SOLD BY BOOKSELLERS GENERALLY.
1836.

This bestseller caused many Americans to be suspicious of nuns

perceived Catholic sisters as their rivals in a struggle to confirm the pre-eminence of American mothers in the moral and cultural life of the nation.

Just as American Catholics defended the compatibility of their religion and republicanism, they also argued for the nun's complementary relationship to American motherhood within the ideology of domesticity.

Compared to the flood of didactic literature emanating from Protestant pens, the amount of Catholic writings on domesticity before the Civil War was but a trickle. Catholic newspapers and periodicals reserved most of their space for theological, political, and economic matters. Nevertheless, in an area like Maryland, with its deep-rooted Catholic elite, and in cities with a nascent Catholic middle-class, the prescriptions of domesticity often appeared in articles in the Catholic press. European clergymen supplied most of this material, which was first translated and then reprinted for American consumption.[16]

An exemplary statement of the Catholic version of domesticity appeared in a series of essays written by Charles Sainte-Foi and collectively entitled "The Mission of Woman." *The Metropolitan,* a popular Catholic journal based in Baltimore, published translations of these articles from September 1853 to August 1854. Though little is known of Sante-Foi, the orthodoxy of his views is attested to by the fact that the magazine's clergyman editor refused to print anything "in the least at variance with the principles of Catholic faith and morals."[17]

Sainte-Foi defined a feminine ideal that in most essentials was virtually indistinguishable from that of mainstream Protestantism. He extolled marriage and motherhood as the proper roles for the vast majority of Catholic women. By their nature, females were expected to follow their hearts over their minds, relying more on intuition than logic. To mothers was entrusted the character formation of their children, especially their early religious training.[18]

Although the family was "the natural and primary sphere of her action," a woman could extend her domain of activities by joining with others of her sex in order to uphold her moral and spiritual responsibilities. Sainte-Foi recommended:

If there are other women around her whom she can associate with herself, let her remember that two are stronger than one, and that in union there is strength. . . . Having on their side

---

16. Gerald P. Fogarty, S.J., "Public Patriotism and Private Politics: The Tradition of American Catholicism" U.S. Catholic Historian 4 (no. 1, 1984): 4–17; Jay P. Dolan, *The American Catholic Experience: A History from Colonial Times to the Present* (Garden City, NY, 1985): 108–109, 304–305. Mary Colleen McDannell, "The Home as Sacred Space in American Protestant and Catholic Popular Thought, 1840 to 1900" (Ph.D. diss., Temple University, 1984), 111–112, 181. Although focusing primarily on the second half of the nineteenth century, McDannell's work is the fullest examination and analysis of Catholic attitudes about domesticity. Especially valuable is her explicit comparison of Catholic and Protestant views.

17. The articles ran in the following issues: *The Metropolitan* 1 (September 1853): 388–390, (October 1853): 435–437, (November 1853): 536–538; (December 589–591); 2 (April 1854): 139–142, (August 1854): 395–398. *The Metropolitan* 1 (February 1853): 1. The magazine had as one of its primary aims to "form a valuable repertory of information for the Catholic family"; *The Metropolitan* 1 (February 1853): 2.

18. *The Metropolitan* 1 (September 1853): 388–390, (October 1853): 435–437.

the power which right and truth confer, they could, in setting about it properly, reform the tone and habits of the city; or at least oppose a salutary check to the evil tendencies that exist.[19]

Like their Protestant counterparts, middle- and upper-class Catholic females might form local benevolent societies to address the plight of orphans, widows, and other unfortunates. The Church considered such female activities outside the home as legitimate and good if carried out in a self-effacing manner and as part of women's apostleship of "preaching Christ" in their everyday acts.[20]

For all their similarities, the glaring difference between Catholic and Protestant interpretations of domesticity was the former's contention that religious life is a higher calling than married life, that for women virginity is superior to maternity. According to Sainte-Foi, "The first and most perfect state that a woman can embrace, is virginity or the religious life." For Catholics, however, this belief in the primacy of virginity remained compatible with the maternal ideal of domesticity for two reasons. First, most women had no vocation for the convent.

140

> The religious life, being a life of perfection, is the portion of but a small number of privileged souls for whom God reserves His most intimate communication, and most precious favors. The greater number of women are called to live in the world, and to serve God in the married state.

Every Catholic woman chose between these two options, "according to her inclinations and the manifestation of the divine will."[21]

Second, even virgins who entered the convent embraced maternity of a sort. "Maternity is for woman the aim of life," asserted Sainte-Foi.

> If to follow a higher vocation, she renounces the joys which the maternity derived from the flesh and blood imparts, it is to consecrate herself to the functions of a more holy and sublime maternity, which is entirely of the spirit in its nature and in its end.[22]

This "maternity of the spirit" derived from the nun's status as a spiritual "bride of Christ" and from her works of teaching, nursing, orphan care, and moral reform.

---

19. *The Metropolitan* 1 (November 1853): 536–538. Sainte-Foi may have been unusual in advocating for Catholic lay women a social role beyond the home. McDannell contends that most Catholic didactic literature of the nineteenth century discouraged Catholic mothers from becoming involved in the type of reform activities occupying their Protestant counterparts, rather the tasks of "social housekeeping" were assigned to nuns.

20. *The Metropolitan* 1 (November 1853): 536–538.

21. *The Metropolitan* 1 (December 1853): 589; 2 (April 1854): 139.

22. *The Metropolitan* 1 (September 1853): 388–389.

Ruins of the Ursuline convent in Charlestown, MA, 1834

She becomes the spouse of Jesus Christ in order to become, through mercy and charity, the mother of the little children whom she feeds with the milk of the doctrine of life, or of the sick and infirm whom she surrounds with her care, . . . or else, . . . she becomes the mother of those poor sinners who have wearied themselves in the ways of iniquity, and she brings them forth to Jesus Christ.[23]

Even contemplative orders of women religious, who dedicated themselves solely to lives of prayer within the cloister, practiced spiritual motherhood. Indeed, they engaged in "a still more exalted occupation" than active works of mercy in the world. Although contemplatives withdrew from the world, Sainte-Foi contended:

They do not on this account forfeit the glorious privilege of maternity; for it is in their heart ever glowing with charity that are formed those germs of salvation and life, which the breath of the Spirit carries into languishing or withered souls, and which are afterwards fertilized by the action of divine grace.[24]

Mary the mother of Jesus embodied this Catholic notion of a "two-fold maternity, that of the spirit and that of the flesh." In her person, Mary

23. *Ibid.*
24. *Ibid.*

united the two states of virginity and maternity. Every other woman had to choose between these two states; but all, whether wife or nun, could share in the functions of maternity.[25]

In their personal and public documents, women religious expressed beliefs and assumptions conforming to the principles of the ideology of domesticity. Although the office of Mother Superior most clearly exemplified spiritual maternity within the convent, all members were committed to this concept in their lives and work. The four qualities identifying the antebellum true woman basically dovetailed with the virtues of the ideal nun as defined in the rules and constitutions of various religious sisterhoods. The convent institutionalized the true woman's attributes of piety, purity, and submissiveness in a nun's religious calling and her vows of chastity and obedience. For example, in recommending a prospective candidate to the Sisters of Charity, a New York priest noted her practical talents, including needlework. "This," he said, "together with her great piety, her modesty, . . . her agreeable manners, leads me [to] think that she will be a good and useful Sister of Charity." Catholic sisters took these virtues seriously as their standard of behavior. Typical was Sr. M. Clotilda Smith of the Visitation Order, who on her deathbed continually repeated the phrase "Obedience makes the religious, obedience and submission."[26]

Although not domestic in the formal sense, women religious often provided to clergymen and seminarians the kind of household services— cooking, washing, sewing—that fathers and sons expected from female family members. Above all, the nun in the cloister shared with the mother in the home a commitment to self-sacrifice for the sake of others. For both women, a spirit of self-denying benevolence formed the core of their being.

With more cleverness than honesty, Catharine Beecher argued a distinction between the self-sacrifice of Catholic sisters and Protestant mothers. "[I]t is often asserted," she remarked, "that the Catholics exhibit more self-denying zeal than Protestants, while these sisterhoods are specially pointed at as evidence." But, she contended, "[I]t has not been

---

25. *Ibid.*
26. Welter, "The Cult of True Womanhood: 1820–1860," 151–174. On convent rules and constitutions, see, for example, *An Abridgement of the Interior Spirit of the Religious of the Visitation of the Blessed Virgin Mary*, translated from the French (Washington, 1834); or *Regulations for the Society of Sisters of Charity in the United States*, printed as Appendix A in Ellin M. Kelly, comp. and ed., *Numerous Choirs: A Chronicle of Elizabeth Bayley Seton and Her Spiritual Daughters: Volume I: The Seton Years 1774–1821* (Evansville, IN, 1981). Rev. James Quinn to Mother Xavier Clark, November 26, 1843, Archives St. Joseph's Central House (Emmitsburg, MD), RG7–10, LV4, #123. "Life of Sr. M. Clotilda Smith," Baltimore Visitation Convent *Vow Book*, Vol. 1, 55, 65.

the benevolent self-denial of Christ, but a selfish and ascetic self-denial, aiming mainly to save self by inflictions and losses." Beecher's argument ignored the innumerable charitable works performed by active communities of women religious like the Sisters of Charity and Sisters of Mercy, of whose existence she was clearly aware. She also misrepresented the motives of contemplative orders, whose prayers were offered not only for the perfection of self but also, and necessarily, for the salvation of others.[27]

Women religious testified explicitly to their practice of maternity of the spirit by the language used in their school prospecti printed annually in the *Catholic Almanac.* Nuns assured parents and guardians of their complementary role to the mother in the nursery. A typical example appeared in the 1848 statement of the Sisters of Mercy of Charleston, South Carolina, promising that "the strictest attention is paid to the health, comfort, manners, and literary improvement of the pupils. The discipline or government, though firm and uniform, is mild and parental. The sick are attended with maternal tenderness." An 1841 announcement for the highly-respected Ursuline academy in New Orleans proclaimed:

143

The object kept in view . . . is the adorning of their pupils' minds with knowledge and the forming of their hearts to virtue. The young ladies are accustomed to habits of order, cleanliness and polite manners. They are never suffered to go beyond the reach of a watchful but maternal superintendence, whose vigilance secures the preservation of morals and the willing observance of the rules.[28]

Catholic sisterhoods applied the same maternal sentiments to the care of orphans and widows and the tending of the sick, a fact to which lay persons bore witness. The Catholic press sometimes published letters of praise for nuns like the one from a visitor to St. Vincent's Asylum in Washington, D.C., who described the Sisters of Charity as "pious mothers of the orphan."[29]

Nuns also encouraged greater awareness of domesticity among others of their sex. After religious training, the chief educational objective of convent academies was to prepare girls to assume positions as refined wives in middle- and upper-class homes. True, nuns welcomed those girls who felt called to a convent vocation, but they recognized that the majority of their pupils would eventually take vows of matrimony not religion. Mother Elizabeth Seton, famous founder of the Daughters of Charity in the United States, explicitly articulated this view to her students at the St.

---

27. Catharine Beecher, *Address to the Protestant Clergy of the United States* (New York, 1846), 32; 28–29.

28. *Catholic Almanac.* 1848, 114; 1841, 158.

29. *Catholic Mirror* (Baltimore), August 27, 1853.

144

*Catherine Beecher, the most
important theorist of domesticity
of her time*

Joseph's Academy in Emmitsburg, Maryland. "Your little mother . . . does not come to teach you how to be good nuns or Sisters of Charity;" she said, "but rather I would wish to fit you for that world in which you are destined to live; to teach you how to be good mistresses and mothers of families."[30]

The curriculum in convent academies was mainly ornamental in intent, concentrating on basic subjects—reading, writing, arithmetic—and the arts—music, painting, and especially French, a must for any "accomplished" young lady. Convent academies closely paralleled the genteel education offered in secular female seminaries of the pre-Civil War years and often were more accessible financially and geographically. This fact explains why many Protestant families entrusted the training of their daughters to Catholic sisters despite the warnings of convent critics.[31]

---

30. Quoted in Charles I. White, *The Life of Mrs. Eliza Seton* (New York, 1853), 362.

31. Edmund J. Goebel, *A Study of Catholic Secondary Education During the Colonial Period up to the First Plenary Council of Baltimore, 1852* (Washington, DC, 1936), 220–230; Mother M. Benedict Murphy, RSHM, "Pioneer Roman Catholic Girls Academies: Their Growth, Character, and Contribution to American Education: A Study of Roman Catholic Education for Girls from Colonial Times to the First Plenary Council of 1852" (Ph.D. diss., Columbia University, 1958). For a detailed examination of curriculum change over time at one of the oldest and most prestigious convent academies, see Mada-Anne Gell, "A History of the Development of Curriculum: Georgetown Visitation Preparatory School 1865–1965" (Ph.D. diss., The Catholic University of America, 1983). Despite its title, this study also contains a good review of the antebellum years.

Convent academies, however, were often too expensive for a Catholic population comprised mostly of working-class immigrants. Yet nuns helped facilitate the acceptance of domesticity among these economically less-fortunate groups as well. Women religious particularly addressed the needs of members of their own sex at each stage of their lives: female foundlings and orphans, school girls, single working women, working-class wives and mothers, and dependent widows.

The tuition from convent academies usually helped fund benevolent schools for orphan girls and daughters of poor families in the parish. Mother Eleanora Walsh of the Order of the Visitation conducted such a free school for seventeen years in the basement of the cathedral in Wheeling, in western Virginia. By her selfless dedication, Walsh "produced such an impression upon the children under her charge, that no fewer than thirty of them became religious . . . while many others have become equally distinguished in domestic life as model wives and mothers of families."[32]

Arriving from Germany in 1848, the School Sisters of Notre Dame specialized in educating girls of that nationality. In 1854, Sr. M. Theresa Gerhardinger, Superior General of the congregation, wrote to Rome about the importance of female education in America. "If the sisters succeed in giving a good education," she predicted, ". . . there will always be enough of these young women becoming mothers, and thus a better generation will spring up."[33]

One of the two congregations of Afro-American women religious established in the antebellum era, the Oblate Sisters of Providence focused on educating the daughters of the free Black community in Baltimore. An advertisement for their school in the 1839 edition of the *Catholic Almanac* revealed that they trained their pupils to serve the ideal of domesticity in either one of two ways:

> . . . these girls will either become mothers of families, or household servants. In the first case, the solid virtues, the religious and moral principles which they acquired when in this school, will be carefully transferred as a legacy to their chldren. . . . As to such are to be employed as servants, they will be instructed in domestic concerns, and the care of young children.[34]

Members of the Sisters of Mercy opened "houses of protection" to relieve the condition of some of the thousands of ill-educated and unem-

145

---

32. "Life of Eleanor Walsh," Mount De Chantal Visitation Convent *Vow Book*, Vol. 1, 35–36.

33. Mother M. Theresa Gerhardinger to Cardinal Protector Clarelli, 1854, in S. M. Hester Valentine, SSND, ed., *The North American Foundations: Letters of Mother M. Theresa Gerhardinger* (Winona, MN, 1977), 116.

34. *Catholic Almanac*, 1839, 95.

ployed females arriving from Ireland, who might otherwise have fallen prey to lives of vice or crime in American cities. The object of these houses was to admit "distressed women of good character" for instruction in religion and domestic service. Each house acted as a kind of employment agency supplying the servant needs of elite Protestant and Catholic families. Convent annals recorded that "Ladies would call at the convent, or again drive up to the door in elegant carriages, to solicit a chambermaid, a nurse, or a cook." By such means nuns introduced immigrant women to middle- and upper-class homes where they became acquainted with the ideology of domesticity, sometimes imbibing its principles and passing them on to their own families.[35]

Women religious, such as the Sisters of Notre Dame de Namur in Boston, also instructed poor Irish mothers in techniques of home management and personal hygiene that encouraged aspiration to middle-class respectability. The nuns educated these women in habits of industry and discipline:

teaching the untaught and overworked creatures how to make everything clean, tidy, and bright about them: helping them to have the children regular in their attendance at school, neatly dressed, with their clothes mended and all marks of degrading poverty removed . . . aiding every wife and mother to be herself, to husband and children, a model of sobriety, thrift, and gentleness.[36]

Nuns had an ambiguous relationship to the ideology of domesticity, but one that was ultimately compatible with a flexible interpretation of it. Superficially, the lives of women religious did transgress several of the outward forms and institutions of domesticity. Nuns renounced marriage, motherhood, and home. The convent served as an alternative to the nuclear household so central to the domestic ideal. Entry into a convent, ironically, provided a woman with unprecedented avenues for participation in the public realm. Catholic sisters were among the first women in nineteenth-century America to work outside the home on a permanent basis, and they became models for the quickly feminized professions of teaching and nursing. As convent superiors, hospital administrators, and academy directors, they held positions of power, influence, and responsibility denied to most women in antebellum society.[37]

---

35. "Annals of the Sisters of Mercy, Baltimore," 10–11. (Manuscript in possession of the Sisters of Mercy Provincialate, Baltimore, MD).

36. Quoted in Hasia R. Diner, *Erin's Daughters in America: Irish Immigrant Women in the Nineteenth Century* (Baltimore, 1983), 131.

37. Most recent scholarly research on women religious in the nineteenth century has emphasized their positive personal experiences and significant institutional contributions. See, for example, Sr. Mary Ewens, OP, *The Role of the Nun in the Nineteenth Century;* "Removing the Veil: The Liberated

147

*Motherine Caroline Friess
of the School Sisters of Notre Dame*

Nevertheless, for women religious such pathbreaking activities and behavior did not reflect or foster changes in their values. There is little evidence to suggest that nuns criticized the male-exclusiveness of the Catholic clergy and hierarchy, or challenged their own subordination, or that of other women, to males generally. In this respect, their belief in spiritual motherhood closely resembled the so-called domestic feminism of women like Sarah Hale, Catharine Beecher, and, in the latter half of the nineteenth century, Frances Willard, president of the Women's Christian

American Nun," in Rosemary R. Ruether and Eleanor McLaughlin, eds., *Women of the Spirit: Female Leadership in the Jewish and Christian Traditions* (New York, 1979), 255–278; and "The Leadership of Nuns in Immigrant Catholicism," in Rosemary R. Ruether and Rosemary S. Keller, eds., *Women and Religion in America: Vol. 1—The Nineteenth Century* (San Francisco, 1981), 101–149; Sr. Frances Jerome Woods, CDP, "Congregations of Religious Women in the Old South," in Randall M. Miller and Jon L. Wakelyn, eds., *Catholics in the Old South* (Macon, GA, 1983), 99–123; and Sr. Barbara Misner, SCSC, "A Comparative Social Study of the Members and Apostolates of the First Eight Permanent Communities of Women Religious within the Original Boundaries of the United States, 1790–1850" (Ph.D. diss., The Catholic University of America, 1980). Mary J. Oates, "The Professional Preparation of Parochial School Teachers, 1870–1940" *Historical Journal of Massachusetts* 12 (January 1984): 60–72; and "Organized Voluntarism: The Catholic Sisters in Massachusetts, 1870–1940" *American Quarterly* 30 (Winter 1978): 652–680 finds a relative decline in the social opportunities and professional training of women religious as they became more restricted to parochial school teaching following the Civil War. For a highly critical interpretation of the effects of religious life on women, see William Jarvis, "Mother Seton's Sisters of Charity" (Ph.D. diss., Columbia University, 1984).

Temperance Union—all of whom justified women widening their traditional sphere of behavior, but who also retained a belief in naturally ordained sex roles and the moral superiority of women. The failure of women religious to question the legitimacy of male domination meant that, as a women's institution, the convent remained at a "prefeminist" stage of consciousness.[38]

Nuns fundamentally accepted the gender distinctions and complementary sex-roles defined by the ideology of domesticity, and attempted to pass these ideals on to other women. Though Catholic sisterhoods pioneered new forms of participation for women beyond the immediate family circle, the effect was only to create new variations on traditional roles, to broaden the meaning of the female sphere without questioning the validity of that concept. Rather than being subversive of domesticity, nuns, by their practice of maternity of the spirit, fulfilled its functions and conformed to its assumptions about the female nature.

148

38. The term "prefeminist" is taken from Estelle Freedman, "Separatism as Strategy: Female Institution Building and American Feminism, 1870–1930," *Feminist Studies* 5 (Fall 1979): 527, f.7. Freedman suggests that "any female-dominated activity that places a positive value on women's social contributions, provides personal support, and is not controlled by antifeminist leadership has feminist political potential." Nineteenth-century convents meet the first two of these requirements but not the last. Freedman further contends, "When the group experience leads to insights about male domination," its members, ". . . often become politicized as feminists." This process failed to occur among religious sisterhoods in the nineteenth century, only becoming evident in the last half of the twentieth century following the Second Vatican Council.

THE BISHOPS *VERSUS* RELIGIOUS ORDERS: THE SUPPRESSED DECREES OF THE THIRD PLENARY COUNCIL OF BALTIMORE

GERALD P. FOGARTY, S.J.
Woodstock College
New York, New York

149

Throughout American Catholic history, the relations between bishops and religious were frequently strained.[1] The issues of disagreement were jurisdiction and the ownership of property. On the latter issue the fathers of the Third Plenary Council adopted two decrees which failed to receive Roman approbation and whose history indicates the American hierarchy's desire to preserve control over the religious orders working within dioceses. The issue centered on the proper person or persons in whom title to property should be vested. At the meeting of the archbishops with the officials of Propaganda, preliminary to the council, the issue was not discussed.[2] The topic was introduced when the various chapters proposed for the council were

---

[1] John P. Marshall, C.S.V., "Diocesan and Religious Clergy: The History of a Relationship, 1789-1969," in John Tracy Ellis (ed.), *The Catholic Priest in the United States: Historical Investigations* (Collegeville, Minn.: St. John's University Press, 1971), pp. 385-422.

[2] There is no reference to the issue of religious holding property in the *schemata* presented to the archbishops in Rome: *Capita praecipua quae Emi Cardinales S.C. de Propaganda Fide censuerunt a Rmis Archiepiscopis et Episcopis Foederatorum Statuum A.S. Romae congregatis praeparanda esse pro futuro Concilio;* likewise the issue is not treated in the *schemata* which resulted from the Roman meetings: *Capita proposita et examinata in collationibus, quas eorum nonnullis Emis Cardinalibus Sacrae Congregationis de Propaganda Fide ad praeparandum futurum Concilium plenarium habuerunt Rmi Archiepiscopi et Episcopi foederatorum Statuum Americae Septemtrionalis Romae congregati;* and finally there is no evidence from the minutes of the meetings that the matter was discussed in Rome: see *Relatio Collationum quas Romae coram S.C. de P.F. Praefecto habuerunt Archiepiscopi pluresque Episcopi Statuum Foederatorum Americae, 1883;* these minutes were translated in "Minutes of Roman Meeting Preparatory to the III Plenary Council of Baltimore," THE JURIST, XI (1951), 121-132, 302-312, 417-424, 538-547.

circulated among the metropolitan provinces for reaction before being formulated into *schemata* for the council itself.

The Province of New York was assigned chapter IX of the Roman *schemata* entitled "De aliis nonnullis capitibus disciplinae." To the *relatio* on this chapter the New York bishops appended a section "De Regularibus" in which they proposed that the apostolic constitution *Romanos Pontifices*, issued for the church in England and Scotland, be extended to the American church as well.[3] The *relatio* cited the three areas for which the constitution legislated: exemption from episcopal jurisdiction, ministries exercised by religious, and temporal goods of missions entrusted to religious.

In regard to exemption, the constitution declared that religious living in residences of missions enjoyed the same exemption as if they lived in their own cloisters. But the rectors of missions and other religious who had received the customary missionary faculties should attend meetings of the clergy and all religious who had the care of souls were to attend diocesan synods.

In regard to ministries exercised by religious, the constitution declared that the bishop could divide a mission entrusted to religious and assign to the new mission either a religious or a secular priest. It gave the bishop the right of visitation of cemeteries and pious places within the limits of a mission conducted by religious and of parochial schools for the poor in religious missions or parishes. It also decreed that religious had to obtain the bishop's permission before opening a new school, church, or any other institution in a diocese.

Finally, in regard to the temporal goods of missions, the constitution decreed that religious missionaries were not bound to give the bishop an account of goods which they possessed as religious, but they were bound in the same way as the secular clergy to render an account of the temporal goods which were given to the mission or the religious for the sake of the mission (*intuitu missionis*). What money and what goods met this specification, the *relatio* stated, were determined by the Second Synod of Westminster.[4]

³ For the background to *Romanos Pontifices*, see J.G. Sneed-Cox, *The Life of Cardinal Vaughan* (2 vols.; London: Herbert and Daniel, 1910), I, 330-357, and Frederick J. Zwierlein, *The Life and Letters of Bishop McQuaid* (3 vols.; Rochester: The Art Print Shop, 1926), II, 305-308.

⁴ *Relationes eorum quae disceptata fuerunt ab Illmis ac Revmis Metropolitis cum suis suffraganeis in suis provinciis super schema futuri concilii praesertim vero super capita cuique commissa* (Baltimore, 1884), pp. 34-36. The text of the constitution *Romanos Pontifices* is given in *Acta et Decreta Concilii Plenarii Baltimorensis Tertii. A.D. MDCCCLXXXIV* (Baltimore: John Murphy and Co., 1886), pp. 212-230; hereafter this edition of the acts and decrees will be cited as *Acta et Decreta* (official edition).

The proposals of the New York bishops were incorporated into Title II, chapter IX "De Regularibus," of the *Schema Decretorum* to be discussed at the council.[5] It was not, however, this section of the *Schema* which gave rise to debate at the council. Rather it was Chapter II "De Episcoporum officiis" of Title IX "De bonis ecclesiae temporalibus," no. 289, which called for all the temporalities of each diocese to be incorporated under civil law: the bishop was either to be constituted as a corporation sole for the goods of the whole diocese or they were to be committed to him in trust or he was to possess them in fee simple—in the latter case he was to be mindful that, while the civil authority gave him full rights of ownership over the goods, canon law designated him merely as the procurator.[6] The bishops debated this section at the council on December 4, 1884, and the rights of religious orders over property were inserted in the discussion when Bishop John Lancaster Spalding of Peoria moved that the following words be added: "the goods of a mission are to be possessed by Religious having the care of a mission under the same title as the other diocesan goods are possessed."[7]

Spalding's proposal raised several questions. First, it went beyond *Romanos Pontifices*, whose extension to the United States had already been requested, by requiring not only a uniform system of accounting for goods of a mission but also a uniform system of ownership. Second, it did not specify whether the goods in question were goods which the religious themselves had provided for the mission or whether they were provided by the diocese. Finally, just what type of "mission" did Spalding have in mind? Was it a church, a school, an orphanage, or a hospital? As the discussion advanced, it became clear that he meant any institution, but especially schools and hospitals, built or maintained with funds collected from the faithful. This raised the further problem that just about every institution operated by a religious order would fall under the proposed legislation since every such institution would depend to some extent on the contributions of the faithful. Bishop Stephan Ryan, C.M., of Buffalo stated that the Second Plenary Council had discussed this matter, but had come to no decision. At his

151

---

[5] *Schema Decretorum Concilii Plenarii Baltimorensis Tertii,* pp. 23-24.

[6] *Ibid.,* p. 80. The manner of holding church property was discussed in Rome; see *Relatio Collationum,* pp. 29-30 and "Minutes of Roman Meeting," THE JURIST, XI (1951), 340-341.

[7] *Acta et Decreta Concilii Plenarii Baltimorensis Tertii in ecclesia Metropolitana Baltimorensi habiti a die IX. Novembris usque ad diem VII. Decembris, A.D. MDC-CCLXXXIV* (Baltimore, 1884), p. xcii; hereafter this edition will be cited as *Acta et Decreta* (private edition).

suggestion the proposal was submitted to the commission on new material.[1]

Bishop Ryan was correct. At the Second Plenary Council in 1866 Archbishop John B. Purcell, representing the Province of Cincinnati, which had been assigned the task of discussing the problem of religious property, submitted a *relatio*. Its first section concerned religious who were pastors or administrators of parishes. In the event that a religious became a pastor or administrator, the title to ownership was to be in the hands of the bishop in the same way as if the parish had a secular pastor. But if a religious order, with the proper permissions of the Holy See and the bishop, formed a congregation and were exempt from the jurisdiction of the ordinary, the latter was to give them a "solemn document" or notarized statement which declared "that the churches are Parochial, administered by them, to be administered by them in the future, with the due presentation of Pastors through superiors and the acceptance of them through the Ordinary." These parishes were to remain in the hands of the religious unless the bishop, with the approval of Propaganda, judged that they should be removed.

The second section dealt with the same problem which came up at the Third Plenary Council. Non-parochial churches, properly established, it said, were to belong to the religious just like monasteries and their goods. It continued:

> But if goods of this kind accrue to the Religious from donations made to them for the intention of the diocese, or from the Ordinary, or from the faithful, or from the Society for the Propagation of the Faith existing in Paris or elsewhere; then goods of this kind, although we allow the legal title to them to be in the possession of the Religious, we judge belong to the diocese; so that if they defect from the diocese, or from the particular purpose of their donations, they are bound to transfer the goods to the Ordinary.

In cases where ownership was mixed, each party was to choose a mediator, who could call in a third party, who would decide how the property was to be dispersed.

The third section considered the property of nuns. Whatever they acquired with their own labor belonged to them. Whatever they obtained

[1] *Ibid.*

[1] *Concilii Plenarii Baltimorensis II., in ecclesia Metropolitana Baltimorensi, a die VII. ad diem XXI. Octobris A.D., MDCCCLXVI, habiti, et a Sede Apostolica recogniti. Acta et Decreta* (Baltimore: John Murphy, 1868), pp. lxxv-lxxvi.

from offerings of the faithful for the intention of the diocese, however, was to be in the possession of the Ordinary, who was to give to the nuns a formal written statement that they were to have the use of the goods.

After the *relatio* was discussed by the conciliar fathers, on the motion of Bishop Michael Domenec, C.M., of Pittsburgh and Bishop John Timon, C.M., of Buffalo, the fathers voted to include the *relatio* in the acts but not in the decrees of the council. They then went on to adopt the following decree:

> But every occasion of controversy would be removed, if, as often as any Religious Congregation or Religious Order wishes to establish a church or house in any Diocese, which can never be done without the consent of the Ordinary, an instrument of contract ought to be exacted between the Bishop and the Superior of the same Congregation or Order, or, if it should be necessary, the Superior General, in which there should be contained clearly and without ambiguity everything which respects the foundation, the rights rising from it, and the duties to be done: and of this instrument there ought to be two copies, so that the one may be preserved with the Superior and the other with the Bishop.[10]

153

The contract provided for in the Second Plenary Council should have prevented difficulties from arising between bishops and religious orders in regard to property, but Spalding and those who supported him wanted more control over religious orders than that of a contract.

On December 5, 1884, the bishops at the Third Plenary Council returned to the discussion of Spalding's proposal. Rupert Seidenbusch, O.S.B., vicar apostolic of northern Minnesota, and Bishop Francis S. Chatard of Vincennes sought to amend the proposal by the phrase "with the rights of Religious preserved." Bishops James A. Healey of Portland and Ryan of Buffalo thought the legislation of the Second Plenary Council was already sufficient and feared that a new law would cause the zeal of religious for serving the missions to decline. Bishop John Ireland of St. Paul denied that the previous council had sufficiently determined the matter and felt strongly the need for new legislation clearly formulated to leave nothing in doubt.

Spalding, with the support of Richard Gilmour of Cleveland, clarified his original proposition and stated that it was not fitting for religious who used diocesan or parochial funds to acquire property to possess it in their own name for fear that they would abuse their power. He was therefore specifying the precise nature of the property in question and, to illustrate that this was no chimerical fear, he told a

[10] *Ibid.*, no. 203, p. 119.

story of a religious order which was invited by the bishop to the diocese, built a school with parochial and diocesan funds, sold the school after a dispute with the bishop, and left the diocese with the money. Spalding asserted that a new law would guard against such abuses in the future and against the possibility of an overly generous bishop giving diocesan goods and institutions to religious orders to be possessed in their own name. Spalding would therefore also limit the rights of bishops in regard to the disposition of such property.

Archbishop Michael Corrigan, coadjutor of New York, who would subsequently emerge as a defender of religious orders, noted that there was already a warning in *Romanos Pontifices* against religious being allowed to take their goods out of the diocese without the bishop's permission. Archbishop John Williams of Boston confessed that he was undecided on the question, but he did have a suggestion. Just as a bishop should not possess diocesan property in fee simple or in trust, but as a corporation sole, he said, perhaps religious orders could be constituted as corporations. Williams' suggestion clearly did not solve the difficulties of the advocates of the proposal, and the discussion was failing to clarify the issue. Therefore, on the motion of Ireland, the matter was referred to a special commission composed of himself, Williams, Stephan Ryan, Corrigan, Gilmour, and Seidenbusch—those bishops who had spoken on both sides of the question at the council.[11]

The next day at the morning session, the minutes of the council cryptically note: "Aberant Abbates omnes."[12] Did "Abbates" refer only to abbots or was it a generic term for all the religious superiors? Was this a protest movement on the part of the "abbots" against the discussion of the previous day? The minutes are silent on this point and do not indicate whether they were present for the afternoon session when the conciliar fathers discussed the special commission's report. Archbishop Peter Kenrick of St. Louis opposed any restrictions on religious holding property, for, he said, they should be admitted to a diocese on their own terms or not at all. Ireland replied that the wording of the proposed decree was general and allowed for every mode of possession, including fee simple. Archbishop Patrick Ryan of Philadelphia thought that religious would be secure enough in possession if they possessed the property in question in trust and such a mode of possession would alleviate the difficulties of which Spalding had spoken. In his intervention at this point, Archbishop Ryan seems to have implied that the legislation of the Second Plenary Council had settled the issue. But Bishop Gilmour was more adamant on the proposal.

154

[11] *Acta et Decreta* (private edition), p. xcvi.
[12] *Ibid.*, p. xcvii.

He believed that religious could find nothing with which to quarrel in the new legislation for it rendered them stable in churches which had rectors, regardless of the mode of possession of the property, but he also thought it would be dangerous to allow them to possess such property in their own name. No pious religious, he said, could take offense at the decree, but it was a precaution against future abuses. Archbishop Ryan agreed with this and cited the example of one bishop at the council, a member of a religious order, who declared that all church property, including that of religious, was to be held in trust.

Bishop James O'Connor, vicar apostolic of Nebraska, argued that the decree was not in accord with the spirit of the Church and noted again that a similar decree had been rejected at the Second Plenary Council. Bishop Ryan added that the decree would restrain the zeal of religious. In response, Gilmour said that there were already in his diocese two religious congregations which possessed property in the name of the bishop and they worked with more zeal than those religious who possessed title in their own name. He then noted what was at the heart of the issue—a desire for uniformity and a certain amount of jealousy of the prerogatives of religious. According to the minutes of the council, he said, "Regulars among us do not labor for the promoting of the salvation of souls more than seculars. Therefore why should they enjoy special privileges?"

Further clarifying his earlier position, Spalding warned that the new decree did not pertain to all the goods of religious orders, but only to those which were properly diocesan or parochial, and these should be held under the same title as other goods of the same nature. He foresaw no difficulty that the zeal of the religious would decline; rather he felt that their own houses and institutions would flourish. This, however, was not sufficient for Bishop Dwenger who wanted to exclude from the decree the case where religious orders began new churches or houses with the approval of the bishop. Bishop William Gross, C.Ss. R., of Savannah agreed with Dwenger and felt that the new decree was detrimental to poorer dioceses which could not provide funds for institutions operated by religious and which would thus lose the service of religious who would fear that the bishops did not trust them. Dwenger and Gross, both religious, had failed to see the point of Spalding's original proposal: that religious who used diocesan or parochial funds for purchasing property or constructing new buildings were not to possess the title. Moreover, Dwenger in particular adhered only to what *Romanos Pontifices* had already stipulated: that a religious order needed the Ordinary's approval for new foundations within his diocese; he would thus exclude from the new decree every institution legally operated by re-

155

ligious. Bishop Patrick O'Reilly of Springfield and Bishop Ireland saw this point and noted that the exception would make the new legislation ineffectual. When a vote on Dwenger's amendment was taken, only twelve of the bishops voted in favor. The decree was then split into two parts. On the first part the fathers of the council voted thirty-three in favor and thirty-one opposed. On Dwenger's call for a new vote, they voted thirty-five in favor and thirty-three against. On the second part of the decree, the fathers voted forty-three in favor, and the opposition is not recorded.[13]

156

The first part of the decree, inserted after a description of the norms established by *Romanos Pontifices* for determining which property truly belonged to religious as religious and to religious as missioners and calling for an account of the latter to the bishop, read as follows:

> In addition, the fathers of this council decide, that ecclesiastical goods, whether of a church, or of a school, or of a parochial house, or any kind whatsoever, which are administered by Religious families, but have been built or acquired through collections of the faithful for the use of a parish or mission, are held in the same form and name, by which all other goods of this kind are held throughout the diocese, and are under the direction of the bishop; not in the name of the Religious family, which administers goods of this type.[14]

The second part of the decree was inserted after the section treating of the incorporation of diocesan property and stated:

> All diocesan institutions of charity and pious benefit, which have been erected and are sustained from money collected from the faithful, are possessed in the name and title as are the rest of the goods of the diocese under the direction of the bishop, whose vigilance should be attentive, lest institutions of this kind under any pretext be deflected from the pious end, intended for them by their founders.[15]

Once the council was completed, the decrees had to be submitted to the Holy See for its approval. For this task Archbishop James Gibbons appointed Denis J. O'Connell, his protege who had accompanied him to Rome for the preliminary meetings and who had acted as a secretary for the council, Bishop John Moore of St. Augustine, and Bishop

---

[13] *Ibid.*, p. xcix.

[14] *Ibid.*, no. 90, p. 27; given also in *Acta et Decreta* (official edition), p. lxvii.

[15] *Acta et Decreta* (private edition), no. 271, p. 90; given also in *Acta et Decreta* (official edition), p. lxvii.

Joseph Dwenger, who had spoken on the issue of religious property at the council. Although there is no evidence that O'Connell discussed the issue with Herbert Vaughan, then the Bishop of Salford, who had been instrumental in obtaining the constitution *Romanos Pontifices* for the English church, O'Connell did visit the bishop on his way to Rome. At the Vatican O'Connell found that American religious superiors had already written in complaint of the conciliar legislation. Abbot Bernard Smith, who had acted as the agent for the American hierarchy in the past, heard the rumor that religious could own no property in the United States in the future. O'Connell was also asked if Spalding and Ireland were not too harsh on the religious. He admitted to Cardinal Giovanni Simeoni, prefect of Propaganda, that "there were some points in the decree distasteful to regulars: the 'Romanos Pontifices' and a decree about the title of diocesan property in the hands of religious," but that "some new laws were necessary" because of the scandal in some areas. Finally, he discovered that Cardinal Johann Baptist Franzelin, S.J., was the most adamant of all the members of the congregation against any deviation from universal canon law.[16]

In the meantime, Bishop Richard Gilmour, who had spoken so strongly in favor of the decree, was trying to get himself commissioned to go to Rome to win approval of the council. To Gibbons he wrote:

> The more I think of it, the more am I persuaded that we need more force than has gone to Rome. Fort Wayne [Dwenger] will not defend the Bishops against the Religious & as I see it, the Religious are but in beginning of an absorbing move, that, if not fully & vigorously stayed, will leave the future with trouble enough. This is a prolific subject.[17]

Gilmour expressed the concept of the strong episcopacy which was shared by the American hierarchy at that time and whose components were independence of Rome, of the lower clergy, and of religious orders.[18]

---

[16] Archives of the Archdiocese of Baltimore, hereafter abbreviated as AAB, 79 F 9, O'Connell to Gibbons, Mar. 8, 1885. On Franzelin's continuing hostility, see also AAB 79 P 2, Gilmour to Gibbons, July 22, 1885. On the Roman approval of the decrees, see Gerald P. Fogarty, S.J., *The Vatican and the Americanist Crisis: Denis J. O'Connell, American Agent in Rome, 1885-1903,* Vol. XXXVI of *Miscellanea Historiae Pontificiae* (Rome: Gregorian University Press, 1973), pp. 48-62.

[17] AAB 79 G 13, Gilmour to Gibbons, Mar. 21, 1885; cf. Zwierlein, *McQuaid,* II, 348-349, 351.

[18] See Gerald P. Fogarty, S.J., "American Conciliar Legislation, Hierarchical Structure, and Priest-Bishop Tension," THE JURIST, XXXVIII (1972), 400-409.

At the end of March 1885, O'Connell, who had then been almost a month in Rome, informed Gibbons that the religious were working against the decree and that it would probably be either eliminated altogether or modified to leave the title of property in the hands of religious, but forbid them to remove it from the diocese.[19] During the next few months little happened in regard to the council. In June, Gilmour, having obtained his commission to join O'Connell, Moore, and Dwenger, arrived in Rome and immediately spoke with Cardinal Simeoni about the tenure of property, but he did not record his conversation.[20] A month later, he took the opportunity of being consulted about a dispute between Bishop Chatard of Vincennes and the Conventual Franciscans over a cemetery to show the disadvantage of allowing religious holding title to diocesan property.[21] Of the delegation in Rome, Gilmour was the most vehement in favor of retaining the decree. As O'Connell remarked in August, "if the clause about diocesan property in the hands of religious does not go through, it will not be Bp. Gilmour's fault and the likelihood is that it will go through."[22] But O'Connell's intelligence at this time was incorrect. At an audience on September 10, 1885, at which the decrees of the council were presented, Pope Leo XIII extended the constitution *Romanos Pontifices* to the American church.[23] The congregation of Propaganda, however, did not submit the decrees on property to the pope. Instead it recommended that the matter be re-examined in the next plenary council.[24]

Propaganda's decision to withhold the matter of religious owning property until the next council should have ended the discussion, but it did not because of a case in which Gilmour was involved and which explains his attitude on the question throughout the council. Gilmour's predecessor, Bishop Amadeus Rappe, thinking to make the property less liable to taxation, had given the title to St. Vincent's orphan asylum in Toledo to the Grey Nuns. The asylum was supported by funds collected from the faithful of the diocese of Cleveland, and Rappe regarded the transfer of title as a formality. When Gilmour attempted

[19] AAB 79 H 11, O'Connell to Gibbons, Mar. 29, 1885.

[20] AAB 79 M 7, Gilmour to Gibbons, June 7, 1885.

[21] AAB 79 O 11, Moore to Gibbons, July 15, 1885; cf. AAB 79 P 2, Gilmour to Gibbons, July 21, 1885, where Gilmour says his position paper on religious holding property is included in the *Ponenza*.

[22] AAB 79 Q 3, O'Connell to Gibbons, Aug. 11, 1885.

[23] *Acta et Decreta* (official edition), p. cv.

[24] *Ibid.*, p. lxvii; see Archives of the Archabbey of St. Paul's outside the Walls, Rome, O'Connell to Bernard Smith, Sept. 23, 1885.

to regain the title, however, the nuns refused and in 1875 they mort-
gaged the property to build a hospital. Gilmour's position was that
which he took at the council and which was embodied in the suppressed
decree: if the asylum was bought and built with money collected from
the diocese, it belonged to the diocese. The issue came to a head in the
summer of 1888 and Gibbons, who was then a cardinal, was appointed
by Propaganda to judge the case.[25] On August 14, 1888, O'Connell,
who was then the rector of the American College in Rome and acted as
the agent for the American hierarchy, wrote Gibbons a letter in which
he referred to a cable he had sent the same day which is no longer extant
and which he hoped would reach the cardinal before his Toledo mission.
In his letter, O'Connell noted vaguely that he had "presented at once
the doubt about that 'hypothetical instruction' of '85 to the Card.
Prefect and today they held a 'congresso' on it, the result of which I cabled you at once."[26] There is no indication as to what this result
referred.

Gibbons in the meanwhile had gone to Toledo and investigated the
dispute, but he was worried that he had incurred an irregularity in
holding sessions on Sunday. He therefore wrote O'Connell to have this
irregularity legalized and then he would submit his report to Propaganda.[27] This O'Connell easily took care of, but about the middle of
September he cabled Gibbons: "Prefect advises withhold judgment.
Await letter explaining." Gibbons was anxious about this letter, but
hoped that he would be left free to reach his decision.[28] O'Connell then
seems to have engaged in some kind of delaying action and failed to
send Gibbons the expected letter.[29] Sometime during this period Gibbons, who had received no clarification from O'Connell, reached his decision. The title to the property, he said, was to remain with the nuns,
and the bishop of Cleveland was to allow them to take collections for
the support of the orphans. The nuns were to renounce all claims for
expenses against the diocese including the litigation. They were not to
sell, mortgage, or alienate the property or make any improvements or
changes without the bishop's written permission. They also needed to
have the bishop's permission for any change in purpose of the property

---

[25] John Tracy Ellis, *The Life of James Cardinal Gibbons* (2 vols.; Milwaukee: Bruce,
1952), I, 325-327.

[26] AAB 84 V 6, O'Connell to Gibbons, Aug. 14, 1888.

[27] AAB 84 W 5, Gibbons to O'Connell, Aug. 23, 1888 (copy).

[28] Archives of the Diocese of Richmond, Gibbons to O'Connell, Sept. 20, 1888.

[29] AAB, 86 W 13, O'Connell to Gibbons, probably Sept. 27, 1888.

and were to submit an annual financial report to him. Gibbons thus followed the norms of *Romanos Pontifices* in mediating the dispute.[30]

On October 8, 1888, O'Connell wrote Gibbons that the pope wished him to use the Toledo case to clarify *Romanos Pontifices* in terms of which all property would belong to a diocese except that actually purchased by religious with their own money.[31] Subsequently he noted that Archbishop Domenico Jacobini, secretary of Propaganda, had asked if there were any further developments on the Toledo case and stated that the suppressed decrees should be approved without waiting for the next council. Jacobini was quoted as saying that the congregation "wanted the Cardinal to judge that one case without pronouncing on the principle." He was also reported as saying that, when the pope approved the decrees, he expressed his regret that the congregation had eliminated the property decrees and stated that he wanted them "brought up and discussed in the next council." To this account, O'Connell added his own reflections:

> This then I take to be the course that things are going to take and I would not like to see you left behind in the move. The Bps. will, most of them, be glad to go in, and it might be better for you to keep at their head. "Franzelin," Mgre Jacobini said, "is now gone." And I suppose Mgre Jacobini and the others here would consider you very wise and administrative if you agreed with them. I have not mentioned this yet to anyone, for I wish you to have the first wise hint and to get ready, so that Gilmour, Ireland &c would not look elsewhere for a leader for a question that can hardly be deferred.[32]

O'Connell may have suspected that Gibbons was still lukewarm, as previously reported, on the subject of the suppressed decrees and wished to cajole him into action in behalf of their approval by flattering him that he alone could take the lead. Whatever his motives, he learned that his cable had confused Gibbons and he wrote on October 31, 1888, to assure him that his judgment would stand with Propaganda. Jacobini, he reported, said there could be no appeal from the judgment, but that Gibbons could "ask for a revision of the sentence." The Propaganda official further urged O'Connell to write Gibbons "to have an understanding with the other archbps." with whom Gibbons would shortly be meeting, and Jacobini promised he would "refer the decree to the

160

[30] Ellis, *Gibbons*, I, 328-329.

[31] AAB 85 F 4, O'Connell to Gibbons, Oct. 8, 1888; see also Archives of the Archdiocese of St. Paul, O'Connell to Ireland, Oct. 8, 1888.

[32] AAB 85 G 2, O'Connell to Gibbons, Oct. 17, 1888.

Pope." Giving his own opinion, O'Connell wrote "I w'd like to see it approved, and the approval w'd remove any acrimony or apprehension any of the bishops may have felt." At the same time, he told Gibbons that he would write a more complete report on the subject.³³

On the same date as he wrote the above, O'Connell wrote Gibbons his report on the suppressed decree:

Your Eminence:

Sometime ago I wrote you what the Card. Prefect and Mgre Jacobini said to me about the decree of the late Council, regarding the tenure of ecclesiastical property, that had been cancelled by the Congregation of the Propaganda; how his Eminence said the Holy Father was of the same opinion as the majority of the council and how he ordered that the principle contained in that decree was not to be encroached upon, and that the decree itself should be brought up again for deliberation in the next council of the Bps. Subsequently, Mgre Jacobini said to me that recent troubles in the United States and others that he saw impending would in his opinion render it necessary to have that decree approved without awaiting a future gathering of the Bps., that when he referred to the Holy Father the action of the Cardinals, His Holiness expressed his regret that the congregation had seen fit to act in that manner and that, tho' he would not now oppose their actions, he wished that decree preserved and brought up again for deliberation. They say that the decree only embodies the provisions already contained in the constitution "Romanos Pontifices," and a few days ago, the Secretary [Jacobini] informed me that I might write you to come to an understanding on the subject with the other Archbishops, and that he would refer the matter to the Pope.

As I learned that there was to be an early meeting of many of the Archbishops in Balto. I deem it my duty to convey this information to your Eminence, that you and they might, if you deem it advisable, take the important matter into due consideration. It seems to present an easy & quiet way of settling a grave question that but for the influence of Card. Franzelin, I am informed, would have been settled long ago.³⁴

Gibbons was then totally in favor of the suppressed decrees and, on O'Connell's advice, consulted Archbishops William Elder of Cincin-

161

---

³³ AAB 85 G 13, O'Connell to Gibbons, Oct. 31, 1888; see also Archives of the Archdiocese of St. Paul, O'Connell to Ireland, Oct. 31, 1888.
³⁴ AAB 85 G 14, O'Connell to Gibbons, Oct. 31, 1888.

nati, Ryan of Philadelphia, and Corrigan of New York about petitioning Rome for the restoration of the decrees. Archbishop Patrick
Riordan, then in Rome, also offered Gibbons his support.[35]

In the meantime, Gibbons' judgment in the Toledo case remained
final, and O'Connell thought that Propaganda would so inform Bishop
Gilmour and at the same time tell him that the pope wanted the restoration of the decrees.[36] Learning of this, Gilmour urged his friend,
Bishop Bernard McQuaid of Rochester, then in Rome and also an advocate of the strong episcopate, to work to have the decrees restored.[37]
But this ended the matter. From the extant documents there is no evidence that Gibbons' petition was ever officially presented to the Holy
See, but this may very well have been because of the other pressing matters which began to divide the American hierarchy: Cahenslyism, the
school question, and the problem of secret societies, to name but a few.

The Toledo case is interesting because it shows why the bishops were
eager to clarify *Romanos Pontifices* in regard to religious possessing
title to temporal goods purchased with funds raised from the faithful.
But the decree proposed by the bishops did not take into consideration
that the religious orders were responsible for providing and training
personnel at their own expense to staff the institutions in question. In
other words, the religious orders were taking a financial risk and were
bearing a financial burden by undertaking a mission within a parish or
diocese.

The suppressed decrees of the council are important for several
reasons. First, they display the desire on the part of the majority of the
hierarchy to maintain a certain amount of control over religious orders,
and the debates on the decrees illustrate that there was tension not only
in regard to financial matters but also in regard to the role which religious orders played in the American Church. Second, the debates at
the council prophesy the division which would take place in the
American hierarchy within the next decade. The position which bishops
took on the question at the council coincided with the positions they
would hold in the liberal-conservative divisions of the 1890s and in the
Americanist dispute. Thus, Ireland, Spalding, and Gilmour would soon
be in the liberal camp. O'Connell's urging Cardinal Gibbons to take the
lead in working for the restoration of the suppressed decrees was typical
of his later role in urging the American church's only cardinal to be the
titular leader of the liberal party. On the other hand, Corrigan and the
religious orders, represented at the council by Bishop Dwenger, were to

[35] AAB 85 H 7, Gibbons to Gilmour, Nov. 13, 1888 (copy). Ellis, *Gibbons*, I, 330.
[36] AAB 85 H 8, O'Connell to Gibbons, Nov. 13, 1888.
[37] Archives of the Diocese of Richmond, Gilmour to McQuaid, Dec. 17, 1888.

162

be leaders of the conservatives. Corrigan clearly recognized that the restoration of the decrees was part of the liberal program. In November 1890 he wrote to Cardinal Camillo Mazzella, former dean of Woodstock College in Maryland and then a curial official:

> . . . A party of advanced views is now seeking to rule the Church in this country. The most prominent members are Archbishops Ireland and Riordan . . ., Bishops [John] Keane [rector of the Catholic University of America], [John] Foley [of Detroit] and Spalding, acting with and under His Eminence of Baltimore. . . .
>
> Again take the two . . . decrees quoted in the Acts of the 3 Pl. Council of Baltimore, page lxvii in fine. Through manipulations with Msgr. O'Connell, it was determined to act in the premises, without notifying the Bishops, and without a word to the Regulars. All this on the strength of a letter from Msgr. O'Connell that he had arranged matters in Rome.[38]

163

The passage of the decrees at the council and the attempt to have them restored afterwards contributed to the general accusation in the condemnation of Americanism that the Americanists or liberals looked down on religious orders.[39] The Holy See's rejection of the decrees illustrated its traditional stance in favor of religious orders, especially in missionary countries. Thus it sought to retain a balance of power between episcopal structure and religious orders.

---

[38] Soderini Manuscript, University of Notre Dame, Corrigan to Mazzella, Nov. 7, 1890.

[39] Leo XIII, *Testem Benevolentiae*, in John Tracy Ellis (ed.), *Documents of American Catholic History* (Chicago: Henry Regnery Co., 1967), II, 544-545.

Prelude To "Americanism": The New York Accademia and Clerical Radicalism in the Late Nineteenth Century

ROBERT EMMETT CURRAN

The Americanist crisis in the last decade of the nineteenth century climaxed the attempt of a group of liberal prelates and their associates to adapt Roman Catholicism to democratic institutions and values. Almost twenty years ago Robert Cross put this complex movement within the context of a growing American Catholic liberalism in the postbellum period.[1] The full dimensions of that liberalism are still coming into focus as archival materials and unpublished sources become more available to the historian. The recent discovery of a remarkable association of New York priests shows another facet of the Americanist controversy that better enables us to appreciate the peculiar lines that the episcopal struggle assumed. It makes clear that as early as the 1860s certain American priests were adumbrating the key issues that would constitute Americanism and that these clerics had an important influence upon the conflict that tore apart the hierarchy in the 1890s.

By 1860 the American priest found himself a prime victim of the power struggle that the episcopacy had waged with the laity during the peak of trusteeism. Autocratic episcopal government might have been an effective means for preventing the schism of various ethnic groups and for consolidating the rapid expansion of the church, but for the American priest it meant chiefly an erosion of his own authority and independence.[2] Groups of priests across the country began pressing for their full rights under canon law. One such group in the Cleveland diocese began to gather for monthly meetings in 1862 to discuss issues related to dogma, scripture, and moral theology, in addition to those regarding canon law. On the eve of the Vatican council its leader Eugene O'Callaghan wrote series of articles written under the *nom de plume "Jus"* for the New York *Freeman's Journal and Catholic Register* which called for

---

1. *The Emergence of Liberal Catholicism in America* (Cambridge, 1958).
2. For an analysis of this development, see Jay P. Dolan, *The Immigrant Church: New York's Irish and German Catholics, 1815–1865* (Baltimore, 1975), pp 163–166. Dolan considers nineteenth-century Catholic theology with its model of monarchial authority to have provided the rationale for the new style of episcopal government and urbanization to have fostered its implementation in America.

Mr. Curran is assistant professor of history in Georgetown University, Washington, D.C.

an ecclesiastical juridical process based upon canon law to replace the existing arbitrary system, in which bishops had the right to transfer or even dismiss priests at will. A thousand clerics responded to the *Journal* in support of *"Jus"*.[3]

Elsewhere canonists such as Sebastian Smith of Newark took the bishops to task for failing to observe not only the provisions of canon law but the hierarchy's own conciliar directives as well.[4] Smith's *Notes on the Second Plenary Council*, published in 1874, became a rallying point for reformers, as had the *"Jus"* letters five years earlier. Smith was part of a loosely associated Newark clerical clique that pressured both James Roosevelt Bayley and his successor, Michael Augustine Corrigan, to change their arbitrary administrative practices as ordinaries of that diocese.

The most notorious of these groups of clerical dissidents was one based in New York City and known, at least in chancery circles, as the Accademia. The focal point of conservative suspicions for over twenty years, the Accademia came to be regarded as the epitome of the unrest fomenting against the established order of American Catholicism, a cabal of liberalism in which the question of priests' rights was only the tip of an ideological iceberg that threatened the faith and polity of t!.e church. Although there was little or no contact among the Accademia and other groups of priests, conservative leaders like Corrigan and Bishop Bernard McQuaid of Rochester became convinced that these groups were deviously promoting what amounted to a national conspiracy against episcopal authority.

The Accademia began in 1865 as an approved theological society of the Archdiocese of New York after the model of a society begun in London by Cardinal Manning. Under the initiative of Jeremiah Cummings, the first American graduate of the Urban College of the Sacred Congregation for the Propagation of the Faith (Propaganda), and of Henry Brann, who had studied at the same college, the society was originally intended as a forum for the continuing theological education of the former Roman students in the area. From the outset, however, the so-

165

---

3. For a short account, see Nelson Callaghan, *A Case For Due Process in the Church: Father Eugene O'Callaghan, American Pioneer of Dissent* (New York, 1971).
4. Both priests and bishops used the law when it suited their interests and ignored it when it did not. That, at least, was the conclusion of George Conroy, the Irish bishop who was sent on a fact finding mission to the United States in 1878 after Vatican officials decided they needed some better information to settle the numerous appeals they were getting from American priests against their ordinaries. Conroy found that few wished to abide by the body of laws set down by the old canon law or the Councils of Baltimore. For an excellent survey of this whole question of the relationship between episcopal and clerical rights, cf. Robert Trisco, "Bishops and Their Priests in the United States," in John Tracy Ellis, ed. *The Catholic Priest in the United States: Historical Investigations* (Collegeville, Minn., 1971), pp. 111–292.

ciety's meetings for the reading and discussion of original papers were open to all members of the clergy. After less than a year's existence, the society voted to disband because many New York priests, according to one member, Richard Burtsell, found it dominated by abolitionists and those trained in Rome. At their last meeting the members appointed a committee to obtain Archbishop John McCloskey's approval for a new society, one presumably more representative and less dominated by Progagandists, those who had studied at the Urban College.[5]

By the fall of 1866 Archbishop McCloskey had not yet taken any initiative toward setting up a new society and Thomas Farrell, the pastor of St. Joseph's Church on Sixth Avenue, was privately threatening to set up his own theogical group if the archbishop did not establish a similar institution for his clergy when he returned from the Second Plenary Council being held that fall.[6] Shortly thereafter Farrell began hosting almost weekly meetings at his rectory. The regular attendants were Farrell, Patrick McSweeny, Sylvester Malone, James Nilan, Thomas McLoughlin, Richard Burtsell, and Edward McGlynn, who would eventually become its most famous member with his controversial support of Henry George in 1886. On the periphery of the group were several Paulists, including the noted converts Isaac Hecker and Augustine L. Hewit, as well as John Moore, a Propagandist who was doing pastoral work in Florida and would later become bishop of St. Augustine. Most of them were young (Burtsell, McSweeny, Nilan, McGlynn, and Moore were in their twenties) and most had been trained in Rome.

We know all too little of their ideology during these years. Outside of Hecker, who was not a regular member, they published virtually nothing. A major source for our knowledge of their thought is the diary which Burtsell kept at the time. We do know that the regular members prided themselves on their radical views. They supported Radical Reconstruction in the South and Fenianism in the North. They defended the public school as a legitimate educational environment for Catholic

5. Archives of the Archdiocese of New York (hereafter AANY), Burtsell Diary (hereafter Diary), 2, April 17, 1866. Propagandists had two special privileges which tended to set them apart from their fellow clergy. They had the right of appeal to the pope upon being removed or disciplined by their ordinary. Second, their letters to Propaganda would not be returned to their ordinaries, as was the standard procedure. In fact they had the obligation of making annual reports to the Sacred Congregation, a tradition that many American bishops considered an undermining of their own authority.

A different version of the official Accademia's demise is given in an unsigned typed manuscript housed in the Archdiocesan Archives of New York and entitled "Private Record of the Case of Rev. Edward J. McGlynn." According to this 1901 account McGlynn himself led the move to dissolve the society. Thereafter—in the "Private Record's" version—the Accademia, now limited to the McGlynn circle, drifted into heterodoxy (AANY 50-3, pp. 517–525).

6. AANY, Diary, 2, September 17, 1866.

children. They were opposed to the temporal power of the pope and had open minds about the inspiration and inerrancy of the scriptures, infallibility, celibacy, and many other topics that were considered beyond discussion in higher circles of the archdiocese.

Monsignor Thomas Preston, Burtsell's pastor during these years, later claimed that the aim of Farrell's Accademia was "to establish an American school of theology with liberal ideas" by minimizing the authority of the Holy See and adapting Catholicism to democratic forms and institutions.[7] Burtsell himself confessed to James Nilan in January 1867, about the time Farrell's group was forming, that "a revision of the fundamental principles of theology" was badly needed and that he considered his theological studies to be commencing *"ab ovo."*[8] The genesis of Burtsell's radical approach to theology, as well as that of the other young priests in the group, apparently did not go back to any Roman education. Although they chafed under the authoritarianism of the Urban College and the aristocratic prejudice of the Roman clergy, especially the Jesuits, both Burtsell and McGlynn, by Burtsell's admission, had been staunchly conservative seminarians with very orthodox ideas.[9] The trauma of the Civil War was evidently the catalyst that radically committed them to American democracy and all its implications for the form that Catholicism should take in America.

As Michael Gannon suggests, the Civil War was "a watershed in the maturation of the American Church," forcing bishops and priests to enter "national politics on an issue not directly affecting Catholicism as such."[10] This seems especially true of clerics like Burtsell, Malone and McGlynn. When Henry Brann in 1865 excoriated the Protestant ministers, north and south, for having brought on the war, and praised Catholics for having "kept aloof altogether" from the sectional controversy that had dominated the Fifties, Burtsell's comment was that Catholics had done so "through cowardice, because we ought to have spoken in favor of the Union and the abolition of slavery."[11] Burtsell had returned to America in the bitterest year of the war—1862—and apparently was disconcerted by the Church's continuing failure to support emancipation as a war goal.

Sylvester Malone was a staunch and outspoken unionist in his Brooklyn parish, which was sharply divided about the war. After Appomatox a tour of the South committed Malone all the more to securing full justice for the freedman. Edward McGlynn had returned on the eve

167

7. AANY 50-3, "Private Record," 521.
8. AANY, Diary, 3, January 25, 1867.
9. AANY, Diary, 2, September 10, 1866.
10. "Before and After Modernism: The Intellectual Isolation of the American Priest," in Ellis, *Catholic Priest*, pp. 311-312.
11. AANY, Diary, 1, May 31, 1865.

of the war in 1860. Before it was over he had charge of a floating parish in Central Park made up largely of Irish squatters and a hospital for Federal soldiers. He was there in July 1863 when the New York Irish began rioting and hanging blacks in protest of the draft laws. It was the perfect setting for some inescapable reflections on the meaning of the war.

Their war experiences evidently made them aware that their fellow Irish were still below the middle class status that the families of the Accademia had attained. Moreover, these priests seemed to sense that the "new freedom" which northern intellectuals saw coming to birth in the fields of Antietam, Gettysburg and Cold Harbor raised new hopes for Irish nationalism as well. Supporting the cause of the Fenians in abolishing English oppression was a natural commitment for one embracing the Radical Republican ideology.

When Brann expressed shock at Burtsell's mercurial change from his Roman conservatism to the radicalism he was exhibiting by the late Sixties, Burtsell told him: "I once thought rulers ought to take care of the people: in America I have learned that the people knows how to take care of itself."[12] For Burtsell and his fellow reformers learned from the war experience of democracy in action, and drew conclusions for American Catholicism. The country had survived because of the basic wisdom and courage of the people themselves, and the structure and principles of the church in America should be determined with the participation of its members. As with another generation of American Catholics a century later, political radicalism fostered religious radicalism.

The inspiration of scripture and the infallibility of the pope were two doctrinal questions the members of the Accademia most frequently discussed. Regarding the former there was a range of opinions. For James Nilan to call the scriptures inspired meant no more than calling Dante's Divine Comedy "inspired."[13] Burtsell, on the other hand, thought that the old and new testaments were uniquely inspired and free of error insofar as they dealt with matters of faith and morals defined by the Church. All its members doubted the authenticity of the Genesis account of the fall of the first parents; indeed they held that there were probably more than one set of such parents, although they did not venture to consider evolution as an hypothesis.[14]

12. AANY, Diary, 2, September 10, 1866.
13. AANY, Diary, 3, January 25, 1867.
14. "We doubted the inspiration of the history of our first parents' fall," Burtsell recorded, "and thought that many Adams may have been created, as long as the whole human race fell from original justice. The reasoning [of] Rom[ans]. 5 about sin entering by one man, is not of faith. . . . St. Paul's reasoning there is very illogical" (AANY, Diary, 3, February 27, 1867). Strangely there is no mention of the theory of evolution al-

With Pius IX's definition of the dogma of the Immaculate Conception hardly more than a decade old, infallibility was a live topic. The Accademians found that neither dogma was sufficient to prove the other. Conversely they interpreted history to prove that the Church had earlier held that the pope could err in matters of faith. With their democratic convictions they preferred to profess the infallibility of the Church as opposed to that of the pope. They were uneasy with the definition of the Immaculate Conception precisely because it seemed to rest on the pope's unique infallibility. The latter claim was particularly unacceptable to Burtsell because he interpreted it to include the pope's indirect power to depose sovereigns.[15]

Many of the practices of the Church they found exceedingly legalistic. Convinced that the material integrity of confession (the exact recitation of one's sins) had not been a prime concern for the Apostolic Church, they felt that their large congregations warranted the use of general absolution. It was absurd, Burtsell and McGlynn concluded, for a priest to waste five hours listening to "the tomfooleries of servant girls!"[16] Other practices such as the wearing of vestments and Latin Masses they dismissed as medieval vestiges which had come to be considered peculiarly sacred. They were promoting the adoption of English in the popular devotions as the first step toward making the vernacular the normal language for the liturgy.

Most of the Accademians opposed mandatory celibacy since it retarded emotional growth and tended to produce too many selfish and lonely priests. Eliminating this requirement, they reasoned, would attract more talented and attractive men to the priesthood. In the present dispensation the influence of the celibate clergy stemmed from "a superstitious reverence" on the part of the laity for a clerical mystique created by the priest's separation from the laity.[17] Religious orders they likewise found outmoded, stifled by their traditions and dominated by small minded men whose vision was fixed on the past. Burtsell remarked in

169

---

though Hecker's *Catholic World* was taking up the issue during these years. This of course was before the publication of *The Descent of Man* in which Darwin explicitly included man within his theory.

15. AANY, Diary, 3, May 19, 1867. The theory of the pope's indirect temporal power asserted that while Church and State are independent societies, the pope has the right to intervene in temporal affairs, even to the point of deposing heretical rulers, when the faith and morals of the people are endangered.

16. "If anyone wishes special advice," Burtsell suggested, "let him confess that special sin privately" (AANY, Diary, 3, January 23, 1867).

17. Nilan, McSweeny, and Burtsell agreed that "celibacy never allows priests to become men, marriage sobers men at once: Celibacy brings lonesome hours to the priest: marriage would give him a perpetual object to be loved; Celibacy makes priests selfish; marriage would make him more social. . . . So few choose celibacy, that few smart and good men become priests. The Protestant clergy has more social influence than the Catholic" (AANY, Diary, 2, July 21, 1866).

1865 that he had once looked to the Jesuits as the leaders of the age; in the light of his subsequent experience he now saw them trying to "fossilize" Americans "with the habits of the Middle Ages." Hecker especially condemned the Jesuits' insistence upon making all the decisions in their direction of others, thus stripping people of their responsibility in making moral judgments.[18]

The Accademians expected authority in the Church to be exercised in a manner suiting mature men. "A diocese or the Universal Church is not to be governed as a large friary or college," Burtsell observed in a discussion with Patrick McSweeny in 1865.[19] Burtsell himself had nearly left the Urban College because of its authoritarian regimen. In democratic America the "boss rule" of a John Hughes appalled Burtsell and his colleagues all the more.[20] What especially irritated them was the growing efforts of the episcopacy to make laws governing the whole lifestyle of the clergy, from the prohibition of beards to the wearing of the Roman collar. This they saw as a further removal of the priest from the general life of the people to be confined to a more cloistered range of activities closely monitored by his bishop. The contemporary style of authority, they were convinced, induced priests to look on bishops as demigods; the laity, in turn, had the same attitude toward priests. It was an enervating situation that impelled the Accademians to seek root changes that would revitalize the Church.

In brief, the Accademians believed that in America the Church had to be radically different from what it had been in the Old World. It had to be open to the uniqueness of its new milieu and reflect that milieu. If only the American Church could break out of its feudal patterns, there was no limit to its possible effect upon the country.[21] American Catholicism had to abandon its tradition of prudent silence on social questions and begin taking the lead in the reform movement. It had to cease its isolation from Protestants and its condemnations of American groups like the Masons, simply on the basis of the reputations of their European counterparts.

By 1867 McGlynn was already preaching this "American Idea" from the secular pulpits that would make him a national figure over the next thirty years. Speaking in Cooper Union McGlynn alluded to the destiny

18. AANY, Diary, 3, December 31, 1866.
19. AANY, Diary, 1, June 20, 1865.
20. When some New York priests had approached Hughes about their rights under canon law, the prelate told them "that he would teach them [County] Monaghan canon law; he would send them back to the bogs whence they came" (AANY, Diary, 1, July 26, 1865).
21. "We agreed," Burtsell wrote of a conversation he had with McGlynn in 1865, "that a different spirit is to be brought into the church's legislation. We have the country whence a new activity may spread throughout the whole Christian world. A little more democracy would be of use" (AANY, Diary, 1, March 30, 1865).

God had given America by creating this continent on such a vast scale, preparing it for a "gigantic race of men not in physical but moral stature of enterprise, intelligence and virtue." To fulfill its destiny America had to become Catholic, McGlynn asserted, because Catholicism, unlike Protestantism, denied the total depravity of human nature, a doctrine that would ever impede human progress.[22] As Isaac Hecker wrote in the *Catholic World* that same year (and likely a chief source for McGlynn's remarks):

> There is no ground [in Protestantism] on which to assert the natural rights of man, for the fall has deprived man of all his natural rights; and for republican equality the reformation [sic] founds at best the aristocracy of grace, of the elect, as was . . . attempted to be realized . . . by the Puritans in New England, who confined the elective franchise and eligibility to the saints, which is repugnant to both civil and religious liberty for all men.[23]

The vision of Hecker and McGlynn was that only under Catholicism could the country achieve its potential and realize true unity. To make this possible, the Church had to Americanize. "It will be [American] in spite of us," McGlynn warned.[24]

With these convictions it was inevitable that conflicts should have early arisen between members of the Accademia and the chancery. Burtsell and McGlynn became archdiocesan gadflies to spur the archibishop to more vigorous measures to serve the pressing spiritual needs of a growing immigrant population among which were many Irish Catholics with little or no contact with the Church. The two priests continually pointed out the lack of churches and accused the chancery of underestimating the number of Catholics in the metropolitan area in order to justify the archdiocese's standpat policies.[25] In his presence they charged the archbishop with being too remote from his people and allowing his clergy to live too luxuriously while spiritual necessities were going unheeded. They attacked the helter-skelter administration of the archdiocesan charitable institutions and the practice of charging fees for dispensations from the laws of the Church. If such fees had to be charged, they insisted that the revenue at least go toward building new churches and training additional priests. Sharing the misgivings of other

22. AANY, Diary, 3, April 28, 1867.
23. "The Church and Monarchy," *Catholic World* 4, no. 23 (February 1867): 638.
24. AANY, Diary, 3, April 28, 1867.
25. Burtsell and McGlynn were arguing that the Catholic population of New York was at least 500,000 whereas the archbishop contended it was not above 300,000 (AANY, Diary, 1, May 25, 1865). Donna Merwick in her study of the Boston Archdiocese during this period finds a similar pattern of polarization between a rising group of Irish-American clerics and a native-born archbishop (John Williams) hesitant to endanger the Church's standing with the Yankee community by responding in a vigorous fashion to the challenges that a rapidly growing immigrant population was raising for the structures of the Church and the larger society *Boston Priests, 1848–1910: A Study of Social and Intellectual Change* [Cambridge, 1973], pp. 61–93.

New York Catholics about the prodigious growth of the parochial school
system, Burtsell and McGlynn argued that the Church in New York was
consuming too much money and energy in building and running schools
at the expense of neglecting the religious ignorance of the vast numbers
of poor immigrant Catholics in the city. Secular education, they
contended, was the proper realm of the State, not the Church.[26]

Burtsell, McGlynn, and Nilan clashed with McCloskey over the latter's
policy of denying the sacraments to the Fenian Brotherhood, the Irish-
American organization dedicated to securing independence for Ireland.
The three priests not only challenged the hierarchy's right to dictate
politics to the Irish but Burtsell and Nilon wrote a pamphlet setting forth
the philosophical and theological justification for the Fenians' position.[27]
Furthermore, the Accademians defended the Masons in the United
States as a legitimate organization that should not fall under the
Church's ban inasmuch as it did not seek the overthrow of religion or the
civil government, the reason for the Church's condemnation of the
Masons in Europe. McGlynn and his colleagues also deepened the suspicions of conservatives by taking part in ecumenical affairs with
Protestant clergymen, such as the Christian United Association.
Cooperating with non-Catholics in charitable work was a measure that
even as intransigent a convert as Thomas Preston could and did
conscientiously support. Joining with Protestants, often in liturgical settings, in pursuit of common traditions and values, was something quite
different.[28]

With the pope's dominions in central Italy reduced to the environs of
Rome, the temporal power of the pontiff was an especially sensitive
issue. When Thomas Farrell publicly questioned certain papal prerogatives, including the temporal power, a special diocesan committee appointed to consider possible disciplinary action against Farrell voted
unanimously for his removal from St. Joseph's, but the recommendation
was stayed by McCloskey's perennial desire for peace.[29] Burtsell
published a series of letters in the *Catholic Standard* of Philadelphia

26. AANY, Diary, 1, May 25, 1865. In that year seventy-five percent of the New York
    parishes had schools with a total student population of 16,000. This was an estimated
    one-third of the Catholic children (Dolan, *Immigrant Church*, pp. 105–108).
27. When Burtsell and Nilan visited Fenian headquarters in Union Square, the officers
    there were surprised to encounter two sympathetic priests (AANY, Diary, 1,
    November 29, 1865). Rome subsequently condemned the Fenians as a secret society in
    January 1870.
28. Burtsell was appalled when Archbishop McCloskey refused to take part in an ecu-
    menical service for Lincoln in April 1865 on the grounds that "it would not look well
    for him to be praying where Prot[estant] clergymen were present! Oh bright
    theology!" Burtsell commented, "Oh cowardice! Does the Catholic Church forbid us to
    bless our countrymen!" (AANY, Diary, 1, April 15, 1865)
29. AANY, 50-3, "Private Record," pp. 522–523.

under the pseudonym *"Excelsius"* in which he attacked the attempt of the Papal States to preserve the temporal power of the pope by raising a loan in the United States. When McCloskey learned that Burtsell was *Excelsius* he summoned him to express his objection to Burtsell's apparent direction, and warned him against any future repetitions.[30]

By May of 1867 the members of the Accademia learned that the archbishop was decrying "a class of young priests" who "pretended to know more than the Church" knows.[31] Five months later he told the pastors of the archdiocese that opinion prevailing outside of New York held that some of his clergy were holding opinions condemned by the Holy See.[32] That same fall the Accademians considered abolishing their society since imprudent members were leaking reports of their freewheeling discussions and the group was widely regarded as systematically opposed to ecclesiastical authority.[33]

It is unclear how long Farrell's theological society lasted. In the wake of the ultramontane victory at Vatican I the intellectual and social ferment of the late sixties ebbed, and the ebullient radicalism of most of the Accademians cooled with advancing age and vested interests within the archdiocesan bureaucracy. Burtsell, for instance, whom even McGlynn in 1866 had accused of being too imprudent in the expression of his radical ideas, had learned the lesson of discretion from his *Excelsius* experience and thereafter was very cautious not to lose his influence within the archdiocese by provocative remarks. In time Archbishop McCloskey's suspicions were overcome and promotions for the Accademia members began to follow. McGlynn was even chosen for the prestigious role of archpriest at the mass in New York celebrating McCloskey's elevation to the cardinalate in 1875.

Nevertheless, stories of the unreconstructed views of Farrell's circle continued. In 1874 Alessandro Cardinal Barnabò, the prefect of Propaganda, instructed McCloskey to warn Burtsell and McGlynn about "the ultra liberal ideas they were indulging in."[34] James Nilan, who had begun a controversial school plan at his parish in Poughkeepsie under which the town government exercised certain controls over the school in return for certain subsidies, heard in 1883 that diocesan authorities were disturbed about bimonthly meetings that Nilan was sponsoring for his fellow priests in the area. Nilan felt constrained to explain that these meetings were not intended to rival the diocesan conferences that had finally been reinstituted but were merely designed to afford entertain-

173

30. AANY, Diary, 3, February 18, 1867.
31. Ibid., May 15, 1867.
32. Ibid., October 8, 1867.
33. Ibid., September 10, 1867.
34. AANY, unclassified, cited in a letter from Archbishop Corrigan to Giovanni Cardinal Simeoni, October 12, 1888, draft.

ment and stimulation of the mind.[35] Such assurances did little to assuage chancery suspicions that Nilan was beginning an upstate branch of the Accademia.

By 1883 Edward McGlynn had publicly cast his lot with the radical Irish nationalists who had discovered Henry George as the messiah who would return the land to the people through his single tax panacea. McGlynn played a key role in persuading Irish-Americans that George's land doctrine was "good gospel, not only for Ireland, but for England, . Scotland, and for America, too."[36] Whether through Michael Corrigan, who had become McCloskey's coadjutor in 1880, or Ella Edes, the American journalist in Rome who had close ties with both Propaganda and the New York chancery, Giovanni Simeoni, the cardinal prefect of Propaganda, received clippings of McGlynn's speech. The Vatican was then in the delicate process of trying to reestablish diplomatic relations with England. Having priests involved in the Irish question would certainly impede any rapprochement. Simeoni informed Corrigan that certain statements attributed to McGlynn regarding the ownership of land contained propositions opposed to the Church's teaching and advised that the clergy abstain from political disputes.[37] Shortly afterwards a second epistle arrived from Propaganda communicating the pope's order to suspend McGlynn from his ministry unless McCloskey judged otherwise. Other prelates such as Silas Chatard of Vincennes and William Henry Elder of Cincinnati were urging McCloskey to take action against McGlynn. McCloskey did drop McGlynn without explanation from a key diocesan committee but declined to impose any further sanctions upon him after McGlynn promised to abstain from future political gatherings.[38]

When McCloskey died in 1885, Corrigan as his successor came to be

35. AANY C-10, Nilan to Corrigan, Poughkeepsie, September 20, 1883.
36. Stephen Bell, *Rebel, Priest and Prophet: A Biography of Dr. Edward McGlynn* (New York, 1937), pp. 26–27. By a fortuitous coincidence, Henry George's *Progress and Poverty* was published in the very year that the Land League was formed. The Land League was the result of the movement known as the "New Departure" that brought together the Home Rule forces of Charles Stewart Parnell, the Irish proponents of social reform led by Michael Davitt, and the American Fenians under John Devoy. George's indictment of the land monopoly as the primary source of economic inequity had an enormous impact upon Irish-American reformers both here and in Ireland (Cf. Thomas N. Brown, *Irish-American Nationalism, 1870–1890* [Philadelphia & New York, 1966].
37. AANY 1-41, Simeoni to Corrigan, Rome, August 9, 1882, Italian. Propaganda was sending similar directives concerning clergy political abstinence to the Irish hierarchy during this summer.
38. McGlynn later claimed that he had voluntarily promised to refrain from making Land League speeches "not because I acknowledge the right of any one to forbid me, but because I knew too well the power of my ecclesiastical superiors to impair and almost destroy my usefulness in the ministry of Christ's Church . . ." (New York *Daily Tribune,* February 4, 1887).

very much under the influence of those who were continuing to smell heterodoxy in the actions and motivations of McGlynn and his clerical associates. Corrigan's vicars general, Thomas Preston and Arthur Donnelly, and the former president of the first Accademia, Henry Brann, were three hard liners who most shaped Corrigan's response to McGlynn's support of Henry George during the mayoralty campaign of 1886 and the sequence of events that extended the controversy for the next eight years. The memories of the radicalism associated with the Accademia continued to color the interpretations that the archbishop and his advisors put upon the position of the clerical dissidents during the controversy. Corrigan, for instance, informed Cardinal Simeoni in November 1886 that McGlynn was persisting in preaching doctrines that were against Catholic teaching. He accused him of denigrating the pope and expounding the heresy that ministry "is not from the bishop but derives its power from the laity," an impudent attempt, Corrigan thought, to democratize "sacred cult in the church," and to substitute George for Leo XIII as the "pontiff of a democratic church without dominion or tiara."[39] In another letter to Simeoni he claimed that McGlynn was denying the principle of *ex opere operato* in contending that the sacraments were valueless without the presence of love.[40]

175

When McGlynn issued a public statement denouncing the right of "Bishop, Propaganda, or Pope" to prevent him from exercising his civil rights as an American citizen, Corrigan concluded that "the poison of anti-Catholic opinions," which McGlynn had long cultivated in private, was now being spread openly.[41] In McGlynn's refusal to respond to the pope's summons to come to Rome in the spring of 1887 Corrigan found the heresy of denying the primacy of the pope in matters that pertain not only to faith and morals but also to the discipline and government of the Church throughout the world. Significantly, the archbishop on his visitations throughout the archdiocese that spring, instructed congregations on this article of faith that Vatican I had declared.[42]

39. AANY, unclassified, [Corrigan] to [Simeoni], New York, November 24, 1886, draft.
40. AANY, unclassified, Corrigan to Simeoni, March 18, 1887, draft. The basis of Corrigan's charge was a letter which McGlynn had written to a Protestant minister at the time of Henry Ward Beecher's death. In his letter McGlynn had stated: "I am glad . . . that the theology of the old church agrees with his [Beecher's] in this, that the essence of religion is in communion with God through the love of Him for His own sake, and in loving all men for God's sake with the best love with which we love ourselves; and that while sacrifice and sacrament, creed and ritual prayer and sermon and song, may be and are powerful helps and necessary manipulations of this religion, which is love; without it they are a mockery, a sacrilege and a blasphemy . . ." (New York *Daily Tribune*, March 14, 1887).
41. AANY, unclassified, Corrigan to Preston, Nassau, February 11, 1887.
42. The definition of the Vatican Council that the archbishop was citing against McGlynn read in part: "If anyone therefore says that the Roman Pontiff has only the office of inspection or direction, but not the full and supreme power of jurisdiction over the

The excommunication of McGlynn in July 1887 for his failure to heed
the pope's order only seemed to increase the threat of schism and made
it all the more imperative to discipline the clerical friends of McGlynn
who were maintaining contact with him and absolving Catholics who attended the weekly meetings of his Anti-Poverty society to listen to
McGlynn's diatribes against "the ecclesiastical machine." In early 1888
Corrigan obtained instructions from Propaganda to impose silence upon
McGlynn's clerical colleagues, forbidding them to advocate or discuss
the theories of George or take part in the Anti-Poverty meetings. None
of the other former members of the Accademia were promoting Geor-
gian theories but they persisted in asserting that McGlynn had been
condemned without the due process guaranteed by canon law for economic doctrines on which the Church had made no pronouncement.

The chancery pressured the clerical friends of McGlynn in various
ways, one of which was to threaten to examine the finances of their
parishes. As early as October 1887 Corrigan had instructed his fiscal
procurator to call Burtsell and Nilan to his court, presumably to examine
their account books, "unless they can explain away their objectionable
utterances on the Land Theory."[43] Another tactic was to eliminate them
from key diocesan positions. Thus in November 1889 Burtsell was
dropped as a synodal examiner, Nilan was removed from the school
board, and McSweeny was discontinued as a diocesan consultor.
Transferral of priests to upstate parishes ("The brains of the diocese are

whole Church, not only in matters that pertain to faith and morals, but also in matters
that pertain to the discipline and government of the Church throughout the whole
world . . . or if anyone says that this power is not ordinary and immediate either over
each and every church or over each and every shepherd and faithful member, let him
be anathema" (Constitutio de Ecclesia Christi, Sessio 4, Conc. Vaticanum 1869–1870,
in Henricus Denziger, *Enchiridion Symbolorum Definitinum et Declarationum, De Rebus
Fidei et Morum* [Karl Rahner, ed., Freiburg, 1955], p. 505.

43. Archives of the Diocese of Rochester (hereafter ADR), Corrigan to Bernard McQuaid,
New York, October 4, 1888. For some reason this instruction was not carried out but
another McGlynn supporter, Thomas Ducey, the pastor of St. Leo's on Twenty-Eighth
Street, was subsequently ordered to turn over his books for examination. When the
examination revealed a deficit of some forty thousand dollars a year, the diocesan consultors began to consider several options, including the removal of Ducey from St.
Leo's and/or the closing of the parish. That the concern was not merely financial,
however, is clearly evident in the minutes of the diocesan consultors for November 5,
1890, when they decided to defer action until they could study Ducey's next sermon
(AANY C-18, Corrigan to Ducey, New York, January 31, 1888; ibid., same to
same, New York, April 5, 1889, copy; AANY, unclassified, Minutes of Meeting of Diocesan Consultors, Wednesday, November 5, 1890.
The financial condition of St. Stephen's was also one of the reasons given by Corrigan to Propaganda for removing McGlynn as pastor in January 1887. In 1886 St.
Stephen's showed an indebtedness of $154,464.54. Even McGlynn's friends admitted
he was a poor administrator but he had reduced his church's debt by more than $142,-
000 during his last four years as pastor (AANY, Financial Report of St. Stephen's
Church, 1886).

up the Hudson" became a common saying during the period), as well as a refusal to promote any priests who were sympathetic to McGlynn, were other sanctions that the chancery exercised.[44]

Since none of these measures successfully stifled the McGlynn controversy, Richard Burtsell drew increasing attention from archdiocesan officials as the major cause of the continuing dissent among the clergy. Burtsell was no McGlynn. He did not support the land theories of George or the Anti-Poverty Society. He was not going to take to the hustings to harangue "the ecclesiastical machine" nor was he about to lead a schism. The lesson of the *Excelsius* experience was not second nature to him. But he was deeply respected at home and in Rome for his understanding of Church law and, in a way, this made him a special menace to episcopal authority. Burtsell was continually a goad as a canonist much in demand to defend priests in their contests with ordinaries across the country. His advocacy of priests' rights was making him a threat to episcopal authority far beyond New York. His book on *The Canonical Status of Priests* published in December 1887 had enhanced his influence.[45] Two months later he was a key witness in a suit brought against the trustees of Calvary Cemetery for refusing burial to a man who had died suddenly at an Anti-Poverty meeting, and contended that since the archbishop had issued no regulation forbidding Catholics from attending the meetings, he could hardly deny Christian burial to someone who in good faith had gone to hear McGlynn. The Church recognized, Burtsell maintained under questioning, that people could disobey out of good conscience.[46]

Chancery officials were sure that to allow Burtsell and his fellows to continue to preach about the rights of conscience of Anti-Poverty people

177

44. From the available evidence it is clear that at least six assistants were moved for their support of McGlynn. Chancery officials obviously regarded three parishes as strategic centers of McGlynnites among the clergy: St. Stephen's, Epiphany (Burtsell's church) and St. Leo's. Thus James Curran, John Barry, Thomas McLoughlin, and P. F. Maughan were transferred from St. Stephen's, John Power from the Epiphany, and Daniel Burke from St. Leo's.

45. "The whole tendency of the book is . . . calculated to do harm," Corrigan wrote his secretary, Charles McDonnell. What especially bothered the archbishop was a note inside the cover requesting recipients to send one dollar to a New York address for the creation of a fund which would be employed "for the defense of priests unjustly deprived of their ecclesiastical positions." The archbishop ordered Burtsell to withdraw it from publication since he had not gotten his approval, but Burtsell claimed that he had not suspected that Corrigan would impose the normal regulations on a pamphlet that had already appeared in a Catholic newspaper (as a series of articles in the New York *Tablet* in the spring of 1887), had been privately printed, and was not for public sale (AANY C-18, Corrigan to McDonnell, New York, December 15, 1887, copy; ibid., Corrigan to Burtsell, New York, December 14, 1887, copy; AANY, Diary, VI, December 16, 1887).

46. AANY, unclassified, Court Record, Philip McGuire vs. Trustees of St. Patrick's Cathedral, November 15, 1888, copy.

would destroy ecclesiastical government in New York. When the archbishop subsequently made attendance at the meetings a case which priests had to refer to the chancery, Burtsell was finally forced to take a stand in the matter. In October 1889 he buried with full honors of the Church a woman parishioner who had been a regular attendant at the Anti-Poverty meetings.

Corrigan, convinced by now that Burtsell was "the backbone of the rebellion," transferred him to a parish in upstate New York[47] and Burtsell thereupon appealed to Propaganda, as was his right as an alumnus.[48] Corrigan defended the necessity for removing Burtsell in an extrajudicial manner rather than going through the normal channels of censuring him for his disobedience. The experience of the McGlynn case was evidence enough for the archbishop that any outright attempt to suspend Burtsell would have renewed the turmoil and mass protest that McGlynn's suspension and removal had first ignited.[49]

Thomas Preston was confident that Rome would sustain Corrigan once more but he was taking no chances. In early January 1890 he laid out to a Vatican official what was at stake in the Burtsell case. It was a question, he said

> of a few priests who are really disloyal to the Holy See. They minimize all the declarations of His Holiness. They were opposed to the Infallibility until its definition, and now are disposed to make it as little as possible consistent with a profession of faith. They are opposed to parochial schools. . . . They have spoken in favor of saying Mass in the English language, of doing away with the vestments and ceremonies prescribed by the church, of getting rid of what they call medieval customs and obsolete practices, and of Americanizing the Catholic Church here, and adapting it to our liberal and republican institutions.[50]

Burtsell was unable to prevent his own transfer but Francisco Satolli, the apostolic delegate sent to America by Leo XIII in the fall of 1892, re-

47. AANY C-18, Corrigan to Ella Edes, New York, Oct. 29, 1889, copy.

48. In his *Canonical Status of Priests in the United States* Burtsell admitted that ordinary rectors like himself were removable at the will of the bishop but "natural equity and the Plenary Councils and the Propaganda," he argued, "have interpreted that this 'will' must be determined by serious motives and be guided by anxious care to save the good name of any one affected by the removal." Since his removal as rector of the Epiphany would inevitably be interpreted as a punishment for some "serious wrongdoing," Burtsell contended that he had the right to a trial to preserve his reputation. Corrigan took shelter in the March 1887 declaration of Propaganda that American bishops were not bound to follow the canonical procedure, so long as there was "serious reason for such action, and full account taken of the past merits . . ." (*Canonical Status*, 46, 101; AANY C-18, Burtsell to Corrigan, New York, December 16th, 1889; ADR, Simeoni to Gibbons, Rome, May 20, 1887, Latin, printed copy; AANY C-18, Corrigan to Burtsell, New York, Dec. 17, 1889; ibid., same to same, New York, December 21, 1889, copy).

49. AANY, unclassified, *Relatio Translationis Statutae Quidem, Sed Nondum Peractae, Doctoris Richardi L. Burtsell, Rectoris Amovibilis Ad Nutum Ab Ecclesia Epiphaniae Ad Ecclesiam Sanctae Mariae, Et Ejusdem Doctoris Recursus ad Superiorem* (1890).

50. AANY S-1, Preston to Archbishop Domenico Jacobini, New York, Jan. 2, 1890, copy.

vived the hopes of the old radicals for the Americanization of the Church, especially when clerical dissidents, including McGlynn, found him an effective court of appeal against their ordinaries. When Satolli lifted the excommunication against McGlynn shortly before Christmas of 1892 the New York *Tribune* found that it meant that American Catholicism was finally "adjusting to the free institutions of the country." Hereafter, it predicted, "the priests of the Church will enjoy a freedom of utterance and action that in many cases has heretofore been denied them, and the whole Church will grow into closer touch with American life and institutions. The ultra-montane type of Churchmanship in this country has received a serious blow from which it may never recover."[51]

It was poor prophecy, for the McGlynn restoration was to be the highwater mark for the dissidents in New York and elsewhere. Archbishop Corrigan's exploitation of divisions within the Roman curia was to be instrumental in ending the alliance between the American liberals and the apostolic delegate.[52] Richard Burtsell experienced at firsthand the changing climate in Rome toward the American liberals in the fall and winter of 1893–1894. After being kept waiting for nearly eight months while trying to obtain a hearing for himself and a parish for McGlynn, he came away with nothing more than some advice from a Vatican official that Americans like himself were wasting their time in trying to "bring Republicanism into the Church."[53]

By the 1890s Burtsell, McGlynn, and Hecker had come to be largely pawns of a new movement toward liberalism which derived its leadership from the hierarchy itself, notably Archbishop John Ireland of St. Paul and Bishop John Keane of the Catholic University of America. Ireland and Keane's attempt to intervene with Vatican officials regarding the McGlynn case in 1886 had been one of the first skirmishes in the ideological struggle that was dividing the American hierarchy into liberal and conservative camps in the last decade of the century. Already in 1890 Corrigan was warning Rome of the "ultra-Americanism" of the liberal party that he saw Ireland and other prelates forming. To Corrigan, Preston, and their conservative allies, the Americanist movement of Ireland and the liberal prelates was the natural outgrowth of the clerical radicalism that had first manifested itself in the sixties.

The relationship of the Accademians to the Americanists is an intriguing one. Sylvester Malone was a close friend of John Ireland, although how much the latter knew of the Accademia is uncertain. Beginning in 1887 Richard Burtsell had regular contact with the Americanist prelates.

179

---

51. *Tribune*, December 25, 1892.
52. For an analysis of this strategy see R. Emmett Curran, S. J., *Michael Augustine Corrigan and the Shaping of Conservative Catholicism in America, 1878–1902* (diss., New York, 1978), pp. 422–427.
53. AANY, Diary, 9, May 5, 1894.

The two groups took basically similar stands regarding secret societies, the rapid Americanization of immigrants, and parochial schools. It is significant that John Ireland adopted James Nilan's Poughkeepsie Plan as the model for his own controversial school arrangements in Minnesota in 1891. Both groups tended to downgrade the relevance of religious orders in a democratic society. They both were pressing for some form of democratization in the church, to enable it to internalize the values of individual initative and freedom that they saw as the hallmarks of American life. While the Americanists restricted their reform aims largely to church polity, the Accademians were raising some basic doctrinal questions that foreshadowed the Modernist crisis in Europe a few years after the Americanist controversy. Changes in the discipline and liturgical life of the Church were also questions that went beyond the concerns of most Americanists although Denis O'Connell's proposal of substituting the common law as a much more appropriate basis than Roman law for the law of the Church had implications for the reform of ecclesiastical discipline that would have been much more radical than the demand of the Accademians for the full institution of canon law in this country.[54]

Both groups favored the Republican Party but by the 1890s the GOP had shed any radical idealism that had attracted the Accademians. It now stood unequivocally for the new capitalism that Ireland thought to be the foundation for the success of American democracy.

Both the Accademians and the Americanists accepted the separation of Church and State as the ideal environment in which the Church could grow in America. An inference of the liberal program as developed by Ireland was that the American Church under liberal leadership would obtain a favored position because of the liberals' ties with the Republicans, and Americanists successfully used this theme in certain Vatican circles in the early nineties to win papal support for their claims to serve as brokers between Washington and Rome. Such posturing was alien to the concept of Church and State that the Accademians were developing in the 1860s. The Americanists, moreover, went much further than the Accademians in touting the American experience as a paradigm for the rest of the world including the Church universal. Just as the American triumph over Spain in 1898 signaled to Americanists like O'Connell that the axis of civilization was providentially passing from Europe to America, so too were they confident that the American Church was to be the fulcrum for the Roman Catholicism of the twentieth century. The Americanists unmistakably manifest a cultural imperialism that makes

54. Cf. Gerald P. Fogarty, S. J., *The Vatican and the Americanist Crisis: Denis J. O'Connell, American Agent in Rome, 1885–1903* (Rome, 1973), pp. 263–265.

Testem Benevolentiae, Leo XIII's encyclical condemning Americanism in 1899, seem a mixed blessing.

No doubt the euphoria of the Spanish-American War accounts for some of the jingoism of O'Connell and Keane in the late nineties but they seem never to have ingested Isaac Hecker's more Christian vision of cultural pluralism. Hecker wrote in 1867:

> The mistake is that people are too ready to make a religion of their politics, and to seek to make the system of government they happen to be enamored of . . . a universal system, and to look upon all nations that do not accept it, or are not blessed with it, as deprived of the advantages of civil society. They make their system the standard by which all institutions, all men and nations, are to be tried. . . . Our government is best for us, but that does not prove that in political matters we are wiser or better than other civilized nations, or that we have the right to set ourselves up as the model nation of the world.[55]

With *Testem Benevolentiae* the liberal prelates got the same message that Burtsell had received in Rome in 1894, and they quietly abandoned their movement. Despite this setback the first years of the new century saw an intellectual fermentation in the Catholic University and several seminaries that promised to renew the spirit of theological openness and investigation that had marked the Accademia. The outstanding forum for this renewal was appropriately enough the *New York Review* which began in 1905 at St. Joseph's Seminary in Yonkers under the spirited sponsorship of Archbishop John Farley, Corrigan's successor. But the suspicion that set in after the condemnation of Modernism in 1907 ended the *Review* and ensured another fifty years of ideological sediment. When the juices finally came to a boil in the 1960s, one could often get the distinct aroma of a century old brew.

55. Hecker, "Church and Monarchy," 639.

THE MCGLYNN AFFAIR AND THE SHAPING OF THE NEW CONSERVATISM IN AMERICAN CATHOLICISM, 1886-1894

BY

ROBERT EMMETT CURRAN, S.J.*

On a Saturday night in June, 1887, an estimated 75,000 people marched in the streets of New York in protest of Edward McGlynn's suspension from his priestly ministry for his support of Henry George. A week later George was telling the thousands who packed the Academy of Music that the mass demonstrations taking place in New York, Chicago, and elsewhere were a resounding message to Michael A. Corrigan, Archbishop of New York, and his backers that they could not isolate McGlynn by the threat of excommunication.[1] Another McGlynn partisan noted: "I think they will have to excommunicate one or two besides Dr. McGlynn; they will have to excommunicate some millions of American Catholics."[2] Recalling those days of protest in his autobiography, Maurice Francis Egan, who had been editor of the New York *Freeman's Journal and Catholic Register* in 1887, described the atmosphere of the city as one of a society reduced to near anarchy with "all the furies let loose."[3]

The controversy between Edward McGlynn and Archbishop Corrigan constitutes one of the most significant cases of dissent within the American Catholic community of the late nineteenth century. Its full significance, however, has not been closely examined within the tapestry of issues that increasingly polarized the Church after the Third Plenary Council of Baltimore in 1884. For the struggle between the Corriganites and the McGlynnites far transcended the economic

---

* Father Curran is an associate professor of history and chairman of the Department of History in Georgetown University.

[1] New York *Herald*, June 27, 1887.

[2] *Herald*, July 4, 1887.

[3] *Recollections of a Happy Life* (New York, 1924), p. 133. A substantial body of literature exists on the McGlynn affair. Stephen Bell's *Rebel, Priest and Prophet: A Biography of Dr. Edward McGlynn* (New York, 1937), is useful but the author's limited sources (mainly newspaper accounts and interviews) enable him to tell little of the

theory of Henry George or socialism or the civil rights of American Catholic priests. What made the McGlynn affair so extraordinary, and gave it such staying power as a controversy, was the number of key issues that made up the sum of its parts. It touched upon, among other things, social reform, Irish nationalism, parochial schools, the relationship between Church and State, and the polity and identity of American Catholicism. Among the factors that began to divide liberal and conservative Catholics in the late 1880's, none was as important as the McGlynn affair in setting in motion the synergistic effects that recast American Catholicism by the end of the century.

Edward McGlynn in 1886 was pastor of St. Stephen's Church on East 28th Street between Lexington and Third Avenues, the largest and one of the most prestigious parishes in the city. As an activist who for twenty years had been working for social reform, McGlynn was extremely popular among both Catholics and Protestants. His parish operations, the largest of which was the St. Stephen's Home for over 500 children, were a forerunner of the methods of the institutional churches that would be the major instrument of the Social Gospel movement later in the century. Intelligent as well as indefatigable, McGlynn's forte was on the speaking platform in the best tradition of revivalism before it parted ways with social reform. He was one of the most charismatic speakers of his day.

183

In 1882 McGlynn had begun preaching the gospel of Henry George

---

internal history of the case. James Roohan makes an illuminating study of McGlynn's relation to the development of Catholic attitudes on social reform in his dissertation written at Yale University in 1952, *American Catholics and the Social Question, 1865-1900* (New York, 1976), pp. 332-383. James Jeremiah Green's "The Impact of Henry George's Theories on American Catholics" (unpublished dissertation, Notre Dame, 1956) is a related treatment of McGlynn's connection with George. Two extensive accounts of the affair are in John Tracy Ellis, *The Life of James Cardinal Gibbons, 1834-1921* (2 vols.; Milwaukee, 1952), I, 549-628, and Frederick J. Zwierlein, *The Life and Letters of Bishop McQuaid, prefaced with The History of Catholic Rochester Before His Episcopate* (3 vols.; Rochester, 1927), III, 1-83. For the campaign of 1886 see particularly Charles Barker, *Henry George* (New York, 1955). For McGlynn's relationship with the radical Irish nationalists, see Thomas N. Brown, *Irish-American Nationalism, 1870-1890* (Philadelphia & New York, 1966), pp. 133-151. None of the above pursues the developments beyond 1892. A wealth of relevant source-material is contained in an unsigned, typed document under the title "The Private Record of the Case of Rev. Edward J. McGlynn," a 1901 manuscript in the archives of the Archdiocese of New York. This article utilizes much of the latter material as does also my book, *Michael Augustine Corrigan and the Shaping of Conservative Catholicism in America, 1878-1902* (New York, 1978).

for the radical Irish nationalists in New York. George's indictment of the land monopoly as the primary source of economic inequity had an enormous impact upon Irish reformers both in America and in Ireland in the 1880's. The Holy See, at the same time, was in the delicate process of trying to re-establish diplomatic relations with England. Even though Rome was unwilling, as a *quid pro quo* for renewed relations, to condemn the Land League's efforts to secure land reform in Ireland, at the very least it did not want priests promoting the movement, especially those whose politics were as socialistic as McGlynn's seemed.[4] Cardinal Giovanni Simeoni, Prefect of the Congregation for the Propagation of the Faith (Propaganda), accordingly instructed Archbishop Corrigan, at that time coadjutor to Cardinal John McCloskey, that certain statements attributed to McGlynn "contained propositions openly opposed to the teachings of the Catholic Church." Simeoni directed that McGlynn abandon his political activities.[5] McCloskey reluctantly rebuked the priest for his "socialistic" addresses and McGlynn promised to abstain from all future political gatherings.[6]

184

Within a short time McGlynn drifted back to the political circuit, but the plenary council of 1884 was absorbing too much of the energy of his ecclesiastical superiors for them to pay much attention to him. By the summer of 1886 he was fully involved in Henry George's campaign for mayor of New York.

The political atmosphere was especially tense, 1886 marking the height of the second of three social earthquakes that shook the country to its core in the last quarter of the century. As in 1877, railroad strikes had swept across the country often leaving a wake of violence and fears of class warfare. By 1886 the meteoric rise of the Knights of

---

[4] Archives of the Archdiocese of New York (hereafter AANY) C-3, Bishop Herbert Vaughan to Corrigan, Salford, December 17, 1881; *ibid.*, same to same, Salford, February 2, 1882. See Emmet Larkin, *The Roman Catholic Church and the Creation of the Modern Irish State: 1878-1886* (Philadelphia, 1975).

[5] AANY I-41, Simeoni to Corrigan, Rome, August 9, 1882, Italian. Propaganda was sending similar directives concerning political abstinence for the clergy to the Irish hierarchy during this summer.

Bernard Smith, an Irish Benedictine in Rome, who was an agent for Archbishop Corrigan, was also the contact for Irish Catholic Whigs who were attempting to secure papal condemnation of the Land League in exchange for diplomatic relations with England. It is likely that Smith was using his influence with Simeoni. See Larkin, *op. cit.*, pp. 59-60.

[6] Archives of the Archdiocese of Cincinnati, Corrigan to Archbishop William Henry Elder, New York, September 18, 1882.

Labor through a series of successful strikes gave substance to the fears. The mayoralty campaign of George was bringing together in an explosive mix the various elements of Irish nationalism, the labor movement, and socialism. Patrick Ford gave George the support of the *Irish World* and toured the tenement districts with him. Terrence V. Powderly, the Knights' Grand Master Workman, came into the city to make speeches in George's behalf. Daniel DeLeon, the radical socialist at Columbia University, as well as Walter Rauschenbusch and Heber Newton, the liberal Protestant reformers, were in his camp. But none was more a key to his success than McGlynn.

When one considers the tenuous balance of power that prevailed between the two national parties in the middle 1880's and the vital position that New York City occupied in that equilibrium, it becomes clear what a threat the George campaign represented to Tammany Hall and the Democratic Party. The source of Democratic power in New York was the vote of the Irish-Americans. In 1886 they most likely already constituted a majority of the population.[7] Reformers and Irish nationalists had for years been trying in vain to wean the Irish from their loyalty to Tammany and the Democrats. McGlynn was an ideal nurse for the weaning. A longtime Republican, his credentials of concern for the poor and the Irish were impeccable, his standing in those communities was unequalled by that of any other Catholic spokesman in New York. His effectiveness in promoting George in the fall of 1886 brought a letter from a Tammany leader to Corrigan's vicar-general, Monsignor Thomas Preston, seeking confirmation that the Catholic Church in New York was not endorsing George's candidacy. Preston obliged by declaring that "the great majority of the Catholic clergy in this city are opposed to the candidacy of Mr. George."[8]

Understandably Tammany made full use of Preston's condemnation of George in trying to offset McGlynn's inroads upon their traditional constituency. Who benefited the most from this ploy is a moot point since some Catholics apparently voted for George in reaction to the chancery's heavy-handed attack upon McGlynn. The Tammany candidate prevailed in the election but George's remarkably strong

185

---

[7] The census of 1890 lists 190,000 Irish-born New York inhabitants out of a total population of 1,489,000. Another 409,000 were second-generation Irish. Beyond these were a considerable number of third- and fourth-generation Irish not identified in the report (William V. Shannon, *The American Irish* [New York, 1966], p. 760).

[8] Preston to J. O'Donoghue, New York, October 26, 1886, cited in Zwierlein, *op. cit.*, III, 6-7, quoting the *Rochester Union and Advertiser*, October 29, 1886.

showing convinced many that McGlynn's influence had been a major factor.[9] Reports later circulated that several Catholic laymen with connections to Tammany were responsible for Corrigan's suspension of McGlynn during the campaign. Bourke Cockran, Tammany's leading orator of the day, boasted that he had convinced the archbishop of the danger of George's candidacy.[10] The New York *World* in 1894 specifically named several prominent. Democrats as having asked Corrigan to suspend McGlynn. That some or all of these individuals complained to Corrigan of McGlynn's actions seems certain. Corrigan later denied that any of these individuals had asked him to suspend McGlynn and there are extant letters that support his denial.[11]

186

Although the archbishop rightly resented the charge that he was in Tammany's keep, he did have close ties with several Tammany figures and was well aware of the local Democrats' longtime support of state aid for Catholic charitable institutions. Corrigan's own background and status predisposed him to have little understanding of the labor movement and of reformers. William Shannon in his study of the American Irish has observed that the Catholic hierarchy in New York has tended to be extremely conservative primarily because of the accidents of personality. But he suggests that another important cause was the fact that the Irish first captured political power in New York and built up a substantial group of upper middle-class property owners. Corrigan's world was really limited to this class. His own father was a perfect illustration for Russell Conwell's thesis that the resourceful could mine "acres of diamonds" in their backyards. Thanks to his father, the archbishop himself was now a man of considerable wealth. He could appreciate the concerns of men of substance about the need to conserve the fabric of society from the attacks of socialists and liberals. He was particularly sensitive to their concerns as contributors to the many churches, schools, and other institutions which the Church was racing to put up in New York to keep pace with a Catholic population that was swelling each year from immigration and a large birth rate. In a year of labor uprisings and fears of impending class warfare he shared the alarm of many

[9] George polled at least 68,000 votes against the regular Democrat, Abraham Hewitt. Many had serious doubts about the honesty of the vote.

[10] Bell, *op. cit.*, p. 35.

[11] AANY, unclassified, Corrigan Memoranda, 1895; AANY G-12, John Crimmins to Corrigan, New York, January 25, 1895; *ibid,* Joseph Daley to Corrigan, New York, January 7, 1895.

conservatives over McGlynn's support of apparently socialistic reform methods.

Thus Corrigan needed no prodding from the Democratic machine to take action against McGlynn. He had begun to pressure the priest to desist from his support of George even before the latter's formal nomination on September 23. On August 21 in a letter to McGlynn, the archbishop expressed his uneasiness about the newspapers' reports of the priest's relations with George and urged him to "leave aside anything that . . . would *seem* even to coincide with socialism."[12] When he learned that McGlynn was to address a mass rally at Chickering Hall on October 1, he forbade him to take part in future political meetings without permission from Propaganda.[13] McGlynn promised to sit out any further political campaigning, but he felt obligated to fulfill his commitment at Chickering Hall that evening.[14] There McGlynn proceeded to anoint George as "the most unselfish man of this country, formed by providence to preach the new gospel."[15] The next day Corrigan privately suspended McGlynn from his priestly duties for two weeks for "so flagrant an act of disobedience," noting that the censure had "nothing whatever to do with this or that political party, but is founded on the instructions of the Holy See, and the nature of Episcopal authority and sacerdotal obedience."[16]

The archbishop had already written to Rome about McGlynn's latest political activities. When Corrigan resuspended McGlynn in late November for a newspaper interview in which the priest urged people to read *Progress and Poverty*, he informed Cardinal Simeoni that McGlynn was persisting in preaching doctrines that were both against Catholic teaching and unacceptable to the vast majority of the American people. Corrigan accused McGlynn of denigrating the pope and expounding the heresy that "ministry is not from the bishop but

[12] Corrigan to McGlynn, New York, August 21, 1886, printed in the New York *Daily Tribune*, February 4, 1887.

[13] AANY, unclassified, Corrigan to McGlynn, New York, September 29, 1886, copy. Ironically the archbishop had not hesitated to use McGlynn's political influence six months previously when he asked him to intercede with President Cleveland on behalf of General John Newton who was seeking a promotion (AANY C-10, McGlynn to Corrigan, New York, March 11, 1886).

[14] AANY C-10, McGlynn to Corrigan, New York, October 1, 1886.

[15] AANY, Burtsell Diary, VI, October 1, 1886.

[16] AANY, unclassified, Corrigan to McGlynn, New York, October 2, 1886. The suspension itself did not become a public issue until after the election.

187

derives all its power from the laity."[17] The increasing attention the press gave to McGlynn led Corrigan to cable Rome at the beginning of December for some prompt action.[18] On December 4 the cardinal prefect of Propaganda cabled Corrigan to have McGlynn proceed immediately to Rome. In January the pope himself issued the same order and took personal charge of the case.[19]

McGlynn maintained that he was unable to go to Rome for three reasons: his poor health, his slender financial resources, and family obligations. Furthermore, he adamantly insisted to the archbishop that he would continue to teach "as long as I live, that . . . private ownership of land is against natural justice, no matter by what civil or ecclesiastical laws it may be sanctioned," and that he would, if given the chance, confiscate all private property in land "without one penny of compensation to the mis-called owners."[20] He denied the right of anyone, "Bishop, Propaganda or Pope," to punish him for opinions in political economy which had not been condemned by the Church.[21]

In May, 1887, Leo approved Archbishop Corrigan's attempt to "crush the vicious seeds of doctrines, scattered under the pretext of helping the masses," and ordered McGlynn to repair to Rome within forty days under pain of excommunication.[22] McGlynn pleaded conscience over obedience and was excommunicated in July.

To grasp the full impact of the McGlynn affair, one must appreciate the extent to which it developed out of a background of growing fear among a sizable portion of American bishops and priests of the mounting liberalism within the American Church. Since the late 1870's a conservative bloc had been forming in reaction to Roman legislation advancing priests' rights and abetting the incipient liberalism among the clergy that was threatening to undermine episcopal authority.[23] Prelates like Bernard McQuaid of Rochester and

[17] AANY, unclassified, [Corrigan] to [Simeoni], New York, November 24, 1886, draft.

[18] AANY, unclassified, Corrigan to Simeoni, New York, December 24, 1886, abstract.

[19] AANY L-3, "Private Record," 21.

[20] AANY C-10, McGlynn to Corrigan, New York, December 20, 1886.

[21] New York *Daily Tribune*, February 4, 1887.

[22] AANY H-5, Leo XIII to Corrigan, May 4, 1887, duplicate; *ibid.,* Simeoni to McGlynn, Rome, May 4, 1887, copy.

[23] For an excellent treatment of the impact of this legislation, see Robert Trisco, "Bishops and Their Priests in the United States," in John Tracy Ellis (ed.), *The Catho-*

Richard Gilmour of Cleveland began to press for concerted action
within the hierarchy that would utilize Rome to bring about uniformity under a strong episcopacy within the Church in America
while maintaining a certain independence from Rome. The question
of priests' rights, they were convinced, was merely a symptom of
more deeply rooted dissent. For the past twenty-five years they had
experienced groups of priests fomenting unrest against the established
order and allegedly questioning everything from celibacy to the inspiration of the Scriptures.

Edward McGlynn had long been one of the most celebrated dissidents. He was the outstanding member of a group of New York
priests who had become notorious for their radical ideas regarding
politics, theology, and the Americanization of the Church.[24] As early
as 1867 McGlynn was publicly proclaiming that the Church in
America had to be radically different from what it had been in the
Old World. In 1870 he created his first sensation by attacking all
public aid to religious institutions as a violation of the separation of
Church and State and by insisting that the Church was misdirecting
its energies in trying to build and maintain schools.[25] Four years later
the Cardinal Prefect of Propaganda, Alessandro Barnabò, warned
him about "the ultra liberal ideas" he was espousing.[26]

In 1882 McGlynn had defied the warning of chancery officials in
Cleveland not to speak to an Irish-American group there, the Parnell
Branch of the Land League, whose women members had incurred
Bishop Gilmour's excommunication for promoting revolutionary poli-

189

---

lic Priest in the United States: Historical Investigations (Collegeville, Minnesota,
1971), pp. 194-292.

[24] This ecclesiastical society or Accademia, as the group was known in the New
York chancery, thrived as an informal association in the late 1860's. Its regular members, besides McGlynn, were Thomas Farrell, Sylvester Malone, James Nilan, Thomas
McLoughlin, and Richard Burtsell. Several Paulists, including Isaac Hecker, were occasional participants. The group generally favored liberal causes including Fenianism,
Radical Reconstruction, optional celibacy for the clergy, the use of the vernacular in
the liturgy, the infallibility of the Church rather than of the pope, and polygenism. For
an account of the Accademia see Robert Emmett Curran, S. J., "Prelude to Americanism: The New York Accademia and Clerical Radicalism in the Late Nineteenth
Century," Church History, XLVII (March, 1978), 48-65. See also Nelson J. Callahan
(ed.), The Diary of Richard L. Burtsell, Priest of New York (New York, 1978), for the
1865-1868 period.

[25] AANY, unclassified, Report of Thomas F. Lynch (n.d.).

[26] Ibid. This is cited in a letter from Corrigan to Cardinal Giovanni Simeoni of
October 12, 1888, draft.

tics. When Cardinal McCloskey was unwilling to order McGlynn to refrain from going to Cleveland, several bishops had seen signs of an impending authority crisis. As William Elder of Cincinnati wrote Michael Corrigan, ". . . if this act of Dr. McGlynn's should pass without adequate reparation, it would be the most disastrous blow to discipline, and to faith itself. . . ." He urged Corrigan to persuade the cardinal to take appropriate action before McGlynn's "poison" had sunk further into the "minds and hearts of the people, perplexing and perverting their ideas of justice, property, of deference for the Church."[27] Cardinal McCloskey, as noted above, eventually reprimanded McGlynn for his "various Communistic addresses," but took no further action after McGlynn promised to discontinue his political activity.

190

With the crisis of 1886 McGlynn was raising those fundamental questions that Elder feared regarding the rights of individual conscience and the limits of ecclesiastical authority over American Catholics, whether clerical or lay. Significantly much of McGlynn's persistent support in his Anti-Poverty Society came not from the working class but from middle-class Catholics, including a disproportionate number of women.[28]

When Archbishop Corrigan sought the advice of his consultors in December, 1886, toward transferring McGlynn from St. Stephen's because of his persistent insubordination, the archbishop contended that he was the heir of a problem which Cardinal McCloskey should have dealt with long before. Monsignor Preston added that the land issue was hardly the only charge against McGlynn. He had refused to build a parish school despite the decree of the last plenary council. He was considered too lax in allowing people to receive communion too frequently and without previous confession. Another consultor maintained that McGlynn claimed that as a Propagandist (one who had studied at the Urban College of Propaganda in Rome), he did not owe obedience to the archbishop. "Dr. McGlynn must be put down," he concluded, "or the Archbishop of New York might as well not be the

    [27] AANY C-2, Elder to Corrigan, Cincinnati, August 20, 1882; *ibid.*, same to same, Cincinnati, August 28, 1882.
    [28] One layman who attended several of McGlynn's lectures in the spring of 1892 found his audience small but largely middle-class and heavily female (AANY, unclassified, E.F. Dunne to Corrigan, New York, April 3; April 10; April 17; April 25; May 1; May 8, 1892). Even when McGlynn was attracting thousands to his addresses, the proportion of middle-class supporters, especially women, seems from the newspaper accounts and other informal reports to have been high.

archbishop of New York."[29] In McGlynn's refusal to respond to the pope's order to come to Rome to explain his position, Corrigan and his advisors found a natural manifestation of McGlynn's heterodoxy, a virtual denial of the primacy of the pope.

Praise quickly poured in to Corrigan when he issued a pastoral letter in which he denounced George's land theory. Patrick Ludden, soon to be named Bishop of Syracuse, congratulated him on taking the offensive against liberalism. Silas Chatard, Bishop of Vincennes, who had issued a similar pastoral at about the same time with much less reaction, thought Corrigan's letter would "do more for the Church in America, than the liberal Priests can do harm." ("The more we strengthen each other's hand," Corrigan owned in complimenting Chatard on his own stand for the rights of property, "the better for discipline, and better for the faithful.") Ignatius Horstmann, chancellor of the Archdiocese of Philadelphia, hoped that now that Corrigan had set the example, "all our Bishops will come out in condemnation of the George heresy."[30]

McGlynn's excommunication in July, 1887, for his refusal to heed the pope's summons only intensified the controversy. The mass demonstrations declined but the attempts of both sides to obtain a favorable solution from Rome persisted for the next eight years with some important consequences for the American Church. The New York hierarchy resorted to various means, including loyalty oaths, the transfer of priests, and the making of attendance at Anti-Poverty Society meetings a reserved sin, to break the backbone of the McGlynn support among clergy and laity. The McGlynn case became a litmus test for judging orthodoxy and establishing one's credentials as conservative or liberal. The pledge of loyalty that New York priests were pressured to sign in the spring of 1887 became for years the norm for promotions and appointments. The laity's involvement in the affair

191

---

[29] This account of the meeting was written by Patrick McSweeny and is found in the archives of Mount Saint Mary's College, Emmitsburg, Maryland, where McSweeny's brother, Edward, was a professor. A passage in Richard Burtsell's diary indicates that it was not composed until 1889 (AANY, Diary, VII, February 14, 1889). Propagandists had the right of appeal to the pope upon being removed or disciplined by their ordinary. This as well as other privileges tended to make American prelates suspicious of them as subjects.

[30] AANY C-16, Ludden to Corrigan, Troy, November 19, 1886; AANY C-15, Chatard to Corrigan, Indianapolis, November 23, 1886; Archives of the University of Notre Dame (hereafter AUND), Corrigan to Chatard, New York, December 28, 1886; AANY C-15, Horstmann to Corrigan, Philadelphia, November 27, 1886.

became a similar criterion. Thus in 1889 when delegates to the Catholic Congress in Baltimore were being chosen, Archbishop Corrigan was allowed to nominate the candidates, all of whom he made sure were "loyal and conservative."[31]

By 1890 McGlynn was becoming a pawn in the ideological struggle that developed between the liberal and conservative camps within the hierarchy. In the new alignment of the prelates a significant addition to the old conservative bloc were the German-American bishops. Prelates like Corrigan and McQuaid were finding that they shared much more in common with Frederick X. Katzer, Archbishop of Milwaukee, than they did with Archbishop John Ireland or Bishop John J. Keane or the other liberal prelates of Irish extraction concerning parochial education or the Catholic University of America or secret societies. The Germans were also drawing McGlynn's fire for their anti-Americanization attitudes. In fact, Corrigan's warming toward the Germans was very likely due in large measure to the strong support he had received from German priests and prelates during the McGlynn crisis. It was the German priests of the archdiocese who had presented him with the first testimony of loyalty. Nor was any German prelate trying to intervene in the McGlynn case, as some of the liberal prelates were.

Corrigan's continuing concern was that his action against McGlynn would be overturned by Rome on the grounds that McGlynn's removal from St. Stephen's had been uncanonical since he had never had the chance of a hearing.[32] The appeals to Rome in McGlynn's

[31] AUND, Brownson Papers, Preston to Orestes Brownson, Jr., New York, April 8, 1889.

[32] Some canonical authorities, such as Richard Burtsell, were arguing that no bishop could transfer or depose even a movable rector for any crime or violation of discipline without the offer of a trial. Propaganda had left this point deliberately vague when the question came up in April of 1887.

Burtsell and others were contending that McGlynn's superiors had denied him equity at every stage of the case. Cardinal Simeoni had ordered him to retract his economic teaching in 1882 without even giving him the chance for an explanation. Four years later the archbishop had dredged up this condemnation to prohibit McGlynn from publicly supporting George's campaign and had suspended the priest for making a scheduled appearance for George even though McGlynn promised to abstain from all further activity in George's behalf. Subsequently, Corrigan had renewed the suspension on the basis of a newspaper report, again without allowing McGlynn any chance to defend himself. Then he had been ordered to Rome without being told what the charges against him were. Corrigan had stated in the press that there were other charges lodged against him in Rome besides his land theories, but none had ever been

behalf by dissident priests like Richard Burtsell or Sylvester Malone were disturbing enough, but even more disconcerting to ecclesiastical authorities in New York were the attempts of other bishops such as Ireland and John Moore of St. Augustine. In September, 1887, Moore attempted to have the American archbishops agree to propose reopening the case in Rome. By November, McQuaid was convinced that the bishops needed to take some joint action to uphold Corrigan. William Elder of Cincinnati agreed to write to Rome warning of the disastrous consequences that would follow any concessions to McGlynn and asked several of his suffragans to do the same. The vast majority of prelates, in fact, even though they might have felt that Corrigan had not acted with prudence, were all too aware of clerical threats to their authority to support a dissident priest in any diocese. As McQuaid wrote Corrigan: "If you are to rule your diocese, you must have all necessary power to inflict discipline on recalcitrant priests. If you can effectively crush this open and defiant rebellion on the part of the McGlynn faction, and you can if Rome sustains you, . . . you will have won a great battle not only for yourself, but for the whole country."[33]

193

The New York archdiocesan officials were also trying to discredit McGlynn in Rome on the grounds of immorality. During the winter of 1887-1888 Corrigan's secretary, Charles McDonnell, presented to Roman officials extensive testimony from several women charging McGlynn with promiscuous behavior and heretical teaching concerning the sixth commandment. That Corrigan and his advisors were predisposed to believe that McGlynn's slippery slope had inevitably led to debauchery is understandable. Convincing Rome that such allegations were true and deserving of censure was another matter entirely, as Cardinal Henry Edward Manning of Westminster was discovering about the same time.[34] Nonetheless, the Holy Office was

---

formally communicated to McGlynn. Nonetheless, McGlynn had authorized Burtsell to write Cardinal Gibbons that he would come to Rome, provided he were first reinstated, and he had even wired Gibbons to that effect. Gibbons had never even acknowledged the letter.

[33] AANY C-16, McQuaid to Corrigan, Rochester, April 5, 1887.

[34] Manning had been attempting for years to have the Holy Office uphold his suspension of Monsignor Thomas Capel, the rector of Manning's ill-fated University College of Kensington, for immoral behavior. Ironically Corrigan furnished the proof that finally convinced Rome. Capel, who had been wandering about America while under suspension, caused a scandal in a New York hotel in 1885 which Corrigan documented for Manning (AANY, unclassified, Corrigan memorandum, February 9, 1885).

persuaded by the evidence that Corrigan forwarded to condemn McGlynn for solicitation and "perverse doctrines in sexual matters."[35] This condemnation would play an important role in Corrigan's reaction to the unexpected restoration of McGlynn in 1892.

Having McGlynn condemned in secret, however, would never destroy his influence. Some supporters of Corrigan were sure that nothing short of a condemnation of the source of McGlynn's ideas would effectively undermine his influence. Urged by his Roman friends to make a direct appeal to Leo XIII for an official denunciation of George's writings, Corrigan in October, 1887, formally petitioned the pope that the Congregation of the Index examine *Progress and Poverty*. Cardinal James Gibbons of Baltimore, with the close support of the Rector of the North American College in Rome, Denis J. O'Connell, co-ordinated extensive appeals from the American hierarchy against any such condemnation on the prudent grounds that George's ideas should be allowed to die the natural death that speculative schemes found in the United States. Even conservatives like Gilmour and Elder thought it better to have Rome condemn the proposition about the injustice of holding private property in land and avoid the whole matter of George's book. A year and a half later the Holy Office compromised by condemning George's writings, but it refused to allow any promulgation of the condemnation. "How *peculiar* to condemn a book," Monsignor Preston understated his exasperation to Corrigan, "& then to keep the condemnation secret! I hope some of the Bishops will leak."[36] None did.

Preston and Corrigan continued to seek a public Vatican condemnation of George as the key to isolating McGlynn. In May, 1890, Corrigan renewed to Cardinal Camillo Mazzella his plea for "some explicit declaration regarding the right of private property" to combat the socialistic theories that the archbishop saw spreading in the United States through such popular tracts as Edward Bellamy's *Looking Backward*.[37] Even some of the hierarchy, Corrigan informed Bernard Smith in Rome, thought that the promotion of liberal doctrines would be "the high road to American favor, and a passport for the claims of the Catholic Church."[38] When *Rerum Novarum* fol-

[35] AANY, unclassified, Corrigan to [Cardinal Lucido Parrocchi], New York, October 12, 1888, copy.

[36] AANY C-24, Preston to Corrigan, New York, April 26, 1889.

[37] AANY L-3, Corrigan to Mazzella, May 16, 1890, in "Private Record," 254-255.

[38] Archives of the Abbey of St. Paul Outside the Walls (hereafter AASPOW), Smith Papers, Corrigan to Smith, New York, April 2, 1891.

lowed in May, 1891, Ella Edes, the veteran American journalist in Rome with close ties to the New York chancery, reported that the pope's aim was to condemn George's theory without condemning his books.[39] Whether it was his aim or not, the encyclical gave the conservatives the magisterial sanction they had been seeking. Declaring that private property was in "perfect harmony with the natural law," Leo condemned "certain obsolete opinions" that denied any individual ownership of land. Corrigan's partisans began hailing the encyclical as the great authoritative vindication of the archbishop's long struggle against McGlynn and George. Corrigan himself stressed the obligation that Catholics had in obeying even such *non ex cathedra* statements as *Rerum Novarum*.

195

In the summer of McGlynn's excommunication Corrigan had mentioned to Gibbons that the crisis had had one good result—it had strongly increased his attachment to the Holy See. "I realize more and more clearly, day by day," he told the cardinal, "the profound truth of the axiom, 'Ubi Petrus, ibi Ecclesia!' "[40] One very concrete way of manifesting loyalty was the yearly Peter's Pence collection. New York as the richest diocese in the United States annually sent the largest amount, between fifteen and twenty thousand dollars in the 1880's. Baltimore, by contrast, was sending between five and ten thousand. At a time when the Holy See had lost its traditional support from the Papal States, such voluntary contributions assumed increasingly large importance. Nor did the New York officials simply let the money speak for itself. When Charles McDonnell went to Rome to lay out the evidence about McGlynn's alleged immorality, his official mission was to present the proceeds of a special collection taken up in honor of Leo's jubilee. But McDonnell was keenly aware of how interrelated his two missions were. "This evidence [of McGlynn's alleged immorality]," he confided to Corrigan, "and the . . . Jubilee collection, will be a powerful offset to the machinations of Smith's [McGlynn's] friends and followers." "I want to bring out the fact that New York's offering is larger now than ever before, a proof of the loyalty of the people in the face of the desperate efforts made to cut down the Peter Pence."[41]

[39] AANY L-3, Edes to Corrigan, Rome, May 28, 1891, in "Private Record," 265-267.

[40] Archives of the Archdiocese of Baltimore, Corrigan to Gibbons, New York, August 5, 1887.

[41] AANY C-16, McDonnell to Corrigan, Rome, December 6, 1887; *ibid.*, same to same, Rome, January 22, 1888. One of the archbishop's fears during the McGlynn

Another effect of the loss of the Papal States in 1870 had been the Holy See's need to secure and invest its funds abroad. As an investment center New York was also unique within the American Church. The year Michael Corrigan became McCloskey's coadjutor, Rome had begun to entrust funds to his custody and management. In 1881 Propaganda had asked him to invest almost $45,000 in securities.[42] In 1889 the Propaganda official in charge of finances, Cardinal Aloisi Masella, decided to withdraw the funds under the belief that the growth rate was too slow. Archbishop Corrigan's realization of the importance of being the custodian of these funds is reflected in his efforts to convince Propaganda officials that the interest rates were much higher than they appeared to be.[43] Fortunately for the archbishop, Masella was transferred from the Sacred Congregation before the securities could be sold and New York continued to be an investor for the Vatican.[44] By 1898 the value of the funds was nearly $172,000.[45]

In the fall of 1889 the announcement of the Peter's Pence collection gave the archbishop an opportunity to issue a pastoral letter on the temporal power of the pope. While it was within God's providence, Corrigan admitted, to devise many ways of ensuring the perfect liberty that the pope needed to exercise his spiritual jurisdiction, "still, as far as human prudence can determine, and as things actually exist, temporal sovereignty is the most natural means, and indeed . . . a necessary means for securing the good government of the Church."[46] This would become an increasingly recurrent theme for the archbishop.

A decade before, Corrigan, along with many of his fellow prelates,

---

crisis was that the size of the collection would greatly decrease. There was some decline in the Pence in the late 1880's but whether this was owing to the poor economy of the period or the boycott of McGlynn partisans is difficult to judge.

[42] AANY, unclassified, Corrigan to Cardinal Cajetan Aloisi Masella, New York, October 18, 1889, copy.

[43] AANY, unclassified, Corrigan to Simeoni, New York, October 25, 1889, copy.

[44] Rome also proposed that Corrigan receive the Peter's Pence collection from all dioceses in the country and directly invest it. The archbishop rightly felt that this would offend some of his fellow prelates and suggested a more indirect procedure whereby the funds would still be sent to Rome while their ultimate investment would take place in New York (AANY, unclassified, Preston to Corrigan, June 6, 1889; *ibid.*, Corrigan to Masella, June 6, 1889, copy).

[45] AANY I-41, [Cardinal Vincent] Vannutelli to Corrigan, Rome, July 28, 1899.

[46] AANY H-3, Pastoral Letter of Michael Augustine Corrigan, Feast of the Holy Rosary, October, 1889.

had been concerned about maintaining a balance between their loyalty to Rome and their collegial independence as American bishops. Corrigan had played a key role in preserving this balance in the Roman deliberations that prepared the Third Plenary Council. But events were now sweeping him along in a way that was forcing him to assume a position that would have a profound effect upon the equilibrium between loyalty and independence that the American hierarchy had long been seeking to attain.

Part of the high priority the American hierarchy had put on unity in the 1880's was the fear that disunity would provide an inevitable occasion for the lessening of their independence by the establishment of a Roman delegation. When Leo appointed Francesco Satolli in August, 1892, as an apostolic ablegate, the announced purpose of his visit was to represent the pope at the World's Columbian Exposition in Chicago. Among his unannounced purposes, however, was to bring about a reconciliation of McGlynn with the Holy See. As Satolli secretly told Corrigan's vicar-general, John Farley, many in Rome felt that Corrigan had acted too hastily in his handling of the case.[47] Cardinal Mariano Rampolla, who as Secretary of State was taking a much more active role in American affairs, had been especially dismayed over Corrigan's actions and his alleged involvement with Tammany Hall. With the proponents of *"ralliement"* holding the balance of power within the Vatican, Corrigan as the leader of the anti-liberal party in America was finding more doors closed to him in Rome.

197

O'Connell and Ireland, having decided that helping the Vatican to establish the American delegation would aid their own liberal program, had been responsible for the invitation to the Chicago Exposition.[48] By August O'Connell could assure Ireland that Satolli was entirely in their hands.[49] Attempts at restoring McGlynn were very much a part of the liberal-conservative struggle that was peaking in 1891-1892. It was a propitious time for such a reconciliation. McGlynn was out of the headlines. Even Burtsell admitted in February, 1892, that the Anti-Poverty Society, now in its fifth year, was "dwindling away."[50] The Academy of Music was a growing cavern of

[47] AANY, Farley Diary, September 24, 1892.

[48] See Gerald P. Fogarty, S.J., *The Vatican and the Americanist Crisis: Denis J. O'Connell, American Agent in Rome, 1885-1903* (Rome, 1973), chapter VIII.

[49] AASPOW, O'Connell to Ireland, Rome, August 3, 1892, quoted in Fogarty, *op. cit.*, p. 231.

[50] AANY, Burtsell Diary, VIII, February 7, 1892.

empty seats for McGlynn's Sunday addresses. This was the background to Satolli's having the McGlynn case as one of his chief priorities when he sailed for America in September. By the middle of December McGlynn was told to prepare a statement of his economic theories. Four professors of the Catholic University of America found nothing in it contrary to Catholic doctrine and Satolli on December 23 restored McGlynn to good standing within the Church without even consulting Corrigan.[51]

The conservatives were dumbfounded. McGlynn's dubious restoration seemed to them to sanction not only the "socialistic" theories he had made his hallmark, but also the defiance of episcopal authority that McGlynn had come to incarnate. "Our people are terribly worked up, particularly the better classes," Corrigan lamented to McQuaid. "Many say they will go to Church no more."[52] Corrigan refused to receive McGlynn back into the archdiocese until the priest made public reparation for the scandal he had given.[53] Roman friends were advising the archibshop to hold firm. By January newspapers were carrying headline accusations against Corrigan as the chief force behind the outpouring of letters and articles against Satolli and Ireland that had begun appearing in newspapers across the country in November when Satolli announced his liberally tilted guidelines on the education of Catholic children, and that had sharply increased in number and passion with McGlynn's restoration. Rumors began to spread that Corrigan would be forced to resign or accept a coadjutor.

Paradoxically the sensational accusations against Corrigan consolidated conservative support for the New York prelate. John Lancaster Spalding of Peoria was but one of many bishops who encouraged Corrigan to stand his ground. To allow McGlynn to be taken back without apology or penance, Spalding wrote, would be "a fatal blow at ecclesiastical authority—a bribe held out to every priest to become disobedient and rebellious."[54] "You are fighting a great fight," Arch-

---

[51] The four professors were Thomas Bouquillon, Thomas O'Gorman, Charles P. Grannan, and Edward A. Pace (AANY, Burtsell Diary, IX, December 20-22, 1892; AANY, Burtsell Letterbook, December 21, 1892).

[52] Archives of the Diocese of Rochester, Corrigan to McQuaid, New York, December 28, 1892.

[53] He also was justifying his stand on the ground that the Holy Office's condemnation of McGlynn for solicitation was unaffected by Satolli's decision about his economic teaching (AANY, Corrigan to Cardinal Monaco, New York, December 27, 1892, Italian copy).

[54] AANY G-4, Spalding to Corrigan, Peoria, January 1, 1893.

bishop William Gross of Portland, Oregon, assured Corrigan. "You are the leader and champion of genuine Catholicity against . . . false liberalism."[55] On no account, Gross urged, should he resign or accept a coadjutor. With Satolli playing into the hands of the liberals by downgrading parochial schools and restoring dissident priests over the protests of their ordinaries, many conservatives were ready for the confrontation with the delegate that Corrigan was providing by refusing to give McGlynn a parish or even to allow him to say a public Mass.

When McGlynn left secretly for Rome in the spring of 1893 Corrigan sent his Italian secretary, Father Gherardo Ferrante, to represent him at the Vatican. Ferrante quickly proved beneficial to Corrigan as he began to win the favor of key officials, including the Prefect of Propaganda, Cardinal Mieceslaus Ledochowski. A larger issue was working in Corrigan's favor. The establishment of Satolli's mission had been the work of the pope, his Secretary of State, and Denis O'Connell. Ledochowski had never even been consulted about Satolli's appointment. O'Connell and Ireland had hoped that the institution of the delegation would free the Church in America from the jurisdiction of Propaganda and increase its independence. But Satolli as well as the American Church still fell under the direction of the Sacred Congregation and Satolli's tendency to deal directly with Leo or Rampolla only increased the hostility toward him in Propaganda. The latter resented Rampolla's assumption of certain traditional prerogatives of the congregation, including being consulted about apostolic delegates to missionary countries such as the United States.[56] This tension was but part of the larger opposition between Leo and Rampolla on the one hand and Propaganda on the other about the restoration of the papal lands and relations with European powers.[57]

Given this Byzantine situation, Corrigan's opposition to Satolli became an asset for him at Propaganda. In supporting Corrigan, Propaganda could help check the designs of Rampolla and the pope.[58] Rampolla warned Satolli in June, 1893, that Corrigan could cause

199

[55] *Ibid.*, Gross to Corrigan, Portland, January 18, 1893.

[56] AANY, unclassified, Ferrante to Corrigan, Rome, June 24, 1893, Italian.

[57] Leo ironically was pursuing his *ralliement* policy partly to gain support against the Triple Alliance, specifically Italy, for a restoration of the temporal power. The American liberals mistakenly interpreted Leo's strategy as a commitment toward democracy.

[58] Denis O'Connell had come to realize this strategy of Propaganda by the fall of 1893. See AANY, Burtsell Diary, IX, October 28, 1893.

much trouble for them, presumably a reference to the New York prelate's new strength at Propaganda.[59] Two months later Leo had
Rampolla suggest to Satolli that he give Corrigan some public sign of
esteem.[60] On August 15 the delegate made his public peace with the
archbishop during a pontifical Mass in St. Patrick's Cathedral.
Realistically both knew a public reconciliation had become mutually
necessary even though suspicion and distrust continued on both sides.

There followed a series of events in which Satolli's stance toward
the conservatives changed radically as he began to support prelates
against the appeals of dissident priests, to praise parochial schools,
and to put pressure upon the liberal Catholic press. The conservatives' confidence in Satolli grew as he came more and more under the
direction of Propaganda. Patrick J. Ryan, Archbishop of Philadelphia, even suggested that Propaganda submit ecclesiastical cases to
the apostolic delegate that had previously been reserved to Rome.[61]

December, 1894, found McGlynn in Brooklyn still waiting for Corrigan to receive him back. The archbishop had learned that the pope
had finally acknowledged that Satolli had acted too quickly in restoring McGlynn and would soon order McGlynn to retract certain propositions. But no order came. By this time the McGlynn case had become such an impenetrable web of issues, facts, and allegations that
Rome was bewildered, as one Vatican official admitted.[62] Leo's apparent tendency to lend encouragement to anyone who had his ear at
the moment seems to have made a final resolution even more difficult.
Moreover, O'Connell was telling Leo that in ordering any retraction
by McGlynn he would effectively be rebuking Satolli and the Catholic
University of America for attesting that no such retraction was necessary.[63] Given the opposition between Leo and Propaganda, the pope
was not about to give such a gratuitous censure to Satolli or the University.

The delegate finally persuaded Archbishop Corrigan to name
McGlynn pastor of St. Mary's in Newburgh, a small town in upstate
New York. The archbishop was sure enough of his position now to

---

[59] AUND, Eduardo Soderini, "Leo XIII and the U.S. of America," unpublished
manuscript, Rampolla to Satolli, June 14, 1893, v. 54.

[60] AANY L-3, Rampolla to Corrigan, Rome, August 4, 1893, in "Private Record,"
377-378.

[61] AANY G-16, McDonnell to Corrigan, Brooklyn, April 21, 1895.

[62] AANY, Burtsell Diary, IX, November 7, 1893.

[63] AANY G-4, Henry Gabriels to Corrigan, Rome, December 21, 1893.

take McGlynn back without it seeming to be a sign of his declining authority. What had become the symbolic goal of the McGlynnites— to have McGlynn restored to a parish in New York—now could be read as an indication of the archbishop's growing power. For by 1895 the signs were increasingly clear that the aims of the American liberals were slowly collapsing. From Newburgh McGlynn continued to vent his unreconstructed views on the single tax, parochial schools, and the plight of American labor. He still believed that the establishment of the Apostolic Delegation in Washington had overturned the "benevolent paternal despotism" of the bishops and created "a new order" that would finally enable the Church in America to be fully American.[64] Neither he nor the liberal prelates were very astute readers of the signals from Rome. Less than a year before McGlynn died in 1900 Leo XIII condemned Americanism.

201

The interplay of events and issues that climaxed in January, 1899, with *Testem Benevolentiae* was a highly complex one. The McGlynn affair was but one of the larger strands of the Americanist tapestry. Given the centralizing trend that both Pius IX and Leo XIII vigorously pursued during their reigns and the growth during this same period of a conservative episcopal bloc seeking to strengthen its authority over clergy and laity, the conservative triumph was probably inevitable. But the importance of the McGlynn affair in relation to this long-term development is that it was one of the most effective shapers of the particular divisions that grew up among the American hierarchy during these last fifteen crucial years of the century and forced a stance toward Rome, on the part of the conservatives, that had extremely serious consequences. The affair dominated Archbishop Corrigan's concerns during those eight years from 1886 to 1894 and critically affected his trust of key liberal prelates like Gibbons, Ireland, and Keane. For many other conservative prelates the McGlynn case confirmed their worst fears of the liberal cancer they saw maturing in the Church.

When they perceived that cancer spreading from clerics like McGlynn and Burtsell to prelates like Ireland and Keane, the conservatives reluctantly resorted to Rome more and more to find a cure. The official purgation that *Testem* provided for them had a higher price than they undoubtedly had anticipated. For by the first years of the twentieth century the American Church was less independent of

[64] Edward McGlynn, "The Results of Cardinal Satolli's Mission," *The Forum*, XXII (February, 1897), 695-705.

Rome than it had been in the 1870's. The old balance between loyalty
to Rome and collegial independence was largely lost, as the veto
power of the apostolic delegate over episcopal appointments clearly
symbolized. Michael Corrigan's tendency to maximize the primacy
and infallibility of the pope set the pattern for the ultramontanism
that would characterize the Church in America in the first half of the
twentieth century. Whereas an older conservative like McQuaid had
found infallibility an inopportune dogma, Corrigan had ended up
flaunting it. In turning so completely to Rome to save themselves
from the designs of the liberals, the conservatives lost some of their
own heritage as well.

Secular Clergy in Nineteenth Century America: A Diocesan Profile

By JAMES HITCHCOCK*

The diocese of St. Louis in 1841 comprised a vast territory, its western boundary largely indeterminate. The pioneering missionary work in the area had been done primarily by religious orders, especially Vincentians and Jesuits.

The coming of Bishop Peter Richard Kenrick at the end of 1841 signalled the beginning of several simultaneous transitions in the diocese which, within a decade, would give it an entirely new character. While not, perhaps, "typical" of nineteenth-century American sees, its growth as seen through the history of its clergy reveals the process by which a missionary center was gradually transformed into a settled metropolitan see.

Bishop Kenrick, who was a Philadelphia priest at the time of his appointment, served as coadjutor bishop and administrator from 1841 to 1843, while the bishop, Joseph Rosati, was on a diplomatic mission for the papacy in Haiti. Bishop Rosati died before returning to St. Louis, and Kenrick became ordinary of the diocese in 1843. He was promoted to archbishop in 1847 and ruled over the see until his retirement in 1895.[1]

Within a decade of Kenrick's coming bishops had been appointed for Arkansas, Illinois, and Kansas and the diocese of St. Louis had been reduced to the state of Missouri. The same decade saw the beginnings of massive European immigration, so that in a double sense St. Louis ceased to be a frontier see. In the process it cut several important ties with its past.

The Vincentians and Jesuits continued to do important work in Missouri, but during the 1840's there seemed to occur a gradual withdrawal from active life of the older missionary generation. The vicars general John Mary Odin and John Timon, both Vincentians, were soon appointed bishops elsewhere.[2] Joseph A. Lutz, an old Indian missionary, was made vicar general but soon left the diocese, ending his life as an obscure curate in New York City.[3] Francis Cellini, a venerable veteran who practiced medicine and marketed his own commercial balm, took up residence in St. Louis and was also made vicar general, but seems not to have discharged any duties; he died in

*Mr. Hitchcock is Professor of History at St. Louis University. The author wishes to thank Msgr. Bernard Granich, vice-chancellor and archivist of the Archdiocese of St. Louis, and Miss Julia Colombo of the chancery staff for their cooperation.

1847.⁴ Peter R. Donnelly, who had ministered to the "Irish-speaking" settlers of rural Missouri and Arkansas, retired and took up residence in the archbishop's house, living on until 1870.⁵ Edmond Saulnier, also a seasoned missionary, was given the undemanding post of chancellor.⁶

Bishop Kenrick found twenty secular clergy attached to the diocese upon his arrival.⁷ The growth in their number over the next sixty-two years (through the administration of Archbishop John J. Kain) was as follows:

TABLE I: NUMBERS OF SECULAR CLERGY

Year	Number	Year	Number
1841	20	1871	136
1851	49	1881	161
1861	77	1891	216
		1903	268

Bishop Kenrick's first decade, the crucial decade of transition, saw the largest percentile increase in the number of diocesan clergy—145%. The largest numerical increase—fifty-nine—was during the 1860's.

The third major change of the 1840's, besides the reduction of the size of the diocese and the transition to secular clergy, was the ethnic shift brought on by immigration, a process which would continue for the remainder of the century.

St. Louis had been founded by French colonizers in 1764, and the character of the city remained predominantly French until the 1840's. The Missouri Jesuits were mainly Flemish, while the Vincentians seem to have been drawn from a variety of nationalities.⁸ Not only the needs of the Irish and German immigrants but also, apparently, the desires of the new bishop led to a swift decline in French clerical influence after 1841.

Bishop Kenrick found the sermons of the French priests at the cathedral "intolerably long" and "not infrequently most scandalous." He also feared that the Jesuits, who had recently opened the second parish in St. Louis (the Vincentians simultaneously opened the third) would attract all the English-speaking parishioners from the cathedral.⁹ He seems, therefore, to have systematically set about discouraging the recruitment of French clergy.

In 1849 two French seminarians arrived in St. Louis, garbed in soutanes and clerical hats. Kenrick is reported to have greeted them correctly, but the next morning at breakfast they found tickets for

New Orleans under their plates.[10] That the need for French priests did not entirely disappear, however, is indicated by the fact that as late as 1886 the archbishop promised to try to find a French-speaking Irish curate for the pastor of Sts. Mary and Joseph's, an old parish in the Carondelet district which had changed from French to Irish pastors after the Civil War.[11]

The French clergy were described as stoical, scrupulous about rubrics and ceremonies, and strict disciplinarians. Their severe Jansenism repelled people, and as a result they could not successfully build up their parishes.[12] At the cathedral in the mid-1850's Edmond Saulnier considered the two young Irish curates lax and neglectful of their duties. One of them was Patrick J. Ryan, who would become a revered archbishop of Philadelphia.[13]

Himself a Dubliner, Bishop Kenrick seems to have recruited Irish clergy most vigorously in the first decade of his administration (see Table II). However, one of his vicars general, Joseph Melcher, was also sent on recruiting trips to Germany, where he had some success.[14] Throughout the nineteenth century Germans were a majority of the population of St Louis. However, since many Germans were not Catholic, Irish Catholics may well have outnumbered their German co-religionists. No other Catholic ethnic group was numerically very significant.[15] Elsewhere in the State German Catholics probably outnumbered Irish.[16]

TABLE II: ETHNIC IDENTITY OF SECULAR CLERGY

Year	Number	% of Total	Year	Number	% of Total
	Irish			German	
1841	4	20.0	1841	5	25.0
1851	26	53.1	1851	10	20.4
1861	38	49.4	1861	25	32.5
1871	63	46.3	1871	60	44.1
1881	74	45.9	1881	76	47.2
1891	85	39.4	1891	105	48.6
1903	91	33.9	1903	153	57.1
	French			English-Scottish	
1841	5	25.0	1841	5	25.0
1851	8	16.3	1851	3	6.1
1861	5	6.5	1861	2	2.6
1871	2	1.5	1871	3	2.2
1881	2	1.2	1881	3	1.9
1891	1	0.4	1891	6	2.8
1903	0	0.0	1903	7	2.6

At various times there were also scatterings of Bohemian-Moravian (five in 1903), Polish (four in 1903), Italian (three in 1903), Dutch (three between 1861 and 1891), and Belgian (two in 1891) priests. Probably many of the clergy with English or Scottish surnames were actually Irish. However, even if they are counted as such the number of Irish clergy did not equal the number of Germans after the 1870's.[17]

Of the forty-nine secular clergy serving in St. Louis in 1851, only nine had been incardinated in the diocese a decade before, further evidence of the radical change in personnel which occurred in the 1840's. Gradually, however, the archdiocese[18] developed a relatively stable body of clergy as evidenced in the average number of years of those in service.

206

TABLE III. SERVICE IN THE ARCHDIOCESE[19]

Year	Average Years of Service	Average Age
1841	9.5	39.6
1851	6.5	36.8
1861	8.4	37.1
1871	8.2	36.0
1881	11.4	38.6
1891	13.3	41.8
1903	15.4	42.9

Thus the twenty-year period between the coming of Bishop Kenrick and the outbreak of the Civil War seems to have been marked by the phasing out of the older missionary clergy and the French clergy in general, vigorous recruitment of Irish and Germans, and reliance on younger men new to the archdiocese. After the Civil War conditions of stability were achieved, and German priests slowly began to outnumber the Irish.

Clerical stability was a relative thing in nineteenth-century America, however. Almost one-third of the secular clergy who served in the St. Louis archdiocese before 1903 eventually left the archdiocese, and about twenty-three per cent were transfers to St. Louis from other dioceses. Seven priests are known to have entered religious orders, and fourteen transferred out of orders.

TABLE IV: CLERGY TRANSFERS

Decade	Number Transferring Out	Transferring In
1840's	17	16
1850's	43	22
1860's	48	29
1870's	33	34

| 1880's | 38 | 11 |
| 1890-1903 | 24 | 32 |

In almost every decade St. Louis, perhaps because of its position as the "gateway to the West," gave up more priests than it received, and its numerical strength was kept up mainly by ordinations (see Table V). However, after the Civil War there was a gradual decline in the number of clergy shifting from one diocese to another.

In each decade of the nineteenth century well over eighty per cent of the new clergy received into the archdiocese were ordained in St. Louis. (The lowest percentages, oddly, were in the 1870's and 1880's.)

207

TABLE V: NUMBERS OF ORDINATIONS IN ST. LOUIS[20]

1840's	30	1860's	69	1880's	67
1850's	48	1870's	74	1890's	84
				1900-03	47

St Louis's role as a feeder for other dioceses is reflected, however, in the number of ordinands who eventually left the archdiocese.

TABLE VI: ORDINANDS TRANSFERRING OUT

Decade	Number	Percentage
1840's	15	50.0
1850's	22	45.8
1860's	15	21.7
1870's	11	14.9
1880's	3	4.5
1890's	6	6.4
1900-03	0	0.0

Again a growing stability is indicated after the Civil War.

The instability and hardship of clerical life in the nineteenth century is also graphically suggested in the number of St. Louis pastors who resigned their pastorates and, often enough, left the archdiocese.

TABLE VII: ST. LOUIS PARISH FOUNDERS LOSS

| | Resigned | | Left |
Decade	Number	Percentage	Archdiocese
1840's	6	100.0	5
1850's	3	50.0	3
1860's	5	83.3	3
1870's	12	42.9	0

| 1880's | 3 | 12.5 | 2 |
| 1890-1903's | 5 | 29.4 | 1 |

TABLE: VIII: St. Louis Pastors Loss

| | | Resigned | Left |
Decade	Number	Percentage	Archdiocese
1840's	8	80.0	7
1850's	11	52.4	8
1860's	10	35.7	5
1870's	12	42.9	3
1880's	3	12.5	2
1890-1903,s	10	23.3	3

Such patterns naturally created extremely unstable parochial conditions in some cases. The cathedral had five pastors in 1857-68; St. Patrick's five in 1845-56 and four in 1870-76; Holy Trinity four in 1849-56; St. Michael's five in 1849-58; Assumption seven in 1861-73; St. Bernard's four in 1874-78; and St Mark's four in 1893-99. (Deaths as well as resignations accounted for some of the turnover.)

There were also some extremely long tenures, such as that of Francis S. Goller at Sts. Peter and Paul's (1856-1910), Joseph L. Hessoun at St. John Nepomuk's (1864-1906), Edward J. Shea of St. Kevin's (Immaculate Conception) (1879-1920), Herman J. Nieters at St. Boniface's (1895-1939), James J. McCabe at Sacred Heart (1871-1916), David S. Phelan at Our Lady of Mount Carmel 1872-1915), Henry Hukestein at St. Augustine's (1884-1925), JamesJ. McGlynn at St. Rose's (1884-1936), Daniel J. Lavery at Holy Rosary (1891-1943), Joseph T. Shields at St. Matthew's (1893-1944), and Urban Stanowski at St. Stanislaus' (1886-1927).

One-third of the German priests and 40.5% of the Irish priests who served in St. Louis at some time between 1841 and 1903 left the archdiocese without a trace, many of them after only a year of service. Few American-born priests disappeared in the same way, and it is reasonable to assume that most of those who left returned to Europe. John F. Bannon, the pastor of St. John's, left without permission to become a Confederate Army chaplain in 1861 and subsequently was a Confederate emissary to England. After the war he became a prominent Jesuit in Ireland and lived on until 1913.[21] Timothy Donovan was expelled from the United States as a rebel in 1862 and was not heard from again until 1903, when he finally sought his release from the archdiocese.[22] John Higginbotham, a poplular early pastor of St.

Michael's and St. Patrick's, was traced in later years by some of his former parishioners, who discovered that he had ended his days as a chaplain in the British Army.[23]

Of the 623 secular priests who served in the St. Louis archdiocese at some time between 1841 and 1903, only twenty-four were ever accused of misconduct (3.1%). The recorded offenses (sometimes unspecified) involved women, alchohol, homosexuality, misuse of funds, and mental illness. Although the St. Louis synod of 1851 had stipulated that accused clergy should be given trials, there is no evidence that any were ever held.[24] St. Louis evidently did not suffer from a shortage of priests, and in virtually every case a priest accused of misbehavior or suspended from his duties left the archdiocese. The sufficiency of clergy was indicated in other ways also. When the young John O'Hanlon arrived in the early 1840's with the hope of undertaking studies, he worked for a time on the riverfront. His attendance at daily Mass attracted the notice of Bryan Mullanphy, St. Louis' first millionaire, who introduced him to the bishop and got him accepted.[25] When John J. Hogan arrived a few years later he was told by the "portly, pompous" rector of the cathedral, Simon Paris, that there were no vacancies at the seminary. Within a few months the archbishop accepted him, however.[26] In 1879 the coadjutor bishop, Patrick J. Ryan, told a priest newly discharged from the hospital that there were no vacancies, and the man left the archdiocese.[27] The year before a student, Jeremiah J. Harty (a future archbishop), was advised by his pastor in St. Louis to delay his ordination, because there were currently no openings in the city.[28] In 1883 the archdiocese was able to reject a newly arrived Irish priest who had given scandal on the boat coming to America.[29] (During the 1870's the archdiocese experienced its smallest net increase in the number of clergy—twenty-five.)

Educational standards for clerical recruits were not particularly high. John J.Hogan, when finally granted an interview with the archbishop, was merely asked to translate a few lines of Latin before being admitted to the seminary. Hogan, himself a future bishop, was candid in admitting that he had volunteered for the American mission because the chances for advancement in the Irish church were not good.[30] Patrick J. Ryan was assigned to teach at the archdiocesan seminary while still a deacon, fresh from Ireland.[31] Not all those who came to America were deemed inferior in their home country, however. John O'Hanlon, who returned to Ireland a few years after ordination because of ill health, became a canon in Dublin and a noted author.[32]

209

When priests left the archdiocese their subsequent histories were rarely recorded, making it impossible to judge how many have left the priesthood. Only one, a St. Louis pastor, is known to have done so prior to 1903. A native St. Louisan, he went on a trip to Europe in 1883 and never returned. Five years later the chancellor of the archdiocese happened to see his name in a German hotel register; he was registered as a physician from Chicago. Two other priests ordained before 1903 (one also a St. Louis pastor) are known to have left the priesthood after that date.[33] A bizarre incident occurred in 1884, when a suspended priest from the diocese of Buffalo gave himself a fatal dose of strychnine in the lobby of the Alexian Brothers Hospital. An itinerant artist and journalist who knew six languages, he claimed to be a Swiss baron but was supporting himself in his alcoholic habits by begging. Among his last words were, "Write the bishop of Buffalo and he will be glad." The bishop of Buffalo was Stephen M. Ryan, C.M., a former St. Louis priest.[34]

Between 1818 and 1837 five Missourians had been ordained to the secular priesthood, and it appeared that the diocese was slowly developing a native clergy. Between 1838 and 1867, however, only one native American was ordained for St Louis. Furthermore, the turnover in priests which occurred in the 1840's lost the diocese two of its sons, George Hamilton and Hilary Tucker, who went to Boston. Tucker was described as a finicky and complaining person, and while a student in Rome in the 1830's Hamilton had expressed embarrassment at the need for American bishops to beg in Europe.[35] Possibly both found the demands of a western diocese uncongenial. But Hilary Tucker's brother Lewis was for many years a beloved rural Missouri pastor and enjoyed a reputation for sanctity.[36]

Beginning in 1868 there was a steady increase in the number of native-born Americans ordained for the St. Louis Archdiocese, although at the end of the century well over half the clergy were still immigrants.

TABLE IX: AMERICAN-BORN ORDINANDS

Decade	Born USA	%	Born Missouri	%	Born St. Louis	%
1840's	0	0.0	0	0.0	0	0.0
1850's	1	2.1	1	2.1	0	0.0
1860's	7	10.1	4	5.8	4	5.8
1870's	18	24.3	11	14.9	8	10.8
1880,s	29	43.3	21	31.3	14	20.9
1890's	44	52.4	39	46.4	29	34.5
1900–03's	22	46.8	20	42.5	15	31.9

Most American-born ordinands were also native Missourians, and of these a high percentage in each decade were also natives of St. Louis.

TABLE X: AMERICAN-BORN CLERGY

Decade	Born USA	%	Born Missouri	%	Born St. Louis	%
1841	4	20.0	3	1.5	1	5.0
1851	1	2.0	1	2.0	0	0.0
1861	4	5.2	1	1.3	0	0.0
1871	10	7.4	5	3.7	3	2.2
1881	25	15.5	15	9.3	12	7.5
1891	53	24.5	33	15.3	23	9.4
1903	111	41.4	83	30.9	56	20.9

Since such information was usually not recorded in the chancery files, it is difficult to judge how many priests were born in Europe but raised in the United States. A sampling of fifty-five Irish-born and twenty German-born priests reveals only one German who came to America when young, as opposed to fifteen Irish (26.7% of the total).[17]

The Irish began producing a native clergy earlier than the Germans, but as time went on the Germans significantly outstripped the Irish in numbers of priestly vocations. Even though Irish Catholics may have outnumbered German Catholics in the city at the end of the century,[18] the Germans were producing far more priests.

TABLE XI: ETHNIC BACKGROUND OF AMERICAN-BORN ORDINANDS[39]

Decade	Irish	German	English-Scottish
1850's		1 (100%)	
1860's	5 (71.4%		2 (28.6%)
1870's	8 (44.4%)	9 (50.0%)	1 (5.5%)
1880's	10 (34.5%)	16 (58.6%)	1 (3.4%)
1890's	11 (25.0%)	29 (65.9%)	3 (6.8%)
1900-03	8 (36.4%)	14 (63.6%)	

During the period 1841-1903 only a single American-born priest was ordained who did not fit one of the above ethnic groups—a man of Belgian ancestry ordained in the 1880's.

Irish ordinands were somewhat more likely than Germans to have been born elsewhere in the United States and to have moved to Missouri later, suggesting perhaps that German immigrant families tended to come directly to a place of settlement and remain there, while the Irish were more mobile. The Irish percentage of ordinands born in the city of St. Louis was in each decade a few points higher than the German, reflecting the well known Irish preference for city life. However, the great majority of German vocations were also drawn from the city, despite the numerous rural German settlements.

TABLE XII: PERCENTAGE OF AMERICAN-BORN
CLERGY IN EACH ETHNIC GROUP

Decade	Irish	German	English-Scottish	French
1841			3 (60.0%)	1 (20.0%)
1851		1 (1.3%)		
1861	2 (5.3%)	1 (4.0%)	1 (50.0%)	
1871	7 (11.1%)	1 (1.7%)	1 (33.3%)	(66.7%)
1881	12 (16.2%)	11 (14.5%)	3 (100.0%)	
1891	22 (25.9%)	25 (23.8%)	5 (83.3%)	
1903	37 (40.7%)	67 (43.8%)	7 (100.0%)	

Thus not only did the German community produce far more priests than the Irish, but by the end of the century a slightly higher percentage of the German clergy were American-born.

TABLE XIII: FOREIGN-BORN CLERGY AS PERCENTAGE OF TOTAL CLERGY"

	Irish	German	French	Italian
1841	4 (20.0%)	5 (25.0%)	5 (25.0%)	2 (10.0%)
1851	26 (53.1%)	10 (20.4%)	8 (16.3%)	
1861	36 (46.8%)	24 (31.2%)	5 (6.5%)	1 (1.3%)
1871	56 (41.2%)	59 (43.4%)	2 (1.5%)	
1881	62 (38.5%)	65 (40.4%)	2 (1.2%)	1 (0.6%)
1891	63 (29.2%)	80 (37.0%)		1 (0.4%)
1903	54 (20.1%)	86 (32.1%)		3 (1.1%)

	Dutch	Bohemian-Moravian		Polish
1841				
1851		1 (2.2%)		
1861	3 (3.9%)	2 (2.6%)		
1871	3 (2.2%)	2 (1.5%)		
1881	3 (1.9%)	2 (1.2%)		
1891	3 (1.4%)	4 (1.9%)		
1903	1 (0.3%)	5 (1.9%)		4 (1.5%)

The number of Irish-born clergy began to decline in the 1890's. The number of German-born continued to increase, despite the plentiful crop of German-American vocations, but the percentage of German-born clergy declined steadily after the 1870's.

Of the 623 secular priests who served in the archdiocese at some time between 1841 and 1903 almost 45% had German surnames and 40% Irish. No other nationality exceeded 3.4% (French). Of those whose birthplaces are known, 31.8% were born in Germany; 28.3% in Ireland; and 29.8% in the United States (21.7% in Missouri and 15.2% in St. Louis). Almost 16% were from Westphalia alone, which provided nearly half of the St. Louis German clergy. (Three-quarters of Westphalians were from the Archdiocese of Paderborn.)

The average age at ordination was not significantly different from modern times, varying from decade to decade between 25.3 years and 27.3 years. However, the average was often a median between extremes. In the 1870's, for example, a third of the new priests were ordained at under age twenty-five, and in the 1840's almost 47% were ordained at over age twenty-seven. There was no particular pattern by nationality or by decade, although those ordained in Europe were consistently ordained at slightly younger age than in America (possibly because their studies were not interrupted). Once ordained, a priest would serve on the average between 32.1 and 38.8 years before death, again with no particular variation according to nationality or time period. Average life expectancies ranged from 59.3 for German priests born in the 1860's to 68.9 for German-Americans born in the same decade, again with no particular pattern according to nationality or time period. Over 30% of those ordained in the 1890's would live to celebrate their golden jubilees, as compared with only 10.8% of the ordinands of the 1870's. Almost 18% of those ordained in the 1850's would die with less than ten years in the priesthood, as compared with only 2.9% of those ordained in the 1880's.

Data show that (see Table XIV on following page), after the period of readjustment before the Civil War, city pastorates were increasingly stabilized and assigned according to a discernable pattern. Not only did fewer pastors resign from office (see Table VIII), but in each decade the majority of parishes were staffed by slightly older men with longer tenures in office than in the previous decade. By the 1890's an appreciable number of native-born clergy had succeeded to city pastorates. In each decade both the number and percentage of American-born Irish pastors exceeded their German counterparts, who were more likely still to be immigrants. (In 1903 about 38% of the Irish pastors were American-born and about 31% of German pastors American-born.)

213

TABLE XIV: St. Louis City Pastors—Secular Clergy[1]

Year	Number	Average Age	Av. Yrs. in Office	Irish	German	Other	Foreign-Born	Native
1851	7	36.5	3.1	3 (42.9%)	3 (42.9%)	1 (14.3%)	7 (100.0%)	0
1861	15	34.7	5.0	8 (53.3%)	5 (33.3%)	2 (13.3%)	15 (100.0%)	0
1871	21	37.8	4.8	12 (57.1%)	8 (38.1%)	1 (4.8%)	20 (95.2%)	1 (4.8%)
1881	34	42.2	9.3	18 (52.9%)	14 (41.2%)	2 (5.9%)	31 (91.2%)	3 (8.8%)
1891	44	48.0	10.9	25 (56.8%)	16 (36.4%)	3 (6.8%)	33 (75.0%)	11 (25.0%)
1903	59	53.9	14.2	31 (52.5%)	21 (35.6%)	7 (11.9%)	41 (69.5%)	18 (30.5%)

TABLE XV: SECULAR PRIESTS APPOINTED
TO FIRST CITY PASTORATES

Decade	*No.*[1]	*Average Age*	*Av. Tenure From Appt. in Years*	*Foreign-Born*	*Native*
1840's	10	32.8	8.5	10 (100.0%)	0
1850's	19	27.0	9.9	19 (100.0%)	0
1860's	22	32.3	13.9	21 (95.5%)	1 (4.8%)
1870's	26	31.6	12.7	24 (92.3%)	2 (7.7%)
1880's	20	36.6	19.6	12 (60.0%)	8 (40.0%)
1890-1903	34	38.7	17.4	20 (58.9%)	14 (41.1%)

The stabilization process for city parishes is again reflected in the above figures, which show that from the time of the Civil War increasingly older men were appointed to city pastorates, and they were likely to have increasingly long tenures in office. By the 1880's native-born priests were being given these pastorates in appreciable numbers. The first native American appointed a pastor in St. Louis was Charles Ziegler of St. Malachy's in 1869. The first native St. Louisan was William H. Brantner of St. Teresa's in 1875.

No rigid pattern existed for clerical assignments in nineteenth-century St. Louis. Some priests, like James J. Bourke at St. Michael's, James T. Coffey at St. John's, and George A. Reis at St. Liborius', were curates who eventually succeeded to the pastorates of their respective parishes. James J. McGlynn, ordained in 1884, spent one day as a curate and then was appointed to found a new parish in the western part of the city, St. Rose's, where he remained for the next fifty-two years. William Klevinghaus and Henry Groll were ordained in 1865 and 1866 respectively. Both held several rural assignments, then in 1871 were appointed curates at Sts. Peter and Paul's in St. Louis, where both eventually died, Klevinghaus in 1915 and Groll in 1926. Joseph A. Connelly, ordained in 1878, was a curate in St. Louis, pastor at New Madrid, again a curate in two St. Louis parishes, pastor at DeSoto, pastor of St. Teresa's in St. Louis, and subsequently vicar general. Michael J. McCabe served for a quarter of a century as curate to his younger brother at Sacred Heart, then spent thirty years as pastor of St. Michael's.

The tenure of rural pastors was often extremely brief, sometimes only a year,[1] quite possibly because of the smallness and poverty of many rural parishes. At least before the Civil War, assignments outside St. Louis were considered somewhat undesirable, so that when

John J. Hogan voluntarily resigned the pastorate of St. Michael's in 1857 to become a missionary in northern Missouri the archbishop promised to restore him to St. Michael's if he should ever desire it and also told him that he would never send a man unwillingly to the places to which Hogan was going.⁴⁴ In 1847 a St. Louis curate, William Wheeler, wrote of the pioneering priest of western Missouri, Bernard Donnelly

216

> I was free to say even to the Archbishop that it was an injustice to Father Donnelly to send him outside of civilization, for there is not a priest in the arch-diocese as well equipped mentally as he. He is an omniverous reader and conversant with several languages, besides his grace and aptitude for ceremonies have properly kept him before the public eye as Master of Ceremonies . . . He will be lost in the land of the Indian and the rude trapper. Besides, his manners are courtly and suited for the culture and refinement of a city.

By 1869, however, Wheeler thought that Donnelly had become "all things to all men."⁴⁵

By 1903 there were sixty-seven parishes in St. Louis—thirty-two designated as Irish, twenty-one as German, five as non-ethnic, three as Italian, two each as Bohemian and Polish, and one each as Slovak, Negro, and Syro-Maronite. Three of the parishes were operated by the Jesuits and one each by the Vincentians, Franciscans, and Redemptorists.

Eastern and Southern European clergy rarely remained in the arch-diocese for very long, and their brief parochial tenures were often marked by bitter quarrels. Except for the Bohemians, the less numerous ethnic groups usually had to rely on priests of religious orders to provide them with pastoral services.

At various times sixteen Bohemian and Moravian priests served in St. Louis, but three-quarters of them quickly moved on. A single patriarchal priest, Joseph L. Hessoun, held the Bohemian community together through most of the nineteenth century.

St. Louis' first bishop, Joseph Rosati, C.M. (1826-43), was an Italian, and Italian priests occasionally served in the diocese in the early years. However, the first attempt at an Italian parish—St. Bonaventure's (1875-82)—was made by the Conventual Franciscans. Bitter factionalism involving some of the clergy split the parish badly, and it was briefly under a secular priest until the decision was made to close it.⁴⁶ Cesar Spigardi, who founded three Italian parishes at the turn of the century and served simultaneously as pastor of all three,

was a Scalabrini Father who was received into the ranks of the archdiocesan clergy.[47]

St. Stanislaus, the first Polish parish (1880), was founded by Franciscans. However, after a few years its pastor, Urban Stanowski, was
also secularized, remaining pastor until his death in 1927. St.
Casimir's was founded in 1889 largely because of strife between
Stanowski and some of his parishioners.[48]

Negro Catholics were under the care of the Jesuits, first at Saint
Louis University, then at St. Elizabeth's. Most of the priests serving
there in the nineteenth century had German surnames.[49]

Ethnic lines among the clergy were naturally strict but not absolutely inviolable, and Americanized priests of German ancestry could
serve in Irish parishes. Charles Ziegler, born in the old French town of
Ste. Genevieve, spent almost his entire priestly career at St. Patrick's
and St. Malachy's and disposed of criticisms by saying that he was as
Irish as St. Patrick.[50] John J. Tannrath was pastor of St. Agnes', John
H. May of St. Thomas of Aquin's, and Raphael Capezuto of the
Assumption, all Irish parishes. However, our Lady of Mount Carmel
in Baden was founded when the Irish majority seceded from Holy
Cross Parish in 1872. Some of the Irish were reportedly angered when
the pastor, Herman Wigger, prayed for the German cause in the
Franco-Prussian War.[51]

Five Belgian and three Dutch priests served in the archdiocese at
various times. One Dutchman, J. A. Stroombergen, founded two St.
Louis German parishes, St. Agatha's and Our Lady of Perpetual
Help, although he stayed only a short time in each. The best-known
Dutch priest, Henry Van der Sanden, did not want to be identified
with the Germans, however. When pastor in the St. Louis suburb of
Kirkwood he heard German confessions and preached German ser-
mons only with reluctance. When chancellor of the archdiocese in
1875 he omitted from the clergy list the name of the venerable pioneer
priest of Chicago, Irenaeus St. Cyr, who was a convent chaplain at
Carondelet. St. Cyr inquired if this were due to national prejudice, but
Bishop Patrick Ryan reminded him that Van der Sanden had favored
the French side in the recent war.[52] (As already noted, many St. Louis
German priests were from Westphalia, which adjoins Holland.)

Especially in the earlier years there were a number of Alsatians
among the St. Louis clergy, useful because they spoke both French
and German. Francis X. Weiss, pastor for many years at Ste.
Genevieve was the last of these pioneers and found his bilingual skills
highly useful as the town changed character from French to German.[53]
In his later years he was assisted for a time by another Alsatian,

August Huettler, who crossed the ethnic barriers to become a close friend of the Gaelic scholar James Keegan, a curate at St. Malachy's.[54]

There were nineteen priests with English surnames and four with Scottish surnames during the period 1841-1903. There were also two Hungarians serving at different times, although there was no Hungarian parish.

Despite semi-frontier conditions some of the clergy were fairly well educated. Henry Muhlsiepen, the German vicar general, did graduate work at Trier,[55] and Engelbert Hoeynck of St. Liborius, studied *Kulturgeschichte* at Bonn before entering the seminary.[56] Martin S. Brennan of St. Thomas of Aquin's and St. Lawrence O'Toole's wrote popular works of astronomy and was a member of the American Mathematical Society, the British Astronomical Association, and other learned groups.[57] Frederick G. Holweck of St. Aloysius' and St. Francis De Sales' had a huge personal library, was a scholarly hagiographer and hymnographer, and towards the end of his life received an honorary degree from Freiburg.[58] The future bishop Thomas Bonacum, although an Irishman, took advanced studies at the University of Wurzburg.[59] Christopher Wapelhorst, who served briefly as chancellor in St. Louis, became rector of St. Francis De Sales Seminary in Milwaukee and later a Franciscan, and wrote standard liturgical works. Joseph F. Selinger, a St. Louis priest, was a professor at the same seminary and one of the first Thomistic philosophers in the United States.[60]

Although Archbishop Kenrick had opposed the establishment of the North American College in Rome, as he opposed most Romanizing tendencies in the American Church,[61] seventeen St. Louisans were ordained from there in the period 1873-1902, nine of them of German extraction. Ten were ordained from Louvain between 1868 and 1900, seven of them Germans. Seven men were ordained after studies at Innsbruck in the 1880's and 1890's, all of them Germans.

There were a few blood relationships among the clergy. In 1873 the archbishop's cousin, Andrew Eustace, transferred from the Diocese of Chicago and was made pastor of St. Michael's, where he served until his death twenty years later. Archbishop Kenrick had been slow in giving his relative preferment, however. Peter Richard Kenrick and his brother Francis Patrick, then Archbishop of Baltimore, had not wanted Andrew to come to America in the early 1850's and for a time the young man had no employment. He served in Chicago fifteen years before being accepted in St. Louis and was described as exceedingly tactless in his manner of speaking.[62]

William Walsh of St. Bridget's had one of his nephews, Thomas J. Walsh, as his curate in the 1890's and later another nephew, Patrick J. Dooley, became pastor of the parish.[63] The most notable clerical family dynasty was that of the Wiggers—two brothers and their three nephews. From 1865 to 1940 the pastorate of Holy Cross Parish was successively in the hands of three members of the family.[64] Besides the Wiggers, there were six other pairs of brothers who served in the archdiocese at various times in the nineteenth century.

Under semi-frontier conditions, St. Louis sometimes attracted priests with unusual personal histories. Joseph A. Lutz had arrived from Germany in the 1820's with a dream of converting the Indians. He travelled as far as Kansas, but witnessing the carnage of an Indian massacre affected his nerves and evidently made him unfit for sustained employment. He left the archdiocese in the late 1840's, reportedly because of the notoriety which ensued when he unknowingly answered a sick-call to a brothel.[65]

Henry Lipowsky, the first pastor of St. John Nepomuk's, had been a Jesuit novice and then an officer in the Austrian cavalry. Aristocratic in attitude, he found his immigrant parishioners uncongenial and returned home.[66] Caspar Doebbener of Holy Trinity had served in the Prussian cavalry.[67] Anton Carius claimed to have been a chaplain to the Emperor Maximilian in Mexico and habitually spoke military slang.[68] James J. McGlynn of St. Rose's had been orphaned in Virginia around the time of the Civil War. He worked his way across country and was eventually adopted by a North Missouri farmer.[69] Thomas A. Butler of St. James' and St. Cronan's had been forced to leave Ireland because of his Fenian associations. Already a priest, he founded a communal settlement in Kansas before coming to St. Louis.[70] Henry J. Shaw was from a well-to-do English family who disowned him after his conversion to Catholicism in France. He became a Redemptorist, transferred to the secular clergy, and finished his days as pastor in a small Missouri town.[71] Joseph Melcher, born in Vienna, had been taken to northern Italy by his family while still a boy. After ordination he served as chaplain at the court of the Duke of Modena until smitten with missionary zeal. He became vicar general in St. Louis and later first Bishop of Green Bay.[72] James B. Jackson, pastor in the St. Louis suburb of Clayton, was born in Ireland, the son of an English squire. At his father's death the estate became entangled in the Court of Chancery and young Jackson emigrated to America. He later got his inheritance.[73]

Some of the clergy gained colorful reputations after coming to St.Louis. William Walsh of St. Bridget's, the leading Irish pastor,

constantly railed against dance halls from the pulpit and on occasion
entered the establishments and flailed right and left with a buggy-whip
to drive out the celebrators. He successfully thwarted a plan to build
an elevated rail line on the street where St. Bridget's was located and
built a huge rectory, dubbed Father Walsh's Hotel, where he enter-
tained visiting priests from all over the United States. Thomas A.
Butler, the ex-Fenian, was not in awe of the redoubtable Father
Walsh, however, and in 1878 grossly insulted him by letter because of
a rumor that Walsh was proposing that Butler's parish be divided.[74]
Michael O'Reilly of St. Columbkille's threatened bodily harm to a
newspaper editor who wrote slightingly of his parishioners and forced
an apology.[75]

220

The most fearless of the St. Louis clergy was David S. Phelan,
pastor of Our Lady of Mount Carmel parish and for almost fifty years
editor of his own newspaper, *The Western Watchman,* which he used
to bestow praise and blame in an independent and often eccentric
spirit. In 1892 Phelan obtained the secret membership lists of the anti-
Catholic American Protective Association and published them in his
newspaper, urging a Catholic boycott of all businessmen belonging to
the organization. Not untypical of Phelan's style of journalism was
his ridicule of Francis M. Kielty, pastor of the fashionable Holy Guardian Angels parish, because Kielty kept gamecocks.[76] Kielty was
believed by many people to have a huge personal fortune, which turned out not to be true. He was also thought to have refused appointment as bishop of Peoria, which was equally untrue.)[77] On Sundays,
Phelan would preach his sermons after Mass, when most of the congregation had left. A stenographer took them down for publication in
the next week's *Watchman.*[78]

One German priest, Sebastian Sennerich, was described by his contemporaries as being "of a jovial disposition, like an Irish priest,"[79]
and evidently a certain puckishness was characteristic of some of the
Irish clergy. One St. Louis alumnus of Carlow College went so far as to
assert that most graduates of the college were plagued by an excess of
levity and irreverence, dating from the days before it was a seminary.[80]
However, the blunt plainness of a nineteenth-century priest is revealed
in the last will and testament of Vicar General Joseph A. Connelly:

> What meaning is there these days sitting up all night with a
> corpse? People become tired and worn out; If the old tim
> [sic] custom would be followed there would be a
> meaning.... Let the doors of residence or Church be clos-
> ed at 11:00 at night; let every one go to bed.

Putting much money in the ground in a high priced casket is out of place for a priest. A neat casket; not too expensive.

Of what good is a funeral sermon? A subject of criticism from priests forgotten by people.[11]

James Henry of St. Lawrence O'Toole's, who as a young curate at St. Patrick's in the 1850's had led a platoon of parishioners in repulsing a Know-Nothing mob, wanted Gaelic taught in the public schools and on one occasion marched his parochial-school children to the neighboring public school to dramatize the denial of tax assistance.[12]

A "state of conflict" between bishops and priests has been characterized as common in the nineteenth-century American Church.[13] Under Archbishop Kenrick such conflicts were not numerous, however, and the overall impression is of an episcopacy characterized by austere aloofness and the general respect of the clergy for their ordinary.[14] In 1880, when the venerable pioneer pastor of Kansas City, Bernard Donnelly, retired, the archbishop's sole response was: "Rev. Dear Father Donnelly: Father Doherty pastor of Kirkwood, will take charge of Immaculate Conception Church on the coming Easter Sunday. Yours truly, +P. R. Kenrick, Abp.'"[15] Kenrick's strong opposition to the definition of papal infallibility in 1870, which may have stemmed from certain Gallican ideas taught to him at Maynooth,[16] seems to have been complemented by an equally strong notion of episcopal authority, which brooked interference neither from above nor below. In addition he was a venerable father figure to the clergy for many years. By 1861, with a third of a century's rule still ahead of him, there were only three priests in the archdiocese older than he was, although he was only fifty-five. He had been ordained longer than any of them.

The Civil War era was a stormy time for the St. Louis Church. John F. Bannon left voluntarily to join the Confederacy. Meanwhile John O'Sullivan, pastor of St. Malachy's was so outspoken in his Southern sympathies that the Federal authorities threatened to arrest him. The archbishop thought it prudent that he leave the city, although rather incongruously he went farther north, to Springfield, Illinois.[17] Kenrick himself, who owned a few slaves, was almost certainly a Southern sympathizer, but acted correctly in public and was always apolitical; he even declined to vote.[18]

After the war the state of Missouri imposed a loyalty oath on, among others, clergy. The archbishop ordered his priests not to take it and promised to support them in their resolves. Several were arrested in outstate Missouri, including the future Bishop Hogan, who met the

221

sheriff in cassock, biretta, and surplice. The embarrassed sheriff asked Hogan to walk to the jail by a different route and meet him there.[19] Another priest, John A. Cummings, refused bail and was jailed for a time while his case went through the courts. The test oath was eventually overturned by the United States Supreme Court as a result of the Cummings case.[20]

Although many Irish priests were Confederate sympathizers, this was not true of all. Hogan, despite his refusal to take the test oath, was an ardent Unionist. While a seminarian at Carondelet in the early 1850's he had written an abolitionist essay, only to be told by a professor that he risked mob violence if he expressed such opinions in public. Hogan was greatly shocked at the treatment of the slaves. "Greed caused it all," was his succinct analysis.

In the 1880's the archbishop clashed with three of his priests. Two St. Louis pastors were accused of scandalous behavior. One, a German, quietly left the archdiocese.[21] The other, an Irishman, fought his dismissal all the way to Rome but lost when it was discovered that he was a member of a religious order and had never received his release. He went to Colorado, got into trouble again, and ended his days as a priest in Oregon.[22]

The most celebrated case involved Cornelius O'Leary, pastor at DeSoto, who espoused the cause of many of his parishioners in the great railway strike of 1886. In the process he became a close friend of Terrence V. Powderly of the Knights of Labor and also of the controversial New York priest Edward McGlynn.[23] In a youthful photograph O'Leary looked handsome and pugnacious,[24] and on one occasion he threatened to cane a railway official who had insulted him. In testimony before a Federal investigating committee he denounced strike-breaking, defended boycotts, claimed that the railroads had bought state legislatures, and warned that their labor policies were spawning Marxists.[25]

Archbishop Kenrick generally disapproved public agitation, and in 1865 had inhibited a Fenian funeral at St. Patrick's Church.[26] He was also influenced against the Knights of Labor by Cardinal Taschereau of Quebec and after a few months removed O'Leary from DeSoto to the St. Louis suburb of Webster Groves. (The railroads had offered to build a new church in DeSoto if O'Leary were removed, but he had built one himself.) Bitter, O'Leary threatened to write a biography of the archbishop (". . . he just struck upon a person who loves to bring tyrants to their knees"), and in Ireland in 1887 he denounced the police and reportedly proclaimed that all true Irishmen were rebels

222

and socialists. In the 1890's he lived in several St. Louis parishes, either as a curate or as a guest."

O'Leary obviously had a fiery temper, and while still a student in 1873 had clashed with Vicar General Muhlsiepen over the courses required for ordination. In 1906, while pastor in the St. Louis suburb of Wellston, he was accused of assaulting a parishioner, a physician who came late for Mass and parked his automobile, decorated with an advertisement, in front of the church." O'Leary died as he lived, killed by a tornado in 1917.[100]

William Faerber of St. Mary's and Francis S. Goller of Sts. Peter and Paul's were among the intellectual leaders of the German clergy in America. Faerber was the author of a widely used catechism. Both were grieved by Kenrick's designation of their German parishes as mere chapels of ease, and they frequently resorted to the press to defend the use of the German language in schools. Their relations with the archbishop were not, perhaps, strained but do appear to have been cool.[101]

By the early 1890's the archbishop was evidently losing his grip on the affairs of the archdiocese. In 1819-93 ten new parishes were established in the city of St. Louis, reportedly because Kenrick would give such a commission to any priest who asked for one, sometimes forgetting that he had done so.[102] His memory was failing in other ways also, and the need for a coadjutor was obvious.

The greatest crisis of his episcopacy, except for the First Vatican Council, was his attempt to designate as his successor his vicar general, Philip P. Brady, the pastor of St. John's. He failed to follow proper procedure, and many priests also found Brady unacceptable. A petition was submitted to Cardinal James Gibbons of Baltimore proposing other candidates for the office and implicitly disapproving the archbishop's choice. Several outstate priests and forty-one of the forty-six secular pastors in St. Louis signed the document. The nonsigners were Jeremiah J. Harty of St. Leo's, Joseph A. Connelly of St. Teresa's, and Francis Jones of St. Columbkille's, who were seminary classmates; Martin S. Brennan of St. Lawrence O'Toole's, who was a friend and classmate of Brady; and Peter A. Lotz of St. Francis de Sales.[103] Among the signers was the archbishop's cousin, Andrew Eustace; and the key organizer of the petition was his former secretary, Charles Ziegler of St. Malachy's.[104]

St. Louis clergy were quoted in the daily press with remarkable frankness and even vituperativeness concerning the archbishop in his last years.[105] Their petition, with John J. Kain, Bishop of Wheeling, as

223

their first choice, was acceded to in Rome, and Kain soon arrived as coadjutor and administrator. Brady had died in the meantime, and Archbishop Kenrick offered the vicar generalship first to Jeremiah Harty, who declined, and then to Joseph Connelly, who accepted, making for a difficult situation until both Kenrick and Connelly resigned in 1895,[106] Connelly was re-appointed vicar general by Archbishop John J. Glennon in 1903.

The troubles of Archbishop Kenrick's last years carried over through almost all of his successor's brief administration. Archbishop Kain's appointment doubtlessly owed much to James and Michael McCabe, who were his classmates at St. Mary's Seminary in Baltimore. Soon, however, his relations with the McCabes were strained. Kenrick had appointed no archdiocesan consultors. Kain did so but failed to appoint the two pastors most favored by their fellow priests—William Walsh of St. Bridget's and Francis S. Goller of Sts. Peter and Paul's. The controversy reached the pages of *The American Ecclesiastical Review.* When the archbishop proposed to hold a banquet for the Apostolic Delegate in 1897, Charles Ziegler objected at a public meeting that this would violate the spirit of Lent and proclaimed, "I hope the pallium celebration will be a great success, but the reception for the Cardinal a great fiasco." Almost half the priests present voted with Ziegler against holding the banquet.[107]

In 1897-98 Kain became embroiled in a lengthy struggle to oust John T. Tuohy from the pastorate of St. Patrick's. Tuohy had been the first priest from the St. Louis Archdiocese to study at the Catholic University of America. The charges against his administration of St. Patrick's although aired in the newspapers at great length, remained somewhat vague, apparently centering on financial mismanagement. Hundreds of parishioners, both Irish and Italian, petitioned for his retention. In 1898, however, he was removed by a civil law suit. He left the archdiocese, returned later under Archbishop Glennon, and held a rural pastorate for the rest of his life.[108]

Archbishop Kain also clashed with the man who was probably the best known, and certainly the most colorful, St. Louis priest of the nineteenth century—David S. Phelan, who thus summarized his own career:

> The first trouble I got into was over the action of some bishops in excommunicating the Ancient Order of Hibernians. I spared no man, no matter how high in the Church, who abused his power to oppress a body of good honest Irish Catholics...
> The next trouble I got into was over the educational clauses of the Third Council of Baltimore. I said they were silly

224

and impracticable and would certainly cause trouble. That war is still on and will last until the last stalwart Lunatic expires. Contrary to the general impression I am not at all a contentious individual. I have been in conflict nearly all my journalistic life, but I have always had for antagonists silly bishops and stupid editors, who insisted in making our people more Catholic than the Holy Father, and more orthodox than the Church. I fired the first gun in the late Cahensly campaign and was the first to withdraw from the field when the Pope commanded a cessation of hostilities. Everybody knows that chicanery and un-Catholic pretense were at the bottom of that miserable movement, and I can only pray the world may long be spared a repetition of the scandal.[109]

225

Phelan's newspaper was condemned on four different occasions, including once by Archbishop Kain. The editor submitted each time, then speedily resumed his old ways. After the condemnation of 1894 he wrote,

The Watchman may be a menace to faith and morals; but the worst articles that have appeared in it were written by bishops, except three that we remember, and they were written by a Jesuit. But they were all right, or we should not let them in.[110]

The gibe was probably directed in part at Bishop Thomas Bonacum of Lincoln, a former St. Louis priest, who had recently condemned the paper.[111] Bonacum had once written for the *Watchman*.[112]

Kain, while still coadjutor bishop in 1894, had condemned the paper because of its criticisms of the Third Provincial Council of Baltimore. He ordered Phelan to retract, which the editor did, and had the condemnation read from all the pulpits. Phelan sneered that Kain had been born in a slave state. (Virginia) and St. Louisans would have to teach him how free men lived,[113] a rather illogical thrust since Missouri had also been a slave state and Kain was from the western part of Virginia, which seceded from the rest of the state because of its Unionist sympathies during the Civil War.

The organization of the St. Louis Archdiocese in the nineteenth century was simple and even careless by modern standards. For a time—1864-1871—there is no record of there even having been a chancellor. The archbishop's secretary for some years—Patrick J. Ryan—was also pastor of a flourishing parish.[114] Henry Van der Sanden was chancellor from 1873 to 1910 and kept the historical archives in a box under his bed; after nis death they were almost lost.[115] There is only sporadic evidence of the archbishop's having had a secretary.

The office of vicar general was important, however, and for a time in the mid-1840's Kenrick had three simultaneously, evidently while he was making up his mind about the administration of the see.[116] Continuously from 1847 to 1927 the archdiocese maintained a vicar general specifically for the non-English-speaking Catholics, mainly Germans. Joseph Melcher held the office from 1847 to 1868 and Henry Muhlsiepen from 1868 to 1903. Muhlsiepen was given wide discretion and was, unlike Goller and Faerber, distinctly not an ethnic militant. He was said never to express himself on controversial subjects, even in private.[117]

The vicar generalship was a demanding office, requiring numerous journeys to rural parishes and ceremonial appearances everywhere. Of the six men appointed vicar general between 1847 and 1893, none was older than forty, although beginning in 1903 the appointees were considerably older.[118] Muhlsiepen had merely been curate to Joseph Melcher at St. Mary's when he was appointed, at age thirty-four. He was also made pastor of the parish but after a year gave it up to serve full time as vicar general.

During the periods 1858-68 and 1895-1903 there was no vicar general for the English-speaking Catholics, but at other times the archdiocese had two vicars simultaneously. Philip P. Brady, who held the office 1884-1893, had already impaired his health by rugged labors in rural pastorates and while pastor of the declining Annunciation Parish in St. Louis lived in one room behind the church and did his own cooking. In 1890 he had a sharp exchange with Bishop John S. Vertin of Marquette over Brady's alledged slowness in replying to a letter. Brady said that he was weighed down with duties and was absent from the city for long periods.[119]

Archbishop Kenrick appointed neither consultors nor irremovable rectors, a lack which his successor remedied.[120] He had wanted the office of canon in his cathedral, an honor not authorized in the American Church, and in the 1850's he evidently did have them for a time.[121] No monsignori were appointed under him, but Archbishop Kain obtained the dignity for three priests—William Walsh, Henry Muhlsiepen, and Joseph L. Hessoun.[122]

Between 1842 and 1868 six Vincentians and three Jesuits from the Archdiocese of St. Louis were made bishops, although most of them were not serving in the archdiocese at the time of their appointments. They included two Spaniards, two Irish-Americans, and one each who were French, Belgian, Italian, Irish, and Irish-Canadian.[123]

Between 1854 and 1903 ten St.Louis secular priests were made bishops. All were Irish except Joseph Melcher and Jeremiah Harty,

226

who was the first native St. Louisan to be raised to the episcopacy. Thus although St. Louis had a preponderance of German priests, virtually none of them was chosen bishop.[124]

Those appointed were: Anthony O'Regan (1854), James Duggan (1857), Patrick A. Feehan (1865), John Hennessy (1866), Joseph Melcher and John J. Hogan (1868), Patrick J. Ryan (1872), Thomas Bonacum (1887), John J. Hennessy (1888), and Jeremiah J. Harty (1903). Except for Melcher, who was sixty-one at the time of his consecration but who had declined a bishopric thirteen years earlier, all of those appointed before 1903 were under fifty years of age. James Duggan was only thirty-two and Patrick Feehan thirty-six. Beginning with Harty, and until after the Second World War, the average age of new bishops in St. Louis was over fifty. Two St. Louis priests ordained before 1903 later became bishops—Christopher E. Byrne and Francis Gilfillan. J. Henry Tihen and Joseph S. Koudelka, both of whom were curates in St. Louis briefly in the 1880's, were made bishops elsewhere. Joseph F. Chartrand was born and raised in St. Louis but did not serve in the archdiocese.

Four (O'Regan, Duggan, Melcher, and Ryan) were vicars general. Three (O'Regan, Feehan, and the first Hennessy) had been seminary rectors. The rest were St. Louis pastors, except for Hogan, who had exchanged his city parish for the rugged missionary life. His bulls of appointment reached him at a remote settlement where he was recovering from exposure suffered by being lost in a blizzard.[125] The chancellorship was not a stepping-stone to promotion, nor was study at the North American College.[126] In the early 1870's a student named Patrick W. Tallon, who would become a prominent St. Louis pastor, was offered the opportunity to study in Rome but declined, because he could see no advantage in it.[127]

Most of those named bishop distinguished themselves. However, Anthony O'Regan, a scholarly seminary rector, resisted appointment as Bishop of Chicago and suffered a breakdown immediately after his consecration. He was unable to travel for two months and resigned four years later.[128] James Duggan, his successor, was an energetic prelate who went insane in 1869 and spent the remaining thirty years of his life in an asylum in St. Louis.[129] Not all St. Louis priests were pleased with the episcopal choices. In 1868 William Wheeler of St. Patrick's wrote to the *New York Freeman's Journal and Catholic Register* that priests suffered from episcopal arbitrariness and that bishops should be elected. "I think now the time has come for the Church to take the girlish pants off her priests and put on them men's

227

breeches..." He called the method of choosing bishops "truly, disgusting" and added:

> It is true we have had hard working, active, and zealous priests nominated from time to time, but this was rather the exception. The rule always was, and is, that the obsequious wirepuller with influential ladies at his back was, and is, sure to succeed rather than the hard-working zealous retiring priest.[130]

Already in the early 1850's, when he was not yet fifty years old, Archbishop Kenrick had wanted a coadjutor, which his brother thought unnecessary.[131] In 1857 he obtained James Duggan, who was taken from him within two years. By 1868 he was again petitioning and included among his choices the German-American Charles Ziegler.[132] The Vatican Council intervened and when Patrick J. Ryan was named in 1872 there were many who thought that the control of the archdiocese was being taken out of Kenrick's hands because of his opposition to the definition of papal infallibility. For the next twelve years the archbishop virtually withdrew from public life and gave all public functions over to Bishop Ryan.[133]

Ryan, one of the greatest pulpit orators of the nineteenth century, was a highly respected and beloved prelate. He was careless of his appearance, and Mrs. William Tecumseh Sherman regularly collected his clothes to mend and patch them.[134] Until 1880 he also served as pastor of St. John's Pro-Cathedral. In 1884 he was made Archbishop of Philadelphia, and the seventy-eight-year-old Kenrick again undertook the administration of the archdiocese. His next coadjutor, John J. Kain, was forced on him.

By 1899 Archbishop Kain was in failing health and sought an auxiliary, an expedient evidently not available to American bishops earlier in the century. He first nominated Jeremiah J. Harty and then Joseph A. Connelly, but Rome acted on neither proposal.[135] Curiously the archbishop chose to promote the candidacies of two of the handful of priests who had not supported his own appointment six years before. Harty was made Archbishop of Manila in 1903, a few months after the St. Louis clergy had again obtained their first choice as coadjutor bishop—John J. Glennon of Kansas City.[136]

Conclusion

The history of the St. Louis archdiocesan clergy in the nineteenth century provides a model by which comparative studies of other dioceses can be made, with a view to achieving a historico-sociological understanding of the American priesthood during the crucial decades of immigration and gradual Americanization.

For St. Louis the Civil War was roughly the watershed between rather unstable, semi-frontier conditions and the gradual emergence of a settled, familiar pattern of clerical life. After about 1865 the Archdiocese could rely on a fairly stable, maturing body of clergy who were promoted to pastorates after a period of probation, ordinarily held those appointments for a number of years, and were likely to remain in the Archdiocese until death. This pattern became stronger as the century wore on, and it marked a reversal of pre-war conditions, when the Archdiocese had to rely mainly on a steady stream of young recruits, most of whom had rather brief tenures and more than half of whom eventually moved on to other vineyards. Beginning in 1868, St. Louis also began to produce its own native clergy, who were over one-third of the total by the end of the century.

229

Despite the stereotype of the Irish as prolific nurturers of clergy, and despite the fact that Irish Catholics may well have outnumbered German in the city of St. Louis, Germans in the Archdiocese were producing many more priests than were the Irish in the last quarter of the nineteenth century, and by 1903 well over half the St. Louis priests were German or of German extraction. The great majority of vocations were from the city of St. Louis itself.

The Irish and the Germans were the only numerically significant Catholic ethnic groups in St. Louis and between them produced virtually all the native clerical vocations. Other ethnic groups had to rely mainly on religious orders to supply them with pastors, although by the end of the century these ethnic parishes were gradually coming under the direction of secular priests. Southern and Eastern European priests tended not to remain long in the Archdiocese.

Priests were generally assigned to definable ethnic parishes, but such lines were not absolutely rigid and were occasionally crossed. In particular German-Americans could sometimes serve in Irish parishes.

Partly because of a steady stream of ordinands from Europe, St. Louis never seems to have experienced a clergy shortage after about 1850. With relatively few exceptions, priests were not highly educated. However, they were only rarely accused of misconduct and seem on the whole to have been faithful and of good character. Misbehaving priests invariably left the Archdiocese. Especially before the Civil War, a high proportion of European-born priests left the Archdiocese after a few years, possibly to return home.

There was no fixed *cursus* for priests to travel in the nineteenth century, and individual cases reveal a variety of career patterns. Most priests eventually became pastors of their own parishes, but at varying ages and after varying kinds of experiences. There were a number of priests who had rather colorful personal histories before coming to St. Louis.

The Archdiocese had a quite simple administrative structure, in which the office of vicar general (separate offices for German- and English-speaking Catholics) was important but in which the chancellor was evidently only concerned with routine administrative duties. Vicars general, with heavy responsibilities, were generally young when appointed and were frequently nominated for episcopal office. The chancellorship was not a stepping-stone to the episcopacy, nor was study at the North American College in Rome.

Despite the preponderance of German clergy, all but one of the twelve St. Louis secular priests appointed bishop between 1854 and 1922 were Irish or of Irish descent. Prior to the turn of the century they tended to be young men, but the average age increased after 1900.

Under Archbishop Peter Richard Kenrick priests were generally quiescent. However, his successor, Archbishop John J. Kain, clashed repeatedly with individuals or groups of priests. Both in 1893 and 1903 the priests were able to obtain their favored candidate for the office of coadjutor bishop with the right of succession, in the first instance directly thwarting the wishes of Archbishop Kenrick.

230

NOTES

1. For the general history of the Archdiocese see William Barnaby Faherty, S.J., *Dream by the River: Two Centuries of St. Louis Catholicism* (St. Louis, 1971). Also still useful, although unreliable in places, is John Rothensteiner, *History of the Archdiocese of St. Louis* (St. Louis, 1928, two volumes).
2. Faherty, *Dream*, pp. 69-70. Rothensteiner, *History*, I, pp. 854-9.
3. Frederick G. Holweck, "Abbe Joseph Anthony Lutz," *St. Louis Catholic Historical Review*, V, 4 (Oct., 1923), pp. 189-204. Paul C. Schulte, *The Catholic Heritage of St. Louis* (St. Louis, 1934), p 207.
4. Mary Constance Smith, *Our Pastors in Calvary* (St. Louis, 1924), pp. 1-4. Rothensteiner, *Chronicles of an Old Missouri Parish—Historical Sketches of St. Michael's Church, Fredericktown* (Cape Girardeau, Mo., 1928), pp. 30-1. The Smith volume is a very useful collection of brief biographies. The basic data agree with that in the chancery archives, although most material of a controversial nature was omitted.
5. Smith, *Our Pastors*, p. 168.
6. Holweck, "Father Edmond Saulnier," *St. Louis Catholic Historical Review*, IV, 4 (Oct., 1922), pp. 189-205. Smith, *Our Pastors*, p. 11.
7. Unless otherwise indicated, material on the secular clergy has been compiled from the priests' files of the Archdiocesan archives, housed in the chancery office.
8. This impression is largely drawn from *Faherty, Dream,* and *Rothensteiner, History.*
9. Holweck, "The Language Question at the Old Cathedral of St. Louis," *SLCHR*, II, 1 (Jan., 1920), p. 17. S. J. Miller, "Peter Richard Kenrick, Bishop and Archbishop of St. Louis, 1806-1896," *Records of the American Catholic Historical Society of Philadelphia*, LXXXIV, 1-3 (Mar.-Sept., 1973), pp. 27-8.
10. Holweck, "Abbe Lutz," p. 201.

11. Archdiocesan Archives, Myles W. Tobyn file.
12. Holweck, "Edmond Saulnier" p. 201.
13. *Ibid.*, p. 205
14. Rothensteiner, *History*, I, pp. 817-35.
15. These calculations are based on census and parish records and are summarized in another article of the author. "Parishes and Neighborhoods in a Nineteenth-Century City" (Unpublished).
16. This surmise is based on the relative proportions of German and Irish priests holding rural pastorates. See Rothensteiner, *History*, II, chs. 7-13, 31-4, 47-54, 67-70.
17. The classification of priests according to ethnic group is here made on the basis of surnames.
18. St. Louis was made an archdiocese in 1847.
19. Prior to 1873 the archdiocese did not keep systematic records on the early history of its priests, so that the birth dates of some priests are unknown.
20. This includes St. Louisans sent to study at European seminaries, which was a very small percentage of the total.
21. Sister Esther Marie Godfrey, S.L., *Catholic Participation in the Diplomacy of the Civil War* (unpublished doctoral dissertation, St. Louis University, 1954), pp. 217-8, 236-43, 246-50, 252-60, 281-92. (Lawrence J. Kenny, S.J.), "Father John Bannon, S.J.,"*Historical Records and Studies*, XXVI (1936), pp. 92-8.
22. Archdiocesan Archives, Timothy J. Donovan file.
23. *Ibid.*, John Higginbotham file.
24. The priests' file does not record any clerical trial in the nineteenth century. For the authorizing of such trials see Robert Trisco, "Bishops and Their Priests in the United States," *The Catholic Priest in the United States: Historical Investigations*, ed. John Tracy Ellis (Collegeville, Minn.: St. John's University Press, 1971), pp. 130, 142.
25. O'Hanlon, *Life and Scenery in Missouri* (Dublin, 1890), pp. 11-2.
26. Hogan, *Fifty Years Ago: a Memoir* (Kansas City, 1907), pp. 96, 99.
27. Archdiocesan Archives, John P. Daly file.
28. *Ibid.*, William Walsh file.
29. *Ibid.*, priests' file.
30. *Fifty Years Ago*, pp. 85, 99.
31. Smith, *Our Pastors*, p. 171.
32. *Life and Scenery*, p. 293.
33. Archdiocesan Archives, priests' file.
34. *St. Louis Republic*, Dec. 31, 1884, p. 8.
35. Rothensteiner, *History*, I, pp. 202, 229, 443, 623, 753-64, 741-9. Donna Merwick, *Boston Priests, 1848-1910* (Cambridge, Mass., 1973), pp. 2, 9, 38, 70, 137, 213.
36. Rothensteiner, *Chronicles*. Also *History*, I, p. 448, II, pp. 90, 97.
37. These figures are taken from the biographies in Smith, *Our Pastors*.
38. See note 15.
39. Categories are based on surnames.
40. Birthplaces are not known in all cases, but for earlier clergy birthplace has been attributed on the basis of surname.
41. Regular clergy held only a handful of city pastorates.
42. Despite the founding of additional parishes in each decade, the number of pastors appointed did not increase dramatically because of the decrease in resignations.
43. See Rothensteiner, *ut supra* note 8. Chancery records confirm this impression.
44. Hogan, *On the Mission in Missouri, 1857-1868* (Kansas City, 1892), p. 12.
45. William J. Dalton, *The Life of Father Bernard Donnelly* (Kansas City, 1921), p. 34.
46. Walter J. Galus, C.R., *The History of the Catholic Italians in St. Louis* (unpublished master's thesis, St. Louis University, 1936). Also Archdiocesan Archives, Salvatelli file.
47. Galus, *History*, pp. 63-9, 82-96.
48. John Stanislaus Mysliwiec, C.R., *History of the Catholic Poles of St. Louis* (unpublished master's thesis, St. Louis University, 1936), pp. 9, 13, 19, 41, 46.
49. John Taylor White, S.J., *Survey of Organized Catholic Activities among the Negroes in the St. Louis District, 1719-1937* (unpublished master's thesis, St. Louis University, 1937), pp. 34, 37-8. Daniel M. Hogan, *The Catholic Church and the Negroes of St. Louis* (unpublished master's thesis, St. Louis University, 1955), pp. 21, 23.

50. Rothensteiner, *History*, II, p. 200. Smith, *Our Pastors*, p. 107.
51. *Diamond Jubilee of Our Lady of Mt. Carmel Church* (St. Louis, 1947), p. 7.
52. Mary Broderick Chomeau, *One Hundred and Twenty Five Years, a History of St. Peter's Parish, Kirkwood* (Kirkwood, 1957), pp. 38 and 45. Archdiocesan Archives, Irenaeus St. Cyr file. The Chomeau booklet is an exceptionally interesting and well written parish history.
53. Rothensteiner, *History*, II, pp. 74, 77, 209, 520.
54. Smith *Our Pastors*, p. 73.
55. Rothensteiner, *History*, II, p. 13.
56. *Andeken an das Goldene Jubilaum der St. Liborius Gemeinde in St. Louis, Mo.* (St. Louis, 1907), p. 28.
57. *Golden Jubilee, 1882-1932, of Saint Thomas of Aquin Church* (St. Louis, 1932), pp. 24-5. In 1891 Brennan also won a contest as the most popular clergyman in St. Louis, sponsored by a newspaper. He received a tour of Europe and the Holy Land.
58. Rothensteiner, *History*, II, pp. 472, 597, 727-30. *New Catholic Encyclopedia* (New York, 1967), VII, p. 60.
59. Archdiocesan Archives, Thomas Bonacum file.
60. Peter Leo Johnson, *Halcyon Days: Story of St. Francis Seminary, Milwaukee, 1856-1956* (Milwaukee, 1956), pp. 90, 228-30. Smith, *Our Pastors*, p. 38.
61. Miller, "Kenrick," pp. 61-2.
62. F.E.T. (ed.), *The Kenrick-Frenaye Correspondence* (Philadelphia, 1920), I, pp. 210, 295-6, 298, 317-8, 393. Smith, *Our Pastors*, pp. 47, 295.
63. Smith, *Our Pastors*, pp. 69, 144-5.
64. *A Souvenier of the Diamond Jubilee of Holy Cross Parish, 1864-1939* (St. Louis, 1939), and *The Centennial History of Holy Cross Parish* (St. Louis, 1964). The first non-Wigger to serve as pastor of the parish was the distinguished liturgist, Msgr. Martin B. Helriegel.
65. Holweck, "Abbe Lutz."
66. *Centennial of St. John Nepomuk Parish* (St. Louis, 1954). Rothensteiner, *History*, II, p. 192.
67. Rothensteiner, *History*, II, p. 115.
68. Smith, *Our Pastors*, p. 46. Carius is not mentioned in standard works on Maximilian.
69. *Fifty Golden Years* (St. Louis, 1934).
70. Smith, *Our Pastors*, p. 60. P. J. O'Connor, *History of St. James Parish, St. Louis, Mo., 1860-1937* (St. Louis, 1937), pp. 21-22. The latter is an exceptionally lively and interesting work.
71. Archdiocesan Archives, Henry J. Shaw file. Shaw arrived in St. Louis in 1890, a year after the death of another Henry Shaw, a millionaire and the city's leading philanthropist. By coincidence both Henry Shaws were from Sheffield in Yorkshire. (See *Henry Shaw, a Biography* [St. Louis, n.d.]).
72. Archdiocesan Archives, Joseph Melcher file. Rothensteiner, *History*, II, 6.
73. Smith, *Our Pastors*, p. 71.
74. Sister Mary George Eppich, C.S.J., *The History of St. Bridget of Erin Parish, Saint Louis, 1853-1917* (unpublished master's thesis, St. Louis University, 1953), pp. 48, 57. Archdiocesan Archives, William Walsh file.
75. Smith, *Our Pastors*, pp. 36-37.
76. Lawrence Edwin Walsh, S.J., *Father David S. Phelan Versus the American Protective Association in St. Louis* (unpublished master's thesis, St. Louis University, 1948), pp. 54, 104 *et seq.*.
77. Smith, *Our Pastors*, pp. 90-91. The names of all the priests proposed for the diocese of Peoria are given in David Francis Sweeney, O.F.M., *The Life of John Lancaster Spaulding, First Bishop of Peoria, 1840-1916* (New York, 1965), pp. 100-06.
78. Walsh, *Phelan*, p. 47. For further information on Phelan see *Dictionary of American Biography*, ed. Dumas Malone (New York, 1954), XIV, 520-21; and *New Catholic Encyclopedia*, XI, 254-55.
79. Smith, *Our Pastors*, p. 117.
80. O'Connor, *History of St. James*, p. 25. The statement was made by Edmund Casey, pastor of St. James's and a Carlow graduate. Casey himself was described as fun-loving. He kept a racehorse and got involved in litigation over its care and feeding.
81. Archdiocesan Archives, Joseph A. Connelly file.
82. Smith, *Our Pastors*, pp. 82-84.
83. Trisco, "Bishops and Priests," p. 270.

232

84. On Kenrick's personality see Miller, "Kenrick," pp. 136-38; Bertha May Ivory, *Fifty Years a Bishop* (St. Louis, 1891); (William Walsh), *Life of the Most Rev. Peter Richard Kenrick* (St. Louis, 1891).

85. Dalton, *Life of Donnelly*, p. 191.

86. Miller, "Kenrick," p. 12.

87. Rothensteiner, *History*, II, p. 198.

88. Miller, "Kenrick," p. 64. Sister Mary Emmanuel White, R.S.M., *Archbishop Peter Richard Kenrick and the Civil War* (unpublished master's thesis, St. Louis University, 1948).

89. Hogan, *On the Mission*, pp. 123-48.

90. Harold C. Bradley, S.J., *John A. Cummings and the Missouri Test Oath: 1865* (unpublished master's thesis, St. Louis University, 1956). White, *Kenrick and the Civil War*, p. 94-100.

91. Hogan, *On the Mission*, pp. 6-7.

92. Archdiocesan Archives, priests' file.

93. *Ibid*. Faherty, *Dream*, p. 107.

94. Faherty, "The Clergyman and Labor Progress: Cornelius O'Leary and the Knights of Labor," *Labor History*, XI, 2 (Spring, 1970), pp. 175-89.

95. Smith, *Our Pastors*, p. 141.

96. Faherty, "Clergyman."

97. Rothensteiner, *History*, II, p. 640.

98. Faherty, "Clergyman."

99. Archdiocesan Archives, Cornelius O'Leary file.

100. Smithy, *Our Pastors*, pp. 140-1. O'Leary's career as a "labor priest" is entirely omitted from this book.

101. Rothensteiner, *History*, II, pp. 220-5, 319-28, 562-8.

102. Archdiocesan Archives, John J. Kain file.

103. Faherty, *Dream*, pp. 123-4. Rothensteiner, *History*, II, pp. 579-82. The letter accompanying the petition stated that only four St. Louis secular rectors had refused to sign. However, five names are omitted from the document as printed in Rothensteiner, p. 580-1.

104. *Ibid*.

105. Archdiocesan Archives, John J. Kain file. This file contains a number of newspaper clippings from the critical period 1893-5.

106. See footnote 103.

107. Faherty, *Dream*, pp. 126-8. Rothensteiner, *History*, II, pp. 601-2.

108. Faherty, *Dream*, p. 132-4. Rothensteiner, *History*, II, pp. 609-10.

109. Walsh, *Phelan*, pp. 50-2.

110. *Ibid*., p. 56.

111. Archdiocesan Archives, Thomas Bonacum file.

112. Bonacum's authorship was noted in *The Watchman* at the time of his consecration, Nov. 30, 1887.

113. Faherty, *Dream*, p. 124-5. Rothensteiner, *History*, II, p. 601.

114. Archdiocesan Archives, Patrick J. Ryan file.

115. Holweck, "The Historical Archives of the Archdiocese of St. Louis," *SLCHR* I, 1 (Oct., 1918), p. 25.

116. The list of vicars general is given in the annual *Yearbook of the Archdiocese of St. Louis.*

117. Rothensteiner, *History*, II, pp. 234-5.

118. The ages have been calculated from the data in the Archdiocesan Archives priests' file.

119. Archdiocesan Archives, Philip P. Brady file. See also Smith, *Our Pastors*, pp. 48-9.

120. Rothensteiner, *History*, II, p. 579. Trisco, "Bishops and Priests," p. 240.

121. Trisco, "Bishops and Priests", p. 142. Peter R. Donnelly is described as functioning as a canon on ceremonial occasions, in a scarlet-piped robe, along with an unnamed French priest, probably Edmond Saulnier (Smith, *Our Pastors*, p. 15).

122. Archdiocesan Archives, priests' file. Rothensteiner (*History*, II, p. 193) gives an incorrect date for Msgr. Hessoun's creation.

123. The list of bishops from the archdiocese is given in the annual *Yearbook of the Archdiocese of St. Louis.* The name of George A. Carrell, S.J., is omitted.

233

124. Of twenty-six St. Louis priests appointed bishop between 1854 and 1976, eight were of German extraction. However, all but one of these was named after 1930.

125. Hogan, *On the Mission*, pp. 193-6.

126. Of Twenty St. Louis priests made bishop between 1887 and 1976 only two had studied at the North American College. Of the twenty-six appointed between 1854 and 1976, only two had been chancellors.

127. Archdiocesan Archives, Patrick W. Tallon file.

128. *The Archdiocese of Chicago: Antecedents and Developments* (Des Plaines, Ill., 1920), p. 35.

129. *Ibid.*

130. Trisco, "Bishops and Priests," pp. 155-6. Wheeler was nonetheless asked to serve as theologian at the First Vatican Council to Bishop Patrick A. Feehan of Nashville, a former St. Louis priest, (Smith, *Our Pastors*, p. 17). At the time of his letter the *Freeman's Journal*, was decrying the high-handed tactics of Bishop Duggan of Chicago, whom Wheeler would have known in St. Louis.

131. *Denrick-Frenaye Correspondence*, II, pp. 328, 363, 356, 336.

132. Miller, "Kenrick," p. 88.

133. *Ibid.*, pp. 129-30. Faherty, *Dream*, pp. 99-107. Rothensteiner, *History*, II, pp. 319-28, 494-501.

134. Anna McAllister, *Ellen Ewing Sherman* (New York, 1936), p. 364.

135. Rothensteiner, *History*, II, pp. 611, 621.

136. *Ibid.*, p. 630.

The Development of an American Priesthood: Archbishop John Ireland and the Saint Paul Diocesan Clergy, 1884–1918

DANIEL P. O'NEILL

BY THE MID-NINETEENTH CENTURY, the Catholic church had become the largest religious body in the United States, primarily as a result of mass emigration from Europe. And between 1852 and 1917, the Catholic population increased eleven-fold—from one and a half to seventeen million. Accompanying this dramatic growth was an expansion of the institutional structure of the church—an increase in the number of dioceses, parishes, priests and nuns. While the scale of this expansion is common knowledge, little is known about the internal development of the church in this period.

The history of the transformation of Catholicism into the largest church in the United States has been written largely from the perspective of the hierarchy.[1] In the eyes of Catholics, however, the church was synonymous with their local parish, not the hierarchy. In important respects, the link between institutional Catholicism at the top and the grass roots was the parish priest. Although priests were under the authority of the bishop in a centralized church, they nonetheless enjoyed a significant degree of autonomy in exercising their ministry in their local communities. Studying the careers of these priests would reveal a great deal about the development of the church at the parish level. How were they recruited? Where were they trained? What were their prospects for promotion? Many individual decisions on each of these scores translated into a larger historical shift as an initially foreign-born clergy became increasingly "Americanized."[2]

The development of an American-born clergy became a deliberate institutional policy. Between 1829 and 1884, the American Catholic bishops met periodically to formulate a common national policy for the church. An area of particular concern was the recruitment, training, and discipline of the clergy. After their 1840 meeting, for example, the prelates summarized their deliberations in a pastoral letter to the laity in which they stated:

> America must gradually become independent of foreign churches for the perpetuation of her priesthood. At present the tide of immigration is too copious to prevent our dispensing with the aid of an immigrant clergy. The people and the priest are derived from the same source; but gradually we must find our own resources within ourselves, and we should make timely preparation.[3]

236

To insure an adequate supply of priests for a rapidly growing church, the bishops repeatedly called for the establishment of diocesan seminaries, the endowment of scholarships for needy students, and the recruitment of worthy candidates for the priesthood. The prelates believed, moreover, that at some time in the future these steps would lead to the development of an American priesthood. The actual implementation of these policies, however, depended on the needs, priorities, and resources of individual dioceses.[4]

An examination of the literature on American Catholicism reveals a curious contradiction, however. While episcopal biographies are a mainstay in the field, they have little to say about the pastoral role of the bishop: for example, his policies on the recruitment, training, and promotion of the clergy in his diocese. Biographies of prominent prelates— John Tracy Ellis' of Cardinal James Gibbons, Frederick Zwierlein's of Bishop Bernard McQuaid, and James Moynihan's of Archbishop John Ireland—concentrate on their role in the national and international controversies of the period, not on their pastoral administration of their sees.[5] In view of the preoccupation with "great men" in writing the history of the American Catholic community, collective biography provides a valuable corrective. Examining the diocesan clergy's origins, training, and career paths highlights the importance of initiative, leadership, and effort throughout this community. The response to the call for indigenous vocations to the priesthood, for example, reveals significant differences among the clergy, ethnic groups, and parishes that constituted the Saint Paul diocese. In short, the making of an American Catholic church was a collaborative effort, not something willed into existence by the pronouncements of the hierarchy.

A collective biography approach is used in an article by James Hitchcock on the Saint Louis diocesan clergy and in my own work on Saint Paul diocesan priests.[6] In his investigation of the origins of Saint Louis priests between 1841 and 1903, Hitchcock found that in most of this period they were overwhelmingly foreign-born—90 percent or more between 1851 and 1880. By the twentieth century, however, a sizeable contingent of American-born priests had emerged: 40 percent of the diocesan clergy in 1903 had been born in the United States. The Irish initially had the lead in producing native candidates for the priesthood, but they were soon outranked by the Germans. Although Hitchcock's findings are interesting, the idiosyncratic manner in which he formulates his data is often confusing. He fragments his data into an unnecessary number of tables and frequently does not label them sufficiently.[7] Hitchcock's failure to formulate his tabular data in conventional form limits the impact of his research, particularly for use in comparative studies.

Given its organizational structure, the diocese is the appropriate unit for the study of the development of the American Catholic church. Among the dioceses established in the era of rapid institutional expansion was that of Saint Paul, Minnesota, which was created in 1850, a year after the Minnesota Territory had been formally organized by the United States Congress. The history of the Saint Paul diocese in some respects parallels that of the country as a whole: initially a rural frontier diocese, by the 1920s it had become a largely urbanized see.

In its early decades, the Catholic church in Minnesota, as in other parts of the country, was an immigrant church. Most of the early priests and many of the parishioners were from abroad. The major ethnic groups from which the Saint Paul diocesan clergy were drawn between 1841 and 1930 can be seen in table 1. The church was established in the area by French and French-Canadian missionaries in the 1840s and 1850s. Later, they were joined by priests from Germany, Austria, Ireland and other European countries. Until the twentieth century, moreover, immigrant priests continued to staff most of the parishes in the Saint Paul diocese. The founding role of the French and French-Canadian missionaries is reflected in their predominance in the early years of the diocese. In the 1840s, Lucien Galtier, Augustine Ravoux, and George Belcourt, the founding fathers of the church in the region, began their missionary work in Minnesota. In the 1850s, Joseph Cretin, the first bishop of Saint Paul, arrived with his pioneer priests and seminarians from western France. Although some of these early missionaries continued to occupy important positions in the diocese for many years, the numerical predominance of the French proved to be of short duration. Mainly, this was the result of the arrival of German and Irish priests in increasingly larger numbers to minister to members of their ethnic groups who were settling in Minnesota. In the 1860s, half of the new priests were German, a quarter Irish and only a fifth French. The predominance of Irish and German priests in recruit cohorts (all priests who began their local ministry in a given de-

237

TABLE 1
The Ethnic Identity of Priests Recruited for the St. Paul Diocese between 1841
and 1930, Combining European and American Recruits into Composite
Ethnic Groups
(number and percent by decade)

Recruit Cohort	French		German		Irish		Bohemian	
	Number	Percent	Number	Percent	Number	Percent	Number	Percent
1341-1350	4	100	0	0	0	0	0	0
1851-1860	12	46	4	15	9	31	0	0
1861-1870	8	13	22	49	12	26	3	6
1871-1880	14	17	17	21	30	37	6	7
1881-1890	15	10	26	13	73	54	5	4
1391-1900	10	8	25	20	64	53	7	6
1901-1910	15	9	38	23	72	44	12	7
1911-1920	3	2	25	21	65	55	4	3
1921-1930	2	1	34	26	55	12	6	4

Source: St. Paul Priests' Data Base.

cade) continued until 1930. From 1880 to 1930, they constituted about 70 percent of each recruit cohort; from two-fifths to half of these candidates were Irish, and a fifth to a quarter, German.

The priests and seminarians who affiliated with the Saint Paul diocese until 1870 were almost all French, German, and Irish. When Bohemians and Poles began to settle in Minnesota in sizeable numbers, they were soon joined by priests from their homelands to care for their religious needs. From the 1860s, Bohemians, and from the 1870s, Poles were found in every recruit cohort. They soon established national parishes of their own in the cities and rural communities of the diocese. As late as 1900, two-thirds of the diocesan clergy were foreign-born. Four-fifths of the candidates ordained for the diocesan priesthood in the 1920s, however, were American-born. Immigrant priests founded the Saint Paul diocese and continued to staff many of its churches until an American clergy replaced them in this century.

The recruitment and formation of the Saint Paul diocesan clergy was the work of many individuals. Parents, priests, religious, friends and bishops all had a role in fostering vocations and in encouraging seminarians and priests from other areas to affiliate with the Saint Paul diocese. But the central figure in the transformation of the diocesan clergy from a

TABLE 1 (continued)

Recruit Cohort	Polish Number	Polish Percent	Other Foreign Number	Other Foreign Percent	American Unspecified Number	American Unspecified Percent
1841-1850	0	0	0	0	0	0
1851-1860	0	0	1	4	1	4
1861-1870	0	0	0	0	0	0
1871-1380	7	3	7	3	1	1
1881-1390	6	4	11	8	3	2
1391-1900	4	3	9	7	2	1
1901-1910	9	5	17	10	3	1
1911-1920	8	7	9	8	5	4
1921-1930	9	7	6	4	13	14

Source: St. Paul Priests' Data Base.

foreign to an American clergy was Archbishop John Ireland. Policies that he adopted in the 1880s contributed to the Americanization of the Saint Paul diocesan clergy after World War I.

John Ireland is best known in Minnesota for his leadership in the temperance movement, his colonizing efforts, and the Faribault school plan. Less known, but probably more important from the perspective of the development of the institutional church, was his role in the development of the Saint Paul diocesan clergy. Head of the Saint Paul diocese between 1884 and 1918, Ireland is most remembered as a strong-willed and outspoken leader in the liberal or Americanizing wing of the Catholic hierarchy. In many speeches and sermons, he argued that there was no conflict between Catholicism and American democracy. Consequently, in the controversies of his era, he opposed those in the church who favored the perpetuation of separate ethnic parishes and even the formal restructuring of the diocesan network along "national" lines.[8]

Archbishop Ireland strongly believed the Catholic church in this country should be served by American-trained and American-born priests. His goal for the Saint Paul diocese was a clergy born, raised, and educated in Minnesota. A diocesan priesthood composed of native sons, he felt, would be more stable, more manageable, and more responsive to the needs of the local church than a clergy recruited from outside of the diocese.[9] The impact of Ireland's policies on the recruitment of the clergy may be tested by examining the background of candidates who were re-

TABLE 2
The Place of Origin of Priests Recruited for the St. Paul Diocese Between 1841
and 1930, Differentiated into American-Born or -Raised and Foreign-Born
and -Raised Recruits (number and percent by decade)

Recruit Cohort	American Born or Raised		Foreign Born and Raised	
	Number	Percent	Number	Percent
1841-1850	0	0	4	100
1851-1860	3	11	23	88
1861-1870	4	9	41	91
1871-1880	7	8	75	91
1831-1890	51	35	93	65
1891-1900	41	34	80	66
1901-1910	55	33	111	67
1911-1920	74	62	45	38
1921-1930	100	77	30	23

Source: St. Paul Priests' Data Base.

cruited into the Saint Paul diocesan priesthood between 1841 and 1930.
Consider, for example, those candidates who began their ministry in the
diocese in the 1880s. These may be considered members of a common
cohort or recruit class. As the number of candidates who affiliated with
the diocese each year varied a great deal, it makes sense to group them in
this manner. Before 1870, from one to ten priests joined the diocese each
year; later, from five to twenty-four. Grouping recruits into cohorts will
facilitate comparison and will show how their place of origin, education,
and ecclesiastical status on affiliating with the diocese changed over the
years.

The place of origin of the Saint Paul diocesan clergy differentiated as
"American" or "foreign" is presented in table 2. Following the common
practice, future priests who emigrated to the United States as infants or
young children are considered American. Saint Paul diocesan priests were
predominantly of foreign origin until the twentieth century. Nine out of
ten recruits between 1844 and 1880 and two out of three between 1881
and 1910 came from Europe or Canada. After the first decade of the
twentieth century, the number of candidates from outside of the United

States dropped sharply; in the 1920s, only one out of four was of foreign origin.

From one perspective, the Americanization of the Saint Paul diocesan clergy was remarkably slow. During the diocese's first sixty years, Americans were a minority in recruit classes. But after 1911, the picture changed. Three-fifths of the 1911–1920 cohort and four-fifths of the 1921–1930 cohort were Americans. This transformation of the institutional church raises questions about the causes and the timing of this change. Were Catholic parents becoming more willing to encourage their sons to enter the priesthood? Did the availability of a local seminary have anything to do with it? Did the diocese adopt policies which made a career in the diocesan clergy more attractive to American candidates?

241

Archbishop John Ireland had long devoted a major part of the resources of the diocese to the development of a local diocesan seminary, which he hoped would encourage Minnesota youths to enter the priesthood. In an 1894 pastoral letter, the Minnesota prelate said that providing "a numerous, learned and holy clergy" was the major responsibility of the bishop.[10] On assuming the direction of the Saint Paul diocese in 1884, he made his first priority not a magnificent cathedral, but a well-run seminary. He explained his rationale for developing a local seminary in a series of pastoral letters to the people of his diocese between 1884 and 1897. Ireland argued that the diocese could not depend indefinitely on Europe and other parts of the United States to supply priests for its parishes and institutions. He claimed that a local seminary would facilitate the recruitment of candidates for the diocese and, eventually, the development of a native clergy. In short, John Ireland proposed diocesan autonomy, a future in which vocations among the young men of Minnesota would supply the diocese's needs for priests.

Ireland's 1885 pastoral letter discussed the impact that the new seminary would have on the recruitment of priests for the diocese. He believed that an increase in the number of vocations to the priesthood among the youth of the diocese would soon occur. He was confident that young men who had been born and raised in Minnesota would be attracted to the priesthood and that their parents would encourage them in their vocations. He held out the great prestige of the priesthood as a reason for Catholic families to make this commitment:

> Christian fathers and mothers there will be, ready in the joy of their hearts to consecrate their sons to the Lord, believing that the crowning honor of a Christian family is to have a representative in the temple praying and offering sacrifice for them.[11]

Although Ireland does not mention it, an additional attraction of a local seminary was that it would enable Minnesota youths to prepare for the priesthood while remaining in close contact with their families. Youths who went to European seminaries, in contrast, might not see their families for years. A local seminary permitted parents to "give" their sons to the service of the church without completely losing contact with them. Parents thus had the assurance that their sons in the Saint Paul diocesan clergy, unlike priests in religious orders, would be educated in Minnesota and stationed there throughout their careers.

Another advantage of a local seminary was that it gave the bishop greater control not only over the recruitment of his future priests but also over their formation—what they were taught and how it was presented. Their training therefore could be tailored to meet local needs.

Attempts had been made earlier to establish a school in Saint Paul to train candidates for the priesthood to serve local requirements. The Cathedral School, which accepted lay students as well as seminarians, operated between 1852 and 1858 and between 1862 and 1867. It was not until Ireland's administration, however, that the Saint Paul diocese was able to establish permanently its own seminary. In 1885, Saint Thomas Seminary, the first institution primarily for training diocesan priests in the Saint Paul diocese, began classes. When James J. Hill offered to build and endow a new seminary, the facilities were turned into an academy and college. That became the main preparatory school for the new Saint Paul Seminary in 1894. The success of other bishops in firmly establishing local seminaries varied from diocese to diocese. This can be seen in the experience of the Milwaukee and Chicago dioceses, both established in 1843. While Milwaukee had its own seminary from 1856, Chicago did not have a permanent institution exclusively for seminarians until the 1920s. In short, a great deal depended on episcopal leadership as well as local commitments and resources.[12]

The early clergy of the Saint Paul diocese were trained in many different seminaries. After the establishment of a local seminary, the clergy's educational background became more homogeneous. The priests recruited into the Saint Paul clergy before 1930 attended over one hundred different schools of theology. Half of them graduated from Minnesota institutions and a tenth from other American seminaries. The other two-fifths graduated from ninety foreign seminaries.

The location of the schools of theology from which Saint Paul's priests were graduated is shown in table 3. Before 1890, the majority of the candidates in each class received their professional training abroad. But even in classes which were predominantly foreign in origin, a significant pro-

242

TABLE 3
Location of Theology Schools from which St. Paul Priests Recruited Between
1841 and 1930 were Graduated
(number and percent of graduates by decade)

Recruit Cohort	Minnesota		Other U. S. A.		Foreign	
	Number	Percent	Number	Percent	Number	Percent
1841-1850	0	0	1	25	3	75
1851-1860	3	18	2	12	12	70
1861-1870	6	17	12	34	17	49
1871-1880	10	15	15	23	41	62
1381-1890	33	26	29	22	68	52
1891-1900	68	57	10	8	41	35
1901-1910	88	53	10	6	68	41
1911-1920	93	78	3	3	23	19
1921-1930	103	81	13	10	12	9

St. Paul Priests' Data Base.

portion received part of their professional training in the United States. Although the 1870s cohort was 90 percent foreign, two-fifths of its members graduated from American seminaries. Between 1881 and 1910, two-thirds of the recruit cohorts were foreign in origin. From half to three-fifths of them completed seminary in the United States. Thus, the Saint Paul diocese had a clergy which had been American educated, at least in part, before it had an American-born clergy.

The proportion of priests trained in the United States increased sharply after the establishment of a Saint Paul diocesan seminary. Three-fifths of the 1891–1900 cohort graduated from this institution and four-fifths of the recruits after 1911 were trained there. Ireland's goal of a locally trained clergy became reality a quarter century after the founding of the diocesan seminary.

The new seminary had two major effects on the recruitment of priests for the Saint Paul diocese. First, it provided a strong selling point in attracting candidates for the priesthood from within and outside of the diocese. Secondly, it enabled the diocese to screen candidates rather than relying on the recommendations of European bishops and seminary rectors who were probably only too willing to foist their weaker candidates upon a missionary diocese in America. After the Saint Paul Seminary was in operation, John Ireland insisted that seminarians from outside his diocese spend at least two years at the new school before ordination. This gave the diocese a chance to evaluate candidates from outside before making permanent commitments by ordaining them.[13]

Another dimension of the recruitment process was the ecclesiastical status of candidates on affiliation with the Saint Paul diocese. This is significant because the Catholic church was committed not just to the development of an American-born clergy but, more specifically, to the emergence of a clergy actually recruited from and trained in the diocese in which they served. Since the Council of Trent in the sixteenth century, Rome had favored this policy believing that priests with local ties would prove to be more stationary and governable. During the early years of the Saint Paul diocese, however, many members of the clergy were "outsiders." Some entered the diocese as priests, after serving in other sees or religious orders. Others were seminarians for other dioceses when they affiliated with the Saint Paul diocese. In contrast to priests and seminarians who transferred their allegiance to Saint Paul were young men recruited from within the diocese itself. The latter, born or raised in Minnesota, were commonly called "the native sons."

The ecclesiastical status of Saint Paul's priests on affiliation with the diocese is shown in table 4. The table accentuates the duration of the "missionary era" in the Saint Paul diocese: as late as the first decade of this century, four-fifths of the clergy were recruited from outside the diocese. From Rome's perspective, the Saint Paul diocese had not yet achieved autonomous status within the Catholic church. Even though the diocese had developed an impressive network of parishes and institutions and no longer relied on the financial assistance of European missionary societies, it still had dependent status within the church. Only when the Minnesota diocese became self-sufficient in producing its own priests would it transcend dependent, missionary status within the Catholic church.

After 1911, however, the Saint Paul diocese was on the threshold of autonomy in recruiting priests for its local needs. Half of the 1911–1920 recruit cohort and almost three-fifths of the 1921–1930 cohort were natives of the diocese. In subsequent decades, it is likely that their proportion increased until the diocese approached self-sufficiency in producing priests. Undoubtedly, a major factor in increasing the number of Minnesota candidates was the establishment of a local seminary. After 1884, the Saint Paul diocese had its own comprehensive training system from high school through the major seminary. In the following years, an increasing

TABLE 4

Ecclesiastical Status of Recruits on Affiliation with the St. Paul Diocese
Between 1841 and 1930, Differentiated into Priests and Seminarians from
Outside the State and Laymen from Minnesota
(number and percent by decade)

| Recruit Cohort | Native Sons Minnesota Laymen | | Outsiders | | | |
| | Number | Percent | Priests | | Seminarians | |
			Number	Percent	Number	Percent
1841-1850	0	0	4	100	0	0
1851-1860	0	0	14	52	13	48
1861-1870	2	4	17	36	28	60
1871-1880	7	8	55	62	26	30
1881-1890	21	14	66	45	60	41
1891-1900	19	15	47	38	59	47
1901-1910	37	22	78	47	50	30
1911-1920	62	52	28	24	29	24
1921-1930	74	57	25	19	31	24

Source: St. Paul Priests' Data Base.

number of its priests were graduates of this system. The initial impact of
the new seminary was to increase the number of candidates from farm
backgrounds. In this century, there were yet further changes in the social
origins of seminarians, reflecting changes in the geographic and occupational distribution of the Catholic community. As Catholics became more
urbanized, the proportion of farmers' sons declined from three-fifths to
two-fifths between 1901 and 1920. Another change resulted from the apparent expansion of the Catholic middle class. In the 1890s, only a tenth
of the native sons were from white collar families; in the 1911–1920
cohort, their proportion increased to a fourth. An analysis of the geographic origins of seminarians reveals that eight of the two hundred
parishes in the diocese produced a fourth of the diocese's native vocations
through 1930. This disproportionate achievement emphasizes the importance of recruitment networks in fostering vocations.[14]

The ethnic stock of native sons who were ordained for the Saint Paul
diocese is recorded in table 5. As noted earlier, candidates who came to
Minnesota as infants or young children are considered to be native sons as
well as those actually born in the state. Among the initial ethnic groups,

TABLE 5
Ethnic Stock of Minnesota Natives in the St. Paul Diocesan Clergy Between
1861 and 1930
(number and percent of Irish-American, German-American,
Bohemian-American, Polish-American, and other candidates by decade)

Recruit Cohort	Irish-American		German-American		Bohemian-American	
	Number	Percent	Number	Percent	Number	Percent
1861-1870	2	100	0	0	0	0
1871-1880	5	81	1	11	0	0
1881-1890	15	71	3	14	0	0
1891-1900	13	68	4	21	0	0
1901-1910	12	32	7	19	11	30
1911-1920	28	45	18	29	2	7
1921-1930	29	39	20	27	7	10

Source: St. Paul Priests' Data Base.

the Irish were the first to produce native vocations to the diocesan clergy. The first two native sons ordained for the diocese were Irish-American, as were 70 percent or more of the native candidates in recruit cohorts until the turn of the century. After then, the Irish proportion declined to less than half. Although the Irish-Americans continued to be the largest supplier of vocations, they no longer constituted a majority of the native candidates. Unlike the Irish, the Germans produced few vocations until the 1890s. The four German-Americans ordained in that decade equalled the number ordained in the previous thirty years. The German-American proportion of native recruits increased to 21 percent in the 1890s; it further increased to 29 percent in the 1911–1920 cohort.

Although earlier settlers than the Germans, the French were even slower in producing vocations to the diocesan clergy. The first French-American candidates were not ordained until the 1920s. In that cohort were two French-American native sons. As late as 1900, there were still five French national parishes in the diocese and several others, although not officially designated national parishes, with a heavy concentration of French-Canadian parishioners. Perhaps partly because of the failure to produce native vocations, the Saint Paul diocese transferred national parishes in Saint Paul and Minneapolis to the Marists, a French order. As a result of the delay in producing vocations, French national parishes continued to be served by foreign priests long after the congregations had become predominantly American-born.

246

TABLE 5 (continued)

| Recruit Cohort | Polish-American | | Other | | Total |
	Number	Percent	Number	Percent	Number
1861-1870	0	0	0	0	2
1871-1880	0	0	1	14	7
1881-1390	1	5	2	10	21
1891-1900	0	0	2	10	19
1901-1910	3	9	3	9	36
1911-1920	7	11	4	7	61
1921-1930	5	7	11	15	72

Source: St. Paul Priests' Data Base.

247

Bohemian and Polish vocations to the Saint Paul diocesan priesthood appeared in ordination classes relatively soon after these groups settled in Minnesota. In the 1901–1910 cohort, were eleven Bohemian-Americans and three Polish-Americans. Each of these groups constituted about a tenth of the following two cohorts. The timing of the Bohemian and Polish vocations to the priesthood is similar to that of the Irish. All three groups showed up in ordination classes within a generation of their settlement in Minnesota.

The comparative lag in the emergence of German-American vocations in the Saint Paul diocesan priesthood needs to be addressed. A possible explanation is that Archbishop Ireland's strong views on the Americanization of the church, which brought him into conflict with the leaders of the German community, might have discouraged German-American youths from joining his diocesan clergy.[15] Instead, they might have entered religious orders, particularly the German Benedictines of Saint John's Abbey in Minnesota. If this hypothesis is correct, youths from German parishes conducted by Saint Paul diocesan priests would be drawn off to the Benedictines rather than entering John Ireland's own local seminary. Between 1877 and 1910, twenty natives of the Saint Paul diocese were ordained for Saint John's Abbey. Seventy percent of them came from parishes run by religious orders, mostly by the Benedictines. Given the importance of role models in fostering vocations in parishes, it is not surprising that these young men were attracted to the Benedictines rather than the local diocesan clergy. In the same period, six German-Americans from parishes run by Saint Paul diocesan priests were also ordained for the Benedictines. Even if these six vocations were included in the German-American column in table 5, they would not change the Irish-American predominance among Minnesota natives in the Saint Paul diocesan priesthood.[16]

Thus, the timing of the production of native vocations among ethnic groups varied. At first, the Minnesota natives in the Saint Paul diocesan clergy were predominantly Irish-American: from 70 to 100 percent of the local candidates between 1861 and 1900. Like the Irish-Americans, the Polish-Americans and Bohemian-Americans produced native priests within a generation of settling in Minnesota while German-Americans and French-Americans lagged behind. After the turn of the century, vocations from other ethnic groups collectively outnumbered those of the Irish-Americans. Between 1910 and 1930, the ethnic background of local candidates stabilized at 40 percent Irish-American, 30 percent German-American, 10 percent Polish-American, 10 percent Bohemian-American and 10 percent miscellaneous. What is noted here is a changing of the ecclesiastical guard—a transition from an immigrant to a second-generation American clergy. This Americanization of the priesthood was a gradual process that occurred at different times and speeds among the various ethnic groups in the diocese. The Irish, Poles and Bohemians produced substantial native vocations relatively early while the Germans and French waited until the twentieth century.

Interestingly enough, in his study of the Saint Louis diocese Hitchcock also found that the Irish took the lead in producing American-born vocations. Unlike the pattern in Saint Paul, however, the Irish predominance proved to be short-lived. Between 1880 and the turn of the century the ratio of Irish to German native vocations in Saint Paul was four to one; in Saint Louis the ratio was one to two.[17] Clearly these figures reveal significant regional variations in the recruitment of the church's religious professionals. Although Germans were the largest ethnic group in the Catholic community in both Missouri and Minnesota, their contribution to the diocesan clergy in Saint Louis and Saint Paul, the largest dioceses in the respective states, was quite different.

Just as Archbishop Ireland's seminary-training policy had clearly fostered native-grown vocations to the diocesan priesthood, his promotion policy also appears to have been directed to this end. An examination of his pastoral appointments and nominations to the hierarchy indicate that he gave special preference to native sons. Ireland's promotion policy can be seen in examining the careers of the members of the 1881–1890 recruit cohort, the first during his tenure as ordinary of Saint Paul. A comparison of the native sons in this class with the outsiders reveals a pattern favorable to the former.

There were fifteen native sons among the sixty-two members of the 1880s recruit cohort still active in the diocese in 1900. At mid-career, 90 percent of them were pastors. The prestige of the parishes held by the native sons and the outsiders differed. Sixty-two percent of the native pastors had urban parishes, the most desirable in the diocese, almost twice the proportion of the total class (33 percent). Among the urban churches held by the Minnesota natives were the Cathedral and Immaculate Conception, two of the largest and most important parishes in the diocese. In addition to the natives in pastoral positions, two were in academic work, one of them president of Saint Paul Seminary. Compared to the outsiders, the native sons as a group had achieved impressive career mobility in the Saint Paul diocesan clergy by 1900.[18]

249

The Archbishop's promotion policy seems to have been related to his recruitment policy. Assigning a large proportion of the highly visible urban pastorates to native sons might have been an attempt to make the church appear an American rather than a foreign institution. Although two-thirds of the clergy were of foreign origin in 1900, Ireland gave half of the urban pastorates to native sons. A more compelling reason for his promotion policy, however, might have been to attract more native candidates into the diocesan clergy. A promotion policy favorable to native recruits told potential candidates that opportunities were open for them.[19]

Another dimension of Ireland's promotion policy is seen in the nominations he made to the hierarchy, specifically to sees established by the division of the original territory of the Saint Paul dioceses. During his tenure, seven new dioceses were established in Minnesota, North Dakota, and South Dakota. Over the course of twenty-one years, Ireland nominated eleven of his diocesan priests to these sees. Seven of eleven episcopal candidates were native sons; ordained in the 1860s, 1870s, and 1880s, they were members of cohorts in which the proportion of native sons ranged from 4 to 14 percent. From these figures, it is obvious that Ireland gave special preference to native sons when making nominations to the episcopate. By his promotion policy he apparently hoped to speed up the transformation of the Saint Paul diocesan clergy from a foreign to a native group of men.[20] An examination of the career patterns of the last recruit cohort (1911–1920) of the Ireland era also indicates a promotion policy favorable to native sons, suggesting that this policy had become institutionalized in the Saint Paul diocese.[21]

A final component of Archbishop Ireland's clerical personnel policy that needs to be addressed is his position on the role of religious orders of priests. The first bishops of the Saint Paul diocese actively collaborated with religious orders, seeking their help in providing priests for a rapidly expanding Catholic population.[22] Bishop Joseph Cretin, for example, ordinary from 1851 until 1857, invited the Benedictines to Minnesota; his successor, Bishop Thomas Grace, ordinary from 1859 until 1884, brought the Jesuits, the Franciscans, and the Dominicans. During Cretin's administration, priests from religious orders accounted for a third of the clergy in the diocese. Under Grace, however, a member of the Dominican Order, this figure fell to a fourth. This decline resulted primarily from changes in diocesan boundaries. After 1875, Stearns County, home base for the Benedictines, the largest clerical order in Minnesota, was no longer in the Saint Paul Diocese. Under John Ireland, ordinary from 1884 until 1918, the diocesan policy on priests from religious orders changed dramatically. During his long administration, Ireland systematically decreased the proportion of priests from religious orders among the clergy. Ireland wanted the diocese to be self-sufficient.

Robert Cross and Colman Barry have suggested that Ireland was, at best, ambivalent, and, at worst, hostile toward priests from religious orders.[23] Much of his opposition to priests from religious orders stemmed from the structural nature of the orders themselves. They were semi-autonomous bodies within the Catholic church. Their constitutions allowed them to be self-governing communities, not under the direct control of the local bishop. Apparently, the strong-willed Ireland was determined to exert his authority over all the priests in his diocese. Moreover, he was confident that his own diocesan priests were fully capable of performing the specialized apostolates that, in the past, had been reserved for priests from religious orders. His ultimate goal was to have a diocese that was not dependent on priests from the semi-autonomous religious orders for parishes and diocesan institutions.

Ireland was effective in implementing these policies. Under his predecessor Bishop Grace a fourth of the priests in the diocese were members of religious orders. The Benedictines, the Franciscans, the Dominicans, and the Jesuits all conducted parishes in rural areas, towns, and cities. During his tenure as ordinary, however, Ireland did not allow these orders to expand their operations in the diocese to any significant degree, and permitted few priests from other orders to establish footholds in the diocese.

As a direct consequence of these systematic actions by Ireland, priests from religious orders assumed neither significant numbers nor prominence in the Saint Paul diocese. In his last year as archbishop (1918), only 16 percent of the clergy were from religious orders. A comparison of the Saint Paul diocese with comparable American sees indicates that the latter had significantly higher proportions of priests from religious orders. In the diocese of Milwaukee, for example, 25 percent of the priests owed their primary allegiance to religious orders; in Cincinnati, 35 percent; in Saint Louis, 40 percent; and in New Orleans, 52 percent.[24] In the Saint Paul diocese, priests from religious orders were not invited to administer colleges, open high schools for lay students, or staff parishes in affluent neighborhoods. In other dioceses all of these apostolates were open to them. In general, Ireland only allowed the orders to run national parishes for German, French, and Polish immigrants.

John Ireland had concentrated his efforts on the diocesan clergy, more subject to his direct control. As a consequence of his policies and the responses of the laity, a substantial Minnesota-born and trained clergy began to be ordained for the Saint Paul diocese sixty years after the establishment of the institutional church in Minnesota. The Minnesotans constituting the native majority in classes after 1911 were born from 1885 on. In this period, there were Catholic families in the state with values which inclined them to encourage their sons to consider the priesthood as a vocation. There was also a network of local institutions for preparing candidates and financial aid for those with limited means.

251

The increasingly American, and more specifically Minnesotan, character of the diocesan priesthood was a stage in the Americanization of the Catholic community in the Saint Paul diocese. This process affected the various levels of this community at different times. After 1859, all of the bishops of Saint Paul were American in origin. By 1900, 70 percent of the population of the state was American-born. At the same time, however, only a third of the diocesan priests were American in origin. Thus, the hierarchy became American first, the laity next, and the clergy last. In 1900, many Minnesota parishes were still being served by foreign priests. If the often stated claim that the church was a major Americanizing institution is true, it is ironic that this function was directed by a foreign clergy for an American laity.

From another perspective, these changes in the clergy, laity, and hierarchy were phases in the de-missionization of the Saint Paul diocese. In its early decades, the diocese had a dependent status within the Catholic church: it relied on Rome and European countries for priests and also for funds to build churches and to subsidize its operations. In time, the diocese became financially independent and eventually self-sufficient in producing priests for its local needs. With autonomy in these areas, the Saint Paul diocese became a mature branch of the Catholic community. Rome acknowledged the maturity of the church in the United States in

1908 by removing it from the jurisdiction of the Congregation for the Propagation of the Faith, the agency for supervising missionary countries, and placing it under the common law of the church. At this point, the Saint Paul diocese was approaching self-sufficiency in the production of vocations to the priesthood. Half of the next recruit cohort, that of 1911–1920, were natives of Minnesota and their proportion increased in subsequent years. With the emergence of a locally trained and recruited clergy, John Ireland's goal of diocesan autonomy was realized.

By the first decade of this century, the Saint Paul and Saint Louis dioceses were on the threshold of producing an American clergy: in that decade the proportion of American priests reached two-fifths in both sees.[25] Given the fact that Saint Louis (1826) became a diocese a generation earlier than Saint Paul (1850) and, moreover, had been an important Catholic center for 70 years when Minnesota was opened to settlement, one would expect that the Saint Louis diocese would take the lead in producing native priests. Considering its later start, the Saint Paul diocese was a generation ahead in approaching clerical self-sufficiency, the result of the collaborative effort of the bishop, clergy and laity.

The emergence of an indigenous clergy in the United States was not an inevitable process. Looking at the history of Catholicism in Latin America, for example, reveals a very different picture. After four hundred years of missionary activity there the church still depends heavily on foreign priests. Forty percent of the Catholic clergy in Brazil, the most populous country in the region, are missionaries from abroad.[26]

Clearly, John Ireland's commitment to the Americanization of the Catholic church was more than a matter of rhetoric for, in fact, it informed the major policy decisions during his thirty-year administration of the Saint Paul diocese. These decisions left a permanent mark on the institutional character of Minnesota Catholicism, producing a clergy recruited from the local laity, and sharing many of their local ties, commitments, and values. With pastors and parishioners from the same bolt of cloth, the cohesiveness of the Minnesota Catholic community was greatly enhanced.

NOTES

An earlier version of this paper was delivered at the annual meeting of the Organization of American Historians, Detroit, Michigan, 2 April 1981. The author wishes to thank Brian Mulhern for his critique of that draft. This paper is based mainly on an analysis of the diocesan clergy's personnel and educational records found in the St. Paul-Minneapolis Archdiocesan Chancery Office and the Saint Paul Seminary, both in St. Paul, Minnesota.

252

1. David J. O'Brien, "American Catholic Historiography," *Church History*, 37 (March 1968): 80–94; Jay Dolan, "New Horizons in American Catholic Studies," in *An American Church: Essays on the Americanization of the Catholic Church*, ed. David J. Alvarez (Moraga, Calif., 1979), pp. 1–7; James Hennessey, *American Catholics: A History of the Roman Catholic Community in the United States* (New York, 1981), pp. 3–8, 331.

2. Given the nature of the sources on which this paper is based—primarily quantifiable biographical and career data on all 855 diocesan priests who served the St. Paul diocese between 1851 and 1930—I limit my consideration of Americanization to the clergy's origins and training. I take what amounts to an operational definition of "Americanization" rather than an ideological one. As the papers of few of these priests have survived, it is hazardous to attempt to chart the emergence of "American" ideas and attitudes on Catholicism among them. Fundamental historical changes in the institutional church must be addressed first. Then the historian is free to make broad conjectures on the implications of these changes.

3. Peter Guilday, ed., *The National Pastorals of the American Hierarchy, 1792–1919* (Westminster, Md., 1954), p. 136.

4. Ibid., pp. 23, 39, 72–75, 112–113, 187–189; Philip Gleason, "The Consolidation of Seminary Studies in the Nineteenth Century," paper in author's possession.

5. John Tracy Ellis, *The Life of James Cardinal Gibbons*, 2 vols. (Milwaukee, 1952); Frederick J. Zwierlein, *The Life and Letters of Bishop McQuaid*, 3 vols. (Rochester, N.Y., 1925–1927); James Moynihan, *The Life of Archbishop John Ireland* (New York, 1953).

6. James Hitchcock, "Secular Clergy in Nineteenth Century America: A Diocesan Profile," *Records of the American Catholic Historical Society*, 88 (March–December 1977): 31–62; Daniel P. O'Neill, "St. Paul's Priests," in *American Church*, ed. Alvarez, pp. 35–42; and "St. Paul Priests, 1851–1930: Recruitment, Formation and Mobility," (Ph.D. diss., University of Minnesota, 1979). Although Hitchcock and I have written on a similar topic, our approach is different. In addition to the ethnic origins of the native clergy—the focus of Hitchcock's article—I also examine recruitment networks, education, career patterns, and mobility within the diocesan priesthood as well as the changing demographic character of the diocese.

7. One example will suffice to illustrate the difficulty that this presents for the reader. In order to get a picture of the patterns of clerical recruitment—the number of American and foreign seminarians ordained for St. Louis each decade as well as priests transferring from other dioceses—it is necessary to consult four tables (his tables I, IV, V and IX). To clarify this point, I consolidated the data in these tables into one and recalculated the percentages. (Unfortunately, Hitchcock does not include the place of origin of the priests who transferred to the St. Louis diocese, an important factor in analyzing patterns of recruitment.)

8. Marian McKenna, "Some Roman Catholic Churchmen as Americanizers," in *Freedom and Reform: Essays in Honor of Henry S. Commager*, ed. Harold M. Hyman (New York, 1967), pp. 167–202.

9. These views are reiterated throughout a series of pastoral letters written by Ireland to the people of his diocese on the seminary fund between 1884 and 1897. Printed copies of these are in the St. Paul Seminary library. Several are cited below.

10. John Ireland, Pastoral Letter on the Seminary Fund, 18 October 1894.

11. John Ireland, Pastoral Letter on the Seminary Fund, 7 November 1885.

12. William Busch, "The Diocesan Seminary Project in St. Paul," *Acta et Dicta*, 7 (October 1935): 56–82; James Reardon, *The Catholic Church in the Diocese of St. Paul* (St. Paul, 1952), pp. 309–317; Gleason, "Seminary Studies"; Emmet H. Weber, "The Diocesan Seminary in St. Paul, Minnesota" (M.A. thesis, St. Paul Seminary, 1952).

253

13. John Tracy Ellis, "The Formation of the American Priest," in *The Catholic Priest in the United States*, ed. John Tracy Ellis (Collegeville, Minn., 1971), pp. 15–22; interview with Rev. Nicholas Finn, St. Paul ordination class of 1919, 11 April 1979.

14. For a more comprehensive treatment of this topic see: Daniel P. O'Neill, "The Development of an American Priesthood: St. Paul's Native Sons, 1861–1930," (Paper delivered at the annual meeting of the Northern Great Plains History Conference, Duluth, Minn., 24 October 1980).

15. A recent discussion of this conflict is found in La Vern Rippley, "Archbishop Ireland and the School Language Controversy," *U.S. Catholic Historian*, 1 (Fall 1980): 1–19.

16. The information on Benedictine vocations was obtained from a collection of biographical sketches of the deceased monks of St. John's Abbey published in *The Scriptorium*, 15 (June 1956). Additional data, notably on the parish origins of the Minnesota natives, was provided by the Rev. Vincent Tegeder, O.S.B., the Abbey archivist, during a visit to the St. John's archives (27 June 1983).

17. Hitchcock, "Secular Clergy," p. 39.

18. O'Neill, "St. Paul's Priests, 1851–1930," pp. 98–100; I have not found any documentation of the European-born priests' response to Archbishop Ireland's policy of favoring native sons. In Chicago, on the other hand, in 1901 a group of Irish-born priests publicly challenged Archbishop Patrick Feehan's selection of an American-born priest to be his auxiliary bishop, claiming that his promotion policy discriminated against Irish priests. For the details of this "Crowley affair," see Charles Shanabruch, *Chicago's Catholics: The Evolution of an American Identity* (Notre Dame, Ind., 1981), pp. 98–104.

19. Otherwise they might have been discouraged by a situation such as prevailed in Latin America where European-born priests were traditionally given preference. Partly because of this policy, the church in parts of Latin Amrica has remained a foreign institution—in terms of the origins of its personnel—and it still depends on foreign missionaries to staff many of its churches.

20. O'Neill, "St. Paul's Priests, 1851–1930," pp. 118-120, 129-130.

21. Ibid., pp. 101.

22. For an extended discussion of John Ireland's policy on clerical orders see Daniel P. O'Neill, "Religion, Churches and the Clergy," in *Historic Lifestyles in the Upper Mississippi River Valley*, ed. John Wozniak (Washington, D.C., 1983).

23. Robert D. Cross, *The Emergence of Liberal Catholicism in America* (Cambridge, Mass., 1958), pp. 176-177; Colman Barry, *The Catholic Church and the German Americans* (Milwaukee, 1953), pp. 19, 35, 50.

24. *Catholic Directory* (New York, 1918).

25. This is based on analysis of the origins of all of the diocesan priests officiating in the two dioceses. In 1903, 41 percent of the 268 secular priests in St. Louis were American-born while in 1910, 39 percent of the 267 priests in St. Paul were of American origin. The tables in this paper, in contrast, focus on decade-long recruit cohorts, not on the total clergy.

26. Thomas C. Bruneau, *The Political Transformation of the Brazilian Catholic Church* (London, 1974), p. 64. *The New York Times* reports that in 1983 half of Chile's priests were foreigners (14 March 1983) as were four-fifths of Nicaragua's (2 March 1983). Another crucial difference between Catholicism in the United States and Latin America is the ratio between priests and parishioners. In 1970 the priest to parishioner ratio (total number of priests/total number of Catholics) in the United States was about one to eight hundred while in Brazil it was one to ten thousand. See Hugo Latorre Cabral, *The Revolution of the Latin American Church* (Norman, Okla., 1978), p. 126. Clearly the church in the United States has been more successful in developing a sizeable, native-born clergy than is the case in Latin America. These factors have a significant impact on the clergy's role in society.

The Ordeal of the Black Priest*

Stephen J. Ochs

From . . . my ordination to the present, my life has been one heavy cross.
John Henry Dorsey, S.S.J., August 7, 1907

On June 22, 1902, the Rev. John R. Slattery, Superior General of the St. Joseph's Society of the Sacred Heart (Josephites), mounted the pulpit of St. Francis Xavier Church in Baltimore to deliver the sermon at the first Mass of one of his newly ordained priests, the Rev. John Henry Dorsey. Dorsey was only the second Black Josephite priest and only one of a total of six Black priests who had ever been ordained for the Catholic Church in the United States.[1] Young Father Dorsey, no doubt, sat transfixed in the sanctuary as he listened to Slattery, the foremost champion of Blacks in the Catholic Church, deliver a scathing attack on prejudice and discrimination within the Church. Slattery especially condemned what he called the "uncatholic" opposition within the Church, especially among the clergy, to the ordination of Black men to the priesthood.[2] With only a few exceptions, that opposition had effectively blocked Afro-American men from Catholic altars in the United States since the seventeenth century.

---

*This article is excerpted from Ochs' Ph.D. dissertation at the University of Maryland entitled, "Deferred Mission: The Josephites and the Struggle for Black Catholic Priests, 1871-1960."

1. Five American Black priests preceded Dorsey: James Augustine Healy, ordained in Paris in 1854; Alexander Sherwood Healy, ordained in Rome in 1858; Francis Patrick Healy, S.J., ordained in Liege, Belgium in 1865; Augustus Tolton, ordained in Rome in 1886; and Charles Randolph Uncles, S.S.J., a Josephite, ordained in Baltimore in 1891. See Albert S. Foley, *God's Men of Color: The Colored Catholic Priests of the United States, 1854-1954* (New York, 1954).

2. Josephite Fathers Archives (hereinafter cited as JFA), John Dorsey File, copy of the Slattery sermon entitled, "John Henry Dorsey, A Colored Man, Was Ordained a Priest by Him Eminence, Cardinal Gibbons."

The exclusion of all but a handful of Black men from the Roman Catholic priesthood in the United States until well into the twentieth century both symbolized and helped to perpetuate the second class status of Blacks within the Catholic Church. Despised by a majority of white Catholics, and deprived of their own priestly spokesmen in the hierarchical, clerical-dominated Catholic Church, Black Catholics, for most of their history, found themselves powerless and persecuted within the Church. The absence of Black priests deprived Black Catholics of symbols of their own dignity and worth and reinforced feelings of inferiority. The paucity of Black priests, moreover, belied the Catholic Church's claims of universality and hindered its efforts to win converts among non-Catholic Black Americans, who regarded the dearth of Black leadership in the Church as proof that Catholicism was "the white man's religion."

256

The few Black men who managed to become priests between 1854 and 1950 remained the exceptions and often paid a staggering emotional price for their vocations. Dorsey's life exemplified the heroic suffering of the pioneering Black priests of the early twentieth century. As a Black priest, he endured misunderstanding, humiliation, isolation, and discrimination, often from his brother priests. Eventually, the strain wore him down, leaving him only a shell of his former self. Dorsey's ordeal illustrated the depth of the racism within the Catholic Church and highlighted the dilemmas which that racism caused for Dorsey's own community, the Josephites, as they wrestled with the issue of Black priests.

John Henry Dorsey, the son of Daniel and Emmaline Snowden Dorsey, was born on January 28, 1874 in Baltimore. In addition to his twin brother, Daniel, John had an older and a younger brother, and a younger sister. His father's family had a long history of Catholicism, but his mother was a convert. The family lived in northwest Baltimore but belonged to the nation's first Black parish, St. Francis Xavier, located in the heart of the city. While serving as an altar boy at St. Francis Xavier, Dorsey caught the eye of John R. Slattery, the foremost advocate of Black priests in the United States.[3]

Between 1878 and 1883, Slattery served as American Provincial of the Mill Hill Josephites, who had come to the United States from England in 1871 to minister to Black Americans. During the 1880's, Slattery became convinced of the need for Black priests to successfully evangelize Black Americans. The enthusiastic response of Blacks in the United States to Father Augustus Tolton, a former slave, who was ordained in Rome in 1886, and stationed in Quincy, Illinois, reinforced Slattery's convictions

---

3. JFA, Epiphany Apostolic College Student Files; interview, Mr. Earl Counters and Mrs. Olga Dorsey, Baltimore, November 2, 1983.

about the viability of Black priests. In 1883, he sent Charles Randolph Uncles, a tall, bespectacled parishioner from St. Francis Xavier to St. Hyacinth's College in Canada to begin studies for the priesthood. In 1888, Slattery sent three young Black men from the Virginia missions to St. Peter's, the Mill Hill minor seminary in Freshfield, England. That same year, Slattery arranged with his friend, John Ireland, the liberal Archbishop of St. Paul, for Dorsey to enroll in St. Thomas College, the prep seminary for the archdiocese. The next year, when Slattery opened Epiphany Apostolic College, his own minor seminary, on the outskirts of Baltimore, Dorsey returned to his home town to continue his studies. In 1891, during his stay at Epiphany, Dorsey witnessed the ordination to the priesthood of fellow St. Francis Xavier parishioner, Charles Randolph Uncles. Uncles was the first Black priest ordained in the United States. Two years later, Slattery engineered the separation of the American Josephites from Mill Hill. Dorsey maintained an excellent academic record at Epiphany and then at the Sulpicians' St. Mary's Seminary, where Josephite seminarians studied philosophy and theology.[4]

257

Dorsey, however, found the road to ordination a rocky one. Despite his relatively advanced racial views and his support for Black leadership in the Church, Slattery still held many of the racial stereotypes of his day. In particular, he believed that slavery and its aftermath had seriously weakened the Black family, resulting in rampant immorality. He viewed the Catholic Church as the only agent that could teach Blacks the morality and self restraint that would keep them from moral degradation. The 1887 prospectus for St. Joseph's Seminary, the Josephites' major seminary reflected Slattery's suspicions about the ability of young Black males, at the height of their virility, to remain celibate. It provided that "No white student should be received under twenty years of age. No Negro under thirty."[5]

By 1894, Slattery's disappointment with Father Uncles, his dissatisfaction with several Black students at Epiphany and St. Joseph's, his fear of possible scandal, and his stereotypical views of Black moral weakness, led him to adopt a more "cautious" approach to the training of Blacks for the priesthood. On July 3, 1894, the Josephite General Chapter, composed of six of the seven priests in the fledgling community, adopted six resolutions "governing the requisites of colored students for admission into the

---

4. John R. Slattery, "Native Clergy," *Catholic World* (March, 1891): 882–893; JFA, 10–N–4, Charles Uncles to John R. Slattery, Quebec, June 7, 1887; 6–Y–10, Rev. Francis Henry to Slattery, Freshfield, November 20, 1888; 9–K–16a, Address of Father Slattery to the First Colored Catholic Congress, January 2, 1889; Foley, *God's Men*, 46, 43; Richard H. Steins, "The Mission of the Josephites to the Negro in America, 1871–1893" (M.A. thesis, Columbia University, 1966), 78–84.

5. JFA, 3–H–12, Prospectus for the Seminary, 1887; 10–S–7A, Rules for St. Joseph's Seminary, 1887.

From 1889–1925 this building served as Epiphany Apostolic College at Walbrook, Baltimore, Md.
(Courtesy: Josephite Archives)

college or Seminary and their promotion to Holy Orders." The heart of the resolutions required that Black students have their studies interrupted. either after graduation from Epiphany, or after completion of their second year of philosophy, for a period of time not longer than two years. in order to test their vocations. During the two year trial period. priests on the missions would employ them "in teaching catechizing, or otherwise." Black students would be readmitted to the seminary only if they could furnish letters of good conduct from the Josephite priests for whom they had worked on the missions. Father Uncles absented himself from the General Chapter in protest against the proposed regulations. Their adoption embittered him and contributed to his withdrawal from Society governance.[6]

Dorsey, along with other Black students at Epiphany and St. Joseph's Seminary felt the impact of Slattery's new policy in the summer of 1894. Slattery advised Dorsey to take up a calling other than the priesthood. Slattery's "advice" unnerved Dorsey, and, after a tearful interview, Slattery suggested that Dorsey teach at the mission school in Keswick, Virginia for ten dollars a month. Slattery confided to Father Lambert Welbers, that he hoped a couple of years at Keswick would "sober Dorsey up and develop

---

6. JFA, Minutes of the General Chapters, July 3, 1894, 6–8. The minutes of the meeting are incorrectly dated 1895 instead of 1894.

him into a good subject." The suspensions and dismissals left five Black students at Epiphany and one at St. Joseph's Seminary in the autumn of 1894.[7]

Initially, Dorsey refused to accept Slattery's decision quietly. He repeatedly entreated Archbishop Ireland to accept him into his archdiocesan seminary. Dorsey's entreaties led Ireland to ask Slattery if he had abandoned the idea of preparing Blacks for the priesthood. Slattery assured Ireland that the Josephites, while making no changes in principle, had decided to go more slowly, not only because of the Black students, but because of Slattery's Josephite confreres, "who may have to live with them when ordained." Slattery charged that Dorsey possessed a violent temper, which he admittedly was trying to overcome, and that his twin brother had drawn a pistol on one of the Josephites "during a drunken bout." Betraying his own subconscious racism, Slattery concluded ". . . of course, taking the Colored people as they are, this militates against Harry." Ireland went along with the recommendation of his friend and declined to accept Dorsey.[8]

Slattery even explored the possibility of sending Dorsey to the Mill Hill Fathers' seminary in England for future service with Bishop Henry O'Hanlon in the Upper Nile of Africa. Dorsey, however, rejected Slattery's proposal that he join a foreign missionary society and spent two years teaching school in Keswick and Baltimore. Evidently, Dorsey's performance on the missions convinced Slattery of the genuineness of his vocation. Dorsey re-entered St. Joseph's Seminary in September, 1897 and on June 21, 1902, was ordained, along with his classmates, by Cardinal James Gibbons of Baltimore.[9]

Initially, Dorsey's public ministry seemed to promise a life of success and acceptance. He was blessed with a "sonorous voice" and spoke with "elegant and flowing diction." Standing five feet eight, Dorsey, with his arching, heavy eyebrows, intense eyes, and missionary's cross hung round his neck and stuck in the sash of his cassock, projected an air of authority. In the nine months following his ordination, and prior to taking up his assignment at St. Joseph's College for Negro Catechists outside Montgomery, Alabama, Dorsey triumphantly toured major cities of the North

259

---

7. JFA, Letter Press Book—2 (hereinafter cited as LPB—2), Slattery to L. B. Welbers, Baltimore, July 20, 1894; Letter Press Book—3 (hereinafter cited as LPB—3), Slattery to Hoffman Brothers, Baltimore, November 17, 1894.

8. Sulpician Archives Baltimore (hereinafter cited as SAB), R G 39, Box 1, John H. Dorsey to Joseph Griffin, Baltimore, July 23, 1894; JFA, 25–G–1, Archbishop John Ireland to Slattery, St. Paul, January 18, 1896; 25–G–2, Slattery to Ireland, Baltimore, January 24, 1896.

9. JFA, LPB—2, Slattery to Rt. Rev. Henry O. Hanlon, Baltimore, April 14, 1896; St. Joseph's Seminary Student Journal, September, 1900; Foley, *God's Men*, 53.

and many of the Josephite missions in the South. In the North, he attempted to enlist white support for the Josephite missions by showing them a "real Black priest." In the South, he hoped that his presence as a Black priest would convince Blacks that the Catholic Church valued them. Their response exceeded Dorsey's fondest hopes. They packed churches to hear Dorsey say Mass and preach. "Their enthusiasm knew no bounds. Some wept openly," reported the Reverend Pierre LeBeau, Josephite pastor in Palmetto, Louisiana. Indeed, LeBeau's parishioners begged him to keep Dorsey in Palmetto, thus giving lie to the commonly expressed belief of many white Catholics that Blacks did not want Black priests.[10]

The triumphant appearance of his tour notwithstanding, portents of impending trouble loomed as Dorsey made his way slowly toward Montgomery. He learned that some priests and lay people in Montgomery opposed his coming on the grounds that Slattery was ". . . purposely ignoring the opinions and sentiments of the southern people on the Negro question. . . ." He also discovered that Slattery had not cleared his appointment with Bishop Edward P. Allen, but had simply presented Allen with a *fait accompli* and then departed for Europe. Dorsey confided to Slattery that he realized that he would have a hard life before he became a priest, but confessed that when bishops and priests, "from whom encouragement ought to come," considered him *personna non grata,* it drained all of the energy out of soul and body. He pleaded with Slattery not to station him in Montgomery, but promised obedience to what Slattery thought best. Slattery advised Dorsey to "play possum," do his duty, and pay no attention to outsiders, despite feeling keenly the opposition. In a well-intentioned, but insensitive ending, Slattery told Dorsey, "We all suffer from race prejudice, myself just as you."[11]

Within two years, Slattery had resigned from the Josephites; in 1906, he publicly embraced Modernism and renounced the Catholic Church. Indeed, Slattery later claimed that he had intended his controversial sermon at Dorsey's first Mass, as his farewell to the Church and to Blacks.[12] Slattery's resignation from the Josephites and subsequent apostasy from the Church almost destroyed St. Joseph's Society and served to discredit

---

10. *The Colored Harvest* (January, 1903): 381; (June, 1903): 414; (October, 1903): 421; newspaper clippings in the Dorsey Family scrapbook in the possession of Mrs. Olga Dorsey.

11. Archives of the Archdiocese of Mobile (hereinafter cited as AAM), Bishop Edward P. Allen Papers, Hugh A. O'Brien to Bishop Edward P. Allen, Montgomery, July 23, 1902; JFA, 23-M-42. Dorsey to Slattery, Montgomery, March 21, 1903; 23-M-43, Slattery to Dorsey, Baltimore, March 27, 1903.

12. JFA, 29-T-9, Rev. Walter R. Yates, S.S.J. to Rev. Thomas P. Donovan, S.S.J., Baltimore, August 27, 1906; John R. Slattery, "How My Priesthood Dropped From Me," *The Independent* LXI (September 6, 1906): 565–571.

the cause of Black priests with which he had identified himself for so many years. Slattery's immediate successors as Superior, Thomas Donovan (1904–1908) and Justin McCarthy (1908–1918), possessed neither his vision nor his leadership. Deprived of their most outspoken champion, Dorsey and the few Black Josephite priests and seminarians began their "time on the cross."

Dorsey stayed at St. Joseph's College for Negro Catechists for seventeen months, charming Booker T. Washington during his fortnightly visits to say Mass for Catholic students at Tuskegee. Shortly after Slattery's resignation, however, relations between Dorsey and Francis Tobin, the rector of St. Joseph's, deteriorated. In September, 1904, therefore, Dorsey was assigned as assistant pastor to the Rev. J. J. Ferdinand at St. Peter's Church in Pine Bluff, Arkansas; a city of 12,000, of whom half were black, located fifty miles from Little Rock in the heart of Arkansas's "black belt." Father Donovan, the new Superior, remarked, "So Colored Priest, Colored Church, and Colored Sisters at Pine Bluff. Let us pray and hope that this move will be blessed."[13] It was not.

Dorsey found himself in an environment marked not only by tense race relations between Blacks and whites, and by the implacable hostility of Black Protestant ministers toward the Catholic Church, but also dominated by the difficult and suspicious J. M. Lucey, pastor of St. Joseph's parish, founder of the Colored Industrial Institute, and self-proclaimed "expert" on "colored people." Lucey had vexed the Josephites since their arrival in St. Peter's in 1898, finding fault with Josephite pastors over the slow pace of conversions, parish finances, relations with the Sisters who taught at the Colored Industrial Institute and the parochial school of St. Peter's, and such "scandalous behavior" as priests "walking with colored people." Extremely sensitive to white southern opinion, Lucey believed that "one of the most important points of the education of colored youth is their bearing and conduct towards the whites." Lucey, therefore, made sure that, in addition to its sewing, literary, music, and woodwork courses, his Colored Industrial Institute also stressed proper behavior for its male and female students.[14]

The glow from the jubilant public welcome accorded Dorsey on his arrival in Pine Bluff, which even featured a speech by the white mayor.

---

13. JFA, 18–E–26, Slattery to Donovan, Baltimore, June 21, 1902; 23–M–21, Booker T. Washington to Donovan, Montgomery, May 15, 1903; AAM, Francis Tobin to Bishop Allen, Montgomery, September 18, 1904; 25–P–8, Dorsey to Donovan, Chicago, August 13, 1907; Donovan to Rev. Justin McCarthy, S.S.J., Nashville, January 13, 1905.

14. *The Colored Harvest* (October, 1901): 272–273; "Diocese of Little Rock," *St. Joseph's Advocate* (April, 1890): 87; *Mission Work Among the Negroes and Indians* (Baltimore, 1902). 18.

quickly faded as the young priest found himself enmeshed in the Byzantine world of the little southern town. Within three months, Dorsey and Father Ferdinand quarreled, with Ferdinand complaining to Donovan that Dorsey did nothing but spend all of his time, "from early morning till late at night with the sisters." Donovan clearly believed that Ferdinand was at fault, and transferred him to Dallas on January 27, 1905, thus making Dorsey the only Black pastor in the United States. Lucey urged Donovan to impress upon Dorsey his great responsibility, and warned that if Dorsey failed, no other Black priest would be tried for years.[15]

Lucey doubted that Black priests "would be as good morally and intellectually as white priests." By the end of 1905, Lucey began to find fault with Dorsey. He complained that stomach trouble barely allowed Dorsey to say Mass and prevented him from giving any parish missions, the Catholic version of revivals. Lucey indicated that Dorsey's ill health seemed to forbode an early departure.[16] The appointment in 1906 of John B. Morris as coadjutor bishop of the Diocese of Little Rock to the incapacitated Edward Fitzgerald helped to harden Lucey's attitude toward Dorsey. Reportedly, Morris, the former Vicar General of the Diocese of Nashville, had objected when Bishop Thomas S. Byrne invited Dorsey to dinner during Dorsey's post-ordination tour and had refused to attend. Morris succeeded to the See of Little Rock when Fitzgerald died on February 21, 1907.[17]

Trouble between Dorsey and the New Orleans based Sisters of the Holy Family, who conducted the parochial school of St. Peter's, soon gave Lucey more ammunition against Dorsey. Many of the Sisters of the Holy Family were light-skinned, Colored Creole Catholics, related by blood, French culture, and religion to white Creole families in New Orleans and along the Gulf Coast. Historically, Colored Creoles identified more closely with their white cousins than with "American blacks." Some of the Creole Sisters looked down on "American blacks" and felt insulted at the prospect of receiving the sacraments from a Black, rather than a white priest.[18] Differences of opinion about Dorsey, coupled with personality conflicts, split the community of Sisters at Pine Bluff. In August, 1906,

---

15. JFA, 24–C–14, J. J. Ferdinand to Donovan, Pine Bluff, January 23, 1905; 25–P–7, Donovan to Dorsey, Baltimore, January 27, 1905; 25–P–14, Rev. J. M. Lucey to Donovan, Pine Bluff, September 6, 1907.

16. *Mission Work Among the Negroes and Indians* (Baltimore, 1902), 18; JFA, 26–B–7a, Lucey to Donovan, Pine Bluff, December 18, 1905.

17. JFA, Diary of Monsignor John E. Burke, 1907, May 17, 1907, 137, copy.

18. Randall M. Miller, "A Church In Cultural Captivity: Some Speculations on Catholic Identity in the Old South," in Randall M. Miller and Jon L. Wakelyn, eds., *Catholics In the Old South: Essays on Church and Culture* (Macon, Ga., 1983), 40–43; JFA, 25–P–13, Adaline Robinson to Donovan, Pine Bluff, August 19, 1907.

263

Father John Dorsey, S.S.J. (1873–1926),
the second Black Josephite priest
(Courtesy: Josephite Archives)

Mother Mary Austin, the Mother General of the Holy Family Sisters, informed Lucey that she feared "criminal intimacy" between Dorsey and one of her Sisters at Pine Bluff. She requested that Lucey ask Bishop Morris for authority to replace Dorsey as the Sisters' ordinary confessor, with a white priest. Bishop Morris granted the request. Mother Austin then reassigned all of the Sisters at Pine Bluff, bringing in a new contingent suspicious of Dorsey.[19]

Lucey became increasingly obsessed with fears about possible immorality and scandal; fears that he strangely failed to communicate to Father Donovan, Dorsey's Superior. Lucey suggested that Mother Austin lay down strict rules governing the relations of the Sisters and their pupils with Father Dorsey. He insisted that Dorsey not visit the Sisters after nightfall, and noted disapprovingly that several small girls visited Dorsey quite frequently. Although Lucey admitted that the girls were so young that "no harm to them can be done," still, he added, it did not look good, and besides, "The little girls at the Colored School are so untidy in dress that they excite thoughts."[20]

---

19. Archives of the Diocese of Little Rock (hereinafter cited as ADLR), Bishop John B. Morris Papers, Report by J. M. Lucey, Vicar General, to Rt. Rev. John B. Morris, Bishop of Little Rock, "The Matter of J. H. Dorsey, Pastor of St. Peter's (colored) Church, Pine Bluff, Arkansas," November 18, 1907.

20. Archives of the Sisters of the Holy Family (hereinafter cited as ASHF), Lucey to Mother Austin, Pine Bluff, August 31, 1906.

During the next year, both Bishop Morris and Monsignor Lucey, who had become the new Vicar General of the diocese, sought ways to remove Dorsey from St. Peter's. Morris considered entrusting all of the Black missions in Arkansas, beginning with Pine Bluff, to the Holy Ghost Fathers. At a meeting in May, 1907, with the Reverend John T. Murphy, the American provincial of the Holy Ghost Fathers, Morris expressed his dissatisfaction with Dorsey and with the Josephites in general. According to Murphy, Bishop Morris believed that prevailing conditions in the South allowed for only white priests. He envisioned raising Blacks only to the level of the diaconate, one step below the priesthood.[21]

In July, 1907, Morris finally asked Donovan to remove Dorsey from Pine Bluff, alleging concern about Dorsey's happiness in view of his isolation from the white clergy. When Donovan asked Dorsey whether he wished to leave St. Peter's, Dorsey indicated his desire to remain at the parish. Donovan, therefore, left him in Pine Bluff. Shortly thereafter, however, Morris sent another letter to Donovan, expressing his surprise that Donovan had not yet removed Dorsey from Pine Bluff and insisting that if he did not, the Sisters of the Holy Family would not return to the Colored Industrial Institute. Indeed, relations between Dorsey and several of the Sisters had become so charged that one of them walked out of the church every time Dorsey gave a sermon. Sister Regina, the local superior and "a Creole lady from head to toe," reportedly wanted Dorsey removed and replaced by a white priest. She even refused to allow two of the Sisters to attend to Dorsey when he came down with typhoid fever. The hostility between Dorsey and the Sisters, in addition to Dorsey's ill health, adversely affected the parish, which failed to register a single baptism or first Holy Communion in 1907.[22] Bishop Morris had no doubts in his mind where the blame for the situation lay.

Dorsey's bout with appendicitis in mid-July 1907, provided further ammunition for Morris and Lucey. Fearing southern doctors and institutions, Dorsey travelled to Mercy Hospital in Chicago for the operation. He assured Donovan that he would be gone only three weeks, that the doctors promised that the operation would solve his recurring stomach problems, and that he had asked Lucey to look after St. Peter's in his absence. Lucey, however, complained to Donovan that Dorsey had failed to secure a priest to look after his parish, and had not bothered to inform either Lucey or Bishop Morris of his departure. Lucey grumbled that

---

21. Spiritan Archives, USA (hereinafter cited as SPAUSA), Very Rev. John T. Murphy to Archbishop Leroy, Conway, Arkansas, May 25, 1907, translated from the French.

22. JFA, 26–B–31, Morris to Donovan, Little Rock, July 20, 1907; 26–B–32, Donovan to Morris, Baltimore, July 25, 1907; 25–P–13, Adaline Robinson to Donovan, Pine Bluff, August 19, 1907.

Dorsey failed to show proper respect to Bishop Morris and warned that the Bishop would no longer tolerate "the way that Father Dorsey has of leaving without his permission in the independent manner that he does." Lucey closed his letter with the revealing observation that "Fr. Dorsey is about like colored people generally, he needs someone to be over him if any work is to be done."[23]

Donovan bowed to the pressure and on August 5, 1907 notified the still hospitalized Dorsey that he should report to St. Peter Claver's in San Antonio, Texas by August 16, to take up his new duties as the assistant to Father Lambert Welbers. At the news of his transfer, Dorsey exploded, claiming that Donovan's action threw a damper over his whole life. He flatly refused to go to San Antonio and declared himself tired of the constant hounding he had endured. "From . . . my ordination till the present," he wrote, "my life has been one heavy cross." He demanded to remain in Pine Bluff until after Christmas and warned, "If I am to be dogged about, I prefer to leave the priesthood out of my life. . . ." Donovan, nevertheless, insisted that Dorsey report to San Antonio.[24]

The Vicar General of the Diocese of San Antonio confounded Donovan's plans, however, by wiring Dorsey and telling him not to come to San Antonio. "Now this is another awful situation. Another insult offered me . . . ," a miserable Dorsey complained to Donovan. The situation so upset him that his doctor ordered him to remain in the hospital for an extra week. Dorsey chided Donovan for failing to protect his priests. "I have been kicked about enough!" Dorsey cried, "I will not be the victim." Donovan finally acceded to Dorsey's demands, pleading manpower shortages as his excuse to Bishop Morris. Dorsey returned to Pine Bluff in August, apparently having won his battle.[25]

Morris reacted with pique to Dorsey's return. In a letter to Donovan, he called Dorsey "a failure" and repeated his desire for Dorsey's removal on the grounds of constant friction with the Sisters, declining attendance at Sunday Mass, and Dorsey's absences from the diocese without permission. Within a week of Dorsey's return, Morris and Lucey conveniently added yet another, more serious, charge to their litany of complaints against Dorsey. They accused him of having sexual relations with Miss Adaline Robinson, a woman whom Lucey described as a public school teacher, a

---

23. JFA, 25-P-4, Dorsey to Donovan, Chicago, July 18, 1907; 26-B-8, Lucey to Donovan, Pine Bluff, August 1, 1907.

24. JFA, 27-H-39, Donovan to Dorsey, Baltimore, August 5, 1907; 26-C-45, Donovan to Rev. Joseph Waering, Baltimore, August 6, 1907; 25-R-9, Donovan to Bishop John Anthony Forest, Baltimore, August 6, 1907; 25-P-7, Dorsey to Donovan, Chicago, August 7, 1907.

25. JFA, 25-P-8, Dorsey to Donovan, Chicago, August 13, 1907; 25-B-35, Donovan to Morris, Baltimore, August 19, 1907; 25-P-14, Dorsey to Donovan, Chicago, August 22, 1907.

recent convert, and a morphine addict. Lucey claimed that, according to the "unimpeachable" testimony of Dr. G. W. Bell and Miss Robinson's sister, Adaline Robinson had frequently spent the night at Dorsey's rectory and had been thrown out of her sister's home by her brother-in-law when she refused to break off the liaison. Moreover, she purportedly attempted suicide, and, in her delirium following the botched attempt, revealed that Dorsey had impregnated her and that she had subsequently had an abortion. Lucey contended that Dorsey's affair with the woman had scandalized parishioners and accounted for the low attendance at Sunday Mass. Lucey did not explain why he had waited so long to act on the alleged Dorsey-Robinson affair, rumors of which had supposedly circulated for more than a year, nor why he had failed to mention such a serious matter to Donovan in their earlier debates about Dorsey's tenure.[26]

Dorsey denied the allegations in a meeting with Morris and Lucey. Lucey insisted on the truth of the charges, though he admitted that he did not care to go into a detailed investigation of them. The Bishop insisted that Dorsey leave the diocese within thirty days. In a subsequent report to Donovan, Dorsey attributed his removal to Morris's opposition to Black priests and quoted the bishop as saying during their interview that the time was not ripe for Black priests and would not be for fifty years. Dorsey explained that Miss Robinson's brother-in-law, whom he called a "narrow, bigoted Baptist," persecuted her when she became a Catholic and threw her out of his house. Dorsey admitted that Miss Robinson, his house-keeper, had attended him during his siege of typhoid, occasionally spending the night in the rectory, but always in the company of two teenage boys. Dorsey told Donovan that Miss Robinson served as his housekeeper because Lucey forbade the Sisters to do so; she acted as his nurse because the Sisters refused to aid him. Dr. Bell, the supposed witness to Miss Robinson's dalliances, had over-charged him for drugs during his bout with typhoid and had made immoral advances on Miss Robinson, which she rebuffed. In retaliation, Bell tried to hurt both Dorsey and Robinson. "Once again," a distraught Dorsey concluded, "I am the victim of southern prejudice." Despairingly he wondered "Where are we drifting?" Dorsey invited Donovan to come down to investigate matters for himself, and assured his superior of his willingness to stand trial in any ecclesiastical or civil court. In words that he would come to regret, Dorsey recommended that ". . . If colored priests must forever suffer and be outcasts, better not ordain them, or . . . get them places in northern cities."[27] Unknown to Dorsey, the Josephites were moving in that direction.

---

26. JFA, 25-P-14, Lucey to Donovan, Pine Bluff, September 6, 1907; Report of J. M. Lucey to Morris, November 18, 1907.

27. JFA, 25-P-18, Dorsey to Donovan, Pine Bluff, September 16, 1907.

Dorsey quickly recovered his spirits, however, and urged a fight. While admitting that he would have to acquiesce in a transfer, he nevertheless advised Donovan that ". . . a good public fight would help the cause immensely. We must not live supinely on our backs. If we do we shall never gain anything."[28] Leading Black citizens of Pine Bluff rallied to Dorsey's defense. In October, 1907, they drew up a petition of support for Dorsey and sent a copy to Lucey. They also addressed a petition to Donovan, urging him to keep Dorsey at Pine Bluff and praising Dorsey's intelligence, high moral character, and labors for his people. The petition was signed by forty-six Pine Bluff citizens, including two of the directors of the Colored Industrial Institute, the former and current principals of the state branch normal college, every Black physician except Dr. Bell, five attorneys, all of the Black teachers in the city's public schools, and numerous Black Protestant ministers.[29]

267

The petition enraged Lucey, who charged that Dorsey had engineered the petition, taking advantage of the ignorance of the Black people of Pine Bluff, and increasing the danger that the scandal would become public; a curious charge given his earlier claim that public knowledge of the affair had caused a decline in church attendance. Accusing Dorsey and Donovan of dilatory tactics, Lucey denied Donovan's request to extend Dorsey's faculties past October 16, 1907. Faced with the inevitable, Donovan transferred Dorsey back to St. Joseph's College for Negro Catechists in Montgomery.[30] William Murphy, Dorsey's successor at St. Peter's, spoke with Dorsey, Lucey, and parishioners about the "affair" and concluded that "Dorsey's crime was a black skin." According to Murphy, Monsignor Lucey, possessed of ". . . an evil, suspicious mind," had been at the bottom of the troubles. Murphy advised his Josephite superiors to take an independent stand and give up the mission at Pine Bluff.[31]

The beleaguered Josephite administrators, however, found it difficult to determine where they might take a stand on the issue of Black priests, for just as Dorsey left Pine Bluff, Bishop Edward Allen of Mobile advised Donovan that he did not favor Dorsey's return to Montgomery "because of certain local circumstances." Instead of reporting directly to Montgomery, therefore, Dorsey went on leave for two months. Though Allen

---

28. *Ibid.*

29. JFA, 25–P–20, L. R. Jones, et al. to Donovan, Pine Bluff, October 2, 1907.

30. JFA, 25–P–21, Lucey to Donovan, Pine Bluff, October 3, 1907; 25–P–22, Donovan to Dorsey, Baltimore, October 10, 1907; Dorsey File, Morris to Donovan, telegram, Little Rock, October 12, 1907.

31. JFA, 26–B–29, Rev. William Murphy, S.S.J. to Donovan, Pine Bluff, October 21, 1907; 27–N–34, Murphy to McCarthy, Pine Bluff, November 27, 1907.

268

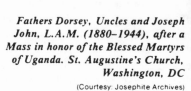

Fathers Dorsey, Uncles and Joseph John, L.A.M. (1880–1944), after a Mass in honor of the Blessed Martyrs of Uganda. St. Augustine's Church, Washington, DC
(Courtesy: Josephite Archives)

finally consented to grant faculties to Dorsey, he advised the Josephites to exercise great caution in accepting any future Black candidates.[32]

In the wake of Dorsey's experiences and in the midst of worsening race relations throughout the country, the Josephite leadership retreated on the issue of Black priests, all but closing Epiphany Apostolic College to Black candidates. On hearing reports about the change in Josephite policy, a number of Black Catholic women, led by Father Dorsey's sister-in-law, Mary Dorsey, founded a society for the support of Black students at Epiphany and St. Joseph's Seminary. On July 28, 1908, they communicated their alarm at the reported exclusion of Blacks from the Josephite college and seminary to the Reverend Justin McCarthy, who was elected Superior General in March, 1908, following the death of Thomas B. Donovan. Father Dorsey himself complained publicly in the pages of the *Freeman's Journal* about the small number of Black Catholic priests. The next year, C. Marcellus Dorsey, Father Dorsey's fiery, younger brother, who operated a printing business in Baltimore, founded the *Colored Catholic* newspaper to fight against discrimination in the Catholic Church and to promote the ordination of Blacks to the priesthood.[33] The refusal, however, in March, 1909, of Archbishop James H. Blenk of New Orleans to allow Father John Plantevigne, a young, Black Josephite priest ordained

---

32. JFA, 32–C–36, Donovan to the M. H. Witzius Company, Baltimore, November 26, 1907; 25–N–1, Allen to Donovan, Mobile, October 22, 1907.

33. *Baltimore Sun* (January 14, 1908); JFA, 28–B–14, Mrs. Rebecca Parker and Mrs. Mary Dorsey to McCarthy, Baltimore, July 28, 1908; 28–B–15, Rev. A. P. Doyle to McCarthy, Washington, D.C., July 28, 1908; Penelope L. Bullock, *Afro-American Periodical Press, 1838–1909* (Baton Rouge, 1981), 164.

in 1907, to enter the city of New Orleans to conduct a mission, further convinced the Josephites of the futility of ordaining Black priests.[34]

Meanwhile Dorsey continued his work in the South, enduring the daily humiliations of the "Jim Crow" system. For example, unlike the white priests at St. Joseph's College, Dorsey did not receive a request from the bishop to attend the annual clergy retreat scheduled for July 5, 1909. Dorsey also had to contend with harassment from the assistant postmaster, who circulated rumors that he mistreated the boys at the college. Those stories nearly led to Dorsey's removal, until an investigation by Father Dan Rice revealed that the assistant postmaster had fabricated them.[35]

In the summer of 1909, McCarthy, attempting to repair the damage caused by Plantevigne's rejection in New Orleans among Black Catholics and non-Catholics along the Gulf Coast, assigned Dorsey to full time work on the mission band along with Fathers John Albert and Sam Kelly. In October, 1909, Dorsey also played an important role, along with Father Conrad Rebesher, in the preliminary meetings which led to the foundation of the Nights of St. Peter Claver, a national fraternal association of Black Catholic men. Dorsey served as the national chaplain of the Knights from 1909 to 1923, often siding with the lay Black leaders in their not infrequent clashes with Josephites like Rebesher, who sought to direct the affairs of the Knights.[36]

269

From 1909 through 1917, Dorsey, billed as the "Great Pulpit Orator," conducted missions throughout the South before large, enthusiastic audiences. The missions had a two-fold purpose: to offer special opportunities for Catholics to renew their faith or return to the sacraments, and to give non-Catholics a chance to hear the Catholic faith explained. Dorsey's lectures during those missions included such topics as: "Why I Am a Catholic," "Bible Reading," "Marriage and Divorce," and "Is One Religion as Good as Another?" Dorsey also used the "Question Box," where he answered non-Catholics' questions about the Catholic Church.[37]

Dorsey appealed effectively to Black non-Catholics. During his travels, he drew generally favorable notices from Black newspapers like the *Memphis Sun.* Realizing that many Protestants would never come to a Catholic Church to hear him, Dorsey employed innovative methods, such as lecturing at meeting halls, Protestant churches, and Black college campuses, and surrounding himself on lecture platforms with local Black

---

34. Copies of the Archives of the Archdiocese of New Orleans in JFA, Archbishop James H. Blenk to Rev. John Plantevigne, S.S.J., New Orleans, March 31, 1909.

35. JFA, 28–R–26, Rev. Daniel Rice to McCarthy, Montgomery, June 4, 1909; 28–R–27, June 15, 1909; 28–R–28, July 29, 1909; 28–R–30, April 4, 1909.

36. Foley, *God's Men,* 56.

37. *The Colored Harvest* (June, 1914): 3–5; (June, 1915): 2–4.

preachers and politicians. In Memphis, he even secured the services of Handy's Band, a popular Black musical group known throughout the South.[38]

Of course, not all Black Protestants reacted favorably to Dorsey. During a 1916 mission at Mobile, for example, Baptist and Methodist preachers brought their congregations to the vicinity of the Catholic Church where Dorsey was conducting his mission and staged competing revival meetings. "Every night," reported Dorsey, "when our bell peals forth, all of the bells of the Protestant churches ring out in a melody of discord."[39]

Dorsey's missions became annual fixtures in the life of Black Catholic communities in the South; the people responded to "Father Harry" with affection and devotion. In 1914, at St. Dominic's in New Orleans, Dorsey gathered in 152 converts and 250 fallen-away Catholics. He created such a good impression, even among whites, that the Vicar General of the Archdiocese even offered some grudging praise. Following the death of St. Dominic's pastor in 1916, the people of the parish petitioned McCarthy to give them Father Dorsey as their pastor. Dorsey also gave missions in non-Josephite Catholic parishes. His missions for the Fathers of the Society of the Divine Word in Jackson and Meridian, Mississippi, helped convince those mostly German missionaries of the feasibility and desirability of Black priests.[40]

Unfortunately, even during his successful mission tours, Dorsey could not escape the burden of racial prejudice. He became a target of the scurrilous anti-Catholic attacks of Tom Watson, the Populist hero turned negrophobe and religious bigot. No issue of Watson's weekly or monthly publications was complete without its exposure of the "papal menace to America." Anti-Catholic articles in *Watson's Jeffersonian Weekly* included, "The Sinister Portent of Negro Priests." The *Jeffersonian* carried a cartoon depicting Father Dorsey as a big ape with a stole around his neck, listening to the confession of a beautiful white girl. The caption read, "This is what the Catholic Church is going to send us, to forgive sins, and to hear the confessions of our beautiful, white, pure virgins."[41]

Loneliness, prejudice, and overwork finally took their toll on Dorsey. He lost control of his weight, swelling to an eighteen and one half collar

---

38. *Ibid.* (June, 1914): 3–4.

39. *Ibid.* (October, 1916): 4.

40. *The Colored Harvest* (October, 1914): 3–4; AANO in JFA, Rev. F. L. Gassler to McCarthy, New Orleans, September 10, 1914; Foley, *God's Men,* 58–60; 32-K–12, A. J. Bell, et al. to McCarthy, New Orleans, January 3, 1916; 32-D–18, Rev. A. Heick, S.V.D., to McCarthy, Jackson, January 4, 1916.

41. C. Van Woodward, *Tom Watson: Agrarian Rebel* (Oxford, 1963), 419 and 421; JFA, transcript of a series of interviews conducted by Rev. Peter E. Hogan, S.S.J. with Rev. Vincent Warren, S.S.J., Baltimore, 1965, 165.

size on a 5'8" frame. In June, 1916, he succumbed to 100 degree temperatures in San Antonio and wrote to McCarthy, "Really, I do not feel able to do any more missionary work just now."[42] Alcohol further exacerbated his health problems. Despite the danger signals, Dorsey's ambitious itinerary in 1917 included Galveston, Mobile, Memphis, Vicksburg, San Antonio, Walter, Mississippi, and Baltimore. In Mobile, he first exhibited publicly the heavy drinking that had apparently begun somewhat earlier. By the time he arrived in Galveston in March, 1917, however, Father Charles Gatley, the Josephite pastor expressed satisfaction with his behavior and observed, "He was on the water wagon the whole time." John Albert, Dorsey's former colleague on the mission band and a strong proponent of Black priests, defended Dorsey to Louis B. Pastorelli, the rector of St. Joseph's Seminary and the man who virtually ran the Josephites for McCarthy. "We ought," Albert told Pastorelli, "to stand behind Dorsey . . . because we must be careful not to give the Colored priest a black eye, even though he might be instrumental in earning one. His life is naturally a hard one and the loneliness which we cannot feel might at times be productive of temporary lapses of sobriety."[43]

271

Dorsey's health finally forced him to give up active missionary work and he returned to St. Joseph's Seminary in Baltimore in 1917. Yet, episcopal snubs still followed him. When illness and death in St. Joseph's Society in the autumn of 1917 forced Pastorelli to assign Dorsey temporarily to Nashville, Bishop Thomas S. Byrne professed fear that Dorsey was "not a man fitted for this place." Byrne suggested that Memphis might suit Dorsey better than Nashville. Taking the bishop at this word, Pastorelli, in December, temporarily assigned Dorsey to Memphis. Byrne, however, curtly informed Pastorelli that Dorsey would not do in Memphis and added petulantly, ". . . you are not allowed to send a Priest into a Diocese without first asking the Ordinary's leave. . . ." After reminding the bishop of his earlier words, Pastorelli withdrew the appointment. Dorsey settled into a sullen and embittered residence at St. Joseph's Seminary.[44]

In June, 1918, Louis B. Pastorelli won formal election as Superior General of the Josephites. He focused his attention on rebuilding and centralizing St. Joseph's Society. He had witnessed first hand the suffering of the first Black Josephite priests. Moreover, he had little faith in Black leadership potential. Convinced that he needed to win the favor of the

---

42. JFA, 32-K-14, Dorsey to McCarthy, San Antonio, June 13, 1916.

43. JFA, Rev. Charles Gatley, S.S.J. to Rev. John Albert, S.S.J., Galveston, March 22, 1917; 32-D-30, Albert to Rev. Louis B. Pastorelli, S.S.J., Mobile, April (?), 1917.

44. JFA, 67-A, Bishop Thomas Sebastian Byrne to Pastorelli, Nashville, September 17, 1917; December 4, 1917.

272

Father John Dorsey, S.S.J.
(1873–1926), in later life
(Courtesy: Josephite Archives)

southern bishops, at whose pleasure the Josephites served. Pastorelli decided to exclude all but an occasional mulatto student from Epiphany Apostolic College and St. Joseph's Seminary. He tried to keep a token light skinned, Black student at the college or the seminary in an attempt "to keep the race from crying out against us."[45]

Pastorelli's policy further alienated him from Dorsey. Indeed, the bitter relations between the two men mirrored the racial turmoil of the post-war years in the United States. They soon became entangled in a public controversy over the Josephite policy regarding Black seminarians. Pastorelli had recalled Dorsey from the mission band in 1917, charging him with drunkenness, laziness, ignoring rural parishes, and keeping money without submitting returns or accounts to the Superior. During the General Chapter meeting that elected Pastorelli as Superior in June, 1918, Dorsey, together with two other Josephites, bitterly attacked Pastorelli—probably over his refusal to accept more Black candidates into the college and seminary. When Pastorelli was elected Superior, on the strength of thirteen proxy votes, Dorsey opposed making the election unanimous.[46]

---

45. JFA, 70–R, Pastorelli to Archbishop John W. Shaw, Baltimore, September, 1933.
46. JFA, Private Data Book, June, 1918, 9 and 45.

Father Louis B. Pastorelli, elected
Superior General of the Josephites in 1918
(Courtesy: Josephite Archives)

Four days after the General Chapter, Pastorelli and his Consultors decided to remove Dorsey permanently from the mission band and to appoint him as pastor of St. Monica's, a poor, rundown Black parish in South Baltimore, whose weekly collection rarely exceeded three dollars. The assignment of Dorsey to St. Monica's upset members of the Dorsey family, who believed that the Josephites should have rewarded Father Dorsey's strenuous years of service on the mission band with an appointment to a more prosperous parish. In February, 1919, relations between Pastorelli and Dorsey deteriorated further when Pastorelli accused Dorsey of neglecting his duties at St. Monica's; charges which Dorsey heatedly disputed.[47]

One month later, the bitterness between Pastorelli and the Dorseys burst into public view. On March 10, 1919, the campaign to raise $15,000

---

47. JFA, Consultors' Minutes Book—1, August 29, 1918, 79; 36-D, Dorsey to Pastorelli, Baltimore, February 5, 1919; interview, Earl Counters and Mary Dorsey, Baltimore, November 2, 1983; 36-D, Pastorelli to Dorsey, Baltimore, February 4, 1919; 36-D, Dorsey to Pastorelli, Baltimore, February 5, 1919.

for the Oblate Sisters, which Dorsey headed, ended with a program at Albough's Theatre-House. C. Marcellus Dorsey, whom Pastorelli regarded as the "mouth" for his brother, read a paper publicly attacking the Josephites, accusing them of mistreating his brother and living like parasites off their Black parishioners. Father Dorsey, seated on the stage, spoke immediately after his brother, but in no way challenged the latter's remarks.[48]

274

Marcellus Dorsey's public attack on the Josephites signalled the beginning of a campaign by two groups of Black Catholics, one centered in Baltimore, the other in Washington, D.C., to force the Josephites to open their college and seminary to more Black students. In September, 1919, the Baltimore Black Catholic dissidents, called "insurgents," formed themselves into a branch of Dr. Thomas Wyatt Turner's Washington organization, known as the Committee for the Advancement of Colored Catholics which evolved into the Federated Colored Catholics. While the Washington Committee concentrated on lobbying the hierarchy, the Baltimore "insurgents," led by Marcellus Dorsey, adopted the more controversial tactic of publicizing its grievances against the Josephites and the Catholic Church in the pages of the *Baltimore Afro-American* newspaper.[49]

Father Dorsey encouraged the Baltimore and Washington groups to pressure the Josephites. He urged Thomas Turner to "Agitate! Agitate!" assuring him that "Constant judicious agitation is bound to bring good results." Dorsey accused the Catholic Church in the United States of doing nothing to stem the tide of race prejudice; rather, he claimed, "prejudice in the Church has kept pace with prejudice in the state." Dorsey confessed to Turner that when, during missions, he had claimed that prejudice did not exist in the Catholic Church, "I knew I was not telling the truth and my inner self rebelled." He concluded, "It is a God-given mission to rid the Church of race prejudice."[50]

Despite the agitation of lay Black Catholics, however, Pastorelli clung steadfastly to his exclusionary policy at Epiphany and St. Joseph's Seminary. The Josephites did not ordain another Black priest until 1941. Not until the election of Edward V. Casserly as Superior of the Josephites in 1942, did the Josephites return to their original policy of encouraging and

---

48. JFA, Private Data Book, March 10, 1919, 45-46.

49. JFA, Pastorelli Miscellaneous Correspondence, Pastorelli to C. W. Wallace, Baltimore, April 12, 1920. For a fine study of Turner and the Federated Colored Catholics, see Marilyn W. Nickels, "The Federated Colored Catholics: A Study of Three Variant Perspectives on Racial Justice As Represented by John LaFarge, William Markoe, and Thomas Turner," (unpublished Ph.D. dissertation, Catholic University of America, 1975).

50. Thomas Wyatt Turner Papers—36 (copies in the possession of Ms. Marilyn W. Nickels). Dorsey to Dr. Thomas Wyatt Turner, Baltimore, May 22, 1920.

recruiting Black candidates for their Society. Nevertheless, the campaign of Black Catholics for Black priests in the early nineteen twenties caught the attention of the Holy See, which in turn put pressure on the American bishops to consider the issue. The result was that the bishops approved the establishment by the Society of the Divine Word (SVDs) of St. Augustine's Seminary in Bay St. Louis, Mississippi, for the training of Black candidates for the SVDs. Leadership in the development of a Black clergy, therefore, passed from the Josephites to the SVDs, although the SVDs did not ordain their first Black priests until 1934. While he welcomed the establishment of St. Augustine's Seminary, Dorsey objected to its segregated nature and insisted that integrated seminary education represented the only truly Christian approach to the formation of priests.[51]

275

Dorsey's tragic death in 1926 seemed to symbolize the sorry fate of the early Black priests. In September, 1924, during a dispute over disciplinary action taken by Father Dorsey toward one of the school children at St. Monica's, the father of the child, an ex-convict, seized a heavy block of wood and struck Dorsey over the head, knocking him down and fracturing his skull. Dorsey never recovered from the blow, suffering progressive paralysis and several strokes. He died at Mt. Hope Sanitarium on June 30, 1926, in the same year as his old patron, John R. Slattery. Dorsey's longtime friend, Father Charles Uncles, and two other Black priests, Joseph John of the Lyons Society of the African Missions, and Norman DuKette, of the Diocese of Detroit, celebrated the funeral mass before three thousand mourners.[52]

The *Afro-American* eulogized "Our Father Harry Dorsey," but white churchmen viewed his death as the end of a "problem." Pastorelli believed that Dorsey had at last found peace, and that his death "would likely quiet an unpleasant commotion." Pastorelli's friend, Archbishop John W. Shaw of New Orleans, wrote, "All things considered, the death of Fr. Dorsey seems providential, as I believe that he was not much consolation." Rumors and gossip led many whites to regard the attack that led to Dorsey's death as evidence of a full-scale rejection of the Black priesthood by Black Catholics.[53]

John Dorsey's life as a priest demonstrated both the heroism and the trials of the Black priest in the United States. He suffered the fate of the pioneer. His devotion to his vocation and to his Church cost him dearly.

---

51. St. Augustine's Seminary Archives. Janser—Christman File, Dorsey to Rev. Joseph Wendel. S.V.D., Baltimore, January 3, 1920.

52. Foley, *God's Men*, 61–62.

53. *Baltimore Afro-American* (July 10, 1926); Welbers to Pastorelli, San Antonio. August 4. 1926; 69–S. Shaw to Pastorelli, New Orleans, August 10, 1926.

Nevertheless, despite the racism that he experienced in the Catholic Church, Dorsey, like many other Black Catholics, steadfastly clung to his vocation and to his faith, prophetically calling the institutional Church in the United States to conversion. He helped blaze the trail for other Black priests who followed him. Although their number rose to more than three hundred by 1985, Black priests still remained a tiny minority of the nation's approximately 50,000 Catholic priests.[54] The shortage of Black priests for the nation's 1.2 million Black Catholics endured as a legacy of the racism that made the life of John Henry Dorsey and other Black priests such a "heavy cross."

---

54. Rev. John Harfmann, S.S.J., *1984 Statistical Profile of Black Catholics* (Washington, D.C., 1985), 9.

"THE GOOD SISTERS": THE WORK AND POSITION OF CATHOLIC CHURCHWOMEN IN BOSTON, 1870-1940

Mary J. Oates

After the burning of the Ursuline convent in Charlestown in 1834, only a few sisters could be found in Massachusetts until 1849. In that year, the Sisters of Notre Dame de Namur arrived to staff a Boston school. Thereafter, the number of sisters increased along with the growing Catholic population; they numbered 221 in 1870 and 4,164 in 1940. Staffing numerous parochial schools, hospitals, orphanages, and social agencies, sisters in the archdiocese of Boston outnumbered the total of priests, brothers, and seminarians combined by a margin of two to one by 1940.[1] Such quantitative indices suggest the importance of organized female groups in the charitable endeavors of the Catholic church. This essay examines the social and religious environments in which Massachusetts sisters worked in the years between 1870 and 1940, the internal structure of their communities, and their position in the organizational framework of the church.

The sisterhoods, like other voluntary organizations, were situated in a context which affected their social acceptability and effectiveness. Organized service to society was an obligatory tenet of these groups of women, which developed after 1820 in the United States. While their efforts were channeled into traditionally female work, the orientation to service outside their own communities, embodying a religious calling to a common and celibate life, became a strongly positive feature attracting new members.[2] The religious motive is

277

[1] Mary J. Oates, "Organized Voluntarism: The Catholic Sisters in Massachusetts, 1870-1940," in Janet Wilson James, ed., *Women in American Religion* (Philadelphia: University of Pennsylvania Press, 1980), 141-169.

[2] In any case, regardless of their personal views about marriage, women desiring long-term professional careers were not usually able to marry. As late as 1920 three-fourths of all professional women were unmarried. See Elizabeth Kemper Adams, *Women Professional Workers: A Study Made for the Women's Educational and Industrial*

especially significant, for if teaching or providing social services were the only goal of a group of women there would be little reason for organizing under the aegis of the church.

In choosing a decidedly unconventional lifestyle, sisters were at variance with mid-nineteenth century social norms governing female behavior, and they aroused considerable hostility in Protestant New England. The Sisters of Notre Dame de Namur did not wear their habits when traveling until about 1870.[3] More than priests, women religious were singled out in Boston society as symbolic of the threat of the Catholic church. George W. Burnap, lecturing at Harvard College in 1853, considered it a particularly ominous sign that "a convent had arisen in the sight of Harvard Yard."[4] The staunch Protestant ethic which imbued charitable agencies and local public schools was not appreciated by the Irish newcomers, and Catholic social agencies and schools staffed by sisters were soon established to counteract its influence. In the half-century following 1870 the number of sisterhoods in the archdiocese increased more than five-fold. In 1920 nearly three-fourths of the sisters belonged to one of the ten largest communities, with the rest scattered among twenty-eight other groups. The dominant communities were the two original teaching groups, the Sisters of Notre Dame de Namur and the Sisters of St. Joseph, which together accounted for 44 percent of all Boston sisters in that year.

A major factor contributing to the increased number of communities was that parishes requiring teachers for schools expanded following the mandate of the council of Baltimore in 1884 that every

278

Union (Chautauqua, N.Y.: Chautauqua Press, 1921), 23. The importance of the work done by Catholic sisters was acknowledged by observers: "I believe more than one half the women who go into the Catholic Church join her because she gives work to her children. Happier by far is a Sister of Charity or Mercy than a young lady at home without a work or a lover"; Barbara Leigh Smith Bodichon, *Women and Work* (New York, 1859), 27, quoted in Nina Auerbach, *Communities of Women: An Idea in Fiction* (Cambridge, Mass.: Harvard University Press, 1978), 195 n.21.

[3] A Member of the Congregation, *The American Foundations of the Sisters of Notre Dame de Namur, Compiled from the Annals of Their Convents* (Philadelphia: Dolphin Press, 1928), 196.

[4] Douglas C. Stange, "The Third Lecture: One Hundred and Fifty Years of Anti-Popery at Harvard," *Harvard Library Bulletin*, 16 (1968): 362, quoting George W. Burnap, "The Errors and Superstitions of the Church of Rome," Dudleian Lecture, Harvard College, May 11, 1853.

parish open a school.[5] Since Boston had been slower than most other dioceses to respond to earlier recommendations to establish schools the edict meant that a surge of school openings was inevitable, immediately stimulating demand for teaching sisters which the established communities were unable to meet. Pastors, determined to find teachers for their new schools, visited motherhouses throughout the country. In the 1880s alone Maryland, Kentucky, Nova Scotia, New Jersey, and Indiana communities first sent sisters to the archdiocese, and the number of teaching communities rose from two to fourteen. In contrast, no growth can be observed in the number of groups engaged in hospital or social work (see Appendix A).

279

A second factor was that the rise of national or ethnic parishes desiring to establish their own parochial schools required that communities whose members could speak the language be introduced into the diocese. French-Canadian, French, German, Polish, and Italian communities began to appear after 1890 as various groups acquired the means to finance their own schools. French-Canadians comprised the largest of these groups, accounting by 1920 for 12 percent of all sisters in the diocese. Italian, Polish, and German communities combined represented only 3 percent of the total in that year. The relatively small number of Boston parochial school children attending the foreign language schools and their cultural distinctiveness meant that the ethnic sisterhoods exerted a largely local influence in a diocese dominated by Irish-Americans. During the period between 1870 and 1940 their schools enrolled less than 20 percent of the children in parochial schools in the Boston archdiocese, while as early as 1900 they accounted for over 55 percent of the total enrollment in the Chicago archdiocesan system, a proportion they sustained over the next thirty years.[6]

Communities not restricted to a single diocese by their rules or constitutions were free to accept invitations from Boston's pastors; frequently they did so over the protests of churchmen in the states where their motherhouses were located. In 1908 one midwestern ec-

[5]*Pastoral Letter of the Archbishops and Bishops of the United States Assembled in the Third Plenary Council of Baltimore* (Baltimore, 1884), 14-17.

[6]James W. Sanders, *The Education of an Urban Minority: Catholics in Chicago, 1833-1965* (New York: Oxford University Press, 1977), 45.

280

Profession ceremony, Sisters of Notre Dame de Namur
(Photo courtesy *The Pilot*)

clesiastic begged sisters to refuse such requests: "Today the East clamors for religious teachers. . . . They invite sisters to come from this section of the country and open schools. . . . I would say to you sisters . . . pray that the Lord send vocations innumerable to the East, but remember . . . that charity begins at home."[7] The expansion of Boston's two original and largest communities suggests that local women were indeed responding to such prayers. In the 1880s alone their total membership, including novices and postulants, increased by 130 percent. Since sisterhoods were highly specialized by profession the young woman considering religious life could determine her life's work through her choice of community. In order for the number of teachers to grow rapidly not only did women have to be convinced that teaching was the essential need of the day, but they also had to find the prospect of convent life attractive. Given this constraint the supply of sisters never adequately satisfied the enormous demand for their services in schools between 1870 and 1940.

281

Who were these young women who joined religious communities and taught in the Boston archdiocese after 1870? Convent records for 764 Sisters of Notre Dame de Namur permit a summary picture of typical teachers. These women staffed flourishing parochial schools in Lawrence (St. Mary's), Cambridge (St. Mary's), and Salem (St. James's). By the 1890s they were predominantly American-born, with most coming from Massachusetts. Over 90 percent of the sisters born before 1880 were of immigrant parentage. Although the proportion declined as the years progressed it remained high. Even for sisters born between 1910 and 1919, 60 percent had foreign-born fathers, the overwhelming majority of whom were from Ireland. The community appears to have modified its policy on the age of admission in the early decades of this century, probably in response to the expanding demand for teachers. Of sisters born before 1900 fewer than one in five had been admitted while still teenagers. Of those born between 1910 and 1919, however, 53 percent were admitted while still in their teens.[8]

[7]Camillus P. Maes, "Comment on 'Promoting Vocations', " *Catholic Educational Association Bulletin*, 5 (1908): 275-276.
[8]Convent records, St. Mary's parish, Cambridge, 1900-1928; St. James's parish, Salem, 1920-1968; St. Mary's parish, Lawrence, 1893-1934: all in Motherhouse Archives, Sisters of Notre Dame de Namur (ASND), Ipswich, MA.

The bulk of the supply of teachers for Boston's schools was by 1880 drawn from working-class Irish families. Teaching was a prestigious profession for women, and the religious community offered working-class youth the opportunity for a useful and long-term career. Personal contact with individual sisters strongly influenced a young woman's choice of a community. Teaching groups, not surprisingly, drew more recruits than communities engaged in other works. Referring to the forty-two postulants expected to enter in 1930, the provincial superior of the Sisters of Notre Dame observed: "They are all, with the exception of one, our own children, so it is the work of the Sisters in the school."[9] This inevitably led to the heavy segregation of communities by nationality. The Sisters of Notre Dame and the Sisters of St. Joseph quickly became Irish because the schools they staffed were mainly in Irish parishes. The former group had its motherhouse in Belgium and made every effort to reproduce in America the conventual traditions and life-style of Namur. The limited success of this endeavor in Boston's convents is reflected in the Gaelic-accented assurance of the provincial superior on the eve of a visit of the mother general from Belgium that "all will be ready and happy to offer her a *caed mille failthe*."[10]

The tremendous expansion of parochial schools after 1884 was viewed by middle-class Protestants as a challenge to their efforts to assimilate foreigners through public institutions. Catholic schools were severely criticized as major obstacles to the transmission of American values, and the struggle over the "sisters' schools," as they were popularly called by Protestant and Catholic alike, soon became more than religious. The mainstream definition of the "moral life" in America conformed to the values of the middle-class. To many Irish as well as non-English-speaking Catholics the parochial schools came to represent one powerful means of preserving both their cultural heritage and their religious tradition. "The contest was a question of whose value system was to be transmitted to future generations."[11]

[9]Sister Mary Frances, "Conference," August 11, 1930, *ibid*.
[10]Sister Mary Frances to Sister Superiors, October 20, 1920, *ibid*.
[11]Paul Kleppner, *The Cross of Culture* (New York: The Free Press, 1970), 77-78. According to Kleppner, on the issue of parochial schools, whether Catholic or Lutheran, the conflict was not only between value systems, but "value systems which had been *sanctified*. In such a conflict there could be no compromise" (74-75).

An indirect but significant outcome of mainstream hostility to the activities of sisters in Massachusetts was the evolution of their own perception of their role within the Catholic church. Their efforts to increase their efficiency and effectiveness in response to external censure provoked in turn greater awareness of conflicting pressures from within the church in matters affecting their daily lives and work decisions. They faced challenges in two environments by the late nineteenth century. They were the most numerous and visible symbols of Catholicism in a heavily Protestant culture, and they were endeavoring to progress as professionals in a religious milieu traditionally governed by men. All the stereotypes about women's capabilities, work, and professional status characteristic of the period were held by churchmen at least as strongly as by their lay counterparts. Since sisters had to work closely with bishops and pastors they were more directly affected by such attitudes than the average Catholic lay woman.

283

Sisterhoods met greater challenges to group autonomy than did communities of priests or brothers. The canon law governing religious was not uniform for men and women. The privilege of exemption from episcopal interference in community affairs and government was reserved to male religious orders. In 1752 Rome refused to approve any new orders; only congregations, which by definition did not enjoy the exemption privilege, were to be permitted. While several of the larger congregations of priests succeeded in obtaining the status through special indults, nineteenth-century clerics increasingly preferred to organize as "pious societies" rather than as congregations. Members of a pious society took no special vows, and so the group could not be classified as a true religious institute, although its constitutions had to have church approval. As a consequence absence of the exemption privilege posed little risk to the autonomy of the pious society.

Women, on the other hand, were not permitted to establish pious societies. The only structure for which they could obtain church approval was the nonexempt congregation. Every female congregation was either diocesan (that is, approved by the local bishop) or pontifical (approved by authorities in Rome). Local bishops were given wider jurisdiction over diocesan communities than over pontifical groups. In the critical matter of the election of superiors, for example, they had veto power: "In congregations of women the election of the mother general shall be presided over by the Ordinary of the place where the election is held, . . . and in the case of a diocesan congregation, the Ordinary has full power to confirm or annul the result of the election."[12] While canon law protected diocesan as well as pontifical communities of women in such matters as "the general relation of subjects to superiors, . . . admission of subjects into the congregation and to the professions, their education and formation, appointments to various offices and employments and transfer from house to house," many American bishops viewed their jurisdiction as extending to those areas.[13]

By 1940 nearly two-thirds of all sisters in the archdiocese of Boston were employed in parochial schools. These schools and their convents were parish-owned, with sisters receiving from the parish their housing and a small annual stipend. Since they were employees of the parish they could be dismissed by its pastor and occasionally they were. The inability of a community to meet pastoral pressures for more teachers for the school was one important cause of dissatisfaction. A Salem pastor, for example, dismissed a group of sisters in 1924 because teachers were briefly unavailable for every grade. The only condition on which the community might remain was that it pay the salaries of the lay teachers he would be obliged to hire in the interim. The sisters, unable to meet his terms, left.[14] Other communities, staffing schools in other parishes and fearing a similar fate, reluctantly accommodated unreasonable requests for more teachers, knowing that the young sisters were not being properly prepared for their work. Annals of sisterhoods during the years of school expansion after 1884 are filled with statements of regret about the persisting dilemma. The provincial superior of the Sisters of Notre Dame commented resignedly: "The Normal School opened

[12]Charles Augustine Bachofen, *A Commentary on the New Code of Canon Law*; vol. 3: *Religious and Laymen* (St. Louis: B. Herder, 1929), 101.

[13]Joseph F. Gallen, S.J., "Religious Clerical Formation and Sister Formation," in Sister Ritamary, ed., *The Mind of the Church in the Formation of Sisters* (New York: Fordham University Press, 1956), 58-59. While John Williams, as archbishop of Boston, did not attend any of the seven elections of the diocesan community held between 1887 and 1907, preferring to send a representative, this was not characteristic of his successor, William O'Connell. See Motherhouse "Annals," 1887-1907, Archives, Sisters of St. Joseph (ASSJ), Brighton, MA.

[14]Sister Marie de Ste. Foi to O'Connell, August 7, 1924, and Haberlin to Sister Marie, September 2, 1924, Institution Files, AABo 16:1.

with a class of twenty-two, but alas! for its hopes, scarcely a day has passed since, but demands from some quarter or other threaten the career of its pupils; and so they have gone."[15] A later superior of the community, writing in 1918, noted that the situation had not ameliorated over time: "Again we must with deep regret, send out a few Novices who have not completed their year in the Novitiate."[16]

Formal professional training was becoming an essential credential for teachers, and pressures for improvement in Massachusetts were especially strong after 1890. Changing public school policy on teacher education can be observed in the stricter requirements of the normal schools and in the hiring of teachers on the basis of qualifications and merit.[17] The tension between the subordinate position of sisters in the ecclesiastical organization and their work as professional educators was nowhere clearer than in the matter of teacher training. On the one hand, strict rules of life required that they remain secluded from society and work under the supervision of pastors, the legal principals of the schools. Many of these men were indifferent to educational reforms and innovative advances. On the other hand, the communities were well aware of their shortcomings in providing adequate pre-service training and were particularly sensitive to criticisms from Catholic journalists on the issue.[18] As more and younger women joined the communities the need to prepare them to meet a standard of certification acceptable in public schools preoccupied sister superiors. In an effort to respond to pastoral requests they tried to train the newcomers in ways that did not retard their rapid flow into the schools. This self-contradictory approach was unsatisfactory to the communities, the schools, and the individual sisters, not only because it was sporadic and lengthy, but also because public school standards were constantly being

285

[15]"Annals," Sisters of Notre Dame de Namur, Waltham, MA, 1 (1889–1896): 127-128, ASND.

[16]Sister Mary Borgia to Sister Superiors, Notre Dame, Waltham, July 28, 1918, *ibid.*

[17]Thomas M. Balliet, "The Problem of the Elementary School," *Report of the Advisory Committee to the Joint Committee of the Collegiate Alumnae and the Federation of Women's Clubs of Massachusetts,* records of the Boston branch of the American Association of University Women, MC 271, Education Committee, IVB.3, manuscript collections, Schlesinger Library, Radcliffe College (SLRC), Cambridge, MA.

[18]See, for example, the criticisms of teaching sisterhoods by Caroline E. MacGill, "The Lost Freedom of Women," *Catholic World,* 118 (1924): 454.

raised, and proper teacher education could no longer be acquired in so casual a way.[19]

While sisters were considered valuable and conscientious workers who gave their lives and possessions in the service of the church, many clerics believed that they alone should determine what nuns would do. It was appropriate for the clergy to define critical needs which women could meet and for sisters to comply, even if, on occasion, they had to modify their present work. In this assumption the hierarchy and parish priests were merely reflecting popular perceptions of the day of women's capacities and place. Why should sisters behave differently from other women? The deference a wife owed to her husband should logically be replicated in the reliance of nuns on their leadership. Sisters never challenged the spiritual authority of the clergy nor argued for participation of women in priestly ministries. In the matter of work choice and the allocation of the labor of community members, however, they were convinced that ultimate authority lay with the community. Collectively they would determine not only the type of professional service they would provide, but also in its modification or expansion. Such disparity of perspective continued over the period and led to considerable, and occasionally heated, exchanges.

A bishop's interest in the work of sisters tended to focus mainly on how it related to the shifting needs of his diocese. Theoretically, with the establishment throughout the country of numerous congregations of women, each highly specialized by work, he could simply invite an appropriate group to enter the diocese to meet the latest challenge. Practically, however, the growing demand for sisters often meant that communities engaged in the desired area of service could not be induced to assume added responsibilities in another diocese. The tendency was therefore to prevail upon groups already working in the diocese to expand their chosen field of endeavor to meet the need of the hour. When this occurred, sisters tried to ensure that the arrangement would be short-term, continuing only until a group specialized in the new work was available. "More especially devoted to serving the sick and caring for the orphan and foundling," the Daughters of Charity staffed the first parochial

---

[19]Mary J. Oates, "Professional Preparation of Parochial School Teachers, 1870–1940," *Historical Journal of Massachusetts*, 12 (1984): 60-72.

school in Boston in 1847, but left two years later when the teaching Sisters of Notre Dame de Namur were finally able to send sisters there.[20] Similarly, the Grey Nuns of Montreal withdrew from a Salem parochial school in 1904 in order to return to their specialty, hospital work.[21]

After 1890, with professionalization of women's fields becoming a matter of wide discussion, sisterhoods became more intent on preserving their various specializations. By 1920, for example, of thirty-four congregations with sisters in the Boston archdiocese, only two were represented in both local schools and social agencies. There was agreement that, given the limitations on financial resources and time available for preparatory training, improvements in the quality of their work could best be achieved through specialization rather than by engaging in a broad range of unrelated activities. When young sisters had to "learn by doing," group loyalty and cooperation were essential for continuing supervision and assistance. Such associational benefits were maximized when all sisters in a community joined in a single corporate work.

When a community's constitutions stated its goals narrowly and unambiguously superiors of pontifical congregations were relatively successful in resisting requests to undertake unrelated works. The constitutions of the Little Sisters of the Poor, for example, were unequivocal: "No establishment shall be accepted and founded with any other aim but that of receiving, feeding and supporting the Aged Poor."[22] At the other extreme, the constitutions of the Sisters of Charity of Nazareth included among the concerns of members "the welfare of the neighbor, the suffering poor, the sick, the insane, the orphans in Hospitals and Asylums; and the Christian education of female youth in Parochial Schools, Academies and institutions of Higher Education."[23] This was the only pontifical congregation in Boston to staff schools as well as social agencies after 1870, and its objectives clearly encompassed both areas of activity.

[20]*Sacred Heart Review*, October 12, 1889.

[21]*The Catholic Church in the United States of America*; vol. 2: *The Religious Communities of Women* (New York: The Catholic Editing Co., 1914), 108.

[22]*Rule and Constitutions of the Hospitaller Congregation of the Little Sisters of the Poor* (Rome: Vatican Polyglot Press, 1936), 34.

[23]*Constitutions of the Sisters of Charity of Nazareth, Kentucky* (Rome: Vatican Polyglot Press, 1922), 18.

Sisters of St. Joseph with students
(Photo courtesy Archives, Sisters of St. Joseph, Brighton)

In contrast, the single sisterhood to depart from its major work after 1900 was the diocesan teaching congregation, the Sisters of St. Joseph, and the change was not made freely. William Cardinal O'Connell never acknowledged that these sisters had authority in determination of their own work. He required that they undertake many projects unrelated to teaching in a period when there was a shortage of teachers for their many schools: "I want the Sisters to do all kinds of work. Some of them don't want to do anything but teach."[24]

If pontifical sisterhoods held firm to their chosen work despite the wishes of a bishop or pastors, they were often asked to leave the parish or institution in favor of a "more cooperative" community. Thus, insistence upon autonomy over work decisions could be costly. The immediate support of all the sisters in the community and the long-term viability of the congregation depended upon the small stipends earned in diocesan establishments. The famous "Boy Question" of the Sisters of Notre Dame de Namur in Boston provides a fine case study of the dilemma confronting sisterhoods. This community specialized in the education of girls and had the largest representation of teachers in Massachusetts parochial schools between 1850 and 1880. At the council of Baltimore in 1884, the bishops mandated that all children attend parochial schools. If the Sisters of Notre Dame refused to modify their chosen work and accept boys through the elementary grades at least, pastors would have to hire brothers to instruct them. The cost of two houses and the higher stipends that brothers could command motivated many pastors to oust the Sisters of Notre Dame in favor of communities of women willing to teach both sexes.[25] The community, though deeply concerned, held to its convictions despite all pressures. Sister Superior Julia wrote to the sisters in 1888: "We are sorry to leave a parish where we have labored successfully, but we prefer doing that to taking a branch of labor that would not be good for our spirit. . . . Massachusetts is not the whole world."[26]

---

[24]Quoted in diary of Sister M. Aloysius, October 15, 1921, ASSJ.

[25]James J. Sullivan, ed., *One Hundred Years of Progress: A Graphical, Historical and Pictorial Account of the Catholic Church of New England, Archdiocese of Boston* (Boston, 1895), 115, 131, 617.

[26]Sister Julia to Sisters, Sixth Street, Cincinnati, February 26, 1888, ASND.

290

In such controversies women's communities had fewer alternatives than male groups. Even though salaries paid religious brothers were approximately twice those provided sisters for the same work the men found them insufficient.[27] When their requests for increases were denied by pastors, congregations of brothers moved out of the parochial schools almost entirely and established private institutions for boys. They, rather than the parish or diocese, controlled these schools and thus were able to charge tuitions high enough to permit them to meet their living costs. A typical justification for such moves was put in a 1922 letter to a West Coast bishop from a brother superior: "Unless, therefore, the dioceses in which we labor find it possible to assist us far more liberally than heretofore, I know not how the problem of educating our young men is to be solved. This condition, and this condition alone, explains our seemingly relentless attitude and our rather sudden withdrawal from Portland. We must look intently to our own interests, now more than ever."[28] Except for some short-term inconvenience the departure of brothers from Boston's parochial schools occasioned few expressions of regret since they could be replaced by sisters at a lower cost to the parish.

Teaching sisterhoods did hold significant power in two key areas. First, they appointed all professional personnel in the parochial schools as well as in their own academies. Teaching sisters were immediately answerable not to the pastor but to their community superiors, who could unilaterally assign them to grades and transfer them to other schools staffed by the community, sometimes in other states. Development of an efficient teaching force was aided by the fact that once a sister entered the classroom as a young teacher she remained there for her entire working life. The female public school teacher of the era, who was forced to resign her position upon marriage, tended to have a much shorter classroom career.[29]

Second, while men held most administrative positions in public schools, from the earliest days of parochial education sisters served

[27]J.A. Burns, *The Growth and Development of the Catholic School System in the United States* (New York: Benziger Brothers, 1912), 23, 100, 282.

[28]Brother Joseph to Christie, July 20, 1922, quoted in Ronald E. Isetti, *Called to the Pacific* (Moraga, Cal.: St. Mary's College of California, 1979), 282.

[29]David S. Tyack, "Pilgrim's Progress: Toward a Social History of the School Superintendency, 1860–1960," *History of Education Quarterly*, 16 (1976): 265.

as *de facto* principals. Two features of Catholic education account for the unusual policy of having women administrators. Sisters were widely known as early as the 1850s for their excellent academies for girls. Unlike parochial schools these institutions were established and entirely managed by the women's communities. They were attended by Protestant as well as by Catholic children before the general development of the public high school.[30] As a result clergy and laity alike were familiar with the image of the sister-principal by the time parochial schools began to open in large numbers later in the century. In addition we can explain the ready acceptance of women leaders in Catholic schools by the fact that the official principals, the pastors, usually had neither the time for nor the interest in their day-to-day management. The typical pastor focused his efforts more on raising funds to construct, furnish, and maintain the schools than on pedagogical concerns. There were, of course, a few notable and often colorful exceptions, pastors who involved themselves heavily in establishing curricula, selecting textbooks, and supervising teachers. Even these rare men did not dispute the ability of women as a group to serve as principals. Most pastors demonstrated their interest in the schools mainly by exhibiting a proprietary attitude toward them, especially by attempting to control decisions of religious superiors in the appointment and transfer of faculty. In 1908, for example, a superior recounted the irritation of an East Cambridge pastor on the transfer of a principal: "Immediately on receiving my letter he telephoned Brighton and said that if his Superior was removed to please remove all the Sisters."[31] Serious disagreements between pastors and sisters were infrequent, and the schools were left to the management of the women. By comparison, as late as 1911 few women in local public schools held the title of master or submaster. Of sixty-seven masters in Boston, for example, only eight were women, "six . . . in the 11 girls' schools, one in the Trade School for Girls, one in the Horace Mann School for the Deaf."[32]

291

---

[30]John Francis Maguire, *The Irish in America* (London, 1868), 48, 503.

[31]Sister Mary Borgia to O'Connell, August 14, 1908, Institution Files, AABo 4:14.

[32]"Report of a Hearing by the Boston School Board," Boston Masters' Assistants Club, March 20, 1911, 1, records of the Boston branch of the American Association of University Women, MC 271, Education Committee, IVB.3, SLRC.

292

Cardinal O'Connell addressing Sisters of Charity, 1932

(Photo AABo)

In contrast to the status of congregations staffing parochial schools, those managing social institutions appear at first glance to have held greater direct authority over their work. Carney Hospital in Boston and St. John's Hospital in Lowell, for example, were incorporated in 1865 and 1867 respectively by the Sisters of Charity, "their associates and successors."[33] Article one of the by-laws of St. Elizabeth's Hospital for Women, established in 1872, stated that "the Treasurer shall always be the Superior of the [Franciscan] community in charge of the Hospital."[34] The original corporation of this hospital was composed of two laymen and five Franciscan sisters. Such a structure, however, cannot be taken as typical of institutions not founded by sisterhoods. The property of the Home for Destitute Catholic Children in Boston, which opened in 1864, was held by a corporation made up of fourteen laymen and one priest appointed by the bishop.[35] Only when the seven male incorporators of St. Mary's Infant Asylum in Dorchester were unable to meet expenses was a new corporation formed "composed entirely of Sisters of Charity."[36]

293

In any case, such authority as women held in these establishments had begun to erode significantly even before 1900. By 1882 the provision that a sister be treasurer had been removed by amendment of the St. Elizabeth's Hospital charter, and in 1900 the board of directors included only one woman, a sister. Although in 1923 six of the ten board members of the House of the Good Shepherd, a reformatory for women in Roxbury, were sisters, they had little decision-making power. Their lack of autonomy was made evident a decade later, when Cardinal O'Connell easily changed the composition of the board by requiring the resignation of two sisters in favor of two priests. By 1940, the board consisted of five clerics and two sisters. In fact, the role of sisters in determining policy in diocesan social institutions had long since become largely token. After 1910, as Catholic charitable agencies and hospitals became larger and more numerous, the sisters staffing them were less likely to be accorded by the archbishop more than nominal representation on their boards.

[33]Sullivan, *One Hundred Years*, 348.
[34]Minutes of the Annual Meeting, February 2, 1880, St. Elizabeth's Hospital for Women, Corporation Records, AABo.
[35]Sullivan, *One Hundred Years*, 248-249.
[36]*Ibid.*, 251.

Their position was clearly subordinate to male boards headed by the archbishop. Ideas for improvement had to have prior approval of these boards, which followed episcopal wishes to the letter. In Boston many controversies ensued between sisters and Cardinal O'Connell over efforts of the women to initiate even minor changes in the institutions. During the 1914 expansion and remodeling of the Working Girls' Home in Boston, for example, the sisters requested than an incinerator be installed, stating also their willingness to pay for it. The cardinal responded simply that he deemed it "unnecessary." When the sisters pressed their case they were reminded that "the Working Girls' Home Corporation is not the proud possessor of untold millions."[37]

Communities of men working in similar establishments were far more resourceful in resisting arbitrary changes in their boards or the introduction of episcopal appointees. When the cardinal proposed to add men of his choice to the board of the House of the Angel Guardian, a Boston home for boys conducted by the Brothers of Charity, the local superior immediately hired a lawyer to protect his group's rights. He firmly told O'Connell: "I have in mind your request but in looking over the by-laws I find that by an agreement between the late Archbishop Williams and our Father General all the members of the board should be Brothers of Charity." The cardinal argued unsuccessfully against the legal opinion that the brothers had the right to conduct the home as they saw fit.[38] Given the canonical status of women's congregations, pontifical or diocesan, neither Archbishop Williams nor any other bishop of the era chose to enter into such an agreement with them.

Progressive ideas initiated by sisters entailing even modest expenditures almost invariably met challenges from institutional boards after 1910. In 1919, for example, the superior of St. Helena's House, a home for over 200 working women, "crowded all the time," suggested that a nurse with training in public health and social work be hired to counsel the younger women on "the social question" and to

[37]Correspondence between J. P. E. O'Connell and Graham, October 16, 17, 19, 23, 24; November 10, 12, 14, 1914; January 18, 1915, Institution Files, AABo 2:16-17.

[38]Brother Jude to O'Connell, February 14, 1908, and O'Connell to Fallon, February 20, 1908, *ibid.* 7:5.

care for residents with short-term illnesses. Her salary of $1,000 per year would be met from ordinary revenues. The proposal was denied without explanation. It is remarkable that, despite frequently discouraging outcomes, sisters persisted in proposing innovations, endeavored to introduce modern practices in institutional management, and participated in professional activities wherever possible. Because of the restrictions imposed on religious women, their goals were not easily achieved. A subsequent superior of St. Helena's House was invited to read a paper on "Homes for Working Girls" at the 1924 convention of the National Council of Catholic Women in St. Louis, but she was forbidden to do so by the cardinal. Although he was more hostile toward the involvement of sisters in professional activities than his colleagues in other dioceses, he was not unusual. Nevertheless, the invitation would not have been extended by a Catholic organization if a blanket prohibition existed. Teaching sisters were permitted by O'Connell to *write* papers on school issues, but at conventions and even local teachers' meetings they had to be read by men.[39] "Father Lyons [the superintendent of schools] asked Sister Mary Ignatius to write a paper for the Catholic Educational Convention . . . in Boston the coming July [1909]," the chronicler of a Hyde Park convent wrote. "Sister selected 'The Problem of the Backward Pupil.' . . . It was read at the Convention by Father Stanton of Stoughton, Mass."[40] By the 1920s sisters were permitted to read their own papers at meetings of religious superiors, probably because men and women superiors met separately, and they did not discuss professional issues.[41]

Sisters may have had only limited influence on the governance of the social agencies they served, but the growing demand on those agencies forced them to assume increasing financial responsibilities. Support for hospitals, homes, and orphanages was consistently less reliable than that for parish schools, and sisters were expected to undertake fund-raising activities. From their inception St. John's

[39]Sister N. M. Coughlan to O'Connell, August 4, 1919, and January 6, 1920, *ibid.* 2:19 and 3:1; Mother M. Duffin to O'Connell, November 3, 1924, and Haberlin to Duffin, November 5, 1924, *ibid.* 3:4.

[40]"Annals," St. Raphael's convent, Hyde Park, 1909, Archives, Sisters of Charity of Nazareth, Nazareth, KY.

[41]*Catholic Educational Association Bulletin*, 6 (1909): 348-350. See issues of this journal throughout the 1920s for additional examples.

Hospital and the Carney Hospital served many poor patients who could pay little or nothing for their care. The resulting heavy debt, "always proved a burden to the sisters in charge."[42] About half the 1895 expenses of the Carney Hospital were met from patients' fees, with the remainder financed through lectures, entertainments, and gifts. Sisters economized severely on institutional costs by doing most of the domestic work themselves. "The Sisters of Charity receive nothing but their living in return for . . . caring for the sick and afflicted. They do a large part of the work of the hospital, such as cooking and washing, etc., as well as taking the direct care of the wards and the patients in them."[43] The City Orphan Asylum in Salem was deeply in debt by 1876, only a decade after opening its doors, and the debt fell on the Grey Nuns of Montreal, who finally paid it in 1890 "after surmounting with much labor and fatigue many trials and difficulties."[44]

By the 1890s some relief came with the introduction of an annual diocesan-wide charities collection. Reports of St. Vincent's Orphan Asylum and the Home for Destitute Catholic Children indicate that these institutions regularly received a share of the proceeds, but the amount varied considerably from year to year. Entertainments and bequests continued to be essential to supplement diocesan allotments.[45] Occasionally, some costs of an institution were met through remunerative work done by residents. The Sisters of the Good Shepherd, for example, directed the women in their reformatory in sewing and laundry work for surrounding parishes and other Catholic institutions. Between 1922 and 1940 their labor defrayed at least 60 percent of operating expenses[46] (see Appendix B). Most institutions, populated as they were by children, the sick, or the aged, were unable to produce such income.

Sisterhoods did not enjoy much discretion over the funds they raised for hospitals and homes through appeals and benefits. Although they were free to make recommendations, they could not expect that they would be routinely honored. Franciscan sisters who

---

[42]Sullivan, *One Hundred Years*, 348.
[43]*Ibid.*, 817.
[44]*Ibid.*, 471.
[45]*Ibid.*, 237, 250.
[46]See reports for St. Vincent's Orphan Asylum in Institution Files, AABo 4:1-11, and reports for the Sisters of the Good Shepherd, *ibid.* 8:11-16.

in 1929 collected $48,000 to enlarge an East Boston orphanage were advised that "the money must be put in the name of the Roman Catholic Archbishop of Boston until it is needed and . . . there is to be no change in the property until it has been approved by him."[47] This policy was uniform for all diocesan-owned institutions. Local superiors of homes and asylums were expected to present a bimonthly report to Cardinal O'Connell throughout his tenure. Only in the exceptional case in which a pontifical sisterhood owned the property of an institution receiving no financial support from the diocese could women control its policies and operations. When questioned by the cardinal on the finances of its Lowell orphanage, for example, the Grey Nuns of Montreal were able to reply that "the property of the Protectory of Mary Immaculate is in the name of our Motherhouse, Montreal. . . . Our General Administration is responsible for the financial status of the institution. . . . Our current receipts and the Community Chest finance the work. We also receive bequests of a few hundred dollars occasionally."[48]

297

The financial health and stability of the women's congregations directly affected their ability to train young sisters and to care for their sick and aged members. It is therefore important to consider the salaries paid to sisters for their work. Payments made to teachers in parish schools during these years appear to have been fairly uniform across the archdiocese. They were also stable, since sisterhoods did not collaborate with one another in negotiating increases, and the archbishop and his pastors had a mutual understanding concerning stipend levels for sisters. The result was extremely slow progress on the salary issue. The experience of the diocesan community, the Sisters of St. Joseph, reflected general practice. In 1910 full-time teachers received housing without board and an annual salary of $200. By 1921 the stipend had risen to about $250, reaching $300 in 1937. At that time the superior argued not only for an increase but also for the establishment of a payment scale based on the grade level taught, maintaining that high school teachers should receive more than elementary teachers or sacristans since they "have all received their A.B. degree and many of them their M.A., which in-

[47]Burke to Mother Marie N. D. des Oliviers, September 9, 1929, *ibid.* 6:4.
[48]Sister Ellen Brennan to O'Connell, November 25, 1929, Brennan to Burke, July 11, 1930, *ibid.* 11:19.

dicates that the Community has spent much on their education."[49] In addition to their full-time work in the schools, sisters taught religion lessons to children enrolled in public schools during after-school hours and on Sunday mornings. Such additional work was compensated only when it was carried on in parishes which had no schools. Then pastors paid fifty dollars per year to each sister for the lessons.

Since the diocesan community was required to report periodically to the cardinal on its financial condition, it is possible to evaluate the adequacy of these stipends for the needs of a growing community. The internal financial condition of pontifical teaching communities was carefully guarded from episcopal eyes, but their situation was probably not unlike that of the Sisters of St. Joseph. While per capita expenses in reporting convents rose by 43.7 percent between 1909 and 1921, teachers' salaries rose by only 24.9 percent.[50] In recognition of this fact, the corporation of the congregation, composed of the superior general and her council, held the central tax levied on each teaching sister to meet community-wide expenses to approximately fifty dollars a year, although central costs were also rising. Receipts of the corporation were used to finance the construction and maintenance of a residence for sick and retired sisters and another for postulants and novices, as well as to cover the medical and educational costs of the entire membership.

The corporation came to rely increasingly on supplementary sources of income to compensate for the insufficient contributions from stipends. Great emphasis was placed on the need for sisters to earn more income after school hours, especially by giving music lessons. One music teacher could account for a disproportionate share of current revenue in a local convent. The maintenance of the motherhouse itself and of sisters engaged in community administration and other nonsalaried work was met entirely from the surplus revenues of a tuition-charging academy for girls, Mount St. Joseph Academy in Brighton. Without these additional revenues and donations the congregation would have been unable to support itself in 1937 (see Appendix C-1). There was little surplus with which to

[49]Sister M. Simplicia to Phelan, December 8, 1937, *ibid.* 4:19.
[50]Compiled from data *ibid.* 4:14-19.

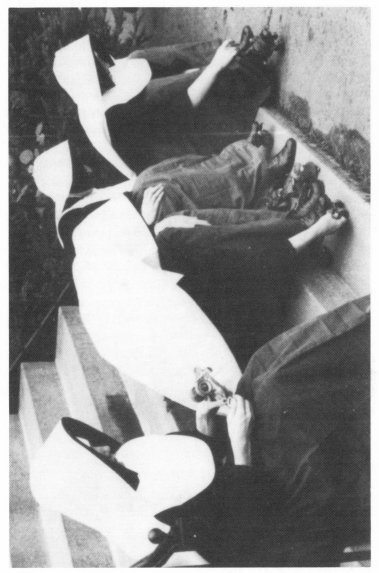

Novice Sisters of Notre Dame at leisure, ca. 1940

(Photo courtesy Archives, Sisters of Notre Dame de Namur, Ipswich)

299

enhance the physical and social environment of the sisters or to further their intellectual development.

Most pontifical congregations with heavy commitments to parochial schools endeavored to open at least one tuition-charging academy and more if possible. In Boston the diocesan community could obtain permission for only one, which probably made its financial status somewhat more precarious than that of pontifical communities with motherhouses located elsewhere. The few sisterhoods which traditionally taught only wealthier populations in academies and boarding schools were uniquely immune to pressures from inadequate finances.[51] Most sisters in the archdiocese belonged to communities which were responsible for parochial schools.

Salaries paid to sisters working in diocesan hospitals, homes, and orphanages exhibited less uniformity than those received by parochial school teachers. On average, sisters in these agencies were by 1909 receiving fifty dollars per year in addition to both room and board. The superior of the Grey Nuns of Montreal, requesting an increase to $100 for her sisters working in Boston, pointed out that although their rule called for employed sisters to support the elderly and novices the Boston contingent was unable to meet its obligations because of their low stipend.[52] The increase was implemented, but only for the two establishments her community staffed. Like their counterparts in parochial school work the communities engaged in hospital and social work did not collaborate on the salary issue. With each group negotiating individually and confidentially the stipends varied substantially among the social institutions. While the Grey Nuns enjoyed a higher stipend after 1909, sisters from another community at the French-American Orphanage in Lowell were still receiving only fifty dollars per year in 1917.[53] Because sisters had little leverage on governing boards stipend levels were occasionally modified unilaterally. In the case of the Lowell orphanage the stipend had reached $150 by 1924. But in 1932 the executive commit-

[51]The Religious of the Society of the Sacred Heart, for example, were for the most part found in tuition-charging academies for girls during this period. "Chief among all the works undertaken by the religious of this institute is the education of the upper classes," *Catholic Church in the United States*, 445.

[52]Sister M. P. Filiatrault to O'Connell, November 9, 1909, Institution Files, AABo 2:15.

[53]Sister Ste. Theodore to S. S. Honore, September 1, 1917, *ibid.* 11:22.

300

tee instructed its secretary to apprise the superior general of the Sisters of Charity "that it was necessary to reduce the salary of each of the sisters at the Orphanage [by] $25.00 per year."[54]

The effect of such varying salary practices on the quality of the professional work of sisters became a matter of serious concern for women's communities in the archdiocese as the years passed. Sisters found themselves increasingly inhibited in their work as educators, nurses, and social workers by the uncertainty of financial support. Drawn away from their primary work to raise funds to support the establishments in which they labored and to supplement the low stipends they were paid, they found social and professional integration a goal difficult to achieve in pre-1940 Massachusetts.

301

Like other women of this period, then, sisters met from church as well as society serious challenges in their efforts to control their own lives and organizations. As a result much potential for good and for genuine personal fulfillment remained untapped. Yet despite all restrictions of cloister and custom the heavy representation of active American sisterhoods in the diocese of Boston signified a major move by thousands of working-class women from the confines of the home into the world. These communities provided unique opportunities for professional careers, benefits which to those who joined them more than compensated for the loss of those offered by the most feasible alternative life path, marriage and a large family. Like other Catholic women sisters appeared to honor the social prescription that "woman's place is in the home" since they lived apart from the world. There was, however, a critical difference. While model Catholic mothers of the era worked only in the confines of their homes in domestic labor and child-care, sisters minimized the time spent by individuals in domestic work by dividing the labor in their convents and undertook outside careers in schools, hospitals, social agencies, and shelters for the aged and the orphan. Popular depictions of the nun as more sheltered from the world than the mother in the home ironically served to legitimate the radical nature of the sisterhoods. Nuns were able to acquire and preserve considerable autonomy by forming lasting female networks and by engaging col-

---

[54]Financial report, October 1, 1924 – October 1, 1925, for L'Orphelinat Franco-Amèricain, Lowell; minutes of meeting of executive committee by L'Orphelinat Franco-Amèricain, November 10, 1932, *ibid.* 11:23.

lectively in significant professions. The varied intellectual abilities and talents represented in large communities were marshaled efficiently and effectively. Sisters were principals of schools and administrators of hospitals and homes, taking these roles for granted in a period when women managers in public schools and state hospitals and agencies were uncommon. They conducted their own large communities with limited means, considerable resourcefulness, and remarkable good humor.

302

Like other American women of the era Boston's sisters were products of their times. One of their primary goals was to be "useful," but they confined their attention to those who shared their religious tradition. They saw themselves as women in the vanguard of social and educational reform, rather than as they were often depicted in the popular press: irrelevant and cloistered from the real world. In a Protestant state they valued their role in the development of Catholic schools, hospitals, and orphanages. With the professionalization of nursing, teaching, and social work in late nineteenth and early twentieth-century Massachusetts they became increasingly aware not only of the concern for social progress which they shared with the Protestant mainstream, but also of the confining aspects of the structures within which religious women were expected to function in the church. Although they, like their lay counterparts, accepted male leadership and intervention in their work, archival records attest clearly that their misgivings about so doing became stronger and more frequent as the decades passed.

Appendix A

DISTRIBUTION OF SISTERS IN ARCHDIOCESE OF BOSTON BY TYPE OF WORK, 1870 AND 1940

	Number of Institutions		Number of Sisters	
	1870	1940	1870	1940
Hospitals	4	6	27	131
Parochial Schools	11	155	102	2,606
Asylums and Homes	6	27	54	383
Academies and				
Boarding Schools	4	18	25	341
Work Unspecified	—	—	13	703*
TOTAL	25	206	221	4,164

303

Source: Compiled from data in official Catholic directories, *Sadlier's Catholic Directory, Almanac and Ordo, 1870* (New York, 1870), and *The Official Catholic Directory* (New York: P. J. Kenedy, 1940).

*Includes 4 missionaries, 32 domestic workers, and 113 cloistered nuns.

Appendix B

EXPENDITURES AND RECEIPTS
HOUSE OF THE GOOD SHEPHERD
1922–1940

	1922[a]	1923[a]	1924[a]	1930[a]	1933–34[c]	1934–35[c]	1939–40[c]
I. Total Receipts	$103,229.48	$90,785.33	$79,764.53	$101,198.34	$73,020.10	$83,165.96	$101,451.54
Interest on Deposits and Investments	2,278.20	2,538.74	2,469.83	29.83	—	—	—
Bequests and Donations	25,659.69	12,160.25	5,026.50	7,619.98	9,040.38	15,050.91	28,118.78
Industries	74,292.99	74,560.57	71,672.59	92,523.53	62,612.22	64,638.38	62,576.04
Board	—	—	—	1,025.00	1,367.50	3,476.67	10,756.72
Other Sources, Entertainments	998.60	1,525.77	595.61	—	—	—	—
II. Total Expenses	$95,449.80	$92,053.37	$85,159.58	$101,703.36	$73,711.35	$81,019.92	$100,605.89
Number in House	380[b]	324[b]	353[b]	337[b]	N.A.	353[b]	N.A.

a. Calendar Year.
b. December 1921; April 1924; April 1925; May 1931; April 1935.
c. April 1933-April 1934; April 1934-April 1935; April 1939-April 1940.

Source: Institution Files, AABo 8:12-16.

Appendix C-1

CORPORATION RECEIPTS, SISTERS OF ST. JOSEPH, ARCHDIOCESE OF BOSTON, 1938-39

Source of Income	Receipts ($)	% of Total Receipts
Stipends from Missions	$54,438.00	60.5%
Music Tuitions from Missions	24,746.99	27.5%
Retreat Offerings	4,880.00	5.4%
Postulants' Offerings	3,084.50	3.4%
Refunds	2,838.60	3.2%
CURRENT RECEIPTS	$89,988.09	100.0%

305

COMBINED MOTHERHOUSE AND ACADEMY RECEIPTS AND EXPENDITURES, 1938-39*

A. Current Receipts**	$69,797.19
B. Current Expenditures	$67,914.88
A ÷ B	1.02

*Includes receipts from all regular motherhouse activities (e.g., sale of altar breads, Sunday school tuitions, stipends from missions without convents, interest on a bequest), and expenditures for school and motherhouse needs. Fifty-four percent of current receipts is from academy board and tuition charges alone.

**$16,702 earned from two special "penny sales" held that year is excluded from this total.

Source: Institution Files, AABo 4:19.

Appendix C-2

ANNUAL INCOME AND EXPENSES IN CONVENTS ATTACHED TO PAROCHIAL SCHOOLS
Sisters of St. Joseph, Archdiocese of Boston, 1909–1922

ANNUAL INCOME OF LOCAL CONVENTS

	1909–1910	1911–1912	1920–1921	1921–1922
Sources of Income				
Teachers' Salaries				
Total	$29,404.00	$36,386.01	$69,895.01	$75,668.29
Percent to Motherhouse	26.1%	27.3%	18.1%	20.5%
(a) Funds Remaining in				
Local Convents	$21,736.07	$26,434.74	$57,272.91	$60,128.49
Music Tuitions				
Total	$ 3,706.23	$ 4,883.92	$21,861.50	$20,479.87
Percent to Motherhouse	65.7%	73.5%	79.6%	85.0%
(b) Funds Remaining in				
Local Convents	$ 1,392.54	$ 1,293.92	$ 4,449.34	$ 3,075.11
Donations Received				
Total	$ 1,133.05	$ 1,656.88	$ 5,341.26	$ 4,855.02
Percent to Motherhouse	24.0%	69.9%	22.3%	19.5%
(c) Funds Remaining in				
Local Convents	$ 861.45	$ 498.88	$ 4,148.76	$ 3,908.52
Total House Income	$34,243.28	$42,926.81	$97,097.77	$101,003.18
Percent to Motherhouse	29.9%	34.2%	32.3%	33.6%
Net House Income	$23,990.06	$28,227.54	$65,871.01	$67,112.12
Net Income per Sister in				
Local Convents	$ 149.94	$ 147.02	$ 203.94	$ 196.81

ANNUAL EXPENSES PER SISTER IN LOCAL CONVENTS

	1909–1910	1911–1912	1920–1921	1921–1922
Living Expenses	$ 119.06	$ 129.79	$ 177.75	$ 178.26
Household Expenses	15.27	16.40	19.21	16.15
Retreat Fee	3.28	2.45	2.83	3.27
(Paid to Motherhouse)				
Total	$ 137.61	$ 148.64	$ 199.79	$ 197.68
Number of Local Convents	10	14	22	23
Number of Sisters	160	192	323	341
Number Salaried	148	183	287	305
Ratio of Net Income to				
Expenses for a Sister in				
a Local Convent	1.09	0.99	1.02	1.00

Source: Institution Files, AABo 4:19.

6

Schools and Sisters

The ethnic leagues were not the only semi-autonomous units within the Chicago archdiocese; numerous religious orders of priests, sisters, and brothers also labored in Chicago, forming separate sovereignties and only loosely subject to the archbishop. Religious orders of men and women came in bewildering variety. Nineteen religious congregations of priests resided in Chicago in 1916, varying in size from the sixty-two Jesuits who staffed three parishes and two large educational establishments to the single Premonstratensian canon who manned the sole Dutch national parish. Altogether, the order priests numbered 340, or 37 percent of all priests in Chicago. Religious brothers were far less numerous, working mainly in a handful of commercial high schools for boys. The sisters, however, greatly outnumbered all kinds of priests and brothers and made an essential contribution to the Church's educational endeavors. In 1916, 2,596 nuns, from at least thirty-six orders, taught in Chicago elementary schools (I say "at least" because many congregations had the same name and followed the same religious rule, but were administered as separate entities from different mother houses. I was not always able to distinguish all these congregations; so the true number in Chicago probably approached fifty).[1]

Religious orders were a tremendous boon for the Catholic Church in Chicago. Since they provided their own manpower and financial resources, they allowed the archbishop to do many things he could not afford on his own. Without them, there would be practically no Catholic hospitals or schools. In addition, Mundelein saw certain advantages in the great plethora of orders at work in Chicago: "Their pressure has led to a worthy rivalry and competition that has upheld the standard." But since religious orders formed separate corporations, with well-defined rights under canon law, they posed a thorny administrative problem for a consolidating archbishop such as Mundelein. He could not discipline a member of a religious order directly, but had to work with and through the religious-order superior. More important, he could not order religious priests and nuns to drive ahead in a straight line toward his goals; rather, he had to play the unaccustomed role of diplomat, negotiating with them as separate sovereignties, trying to persuade them to enlist their money and personnel in his projects. In Catholic education, Mundelein could not exercise the direct, unquestioned authority of the corporation sole. Forced to deal with the orders as equals, he encountered numerous frustrations and compromises while attempting to reorganize the school system, to bring a Catholic women's college to Chicago, and to cap his work with a great theological seminary and Catholic university.[2]

308

The reorganization of Catholic school administration had proceeded slowly after the "English only" order, announced at Mundelein's first clergy conference in March 1916. Uniform textbooks were settled upon during the summer of 1916, after much hard work by the three members of the newly formed school board and the superiors of the fifty or so teaching orders of sisters in the archdiocese. A brief controversy had developed over the choice for a Polish-language catechism when Father Felix Ladon, C.R., blasted the school board's selection as outdated. Mundelein quashed this rebellion by ordering Father Ladon's superior to remove the faculties of the archdiocese from him (i.e., refuse him permission to function as a priest in Chicago) until he withdrew his attack. Father Ladon apologized and the school board's chosen textbooks were adopted for the new school year in the fall of 1916,[3] but not all the obstacles to school reorganization could be ordered aside so peremptorily.

The Catholic schools were an administrative nightmare. The pastors hired the sisters, negotiated their salaries, and built and maintained the school buildings; the sisters decided what to teach and how to go about it. The bishop, though he had, theoretically, complete authority over Catholic education, had no real control. As Professor James W. Sanders, the historian of Catholic education in Chicago, put it: "More uniformity in textbooks, curriculum, and methods of instruction existed among the schools of a single religious order, even when spread over the entire country, than among the schools of different parishes within Chicago."[4]

Mundelein's reorganization plan called for the school board to standardize curriculum, which it did, and then for a full-time superintendent to monitor curriculum changes. In addition, he set his financial advisory council, the Board of Consultors, to work on a uniform salary schedule for paying the sisters. But of course, all of this took time. Mundelein was unable to train and assign a priest-superintendent as soon as he had hoped since the wartime demand for chaplains drained his manpower; therefore the three-man school board had to undertake the onerous task of regularly visiting the 200-plus schools to observe the progress of curriculum reform. Since the school board members were also full-time pastors of parishes, they soon found this duty too much for them. As a stopgap measure, Mundelein expanded the board by adding two pastors, but this did little to improve the situation.[5]

309

Finally, in 1919, Mundelein sent two young priests, John Ford and John Kozlowski, for a year's training at Catholic University's recently established School of Educational Administration, and upon their return he appointed them cosuperintendents of schools. In the meantime, the Board of Consultors had labored over a uniform contract and salary schedule for the teaching sisters. They settled on a monthly salary of $35 per sister and the new contract system was presented to the pastors, to begin in the fall of 1920. By this time the school reorganization was nearly complete, on paper. Uniform curriculum, contracts, and salaries had been negotiated and two professionally trained superintendents appointed to monitor performance and compliance.[6]

Running the school system, however, proved to be more a problem of human relations than of paper efficiency. It took several more years before Mundelein found the right man to make the schools run smoothly. The bishop and the superintendents could formulate plans and issue orders, but the sisters did the work and the pastors raised the money to pay them. Their individual whims and sensitivities had to be respected. Fathers Ford and Kozlowski worked fairly harmoniously with all parties, but in 1923 Father Ford was shot by a robber who had broken into his rectory. Seriously injured, he gave up his duties and retired to California. His successor, Father Patrick Henry Matimore, was a tactless, efficiency-minded "professional" who relentlessly gathered statistics and bothered the sisters with long reports and forms to fill out. He even developed a rating system whereby he ranked the religious orders according to their competence and efficiency. The sisters felt this was carrying "worthy rivalry and competition" too far.[7]

Eventually, Mundelein realized his mistake. He removed Matimore from his post in 1926, and instead of replacing him with another professional, he appointed Father Daniel Cunningham, a gregarious Irish curate from the cathedral parish, who had occasionally been his golfing partner. Belatedly, Mundelein understood that the post of superintendent required a politician with the gift of gab, not an expert with a slide rule. Cunningham swiftly smoothed the ruffled feathers of pastors and sisters; Mundelein eased Father Kozlowski out of office, awarding him a pastorate; and Cunningham became sole superintendent. Viewing his job mainly as public relations, he succeeded admirably in this post for nearly thirty years. The reorganization of the schools took longer than originally foreseen, but Mundelein eventually got what he wanted: a reasonably standardized, smooth-running system for coordinating the many parishes and teaching orders in primary schooling.[8]

310

He also got about as much as he could hope for in secondary schooling, but the situation at the high school level remained less than ideal. Before the twentieth century, secondary education had been a privilege available only to the few. Many parishes attempted to add high schools to their elementary schools, but the attrition rate was high and the instruction usually substandard. Of greater importance for the future of Catholic education, religious orders of priests had founded several "colleges" (what we would call "collegiate preparatory schools" today) in Chicago, with the Jesuits' St. Ignatius College on the Near West Side leading the way in 1870. Modeled after what the French called a *collège classique,* St. Ignatius attempted to train an elite in the basics of a classical, liberal arts education. Middle-class Irish Catholics sent their boys to St. Ignatius to acquire a foundation in the arts before entering law, medicine, or the priesthood. During the long years when Chicago had no seminary of its own, many of the native-born clergy "did their classics" at St. Ignatius before going away to study philosophy and theology at a major seminary elsewhere. Other religious orders founded similar schools: St. Vincent's College on the North Side (1898), St. Cyril's (1902) and St. Rita's (1905) on the South Side, the Bohemian St. Procopius (1887) in Lisle, and the Polish St. Stanislaus (1890) on the North Side. These institutions evolved in different ways. St. Ignatius and St. Vincent's became full-scale universities, Loyola (1910) and DePaul (1907), while St. Procopius became a small liberal arts college with a heavy ethnic tinge (now called Illinois Benedictine College). The others gradually broadened and modernized their curricula until, by the 1920s, they had become regional high schools for the parishes in their areas.[9]

Women's education was far less developed. A number of small

academies provided the only semblance of Catholic secondary education in the nineteenth century, but the women who attended these exclusive institutions (many of them boarding students) learned more about good manners and fine sewing than anything else. In 1900 the Sisters of Charity of the Blessed Virgin Mary (B.V.M.s) opened St. Mary's regional Catholic high school for girls, in the same West Side neighborhood where St. Ignatius had opened for boys thirty years previously. Possibly the first such women's high school in America, St. Mary's took no boarders, drew from a wide range of social strata and geographical areas, and provided a decidedly practical education, training many Irish girls sufficiently to pass the state exams for public school teacher certification.[10]

Mundelein viewed the regional high school, such as St. Mary's for girls or the modernized "colleges" for boys, as the best way to provide Catholic secondary education. After he had persuaded the B.V.M. order to open a second high school, Immaculata, on the North Side lakefront, he stated his opinions at the school's first commencement in 1925:

> When I came here from the East some years ago, I was unfamiliar with this type of school. We had academies. Oh, yes—I had one in my own parish. I could never see that they meant much for scholarship, nor did they develop religious vocations. . . . But when I came here I found St. Mary's high school, a school where girls of all classes meet on an equal footing, where the only aristocracy is the aristocracy of brains. The methods of this institution are marked by briskness of attack. The girls are prepared for active service in the school, in commercial life, and in the home.[11]

Too tied up with other costly projects to attempt to build high schools with archdiocesan funds, he requested the religious orders of priests, nuns, and brothers to expand their colleges and academies, wherever possible, into high schools. He also tried to persuade the teaching orders to locate their schools in easy-to-reach, strategically placed spots throughout the city so that they would be, in effect, regional high schools. This strategy, announced publicly in 1922 when Immaculata first opened its doors, enjoyed some success. Though the numbers of Catholic high schools in Chicago declined in the 1920s (as many parish high schools folded), the new emphasis on large, centrally located regional high schools resulted in a rise in Catholic high school attendance.

Nevertheless, Mundelein's plan proved frustrating at times. Since someone else—a religious order—was paying for the school, the archbishop could only ask, not command, the order to open it when he wanted and locate it where he wanted. In 1924, for instance, Mundelein offered the Bohemian Benedictines, whose St. Procopius College in Lisle was too ethnic and isolated to serve as a mass high school, any parish they wanted in the city if they would agree to open a high school near it within two years; but the monks refused, pleading lack of manpower. Therefore, though Catholic secondary education grew notably in the 1920s, it never became as widespread as elementary education. The high schools were scattered about the city in a largely accidental pattern, with little order or system, depending totally on the decisions of sovereign religious orders.[12]

When Mundelein attempted a similar scheme of regional, commuter locations for women's colleges, he encountered even greater problems. Running head-on against an older tradition of female education, he came away with considerably less than he desired. The only local women's schools with any pretensions to higher education, St. Xavier's College on the South Side and Barat College in the far North Shore suburb of Lake Forest, were small and exclusive. The Barat site was too removed from the city to figure in Mundelein's plans, but he felt he might persuade the Sisters of Mercy to expand St. Xavier's sufficiently to make it a regional college for the South Side. Thus he concentrated on securing new women's colleges for the West and North sides.[13]

Mundelein had definite ideas about women's education. He recognized that little had been done by Catholics to educate women:

> The need of a Catholic college for women is patent to everyone and becomes more urgent every day. More and more are women taking the places formerly occupied by men in the professions, in business, in literature, in the shaping of public opinion, even in science. The time has come when they are receiving the advantages and responsibilities of equal suffrage with men. It stands to reason then that we must provide equal educational advantages for our Catholic girls.

The archbishop did not hold "advanced" views on the role of women, but he realized that if the Church did not provide higher education, Catholic women would obtain it elsewhere. He once remarked to a group of sisters: "An excellent young girl in this city attended the University of Chicago, and her remarks after her

312

course of study . . . showed the bad influence that training had on her character and in turning her away from religion.''[14]

Mundelein wanted to provide women with a practical educa- tion, available to as many as possible; so his plans called for a ''commuter college,'' conveniently served by public transportation. Furthermore, when he came to Chicago in 1916 he wanted to imple- ment his plans right away; he hoped that at least one new college would open by September 1917, and, he wanted it to be a women's college ''taught and controlled by women, and not by men.'' The Vincentian Fathers, who operated DePaul University in Chicago, wished to establish a separate college for women or else open up DePaul on a coeducational basis; but Mundelein denied them per- mission to do either.[15]

The Chicago archbishop got a ''women's college controlled by women,'' but he didn't get it quickly nor did he get it in a conven- ient, commuter location. In striving to obtain a women's college for Chicago, he ran against a sister superior, Mother Mary Samuel, O.P., of the Sinsinawa Dominicans, who easily matched him in shrewdness and tenacity. When finally completed, Rosary College resembled Mother Samuel's dreams far more closely than Mundelein's.

On April 24, 1916, Mother Samuel met with her General Council in the Dominican motherhouse at Sinsinawa Mound, Wisconsin, and decided to move St. Clara's College, which adjoined the motherhouse, from its isolated location. The Mound was so far off the beaten path that it would be difficult to bring in building materials if they decided to expand on the present site. Furthermore, modern women might think twice about cloistering themselves so far away from a city. Mother Samuel therefore wrote the newly installed Archbishop Mundelein, asking permission to move St. Clara's to Chicago as one of his proposed colleges for women. As Mundelein had already been turned down by other orders of sisters when he had inquired about founding a college, he accepted the Dominicans' of- fer and began negotiating personally with Mother Samuel.[16]

That the two were working at cross-purposes became clear at the outset. The original letter from Mother Samuel suggested that a boarding school should accompany the commuter college. The Dominicans wanted to be closer to the city, but they did not want to abandon the tradition of female seclusion. Mother Samuel and the archbishop disagreed sharply over a location for the college. Mundelein wanted a city location, with a building already on the site, so that classes could begin almost immediately while plans were

313

made for a newer edifice. He discovered that Oak Park High School was abandoning its building at Lake Street and East Avenue and that the location, though in a suburb, was easily accessible to the West Side of Chicago by bus, rapid transit line, and commuter railroad. Mother Samuel inspected the building but turned it down as unsuitable. The archbishop, in a great hurry during his first year in Chicago, purchased the property himself in the hope of changing her mind, and when he found her adamant, he used the building for another project, Bishop Quarter boys' school.[17]

314

Like a married couple arguing over where to build their dream house, the archbishop and the sister superior continued to search for a site. Mother Samuel discovered peaceful, secluded spots in distant suburbs on the North Shore and in areas west of Oak Park. When Mundelein heard about a site in River Forest that she was considering, he exploded and wrote her that it was "entirely out of the question." In late June, he persuaded her to purchase property in Oak Park: 16 acres at Division Street and Oak Park Avenue. Still not certain whether she had been converted to his line of thinking, he began to press her to start building. After announcing his plans for a women's college in general terms in October (without naming either the teaching order or the location), he was eager to get under way. He still hoped for a modest building which could be erected cheaply and opened swiftly; so he sent Mother Samuel a practical suggestion:

> That you erect three . . . different parts of the structure, each one running about fifty to seventy-five thousand dollars, one to be raised by the funds that the Community now has; another perhaps to be raised by your Alumnae and a general campaign here in Chicago, for which purpose I am quite sure that the Catholic Women's League will stand as a sponsor behind you; a third one you might perhaps obtain by private donations from your more wealthy and influential friends.

This was precisely the plan he was using to build Quigley Seminary: one wing financed from current cash, one paid for by a public campaign, and one donated by a wealthy "angel." To encourage the sisters, he offered to head the list of contributors with $1,000 from his personal funds.[18]

In December the sisters engaged Ralph Adams Cram as architect. Mr. Cram, a non-Catholic, and probably the most distinguished architect of the Gothic Revival style, had designed the Graduate College of Princeton University as well as the Fourth

Presbyterian Church on Michigan Avenue in Chicago, the "society church" for residents of the Gold Coast. The choice of Cram as architect signaled to Mundelein that the sisters were going beyond his idea of a modest commuter college. In resignation, the archbishop warned Mother Samuel:

> There is but one observation that I would make regarding him [Cram]. . . . He had always built for people whose pockets were well filled with money. . . . Whether he will be able to produce like results for people with slender purses like the Dominican Sisters is something which time alone can tell.[19]

The architect began work on preliminary sketches, but when the United States entered World War I, in April 1917, the mother superior immediately ordered: "We must desist from building our College during war. Lawyer and architect both advise this." Mother Samuel, who must have been grateful for the respite the war gave her from Mundelein's bullying, took immediate advantage of the lull to change plans completely. In May 1917 she sold the Oak Park property for a profit and purchased almost 30 acres in exclusive River Forest, a scenic site near the Forest Preserves on the Des Plaines River. Mundelein's reaction is not recorded, but he seems to have realized he had met his match. He acquiesced in the Dominicans' slow, step-by-step approach, granting permission in 1917 for the sisters to teach painting and music in a small house on the new property and to begin a high school department in 1918. Instead of urging more speed, the archbishop wrote Mother Samuel: "It will be . . . a little beginning of the great work that your Sisters at none too distant a day will begin in the great cause of Catholic education."[20]

Since Mundelein had announced the college publicly and placed his prestige behind it as a priority project, he needed the Dominicans more than they needed him. No other teaching order was willing to take the financial risk of building a women's college in Chicago; so Mundelein had to go along with Mother Samuel on her terms. He wrote to a woman he was trying to recruit for the college fund drive: "Should you hesitate, I would at least advise that you see Mother Samuel first, for I know you could hardly refuse her, for even I have found this to be a difficult task."[21]

Mother Samuel had the upper hand, but she needed Archbishop Mundelein's help; his backing was necessary for a successful fund-raising campaign. Even during the war the sisters were trying to scrape up money for the college fund, using such measures

315

as "decade of dimes" cards in grammar schools where they taught. Mundelein suggested a better wartime plan: a campaign asking friends and alumnae to donate war-bond savings stamps to the sisters.[22]

The school was formally incorporated as Rosary College on October 22, 1918, but serious work on the building did not begin for over a year. After a good deal of searching, an active laywoman was found to head the major fund-raising campaign. Mundelein recommended Mrs. Edward Hines, the wife of a large lumber company owner in Chicago, as a woman with "energy, position, wide acquaintanceship and the experience acquired in the Liberty Loan." Privately, he wrote Mrs. Hines: "We did not consider the position exactly a sinecure"; and as if to emphasize the point, he vetoed a suggestion that professional fund raisers be hired to help. A ceremonial groundbreaking at River Forest was arranged for February 2, 1920, to inaugurate Mrs. Hines's campaign. The drive netted about $140,000 and construction finally began on Ralph Cram's "collegiate Gothic" building. Still, the work and the money gathering dragged on. In 1921 Mother Samuel told Mundelein that she was waiting for interest rates to drop before floating a bond issue for the college. She added: "The fact that almost no work is going on makes it easy to wait."[23]

Rosary College opened its doors late in the fall of 1922, on October 6. Mundelein had hurried home from the general meeting of the American bishops in Washington to preside at the formal dedication of the college on October 1, Rosary Sunday. Only about half of the three-wing Gothic structure was finished and usable, and the very next day was scheduled as a tag day to help raise badly needed funds, but at last the archbishop had a new women's college in the archdiocese, as he had promised six years previously. It had been a frustrating experience for this impatient man, who had naively written Mother Samuel in 1916: "When I want anything, I want it now and I don't want to wait a long time until I get it." He *did* wait a long time, and what he got was a long way from a commuter college, since it was a long way from the city.[24]

The Dominican Sisters were competent teachers and their new college won accreditation from the prestigious North Central Association of Colleges less than a year after it opened. They had risked a great deal in coming to Chicago, spending well over a million dollars and mortgaging their property at the Mound in the process.[25] Mundelein, who desperately wanted a college, could offer the sisters nothing but his permission and a small portion of his

316

energy as a fund raiser. Mother Samuel must therefore have felt justified in building the college she wanted, rather than the one desired by the archbishop. Rosary College continued the tradition of sheltered female education in a sylvan setting. It has never functioned as a commuter school, except for wealthy inhabitants of the nearby suburbs.

Mundelein never gave up his plans for a practical, accessible, commuter college for women; so after his defeat by Mother Samuel he directed his energy toward securing such a college for the North Side of the city, and there was only one plausible candidate to provide the kind of school he wanted, the Sisters of Charity, B.V.M. An able and ambitious teaching order, the B.V.M.s conducted seven large parish schools on the North Side, eighteen in all in the city, and the two regional high schools of St. Mary's and Immaculata. They had more sisters—over 300—working in the archdiocese of Chicago than any other women's order. Furthermore, they had been planning to build a college in Chicago as early as 1911, had sent six sisters to Catholic University in Washington for training, and had discussed building plans with Archbishop Quigley. Many obstacles, however, blocked their path. Catholic University would not permit the sisters to attend regular classes at its all-male institution; so the six sisters could only study with tutors during the summer in Washington. The archbishop of Dubuque, where the B.V.M.s had their motherhouse and a small college, did not want them to mount a major effort outside his archdiocese; so he strongly discouraged the Chicago project. As a result, nothing had come of the college proposal in 1911.[26]

Less than two weeks after Mundelein's arrival in Chicago, the mother superior of the B.V.M.s, with two other sisters, paid a courtesy visit to the new archbishop, on February 22, 1916. Mundelein mentioned the need for women's colleges in the city, and when the sisters replied that they would like to build such a college, he asked them how soon they could start. Before the sisters could catch their breath, the archbishop was discussing specifics of location, cost, and timing. Mundelein's impatience to begin must have frightened the sisters, for upon their return to Dubuque they informed him that "the time is not opportune for our Congregation. We are not in a position to finance an undertaking which involves so great an outlay." The archbishop of Dubuque, moreover, had intervened again; he not only talked the B.V.M.s out of the Chicago school but persuaded them to buy more land and equipment to expand their Mt. St. Joseph College in Dubuque. When news of this

317

expansion at the Mount—at the same time that the mother superior was pleading poverty—reached the sisters in Chicago, they were outraged. Considerable support for a Chicago college remained, therefore, among the sisters of the order, and after Rosary College opened in 1922, Mundelein badgered the B.V.M.s for six years until they gave in.[27]

A new superior, Mother Isabella Kane, had taken office in the meantime, and on April 25, 1928, she arranged an interview with the cardinal. Determined not to repeat his Rosary College fiasco, Mundelein took no chances. He flattered the B.V.M.s, praising their wonderful work in Chicago and avowing that his best seminarians came from schools taught by their sisters; then he told Mother Isabella precisely what he wanted: "a city day college built in the modern skyscraper style, in order not to expend too much money on property." He suggested that it be located near Loyola University, on the rapid transit lines, and that little money be spent on landscaping or recreational grounds (no sylvan seclusion this time). Finally, he assigned his own architect, Joseph W. McCarthy, who had recently completed the major seminary for the archdiocese, to begin preliminary plans.[28]

Mother Isabella, who was in poor health and suffering from a series of freak accidents, recoiled from the cardinal's bullying. She remarked in a memorandum written after the interview: "The Cardinal is a very rapid talker and it was difficult for me to get in all the points I had in mind." Looking for excuses to avoid such a large and expensive task, she found plenty: "We must remember that Lake Shore property has trebled in value since we purchased the Immaculata in 1920." But Mother Isabella wanted to complete the plans her predecessor had postponed; so in March 1929 the order purchased 250 front-feet of prime lakefront land on Sheridan Road, next to Loyola University. Under the supervision of architects Joseph McCarthy of Chicago and Nairne Fisher of Dubuque, work began on a fifteen-story skyscraper college, faced with gray limestone and constructed in the popular set-back style of the 1920s. Mother Isabella, an artist in her own right, designed much of the interior ornament, particularly the Art Deco grillwork in the main lobby. Though the stock market had crashed just a few days before the work began, the B.V.M.s obtained financing from the Continental Bank with the cardinal's backing. The Depression made fund raising difficult and the sisters virtually starved their smaller foundations to meet the $90,000 per year interest costs on the $2,375,000 price of the college. One downtown banker reportedly told Mother Isabella: "You ladies launch and carry through projects that would make a business man tremble." But in one respect, the Depression proved an advantage: since labor was readily available, the building contractor drove forward in double shifts and completed the structure in less than a year. The new school for women, which the B.V.M.s named Mundelein College, opened its doors in September 1930 with Sister Justitia Coffey, a shrewd and able administrator who had guided Immaculata High School through its initial years, as president.[29]

Far more than Rosary College, this institution, bearing his name, fulfilled Mundelein's desire for a practical, in-city education for women. The college offered twenty-five courses of instruction, from the classics to home economics. The sisters soon opened a noncredit secretarial course, a summer program, and, at the request of the cardinal, a department of social service, affiliated with Catholic Charities. An overenthusiastic writer in the Jesuit magazine *America* contrasted Mundelein College's modern lines with the Gothic trappings of the secular University of Chicago: "The old Faith is too sure of itself to put on the false face of a long-past architecture, and, because it finds itself at home in the world of today, it symbolizes its eternal youthfulness in this most modern of buildings." Cardinal Mundelein may well have made similar comparisons between "his" city college and Mother Samuel's Gothic preserve in River Forest.[30]

319

Mundelein took a personal interest in the college during its early years, not least because his only niece, Rita Eppig, was a member of the first graduating class in 1934. He donated a massive pipe organ for the auditorium, as well as some of his countless autographs and collector's trivia. In Sister Justitia the cardinal found a kindred spirit, every bit as nervy and enamored of ceremony as himself. At commencement exercises, when the cardinal appeared in person, Sister Justitia persuaded the Chicago police to block off Sheridan Road for four blocks and to provide a mounted-police honor guard for the visiting Prince of the Church. Knights of St. Gregory, in full regalia of plumes and swords, then escorted the cardinal up the college steps to the blare of silver trumpets. A practical school conducted with flare—Mother Isabella, Sister Justitia, and the B.V.M.s finally gave the cardinal what he wanted in women's education.[31]

The long-protracted negotiations for a women's college, as well as the reorganization of primary and secondary schooling in the archdiocese, illustrate the limits within which even the most energetic and authoritarian of bishops operated. Mundelein was the autocratic "Dutch Master" to priests directly under his authority and in all matters of doctrine and discipline, as Father Ladon of the Polish Resurrectionists discovered, but the Catholic Church contained many separate sovereignties that he could not order around (except in doctrinal matters). Religious orders of priests, teaching brothers, pastors who held influential positions, and ethnic bosses were some of these sovereignties, but perhaps the most independent of all were the teaching sisters.

The "good nuns" may have been the subject of jokes in male-chauvinist rectories and their outlandish costumes no doubt induced nightmares in many a schoolchild (an old schoolboy joke held that "B.V.M." stood for "black veiled monsters"). Subjected to numerous petty restrictions by the rules of their orders and by the archbishop's delegate for religious communities of women, they were often unappreciated and taken for granted by Catholics. Yet the sisters were absolutely essential for Catholic schools. The American bishops had solemnly decreed at the Third Plenary Council of Baltimore in 1884 that every Catholic child should go to a Catholic school; but without the sisters, they would have been powerless to execute the decree. The sisters worked for next to nothing, and their dedication could not have been purchased with money.

In the mid-1920s the average parish in Chicago spent roughly 10 percent of its annual revenue on school expenses. This figure is very low, and can be misleading. Pastors did not generally reveal the full cost of maintaining a parochial school in their annual financial reports. Capital expenses—the cost of constructing, heating, and lighting a school building—were buried in the general capital costs of the parish. Frequently, school and church were under the same roof; but even if they were separate, the pastor considered them part of the parish "plant." The reported item, "school expenses," reflected merely the teaching sisters' salary ($35 a month for a ten-month year) and some school supplies. Even so, Catholic schools were a real bargain. Imagine running a system of 323 schools and 160,000 pupils with a salary budget of less than $1.5 million![32]

In the years since the upheaval of Vatican II, vocations to the sisterhood have declined sharply, and the bishops, faced with the necessity of paying lay teachers, are recoiling from their commitment to Catholic education.[33] Nowadays, with lay teachers predominating, a school takes 40 to 60 percent of a parish budget. When Catholic schools were still expanding, as in the 1920s, the

320

sister superiors knew that their work was essential and they did not submit to autocratic pastors, school superintendents, or archbishops. Mundelein eventually realized this. He had to appoint a diplomat-politician to keep peace in the grammar school system and he could only *request* high schools and commuter colleges. When a strong-willed superior, such as Mother Mary Samuel of Sinsinawa, nurtured different plans from Mundelein's, her wishes prevailed.

Mundelein turned then to the capstone of his dreams for Catholic education, the building of his theological seminary, and this time he tried to keep all the lines of finance and control in his own hands. But even so, as we shall see, separate sovereignties in the Church impeded his efforts.

321

6. Schools and Sisters

1. Data were compiled from the *Official Catholic Directory* for 1917.

2. The precise relations between a bishop-ordinary and the religious orders of men and women are defined by lengthy and complex regulations in canon law. Most orders of men were removed (for all practical purposes) from the jurisdiction of the local bishop and subject only to their own superiors and to Rome. Orders of women were more restricted; the bishop and his delegate for religious communities of women were supposed to exercise a kind of fatherly protection of their morals. Still, the main lines of authority ran through the women's superiors to Rome. For more details, see the *New Catholic Encyclopedia;* a standard textbook of canon law, such as John A. Abbo and Jerome D. Hannon, *The Sacred Canons* (St. Louis: Herder, 1966); or Joseph D. O'Brien, *The Exemption of Religious Orders in Church Law* (Milwaukee: Bruce, 1942).

3. *New World,* April 28, 1916, p. 1; June 23, 1916, p. 1; August 11, 1916, p. 1; Mundelein to Archbishop Joseph Weber, C.R. (undated), and Rev. Felix Ladon to Mundelein, August 29, 1916, AAC 3-1916-W-35.

4. James W. Sanders, *The Education of an Urban Minority: Catholics in Chicago, 1833–1965* (New York: Oxford University Press, 1977), p. 145.

Sanders gives a complete and readable survey of the elementary and secondary schools in Chicago; for this reason I have kept my remarks on elementary schooling brief and given more attention to higher education, which Sanders covers only sketchily.

5. Mundelein to Rev. Joseph Heimsath, September 5, 1916, AAC 2-1916-H-23; Mundelein to Rev. Thomas Bona, February 18, 1918, AAC 4-1918-B-2.

6. Sanders, *Education of an Urban Minority,* pp. 141-160; Rev. Edward F. Hoban to Mother M. Cleophas, July 7, 1919, AAC 5-1919-C-30; Mundelein to Rev. James Jennings, November 24, 1919, AAC 5-1919-J-3; Mundelein to Mother Mary Isabella, March 30, 1920, AAC 6-1920-I-1; Rev. Edward F. Hoban to "Rev. Dear Father" (form letter), July 13, 1920, AAC 6-1920-H-21.

7. Examples of Matimore's reports are Rev. P.H. Matimore to Mundelein, June 22, 1923, AAC 7-1923-M-81, and Matimore to Mundelein, December 18, 1924, AAC 8-1924-M-142.

8. Sanders, *Education of an Urban Minority,* pp. 157-158; personal interview, Msgr. Daniel Cunningham.

9. Sanders, *Education of an Urban Minority,* pp. 167-170; Sr. Mary Innocenta Montay, "The History of Catholic Secondary Education in the Archdiocese of Chicago" (Ph.D. diss., Catholic University of America, 1953), p. 312.

10. Sr. M. Jane Coogan, B.V.M., *The Price of Our Heritage* (Dubuque: Mt. Carmel Press, 1978), 2:270-272; Sr. M. Anna Rose Callan, B.V.M., "The Sisters of Charity of the BVM and Their Schools in Chicago, 1867-1940" (M.A. thesis, Loyola University, 1941), chapter 4.

11. Coogan, *The Price of Our Heritage,* pp. 272-273, 399-400.

12. *New World,* September 8, 1922, p. 4; June 15, 1923, p. 1; July 1, 1977, p. 1.

13. Mundelein felt Catholic men had adequate facilities for higher education. The Jesuits operated Loyola University and the Vincentian Fathers conducted DePaul University, both conveniently located near the "L." See Sanders, *Education of an Urban Minority,* pp. 170-175.

14. Mundelein to Mother Mary Samuel, O.P. (undated), AAC 5-1918-S-30; "Copy of a Report of the First Interview of Mother M. Cecilia et al. with George W. Mundelein, February 22, 1916," obtained for the author by Sr. M. Jane Coogan from the B.V.M. Archives at Mt. Carmel Motherhouse, Dubuque, Ia.

15. Mundelein to Mother Mary Samuel (undated), AAC 5-1918-S-30; Mundelein to Mother Samuel, June 2, 1916, AAC 3-1916-S-73; Marion E. Hogan to Dennis J. Dunne, September 11, 1917, AAC 3-1917-D-41; Rev. F.X. McCabe, C.M., to Mundelein, September

14, 1917, and Mundelein to McCabe, September 25, 1917, AAC 4-1917-M-29; Mundelein to Mrs. Howard Spaulding, October 13, 1917, AAC 4-1917-S-47.

16. Mother Samuel to Mundelein, April 24, 1916, AAC 3-1916-S-74; Sr. Mary Eva McCarty, O.P., *The Sinsinawa Dominicans: Outlines of Twentieth Century Development, 1901–1949* (Dubuque: Hoermann Press, 1952), pp. 186–187.

17. Ibid., p. 187; Mother Samuel to Mundelein, April 24, 1916, AAC 3-1916-S-74; Mundelein to Mother Samuel, June 2, 1916, AAC 3-1916-S-73.

18. McCarty, *Sinsinawa Dominicans*, pp. 188–190: *New World,* October 13, 1916, p. 1; Mundelein to Mother Samuel, October 4, 1916, AAC 3-1916-S-70.

19. McCarty, *Sinsinawa Dominicans*, p. 190; Mundelein to Mother Samuel, December 29, 1916, AAC 3-1916-S-69; "Ralph Adams Cram," in *Dictionary of American Biography,* supplement 3, 1941–45 (New York: Scribner's, 1973), pp. 194–197.

20. McCarty, *Sinsinawa Dominicans*, pp. 191–192; Mother Samuel to Mundelein, May 21, 1917, AAC 4-1917-M-296; Mother Samuel to Mundelein, July 12, 1917, and Mundelein to Mother Samuel, July 16, 1917, AAC 4-1917-S-76; Mother Samuel to Mundelein, April 17, 1918, AAC 5-1918-M-360; Mother Samuel to Mundelein, May 7, 1918, AAC 5-1918-M-359.

21. Mundelein to Mrs. Howard Spaulding, October 13, 1917, AAC 4-1917-S-47.

22. McCarty, *Sinsinawa Dominicans*, pp. 194–195; Mother Samuel to Mundelein, February 20, 1918, AAC 5-1918-M-23.

23. McCarty, *Sinsinawa Dominicans*, pp. 196–213; Mundelein to Mother Samuel, July 17, 1919, AAC 5-1919-S-35; Rev. Hugh J. O'Connor, C.M., to Mother Samuel, July 21, 1919, and Rev. Thomas V. Shannon to Mundelein, July 25, 1919, AAC 5-1919-M-216; Mundelein to Mrs. Edward Hines, November 15, 1919, AAC 5-1919-H-30; *New World,* February 6, 1920, p. 1; October 13, 1922, p. 2; Mother Samuel to Mundelein, October 15, 1921, AAC 6-1921-M-33.

24. *New World,* July 14, 1922, p. 2; September 22, 1922, p. 7; October 13, 1922, p. 2; Mundelein to Mother Samuel, September 8, 1922, AAC 7-1922-S-3; Mundelein to Mother Samuel, June 2, 1916, AAC 3-1916-S-73.

25. G.V. Tuttle to Sr. Mary Clementine, O.P., March 22, 1923, AAC 7-1923-M-15; Mother Samuel to Rev. Edward F. Hoban, December 7, 1921, AAC 6-1921-H-34.

26. Coogan, *The Price of Our Heritage,* 2:344–350, 415–416.

27. Unless otherwise noted, the following unpublished material on the B.V.M. order was obtained for me from the B.V.M. Archives, Mt. Carmel Motherhouse, Dubuque, Ia., by Sr. Jane Coogan. "Report of the First Interview of Mother M. Cecilia et al. with George W. Mundelein, February 22, 1916"; Mother Cecilia to Mundelein, May 15, 1916; Mundelein to Mother Cecilia, May 18, 1916; notes for a biographical sketch of Mother M. Cecilia Walsh. Mother Cecilia's successor, Mother M. Isabella Kane, who finally heeded the archbishop's request, cryptically jotted in her notes for November 15, 1929: "Mundelein—6 yr. agitating."

28. "Report of an Interview with Cardinal Mundelein, April 25, 1928."

29. During the years when Mundelein College was in the planning stages, Mother Isabella broke her arm and wrist, dislocated her shoulder, and suffered from fainting spells. "Report of an Interview with Cardinal Mundelein, April 25, 1928"; "Report of Interview with Mundelein, October 29, 1928"; "Report of Interview with Mr. Lewis, Continental Bank, November 1, 1928"; *Chicago Tribune,* September 27, 1931, p. 1; Sr. Madelena Thornton, "Mundelein Then, 1911–1940," in *Mundelein Now,* 6 (May 1980), 5–8. A biographical sketch of Sr. Justitia is in Coogan, *The Price of Our Heritage,* 2:438–439.

30. Thornton, "Mundelein Then," p. 7; Edward D. Reynolds, "Ivy and Rectangles," *America,* January 10, 1931, pp. 336–337.

31. Mundelein to Sr. M. Justitia, October 17, 1932; *Chicago Daily News,* June 6, 1934, p. 3; personal interviews with Sr. M. Jane Coogan, B.V.M. historian, and Sr. M. Cecilia Bodman, Mundelein College archivist.

32. Figures calculated from parish financial reports, 1926, at AAC.

33. See Greeley et al., *Catholic Schools in a Declining Church,* for an expansion of this point.

BENEFICIAL RELATIONS: TOWARD A SOCIAL HISTORY OF THE DIOCESAN PRIESTS OF BOSTON, 1875-1944

Robert E. Sullivan

Every effort to interpret history is unavoidably selective and potentially ironic. An observer selects some events as noteworthy, discerns a pattern in them, and evaluates the result. Others may accept the pattern he has discerned, only to reverse his evaluation of it. They indict what he has celebrated. By the 1920s William Henry Cardinal O'Connell was developing an interpretation of his tenure as archbishop of Boston. His "herculean and never ceasing" labors had resulted in the consolidation of the archdiocese. Almost twenty years later the cardinal's conception of his historical role assumed a monumental form in the official *History of the Archdiocese of Boston*. At O'Connell's direction the authors of the study organized it around the lives of the ordinaries of Boston.[1] O'Connell's accession on August 30, 1907, marked "The Dawning of a New Era." Its hallmark was the "reorganization of the diocesan administration and institutions and of Catholic activities generally with a view to attaining the maximum of unity and efficiency." To this end O'Connell sought to place "all Catholic activities in the Diocese under the direction of the constituted authorities: the Archbishop, in the first place, and, above him, the Holy Father."[2] He eliminated the virtual autonomy enjoyed by pastors, parishes, and Catholic organizations under his predecessor, John J. Williams. By 1911 Cardinal O'Connell was on the verge of transforming the archdiocese of Boston into a monolithic regime.

In 1973 O'Connell's supposed achievement was subjected to a harsher evaluation. Donna Merwick, in *Boston Priests, 1848-1910: A Study of Social and Intellectual Change*, accepted the principal contention of the authorized version bequeathed by O'Connell. He had accomplished "a swift and total centralization of the diocese." She, however, decried it as an expression "of an authoritarian scheme of

---

[1]Draft review of John E. Sexton, *Cardinal O'Connell: A Biographical Sketch* (Boston: Pilot Publishing Company, 1926), April 12, 1927, *Pilot* File, AABo 5:2; Lord to Minihan, November 10, 1943, Chancery Central Subject File M-6, *ibid.*
[2]*HAB*, 3:501.

things that was basically medieval." His was "a reactionary notion of authority," which issued in policies that had "little or no reference to the particular needs of individuals or situations."[3] Although the authorized version and the reevaluation differed radically in their appreciation of O'Connell's effort, they were agreed about its nature. Merwick was aware of the widespread distress in Boston and elsewhere that followed O'Connell's precedent-setting appointment in 1906 as coadjutor with the right of succession to Williams. Since her original research into the early years of O'Connell's tenure was sketchy, she acquiesced in the contention that he had rapidly created a monolithic regime out of a refractory feudalism. If Merwick and subsequent historians have turned the authorized version on its head, they have nonetheless preserved it intact.[4] They have offered a change of perspective rather than a new analysis.

327

The *History of the Archdiocese of Boston* and *Boston Priests* are surface narratives. Their point of view is essentially biographical, and they reduce the complex history of a religious culture to the life —or lives—of one individual or of a small group. History written from the top down is explanatory as well as descriptive, but the explanations it offers tend to be implausibly neat because the descriptions it embodies are unduly impressionistic. By magnifying the impact of manifest change this approach intensifies the simplification of past reality that afflicts every historical enterprise. Not even the most comprehensive history can recover the full reality of the past. Yet insofar as an account tries to probe deeply by using evidence from a variety of sources, it must expose the diversity of the past, which, like the present, mixes continuity and change.

This essay attempts to explore the history of the secular clergy of the archdiocese of Boston from its elevation to that status in 1875 until O'Connell's death in 1944. Neither date is a watershed, but together they mark the approximate boundaries of adequate evidence. Resting on samples of that evidence, the effort is

[3]Donna Merwick, *Boston Priests, 1848-1910: A Study of Social and Intellectual Change* (Cambridge, Mass.: Harvard University Press, 1973), 177, 181.

[4]*Ibid.,* 243-244 n. 83; James Gaffey, "The Changing of the Guard: The Rise of Cardinal O'Connell of Boston," *CHR*, 59 (1973): 225-244; Edward R. Kantowicz, *Corporation Sole: Cardinal Mundelein and Chicago Catholicism*, Notre Dame Studies in American Catholicism (Notre Dame, Ind.: Notre Dame University Press, 1983), 2-3.

preliminary. The questions it raises are perhaps more numerous than the answers it offers, and these answers invite correction. Notwithstanding its limitations this study of the origins, beliefs, and careers of the approximately 1,600 priests who served, taught, and ruled the church of Boston for almost seventy years suggests the partiality of both the authorized version and the reevaluation. Their history fails to reveal the easy triumph of fundamental change.

Throughout this period Catholicism in Boston was stable in a way that now seems alien.[5] The structure of the social relations of the Catholic community of Essex, Middlesex, Suffolk, Norfolk, and Plymouth counties was articulated and cohesive. If these people were not legally segregated, most of them remained set apart, viewed with suspicion by others, and jealous of their own identity. Their religion consisted of traditional symbols, which provided them with a uniform system of meaning and ensured the persistence of their cultural memory, despite frequent local moves. The psychological processes of the Catholics of Boston defy scrutiny, but the recoverable words and behavior that can evince them point to the existence of relatively coherent habits of mind. Change touched the community without transforming its life. Although institutional arrangements are peculiarly sensitive to the movement of events, the life of even strictly hierarchical organizations usually owes more to the society and culture that support them than to the aspirations and directives of any leader, no matter how forceful. The collective biography of Boston's priests conforms to this generalization. The governance of their church never experienced either "the maximum of unity and efficiency" or "a swift and total centralization." Instead it was marked by the attenuation of feudalism.

The detailed research of Joseph B. Fuller into the family histories of the priests of Boston ordained between 1875 and 1924 has yielded a remarkably clear picture.[6] These men were ethnically

328

[5]For the interdependence of social structure, psychology, and religious culture, see Mary Douglas, *Natural Symbols: Explorations in Cosmology*, rev. ed. (New York: Vintage Books, 1973), and Clifford Geertz, *The Interpretation of Cultures: Selected Essays* (New York: Basic Books, 1973), 87–141.

[6]This and the following paragraph summarize Joseph B. Fuller, "At the Very Center of Things: The Catholic Secular Clergy in the Redirection of Catholic Boston" (Honors thesis: Harvard College, 1979), 69–90. Mr. Fuller's research was based on a random sample of 10.25 percent of the diocesan priests ordained between 1875 and 1924. I am indebted to him for assistance on this and other subjects.

329

A montage: Archbishop Williams and the priests serving the archdiocese, 1902
(Photo AABo)

homogeneous. By 1875 almost two-thirds of those being ordained had been born in the archdiocese, but Irish-Americans exercised a near-monopoly on the diocesan priesthood. Irish immigrants were a steadily declining percentage of the total body, never amounting to 10 percent of any ordination class after 1910. During this half century nearly 80 percent of the ordinands were either first or second generation native-born Irish-Americans or of Irish extraction. Although Irish and Catholic were virtually synonymous terms in Boston, the national origins of the population of the archdiocese became more various with every federal census beginning with that of 1880. French-Canadians were the first to arrive in large numbers. By 1910 they were contributing as many foreign-born ordinands to the archdiocese as the Irish. The representation of the French-Canadians in the diocesan clergy continued to grow without ever becoming proportionate to their percentage of the total Catholic population. Even before 1900 most French-speaking priests were serving in national parishes made up of their fellow ethnics; they formed their own group marked by distinctive patterns of assignment and promotion. Slavic- and Italo-Americans began regularly to contribute sons to the secular priesthood only during the 1930s. They too tended to serve in non-English-speaking assignments.

The diocesan clergy also formed a socially coherent group. As early as 1875 priests usually derived from the more prosperous families in their community. The sons of unskilled laborers were consistently less than 10 percent of those ordained after 1900, even though they constituted over half of the Irish-American working population in Boston into the 1920s. Foreign-born Irish ordinands tended to come from the lowest levels of the occupational scale; their fathers were equally divided between skilled blue-collar workers and semi-skilled and unskilled laborers. In excess of 40 percent of the fathers of first generation Irish-American priests held skilled blue-collar positions. An absolute majority of second generation Irish-American priests had white-collar origins. Although only about one-third of the priests ordained between 1875 and 1924 were the sons of fathers born in the United States, over 60 percent of them came from families whose social standing was typical of second generation Irish-Americans. Their brothers rarely succumbed to the occupational slippage that beset the community. On the contrary most of them achieved occupational upward mobility. Fewer than 8 percent

330

of the fathers of clerics reached professional status; over 30 percent of their brothers did. There seems to have been no appreciable change in the ethnic and social character of the priests ordained between 1925 and 1944; they remained preponderantly of Irish-American stock and lower middle class.

The upward mobility of the families of many priests suggests the high social prestige that the clerical state enjoyed among a group regularly underrepresented in the professions. The archdiocese never had a serious problem in recruiting an adequate number of candidates for ordination. Family reconstruction helps to explain who the priests of Boston were, but it sheds scant light on why these men chose to become priests. Individual motivation is seldom transparent, and few clerics recorded how they discerned their particular calling. Robert Howard Lord, one of the least typical men whom Cardinal O'Connell ever ordained, left the most detailed written account of such an effort.

Raised as a Protestant in Illinois, Lord thought of becoming a minister while an undergraduate at Harvard. Instead he became an historian. Groomed to be his university's specialist in Eastern European history, Lord pursued doctoral studies which took him to tsarist Russia. The steady progress of his academic career at Harvard was enhanced by his service as the American expert on Russia at the Versailles Conference. In 1920 Lord entered the Catholic church. Conversion rekindled in him the clerical aspirations that he had felt as an Episcopalian. Although he only resigned his professorship and enrolled in St. John's, the archdiocesan seminary, in 1926, Lord was already considering the step in the autumn of 1921. Then he drew up a number of lists in which he weighed the "reasons in favor of entering the priesthood" against those for "remaining where I am."

The principle governing Lord's deliberations was simple: "My whole life must be given to [God's] service. He must have my whole heart, mind, soul." Becoming a priest seemed to entail immediate loss and ultimate gain: "The priesthood is the noblest and most sacred of callings. If it demands the greatest sacrifices, it brings the greatest rewards. It ought to call forth all that is best in a man and stimulate him to lead the fullest, richest, most ideal life of which he is capable. By the sacrifices it involves, the renunciation of self, the constant intercourse with God and the daily contact with the Divine

331

Mysteries, it ought to keep a man in a higher spiritual plane than is possible, save in rare cases, with any secular calling."[7] Lord was conscious both of the role that "certain half-selfish sentimental motives" played in prompting his inclination and of " 'experiences' which, if they are valid and not illusions," appeared to indicate a genuine vocation. Conceding that he might be impelled by the natural desire to cling to the security of routine, Lord held back because he lacked certitude that God was calling him and suspected that he was "fitted for my present work and nothing else." Even so, he sensed that his "values in life" had changed, that he "no longer cared much for the pleasures, the honors or the comforts of 'the world.'"[8]

Lord's personal distinction might seem to disqualify him as a specimen had not more typical men also approached the seminary professing symptoms of the psychology of renunciation. Writing in 1895, one matriculant, an Irish-American alumnus of Boston College, noted his feeling of "repugnance for the world."[9] He was perhaps too callow to know enough about the world to have acquired real distaste for it. He was, however, a Catholic and fell effortlessly into the stylized language with which his religion had traditionally defined the detachment that was necessary for every Christian, and especially for the priest. Thus William O'Connell was given to complaining that "the world . . . is utterly selfish. Its life is folly, and its heart frozen and utterly unfeeling for all those who ought to be very dear to it as they are to Christ."[10] Insofar as the attitudes of the Catholic community of Boston toward education, thrift, and consumption were incompatible with an ethic directed toward worldly success, its young men who were candidates for ordination must have found the vocabulary of renunciation doubly congenial.[11] They were probably insensible to the irony that they were perfecting its use while preparing to assume a leading role among their fellows.

Social factors worked to promote, or at least to support, the

---

[7] Account of October 21, 1921, Lord Papers, AABo.

[8] Accounts of November 21 and 27, 1921, *ibid.*

[9] Diary of William L. Sullivan, February 15, 1895, Sullivan Papers, Andover Library, Harvard Divinity School, Cambridge, MA.

[10] *S&A*, 10:14.

[11] Stephan Thernstrom, *The Other Bostonians: Poverty and Progress in the American Metropolis, 1870-1970* (Cambridge, Mass.: Harvard University Press, 1973), 168-169, 321-322 n. 30.

discovery of a priestly vocation. Innocent of the apprehensions recurrently felt by clerics, many Irish-American families remained willing to hold up the priesthood to their sons as pleasing to God and humanly dignified.[12] The number of siblings who became priests— both entering the service of the archdiocese on occasion; more often, one electing to join the ranks of the seculars and the other those of the orders—suggests the importance of early nurture. Custom symbolized the ties between a priest's vocation and his parents. During the rite of ordination the hands of each man were anointed with chrism and bound with a linen strip called the *manutergium*. This binder, which was often made by his mother, was immediately taken off and put away until a parent died. In Europe the *manutergium* had traditionally been wrapped around the hands of whichever died first when he or she lay in the coffin. In the United States it was usually wrapped around the hands of the mother of the priest.

333

Maternal influence appears to have been decisive for many. In describing the genesis of his vocational aspirations, O'Connell remembered that his days as a fatherless altar boy had left him in awe at "the sublimity of this service of God," but that in adolescence he had been led "by a gentle attraction, which seemed like nothing else but a mother's love, . . . to wish and pray that I might be worthy of a call which could come from God alone." For their part the official historians of St. John's Seminary were sure that every priest had known "indescribable joy" at his first Mass "and the meeting then with his mother."[13] Such impressionistic evidence points to conclusions that social scientists would later formulate in their characteristically cool phrases. Writing in the early 1970s, one psychologist suggested that a priest's "relationship with [his] mother is . . . related to the tendency to define the priesthood in sacred terms and the willingness to accept celibacy, as well as to perseverance in the seminary."[14]

[12]Joseph V. O'Conor, "Is Catholicity Spreading in the United States?" *Donahoe's Magazine*, 3 (1880): 330, and Murray to Minihan, April 4, 1939, Seminary File, AABo 7:11; Faculty Minutes, St. John's Seminary (SJS), June 3, 1896, *ibid.*; John E. Sexton and Arthur J. Riley, *History of Saint John's Seminary Brighton* (Boston: Roman Catholic Archbishop of Boston, 1945), 231-232.

[13]William Cardinal O'Connell, *Recollections of Seventy Years* (Boston: Houghton Mifflin, 1934), 47; Sexton and Riley, *History*, 228.

[14]John J. Rooney, in Eugene C. Kennedy and Victor J. Heckler, *The Catholic*

Influences outside the family were also weighty. In Boston and the other urban areas of the archdiocese where most Catholics lived and a majority of diocesan priests were born, the parish was central to the lives of many of its members. They looked to it as the focus of solidarity as well as of worship, but were less likely than their co-religionists elsewhere to see it as a place where their children should be educated. The archdiocese of Boston failed to create an educational system as extensive as those of other major sees like Chicago, and most of the priests ordained for its service between 1875 and 1944 had attended public schools.[15] Nonetheless, the outsize buildings of many large parochial complexes expressed and helped to shape the distinctive neighborhood identities of Catholic city-dwellers.

Perhaps exemplary of this kind of center was the Mission Church, Roxbury, which was operated by the Redemptorist order and became a parish in 1883. In addition to big primary and secondary schools, it sponsored outings, athletic teams, drama groups, a marching band, and an association that offered youths facilities for activities ranging from bowling to reading.[16] Officially named Parker Hill, the area dominated by a square block of church facilities became known as Mission Hill to the thousands of Catholics who lived within its precincts. Less lavishly equipped city churches also provided diverse activities that made them a vital presence in their communities and thus exhibited the priesthood as a visible option to the young.

Priests were frequently able to recruit possible successors. The mean length of each of their parish assignments, exclusive of temporary placements, was in excess of eight years. If he was so disposed, a well-established priest could nurture a protégé almost from boyhood. A pastor or curate might undertake to help support a former altar boy through college; he continued his aid if the young

334

Priest in the United States: Psychological Investigations (Washington: United States Catholic Conference, 1972), 209–210.

[15]James W. Sanders, "Catholics and the School Question in Boston: The Cardinal O'Connell Years," elsewhere in this volume; Faculty Minutes, SJS, June 3, 1896, AABo.

[16]John F. Byrne, *The Glories of Mary in Boston: A Memorial History of the Church of Our Lady of Perpetual Help (Mission Church), Roxbury, Mass., 1871–1921* (Boston: Mission Church Press, 1921), 200, 416–453.

man became a seminarian.[17] The majority of Boston's priests went on from the public schools to Catholic colleges before beginning their clerical studies. Over 70 percent of those ordained between 1900 and 1944 had been students at Boston College; others were alumni of the College of the Holy Cross in Worcester. Many had not graduated from these institutions, since it was possible to be admitted to St. John's Seminary after only two years of college. Jesuit professors were disposed to encourage their students to consider becoming candidates for the secular priesthood as well as for their own society. Himself an alumnus of Boston College, O'Connell resourcefully deflected attempts by the Vatican during the early 1930s to disrupt this long-standing symbiotic relationship by requiring the archdiocese to conform to Latin practice and support a minor seminary that would admit youths immediately after high school. He finally acquiesced in this recommendation in the summer of 1939 as Europe was preparing to go to war once again. Should America become involved, the federal government was unlikely to renew the concession it had granted in the spring of 1917 and declare Boston College a minor seminary whose undergraduates were exempt from conscription.[18]

Both absolutely and in per capita relation to the faithful of the archdiocese, the clerical population grew between 1875 and 1944. A relatively greater increase occurred in the number of priests belonging to religious orders. During these years their ranks expanded from 38 to 216, an increase of 570 percent. Staffing seven parishes in the beginning, they operated forty-four by the end; nearly all were non-Irish. Although most of the order priests did extra-parochial work, their parishes virtually constituted a diocese within the archdiocese, not quite autonomous but clearly differentiated. The increase in the numbers of diocesan priests was almost as dramatic. With a few exceptions they did parochial work. In 1875, 137 secular priests served 93 parishes; by 1944, 986 secular priests were staffing 281 parishes, an increase of 563 percent. If the officially reported estimates of the population of the archdiocese are ac-

---

[17]Sexton and Riley, *History*, 18-19; Neagle to O'Connell, September 20, 1920, Parish Files, AABo 56:22; Sullivan to Peterson, April 23, 1913, Seminary File, *ibid.* 2:3.
  [18]Bisleti to O'Connell, February 16, 1933, and O'Connell to Bisleti, May 4, 1933, Seminary File, AABo 6:7; Sexton and Riley, *History*, 219, 170.

cepted, there was one diocesan priest for every 2,262 Catholics in 1875, and one for every 1,149 in 1944. When the orders are included in the total, the evidence of growth is even more striking. There was one priest for every 1,771 Catholics in 1875, and one for every 943 in 1944. The work load of the progressively more numerous diocesan clergy grew somewhat lighter in every decade. Clerical duties in 1944 were much the same as they had been in 1875, but most priests during the Second World War were celebrating fewer Masses, as well as baptizing, marrying, and burying less frequently, than had their late nineteenth-century predecessors.[19]

336

It lay with the ordinary to determine how many priests he needed in order to conduct his diocese efficiently. There was no accepted yardstick for him to consult. Because of the ample number of suitable applicants after 1890, the willingness of pastors to receive additional curates formed the primary limitation on the archbishop's discretion. In the mid-1880s many of them had been eager to receive more assistants, but by 1900 the seminary was curtailing admissions because its "graduates had no places awaiting them at ordination." Although on average over three new parishes were erected every year from 1868 until the end of Williams's regime, the archbishop felt obliged to loan priests to other dioceses.[20]

Shortly after his accession O'Connell determined that Boston was suffering from a shortage of priests, and the seminary responded to his judgment by gradually increasing its enrollment. In September 1907 about 60 students for the archdiocese had been registered there; nine years later the number stood at 159. During his first sixteen months as archbishop O'Connell created twenty additional parishes, by either raising existing missions to independent status or carving entirely new parishes out of a few large units. He could not sustain this burst of expansion. Throughout the remainder of his tenure, a period of over thirty-five years, he founded new parishes at an annual rate slightly below that maintained by Williams. While

[19]Throughout this essay figures for the clerical and lay populations and number of parishes of the archdiocese of Boston have been drawn from the official reports in the national *Catholic Directory* (various imprints: 1875–1944). The work loads of Boston's priests have been calculated from the Parish Census Records, 1908–1944, AABo. The method of computation is adapted from François Houtart, *Aspects sociologiques du catholicisme américain* (Paris: Editions ouvrières, 1957), 227–234.

[20]See Fuller, "At the Very Center," 118 and references; Sexton and Riley, *History*, 109.

steady, the increase of the Catholic population was too slow to justify the wholesale multiplication of parishes unless the pattern of extensive entities that had obtained in Boston were abandoned. O'Connell clung to the existing system and continued to ordain additional priests with little regard to the rate of growth of the lay population. Between 1915 and 1925, for example, he augmented the supply of active diocesan clergy in Boston by almost 34 percent; the total number of Catholics in the archdiocese grew during this decade by about 6.7 percent. By the mid-1920s a few pastors were reluctant to keep their junior assistant lest he grow indolent from lack of work.[21] Their apprehensions had no effect on the cardinal's policy.

337

Two considerations seem to have encouraged O'Connell's resolute ordaining. The Catholic belief that a life of ordained service is the highest human calling has recurrently fostered the idea that the church is the concern of its priests. Widening access to the priesthood easily expanded to accommodate the use of increased numbers to maintain—or to strengthen—the influence of ecclesiastics within both the church and society. Pope Pius X's attitude toward lay initiatives was clearly unsympathetic, and the cardinal, ever his disciple, made it his own. Moreover, O'Connell appears to have been eager to increase the number of younger priests who had not known the less demanding rule of Williams.[22] They would help to vindicate the truth of his dictum that "there is only one Church militant—only one real régime in the Church—the present one."[23]

In the wake of the Great Depression O'Connell hesitantly reversed course. Although he had ordered that the eleven weakest members of the class of 1931 be dropped in the spring, weeks before their scheduled ordination, the seminary that autumn admitted a class as numerous as its immediate predecessors. Whether in response to the unwillingness of his pastors to employ more curates or to the failure of the hoped-for rapid economic recovery, O'Connell initiated far-reaching measures in January 1933. At the end of

[21]*HAB*, 3:528; "Report on St. John's," n.d. [1938?], 5A, Seminary File, AABo 6:6; Sexton and Riley, *History*, 169. See Fuller, "At the Very Center," 124 and references.

[22]See "Il fermo proposito," *Acta Sanctae Sedis*, 37 (1904–1905): 741-767; Peterson to Sullivan, April 23, 1913, Seminary File, AABo 2:3; Sexton and Riley, *History*, 169.

[23]Draft editorial, December 4, 1909, *Pilot* File, AABo 1:10.

338

"Along the lines of a Norman castle": seminary procession, 1923
(Photo AABo)

the academic year twenty students were let go, and the course of studies for those who remained was lengthened by at least two semesters. Overall, the seminary's enrollment was reduced from 253 students in September 1930 to an average of 150 students during each of the years between 1933 and 1938.[24] The slow increase that began during O'Connell's waning years would again become a striking expansion after 1945 because Richard J. Cushing, O'Connell's successor, determined that the archdiocese was suffering a shortage of priests.

After Archbishop Williams opened St. John's Seminary in an isolated part of the Brighton area of Boston in 1884, it was no longer necessary for candidates to be trained in various places outside the archdiocese. Boston was finally able to standardize the formation of its priests, but attendance at St. John's became a rule that admitted of exceptions. If nearly 90 percent of those ordained by Williams after 1885 received a uniform preparation from the Sulpicians who directed the new seminary, some had been sent to Baltimore, Montreal, or Europe for their studies. Moreover, the presence of seminarians from other dioceses in New England diversified the student body. Only under O'Connell would external candidates be all but excluded and the alternatives for Bostonians be reduced to Brighton or the North American College in Rome.

The structure which Williams provided for the new institution took as its model the Seminary of St. Sulpice in Paris. Constructing an educational building along the lines of a Norman castle was more than a reflection of Victorian medievalism. It was a reaffirmation of the militancy that had animated the church of the Counter-Reformation. The bishops of the United States were meeting in the Third Plenary Council of Baltimore as St. John's was opening. The prelates decreed clear standards for seminary faculty members. They had above all to be able to teach their students, "by example as well as word, the virtues of humility, unworldliness, industry, solitude and assiduous prayerfulness"; conveying "true doctrine" to students was essential to inciting "their minds with zeal for the glory of God and the salvation of souls."[25]

[24]Memorandum titled "Dropped 1931, June," Seminary File, *ibid.* 6:2; Finn to Burke, May 4, 1933, and Burke to Finn, May 5, 1933, *ibid.* 6:7; "Report on St. John's," 5A, *ibid.* 6:6; Sexton and Riley, *History*, 202.

[25]*Acta et Decreta Concilii Plenarii Baltimorensis Tertii* (Baltimore, 1886), 81-82.

Williams had been a student of the Sulpicians both in Montreal and in Paris, and he counted on his old teachers to inculcate in his own seminarians their traditional principles of discipline, piety, and sound doctrine. Students were not admitted to Brighton before completing their sophomore year of college. If they entered then, they would ordinarily spend two years studying philosophy and four learning theology. As a rule, those who were admitted after their junior year or with a baccalaureate from a Catholic college followed a five-year course. Admission depended on passing an examination that sought to test the students' basic competence in the liberal arts and their grasp of the content of their last year of undergraduate studies. They also had to produce letters recommending their character and devoutness from their pastors and other priests who knew them.[26] Although often unimpressed with the general academic fitness of applicants, the seminary faculty was particularly concerned about the weakness of their Latin. Most seminarians appear to have been ill-at-ease with the essential hierophantic language.[27]

340

The effort of the teachers, many of whom were French or at least Frenchified, to prepare a group of predominantly Irish-American youths for the priesthood inevitably resulted in cultural tensions. In the eyes of the professors all except those who had received their undergraduate education under Sulpician auspices seemed spiritually immature. The majority had failed to advance beyond the sentimental devotion which they had learned from their parents. They had to be introduced to reading the breviary every day, a practice which would be binding on them under pain of sin when they were advanced to major orders. It proved harder to accustom them to regular mental prayer or meditation, discursive reflection on a theme or passage meant to deepen their spiritual insight and to strengthen their will and love for God. Like most Americans, they naturally identified religion with personal morality. If they were for the most part upstanding, they consistently found Christian mortification inconvenient, if not incomprehensible. Aware that

[26]Faculty Minutes, SJS, May 31, 1886, AABo; Results of Entrance Examinations, 1889–1966, 2 vols., St. John's Seminary, Brighton; Thomas C. McGoldrick, "St. John's Seminary," *Donahoe's Magazine*, 30 (1893): 59-64.

[27]Faculty Minutes, SJS, February 1 and May 31, 1886, June 3, 1896, and May 15, 1901, AABo; Sexton and Riley, *History*, 157.

Boston's priests suffered from a reputation for coarseness, the faculty of St. John's scrutinized the deportment of the seminarians.[28]

When evaluating the basic dispositions of students, the Sulpicians and their diocesan auxiliaries often arrived at an apparently self-contradictory judgment. The seminarians exhibited on the one hand a docility toward their superiors that could merge into passivity and on the other hand signs of disquieting independence. Content with explaining the cultural origins of two distinct kinds of behaviors, the evaluators did not seek to explore the psychological significance of their conjunction in the tight environment of the seminary. They traced the docility to an inbred awe (*crainte révérentielle*) of the person and words of every priest and the independence to a bias of the American character reinforced by the experience of self-sufficiency gained by men who had been obliged to put themselves through college.[29]

341

Evidence of the feelings of students toward St. John's is mostly indirect and far from clear-cut. From their arrival many saw the foreign accents and mannerisms of certain Sulpicians as droll. Driven by adolescent playfulness or by grimmer impulses, they would occasionally disrupt classes with "petty applause and the stamping and shuffling of feet."[30] The austerity of their teachers hardened in a few cases into officiousness, which left some alumni with a "deep-seated and persistent resentment against the faculty, and the whole idea of Brighton." Yet by choosing Sulpicians as their confessors after ordination, others testified that enduring ties of personal respect and affection had been forged there.[31]

Pedagogy at Brighton held back from the course being taken by contemporary American professional education. Academic specialization tentatively appeared in the seminary only in the mid-1930s. The career of John B. Peterson illustrates the combination of thin preparation and abundant demands that beset the faculty of the seminary. Immediately after being ordained in 1899, Peterson was sent away for graduate study in history, which consisted of two years

---

[28]Faculty Minutes, SJS, June 3, 1896, June 3, 1886, September 21, 1904, AABo; Diary of John B. Hogan, November 22, 1884, Sulpician Archives, Baltimore, RG9, Box 6 (photocopy in AABo), and Faculty Minutes, SJS, May 23, 1886, AABo.

[29]Faculty Minutes, SJS, May 31 and June 3, 1886, and June 3, 1896, AABo.

[30]Sexton and Riley, *History*, 66, 98, 110-111; Faculty Minutes, SJS, September 17, 1901, AABo.

[31]Sexton and Riley, *History*, 114, 70.

divided between Paris and Rome. He then began to teach. Within a decade he had offered courses not only in church history of every period, but also in moral theology and in canon law; he was dabbling in administration as well. Although Peterson lacked any parochial experience, he assumed responsibility for giving regular talks on clerical life called "Spiritual Readings" when O'Connell appointed him to head St. John's in 1911. The institution's official history lauded them as "the very backbone of the whole Seminary curriculum."[32]

342

Even when allowance is made for the celebratory tone appropriate to such volumes, the description remains telling. Specific course work played a subordinate part in the making of Boston's priests. If the educational procedures of the seminary were indebted to the "whole man" ideal common to mid-nineteenth-century American colleges, they owed even more to the essentially objective conception of Holy Orders that the Council of Trent had shaped and subsequent ecclesiastical legislation and practice enforced. St. John's sought primarily to form men to be made priests. Teaching them how to become priests was an incidental part of its design. The official theology of the Catholic church, which provided believers with the common vocabulary of their faith, held that ordination allowed a man to share in the priesthood of Jesus Christ and to be conformed to His person. Such configuration differed from that given to every Christian at baptism because it entailed the special powers of consecrating the Eucharist and absolving from sin. The priest was dependent on the episcopate, which alone enjoyed the fullness of Holy Orders. It was through episcopal ordination that he participated in the special form of Christ's priesthood and by episcopal license that he was able to use its powers. They were the basis of the jurisdiction or rule which a pastor exercised over the flock to which his bishop assigned him. Three binding relations were thus integral to the diocesan priest: to Christ and His sacramental manifestations; to the bishop to whom he owed respect and obedience; and to the people whom he was charged to lead to eternal salvation.

Although a sinner could validly exercise priestly powers, this complex of transcendent and mundane relations bound the priest to strive for increasing holiness of life. When he was ordained, he had

[32]*Ibid.*, 146.

been charged to "let the odor of your life be the delight of the church of Christ, that by preaching and by example you may edify the house that is the family of God."[33] The injunction had profound implications for the interior life of every priest. In order to make them tangible the Council of Trent identified them with a demeanor it judged to exhibit perfection. In his actions, his gestures, his words, and even his gait the cleric should show himself to be grave, modest, and pious. Faithfully adhered to, this demeanor would keep him blameless and evoke universal veneration.[34]

The ascetic and uniformly exacting order of the Tridentine seminary aimed to impress such attitudes on future priests. Its rationale derived from the theory of moral activity of Thomas Aquinas.[35] In his view the quality of every human life was determined by the performance of operations and actions. Moral virtues were acquired habits, willed patterns of behavior that at once expressed goodness and worked to dispose individuals to do good readily, easily, and regularly. Aquinas taught the prelates at Trent that there is a universal ideal of human development and integration. He also taught them that the fact of social differentiation meant that the ideal could not be realized uniformly by distinct groups. Like the rest of them, the clergy were subject to a particular expression of the common norm. Because they were celibate and set above the laity, they could acquire the virtues appropriate to their state only by submitting to an especially rigorous habituation. Such a regimen also provided a means of excluding the deficient or the undesirable. Although the Tridentine design was occasionally questioned at the turn of the century, Pius X insisted on it in several documents issued between 1904 and 1910.[36] His firm will ensured that his endorsement would command general attention.

The institution where John Peterson had been shaped and which

343

[33]*Pontificale Romanum* (Mechelen: H. Dessain, [1934]), 117.

[34]Council of Trent, session 22, "Of Reformation," c. 1, in *Canones et Decreta Concilii Tridentini*, ed. Emil Ludwig Richter (Leipzig, 1853), 149-150.

[35]F. C. Copleston, *Aquinas* (Baltimore: Penguin Books, 1955), 214-217, and Etienne Gilson, *The Christian Philosophy of St. Thomas Aquinas*, trans. L. K. Shook (New York: Random House, 1956), 256-258.

[36]See "Iacunda Sane," *Acta Sanctae Sedis*, 36 (1903–1904): 513-529; "Haerent Animo," *ibid.*, 41 (1908): 555-577; "Ordo Servandus" of the Congregation of the Consistory, *Acta Apostolicae Sedis*, 2 (1910): 21-22, 26-28; "Sacrorum Antistitum," *ibid.*, 655-680.

he eventually led was governed by these aspirations. It aimed to form young men to assume the "priestly office and character." There Peterson had deliberately "sunk his whole personality" into the priesthood and offered himself as a model to others.[37] In both its form and content the priestly office was seen as objective and owing nothing essential to subjectivity. Suitable men could acquire and exercise its liturgical and extraliturgical responsibilities in a prescribed and uniform fashion. St. John's Seminary tried to prepare candidates so that they could absorb a sacramental character at ordination, much as softened wax is impressed with a seal.

344   Throughout this period any expression of distinctiveness of personality in and through the priesthood was suspect. During the winter of 1899 an original young alumnus of St. John's was visited by a "Protestant lady torn with a question of faith." Though attracted to some features of Catholicism, she found an Episcopalian minister particularly consoling. "I exhorted her to pray," the priest wrote in his diary, "not to attach herself to the personality of any minister or priest. Protestants are so accustomed to depend on a personality for continued interest in their religious life that the same habit follows them into the Church."[38] Over thirty years later William O'Connell articulated the same conviction with his usual assertiveness: "There is no such thing as the personality of a Bishop or the personality of a parish priest. Personal qualities are subject to change. These are transient things on which depend nothing of the certainty of the Catholic Faith."[39]

The regulated little world of the seminary did not encourage individuality. Its schedule underwent minor changes during the first sixty years of its existence. For the most part they consisted of matters of detail rather than of substance. The hours of rising and retiring were altered, along with those of the mandatory "strenuous exercises of hand-ball, baseball and tennis." The amount of time spent attending lectures—the only form of instruction available—was lengthened.[40] Such adjustment had slight effect on the life of the place. The students' time remained strictly allocated and largely outside their control. While dramatic, O'Connell's removal of the Sulpicians in

[37]Sexton and Riley, *History*, 147.
[38]Diary of James A. Walsh, March 12, 1899 (overleaf), AABo.
[39]*S&A*, 10:102.
[40]Sexton and Riley, *History*, 150-152.

"Strenuous exercises": seminarians playing tennis, 1920s
(Photo AABo)

1911 in favor of a teaching staff made up of his own priests did not revolutionize the curriculum of the seminary. Dogmatics, moral theology, and canon law still predominated, and instruction continued to depend on apologetic manuals which, though reflecting the prescribed neo-Thomism, failed to partake of the intellectual distinction of the *Summa Theologiae*. That book was persistently commended rather than read.

The cardinal's assumption of direct control over St. John's resulted in other changes. Taken together, they deepened its isolation from external influences and magnified docility or obedience as a criterion of suitability for promotion to Holy Orders. O'Connell's attitude toward his candidates was severe: "The Seminarians are not Angels, but untrained boys who must be made to feel the hand of authority, lightly, whenever possible, but, nevertheless, it must be there. They must feel under orders at all times." The cardinal was partial to military imagery when depicting his relationship to his ecclesiastical subordinates. In the tense atmosphere that had prevailed when he assumed the coadjutorship in 1906, he had informed his fellow priests that the church was an "immense army" whose ranks included the "humblest soldier" as well as "great generals."[41] His own conspicuous promotion offered him an opportunity to remind them of the chain of command that ran from Rome to Boston through its archbishop. With the death of Williams it was inevitable that he should treat his seminary as a kind of basic training camp in which recruits could learn how to transform a metaphor into an organizational reality.

The intensification of existing currents and arrangements was central to the effort. Unprecedented moves were rare. In 1911 seminarians were prohibited from receiving all newspapers and reviews both religious and secular. "Not even *The Boston Pilot* has been excepted," Peterson noted, "nor such a useful journal for our class-work as the *Ecclesiastical Review*." Far from being a departure the action completed the limitation on the students' access to periodicals that had begun in the mid-1890s.[42] O'Connell also

---

[41] O'Connell to Finn, May 21, 1929, Seminary File, AABo 5:15; *S&A*, 3:10.

[42] Peterson to Walsh, February 20, 1912, as cited in Merwick, *Boston Priests*, 192; Faculty Minutes, SJS, June 6, 1896, and November 18, 1900, AABo; Sexton and Riley, *History*, 58, 96.

346

moved to separate instructors from the outside world. As the Sulpicians were departing, he required the new faculty to "maintain a certain distance and aloofness from the Clergy of the Diocese, contenting themselves with the companionship and friendship that they will find among themselves." Whatever the cardinal's motive—whether to contain or to exclude—this measure had precedents in the inwardness which had ruled the lives and work of the Sulpicians.[43] When he instituted novelties, he usually did so gradually. From the beginning the calendar of the seminary had been like those of other schools, and the seminarians had been left to their own devices during the long summer vacation. Although he believed in the Roman custom that required them to live for a period in the controlled environment of a summer villa or camp, O'Connell was slow to introduce the practice in Boston. In 1918 he made property in New Hampshire available to the seminary as a vacation resort for a few students, and only later did it become obligatory for each of them to spend about half his summer there.[44]

347

Docility had been valued by the earlier Sulpicians, and during the O'Connell regime it sometimes became a watchword. In 1902 the rector praised a model candidate for being "industrious, pious, gentlemanly in manner and exemplary in conduct." Peterson also defined his standards of excellence variously. For the class of 1913 they were "maturity, docility, and priestly spirit," but the following year his key criteria were academic standing, good discipline, and physical health.[45] Peterson's flexible emphases reflected the complexity of O'Connell's own aspirations for the seminarians. Docility was a virtue he consistently prized, but it did not for the most part obsess him. He was a realistic administrator who desired to employ serviceable men and appreciated that serviceability is a plural quality. He was thus concerned to impress on his candidates that they had "a grave duty in equipping themselves mentally for the Priesthood."[46]

---

[43]O'Connell to Peterson, May 17, 1911, Seminary File, AABo 1:15; Sexton and Riley, *History*, 61, 70.

[44]Sexton and Riley, *History*, 171.

[45]Maher to [Williams], August 28, 1902, Seminary File, AABo 1:1; Peterson to Sullivan, March 13, 1913, *ibid.* 2:3; Peterson to Sullivan, February 3, 1914, *ibid.* 2:5.

[46]O'Connell to Nilan, December 5, 1907, *ibid.* 1:2.

Only from 1927 was the routine of St. John's affected by actions that might be construed as enforcing total docility. The development owed more, however, to proximity than to ideology. Early in that year the cardinal moved into a new house on the grounds of the seminary in Brighton; Peterson had resigned the rectorship the previous November. For the first time O'Connell was in a position to exert close supervision over minute details of the life of the institution. He considered himself "to be practically the Rector."[47] Many of his decisions were sudden, ambiguous, and short-lived. He decreed in May 1927, a time of general prosperity, that eggs be removed from the diet of both faculty and students, that their breakfast rations be restricted, and that the customary preordination banquets be ended.[48] The decision may have been the result of a desire to instill greater mortification, to economize, or to impress on these subordinates that they were in fact "under orders at all times." It was first obeyed and then relaxed.

The five or six years that Boston's priests spent at Brighton were the end of the beginning rather than the beginning of the end. Under O'Connell established public manifestations of clerical solidarity, including the Feast of Priesthood, a yearly reunion of all diocesan priests, and the *Anciens Elèves*, the seminary's alumni association, disappeared. Nonetheless, priests still congregated together both formally and informally; friendships made at the seminary were often lifelong. Such fraternity, together with the dispersed nature of the lives and work of the clergy, tended to qualify the imposition in the field of the military conventions observed in the shadow of headquarters. No newly ordained man lived alone. All of them learned to adopt an ethos from older clerics. A priest's first permanent assignment constituted his real introduction to clerical life.

Throughout this period two elements determined the place to which a new priest was sent. First, a parish had to need someone and its pastor be willing to accept an untried man. Then, the archbishop had to decide whether and, if so, how to match an opening with one of the ordinands available to him. There is no way of determining the procedures by which Williams made his appointments, but the documentation of O'Connell's personnel arrangements, while spot-

---

[47]*S&A*, 10:35.
[48]Memorandum, May 17, 1927, Seminary File, AABo 5:3.

A first Mass, 1922
(Photo AABo)

ty, suggests that he developed and tried to apply a clear method based on his evaluation of the components of the archdiocese. In 1915, for example, both parishes and candidates were divided into five groups. Parishes were ranked according to their size, location, or ethnic composition, and candidates in descending order according to their abilities or nationality. The four members of the first group of men—three of Irish descent and one Franco-American— were deemed "suitable for the most exacting places"; the best regarded man was sent to the Catholic University of America for graduate studies, the next two to large parishes in Boston, and the fourth to a town on the North Shore. Group two also had four members; judged to be "generally serviceable," though not as bright as those ranked above them, they went to parishes in four large towns within the ten-mile radius of Boston. The men in group three were consigned to four "places of medium importance," which ranged from working-class parishes in Boston and Lawrence to two in seacoast resorts; these priests were not "as vigorous or as talented" as those in the higher groups. Docile, sensible, agreeable "but not highly gifted intellectually," the two men in group four were dispatched respectively to a small parish within the ten-mile belt and to the same Boston parish found in group three. Finally, there were three "Canadians best suited for work in French parishes"; since only one place of this kind was then open, two men were sent to isolated rural parishes until they could be placed in their own group.[49]

Once assigned, a priest found himself serving a pastor who could embody virtually any human type—the exemplary, the dutiful, the eccentric, the tyrannical, and the antisocial. Nowhere were official attitudes less congruent with reality than in the insistence on the essentially impersonal nature of the priesthood. From William Henry O'Connell downward individuality marked the personalities of Boston's priests. By law assistants were subject to their pastors, who were bound to give them paternal instruction and direction in the care of souls, to watch over them, and to report annually to the ordinary on their conduct.[50] Practically, this canon meant that the sphere of activity and living conditions of a junior priest depended on the inclinations of his pastor. There were no

[49]"Report on Serviceability of Newly Ordained Priests, May 1915," *ibid.* 2:8.
[50]*Codex Iuris Canonici* [1917], canon 476, s.7.

350

fixed terms of assignment. Whatever their fate, curates seldom applied for quick reassignment. The needs of the archdiocese, the
satisfaction of a pastor, and the seniority and desires of an assistant
were the unequal factors that determined when a transfer was
granted. The approval or disapproval of the parishioners was irrelevant to the decision. The relative stability of Boston's priests testified
not only to their contentment but also to the difficulty of securing
relief from disagreeable or harsh situations. It owed something as
well to the hold on their minds of a traditional outlook that valued
duty more highly than self-fulfillment.

Any cleric who judged that his first responsibility was to his social   *351*
role rather than to his individual development shared this mentality.
An extreme case illustrated its tenacity. Having served as a temporary replacement for three months after his ordination in May
1936, one new priest found himself assigned to Monsignor John T.
Creagh, pastor of St. Aidan's, Brookline. The circumstances of
Creagh's life so baffled a psychiatrist that he preferred to leave their
description to the genius of a Dickens. After five-and-a-half years the
curate requested a transfer. He had served Creagh longer than any
assistant in the past.[51] About thirteen months earlier a priest ordained in 1922 had joined the staff. He quickly reached what he
imagined to be his breaking point and wrote a month after his junior
colleague asking to be removed. In doing so, he truthfully reported
that during twenty years of priesthood he had never complained,
even when he suffered "harsh and unfair treatment from the hands of
misguided pastors." Since he had always thought he was doing his
"duty to God and to [O'Connell] by accepting such crosses," he
regretted that in taking this step he now appeared to be "such a
baby." He felt that he had done his share but had qualms because his
departure would "put some other priest in my undesirable position."
He suggested that in the future no one should be sent there for more
than a year.[52] In the end the younger but longer-serving assistant
was reassigned, while his older colleague was kept at St. Aidan's for
another three-and-a-half years to manage as best he could.

The parish to which a newly ordained priest was assigned had a

[51]Kelly to Minihan, September 16, 1938, Parish Files, AABo 31:17; Gough to
Minihan, January 1, 1942, *ibid.* 99:1.
[52]Madden to O'Connell, February 19, 1942, *ibid.* 99:1.

specific identity throughout this period. It was a benefice. Creagh, the pastor who tried a succession of curates, was also a learned canonist and in 1907 provided an authoritative account of this legal concept. It was narrowly defined as "the right given permanently by the Church to receive ecclesiastical revenues on account of the performance of some spiritual service."[53] Its purpose was to support a priest and to ensure that a particular community received the sacraments and other ministrations it required. A legacy of medieval Frankish feudalism, it survived into the twentieth century in both the Catholic and Anglican churches. In Creagh's judgment only the bishoprics of the United States certainly met the legal standard, but he advanced the opinion that permanent rectorships—those whose incumbents enjoyed legal stability—might do so too.

352

The practice of the archdiocese of Boston was even more generous and impervious to changes in canon law. Until 1952 its entire fiscal organization was modeled on the benefice system. In the instrument certifying his canonical installation, every pastor was designated as the possessor of a parochial benefice. In addition to an annual salary that was set by statute at $600 in 1886 and remained unchanged into the 1920s, he owned all the free-will offerings of his parishioners except for those received from a few special collections for designated purposes. Such offerings constituted the greatest part of the parochial revenues, and from them a pastor had to meet the capital and operating expenses of his benefice, including the board and salaries of his assistants. Their pay was fixed at $500 to $600 a year in 1886 and standardized at $600 by the archdiocesan synod of 1919. From their salaries, sacramental stipends, and any bonuses their pastors chose to award them they were obliged to support themselves. The parish surplus was effectively a pastor's to dispose of or to retain as he saw fit. Some deposited the bulk of this revenue in accounts in the names of their parishes and used it to provide comprehensive educational and social services for the parishioners. At St. Columbkille's, Brighton, for example, the Reverend Joseph V. Tracy built a complex of buildings to house organizations and activities nearly as extensive as those of the Mission Church.

Other pastors chose to accelerate the upward social mobility of their families by means of subsidies or legacies. If parish priests en-

[53]*Catholic Encyclopedia*, s.v. "benefice."

joyed long tenures, they could accumulate large estates. Peter Crud-
den, pastor of St. Peter's, O'Connell's home parish in Lowell, for
thirty-eight years, left $500,000 to his sister on his death in 1885.
Although the cardinal's warnings against such conduct were
strenghtened by canon law after 1917, it was difficult either to define
the superfluous income of a beneficiary or to compel him to spend it
for charitable purposes.⁵⁴ Unlike monks and other religious priests,
seculars took no vow of poverty. In the end the consciences of
pastors governed their financial behavior.

The benefice system antedated O'Connell's accession, and it
would survive him. Throughout his reign he was a participant in it.
Because the cardinal served as titular pastor of St. Cecilia's in the
Back Bay section of Boston from 1911 to 1943 and enjoyed the per-
quisites of the cathedral rectorship for many years after 1908, he
possessed a secure income. It enable him both to meet his official
and personal expenses and to support numerous charities.⁵⁵
Although O'Connell left the archdiocese in a prosperous state on his
death, he never attempted to centralize archdiocesan finances even
on the limited scale achieved in Chicago by his near contemporary,
George Cardinal Mundelein.⁵⁶ Rudimentary central banking was
introduced in Boston only in the reign of Richard J. Cushing after
1944. Evidence survives that ordinary people in the pews accepted
this state of affairs. A housemaid from the Chestnut Hill section of
Newton once write to O'Connell requesting that he override her
pastor's decision to bar her and some of her friends from attending a
convenient daily Mass in the chapel of Boston College. Despite her
grievance, she admitted that "we are obliged to contribute to the support of our pastor and if it is a case of money we are willing to pay
any dues that our parish priest may think just."⁵⁷ Pastors for their
part insisted that accepting the obligation to donate was a note of
membership in the parish. As Creagh observed of a discontented

⁵⁴*Donahoe's Magazine*, 16 (1886): 185; Boston *Evening Transcript*, February 14,
1910; *Codex Iuris Canonici* [1917], canon 1473.
⁵⁵McGarry to Haberlin, November 18, 1922, Parish Files, AABo 7:11; Ryan to
Haberlin, October 20, 1923, *ibid.*; Phelan to Garrity, September 30, 1935, *ibid.*
7:21; Finigan to Haberlin, July 2, 1920, *ibid.* 1:15; Dacey to Minihan, December
29, 1934, *ibid.* 3:6.
⁵⁶See Kantowicz, *Corporation Sole*, 37.
⁵⁷McPartland to O'Connell, September 28, 1921, Parish Files, AABo 62:8.

parishioner in 1917, "She says something about her impressions of the Catholic Church, but among these I know that the duty of contributing to its support has no place."[58]

The security of beneficial rights guaranteed that pastors who were determined to assert themselves would enjoy considerable latitude. Richard Neagle, who ruled Immaculate Conception, Malden, from 1896 until 1943, was such a parish priest. He was legally irremovable and had been on the *terna* of candidates drawn up by the bishops of New England to nominate a coadjutor to Williams. Knowing that O'Connell had been omitted from the list, Neagle regularly behaved with the self-confidence of a man who was a law unto himself. On May 15, 1931, he informed the cardinal that he proposed to construct a parochial high school at a cost of $100,000. The next day the chancellor of the archdiocese, writing at O'Connell's direction, expressed surprise that no plans for the school had been received. He was irritated that the press had announced Neagle's intention before the cardinal had been consulted and puzzled about how the project was going to be financed, since the officially reported assets of the parish treasury amounted to only $6,061.49. Replying to the cardinal on May 20, Neagle voiced discomfiture that the plans had not reached the chancery and that the newspapers had disclosed his undertaking. Financing the new school raised no problem: "the cost . . . (about the surplus revenue of the coming year) will be met by a gift from a friend. The money is in my hands, to be used as needed." He received permission to proceed by return mail. The exchange had a postscript. On November 2, 1931, Neagle decided that he had overlooked a nicety and wrote to the cardinal: "I have asked the Xaverian Brothers to take charge of our Boys' High School next year. As they are already in the diocese I assumed your approval, but it is no harm to ask it formally."[59] He was correct in his assumption.

Unlike Neagle, most pastors were always careful to end their correspondence with the cardinal-archbishop by "kissing the sacred purple." There is a risk of exaggerating the import of such ornate formulas. The majority of priests used them routinely, out of respect

[margin: *354*]

[58]Creagh to O'Connell, November 26, 1917, *ibid.* 31:13.
[59]Neagle to O'Connell, May 15, 1931; Burke to Neagle, May 16, 1931; Neagle to O'Connell, May 20, 1931; Burke to Neagle, May 22, 1931; Neagle to O'Connell, November 2, 1931, all *ibid.* 56:24.

for their ecclesiastical superior. Some invested the formulas with real feeling for either the office or the man who held it. A few saw themselves as personally dependent on that man. One of these dependents wrote in 1915 to thank the cardinal for an appointment and to renew his allegiance: "In taking up my new work I shall endeavor so to act as to carry out at all times what will be your wish and desire. I have no other purpose in life save to please and to serve you in the highest manner possible."[60] Although the implications of the pledge of obedience to his diocesan which this priest, like every other, had taken at ordination were fuzzy, its purpose was to ensure that he fulfilled his duties as a minister of the church by remaining subject to his proper superior. He was meant to be neither autonomous nor servile.

355

Servility to the person of the archbishop was as infrequent among Boston's priests as disdain of it. Most pastors and curates worked correctly with their ordinary. John T. Mullen, the parish priest of St. Michael's, Hudson, from his discharge as rector of the cathedral in late 1907 until his death in June 1928, was not among them. His endurance testifies to the limitations of the canonical process for deposing a pastor. It was so cumbersome as to be virtually impracticable. Mullen was an implacable and well-known foe of O'Connell, who often complained about him and once accused him of assault. Despite their mutual animosity, Mullen kept his remote benefice. The cardinal was reduced to gestures of frustration. In life he transferred Mullen's curates against his will and created a French national parish within his territory; afterward he ordered that a sermon on the evil of priestly disobedience supplant the customary eulogy at Mullen's Requiem. His clerical friends printed a memorial card that included a catena of scriptural verses. First among them was 2 Timothy 4:7: "I have fought a good fight. I have finished my course."[61]

The early 1920s were dangerous years for the cardinal. Monsignor James P. E. O'Connell, his nephew and chancellor, was one

[60]Splaine to O'Connell, March 1, 1915, Priests' Correspondence Files, AABo.
[61]O'Connell to "Excellency" [Fumasoni-Biondi], draft of September 11, 1923, *ibid.*, John T. Mullen. William Wolkovich-Valkavičius, "Cardinal and Cleric: O'Connell and Mullen in Conflict," *Historical Journal of Massachusetts*, 13 (1985): 129-139; the memorial card is in AABo.

of only a handful of priests of the archdiocese who abandoned orders between 1875 and 1944. Most of them became nonpersons, but the scandalous circumstances surrounding his departure set off reverberations long after November 1920. The actual extent of these troubles is as yet impossible to determine, but real and suspected enemies seemed to multiply on every side.[62] Clerical informers thrived in this atmosphere and filled the cardinal's ears with alarms of plots. Early in 1923 one of them set at the energetic Father Tracy of Brighton, who was a veteran of late nineteenth-century liberal Catholicism. He was accused of having both elevated the parish so "as to minimize the importance and authority of the diocese and the bishop" and abetted "Sulpician intrigue"—a code phrase for supporting the cardinal's enemies. When O'Connell confronted Tracy with the accusations, he responded with dignity. Far from denying his Sulpician friendships, Tracy acknowledged them as "part and parcel of whatever good there may be in me" and repudiated charges that there was something "conniving, mean, [or] disloyal about them." "Death and I," he concluded, "are not at most far apart, for which reason I am all the more anxious to see these things and all others as they are in the sight of God, not blinking the poor and unprofitable servant of His I know myself to be." It is difficult to believe that priests of Tracy's character were fit subjects of the "thought control" that Merwick has imagined to have fettered the archdiocese of Boston by 1911.[63]

356

O'Connell was not convinced by the apologia, but he knew that he had to live with Tracy and proceeded carefully. Shortly after this episode he encouraged the Passionist order to enlarge their chapel in Brighton in order to accommodate other worshipers. When Tracy protested to the apostolic delegate in Washington, the cardinal was moved to explain his action. Although he judged Tracy to be morbidly preoccupied with the idea that the monks were "going to infringe on his infallible rights as Parish Priest" by luring away parishioners, he made no effort to designate the chapel as a

---

[62]John Tracy Ellis, *Catholic Bishops: A Memoir* (Wilmington, Del.: Michael Glazier, 1983), 73.

[63]Robert D. Cross, *The Emergence of Liberal Catholicism in America* (Cambridge, Mass.: Harvard University Press, 1958), 73, 138-139; Tracy to O'Connell, February 25, 1923, Parish Files, AABo 10:12; Merwick, *Boston Priests*, 192.

separate parish until 1934.[64] Moreover, within three years of this action he arranged for Tracy to be named a monsignor by the Holy See.

The cardinal was a skillful tactician whose conduct toward his pastors defies facile characterization. He aimed to create a strong government, but he appreciated the value of accommodation as well as of confrontation. At the beginning of his reign he had relied on both in an effort to secure the compliance of John O'Brien, pastor of Sacred Heart, East Cambridge, and editor of the *Sacred Heart Review*. The results were dizzying. On the one hand he established two parishes at the expense of Sacred Heart in 1908. On the other hand he made O'Brien a diocesan consultor, one of his official group of advisers, in that year and successfully petitioned the pope to appoint him a domestic prelate in 1909.[65] Termination of the *Review*, an independently controlled journal, was presumably among O'Connell's goals, but it eluded him until 1918, the year after O'Brien's death. As with Mullen, he was able to prevail over a trying subordinate only by outliving him. The cardinal's longevity served him well.

357

From 1897 the civil law of Massachusetts has recognized the archbishop of Boston as a corporation sole, a perpetual moral personality owning the mass of the church's real property. Since the bulk of it was not income-producing, the statute had little effect on the financial relations of pastors with their ordinary. Funding of the central operations of the archdiocese depended on the *cathedraticum*, an annual tax of 2 to 3.12 percent on the total "seat offerings" of every parish, gifts, and a regularly scheduled series of collections. Because pastors were their own unaudited accountants and sometimes quibbled over assessments, the archbishop of Boston needed their cooperation in order to meet the expenses of the see.[66] Although this arrangement had served to keep a greater measure of harmony between the ordinary and his pastors than had obtained elsewhere in the church in America during the nineteenth century, it seems to have been a source of regular frustration to O'Connell.[67] From time

[64]O'Connell to Tracy, February 27, 1923, Parish Files, AABo 10:12; O'Connell to Fumasoni-Biondi, April 23, 1925, *ibid.* 10:21.

[65]O'Connell to Curtin, October 27, 1926, *ibid.* 62:9; J.P.E. O'Connell to Tampieri, March 13, 1913, Chancery Central Subject File M-1693, *ibid.*

[66]Neagle to Burke, March 21, 1928, Parish Files, *ibid.* 56:23.

[67]See Robert Trisco, "Bishops and Their Priests in the United States," in *The Catholic Priest in the United States: Historical Investigations*, ed. John Tracy Ellis (Collegeville, Minn.: Saint John's University Press, 1971), 126-150, 194-273.

to time his frustration expressed itself in impatient actions directed against individual parish priests.[68] Their hold on the revenues of their benefices was both a personal affront to the cardinal and a tenacious check on the achievement of his aspiration to consolidate and expand the operations of the archdiocese. The failure of its educational and charitable services to fulfill his ambitious projections for them owed much to the persistence of local control over most church funds. O'Connell was sometimes able to single out amenable donors among pastors, but even they could haggle with him.[68] In the end such donations were not an adequate substitute for some form of central regulation of finances.

The economic aspects of the institutional history of the archdiocese of Boston are less murky than those of most other churches and denominations in America. It is clear that Cardinal O'Connell had—or chose—to content himself with partial measures. He succeeded, for example, in imposing a series of detailed checks on the capital expenditures of pastors of a kind unknown in Williams's time. In a few instances they had the formalistic quality of an elaborate etiquette. Throughout 1928 letters passed back and forth between the pastor of St. Ambrose's, Dorchester, and the chancery. Responding to an allegedly popular desire "to have a new rectory here," he submitted plans for a $70,300 building. He was told that "a less extensive house would be more serviceable." In the end, the pastor effected a savings of $3,000 by directing his architect to chop one foot off each side of the building. He submitted the revised plans, which were approved.[70] Legislating was easier than attaining effective enforcement.

The most important and sought after benefices were the larger urban parishes within Boston and its adjacent communities. As auxiliary bishop to O'Connell, Francis J. Spellman was angry at having been made pastor of Sacred Heart parish in suburban Newton Centre in 1933. He felt that his episcopal dignity would have been better served by appointment to another church of that name located in the

358

[68]Mitchell to O'Connell, August 4, 1919, and Haberlin to Mitchell, August 9, 1919, Parish Files, AABo 45:1; Higgins to Haberlin, October 1, 1917, Wills Correspondence Files, *ibid.*

[69]Mark Sullivan, memorandum of April 16, 1931, Parish Files, *ibid.* 19:13.

[70]Correspondence between Harrigan and Burke, January 4, 10, 14, 1928; April 10, 21, 23, 27, 30, 1928; November 16, 1929, *ibid.* 11:25.

crowded Roslindale neighborhood of Boston.[71] A high volume of small contributions gave such parishes their luster. Since the work load in densely populated units was naturally heavier than that in smaller suburban or rural parishes, the expectation of a proportionately greater reward was understandable.

The tracking system which governed the assignment of the newly ordained during the O'Connell years may have had its origin in the traditional conception of the relative importance of different kinds of pastorates. After a series of curacies a priest could aspire to be named a pastor, most often of a small or outlying parish. If he was ambitious, he might aim to receive a large urban parish as his benefice sometime later.[72] The experience of a sample of 344 priests ordained in the period from 1875 through 1944 suggests that the interval between ordination and promotion to a first pastorate lengthened over the years. Since the demand for Francophone priests consistently outstripped their supply, they came to enjoy a clear advantage over the Irish-Americans who staffed ordinary territorial parishes. In the late nineteenth century seniority seems to have been a subordinate element in making appointments. Of those in the sample ordained in 1881, for example, one was made a pastor after only thirteen years of service, while a classmate had to wait for twenty-three years. Under O'Connell's regime seniority came to play a decisive role. None of the members of the sample ordained in 1920 was given a pastorate before his twentieth year in the priesthood; 83 percent of them had to wait for twenty-five years or more. Because the number of diocesan priests steadily increased, their average life expectancy lengthened, and the custom of identifying the viability of a parish with relative populousness endured, extension of the length of service in the ranks of assistants was inevitable.

Church law recommended that ordinaries use examinations and other objective methods to help determine which candidate for a vacant pastorate was the most qualified. In practice the diocesans of the United States effectively controlled all appointments and after 1931 could disregard the examination procedure. The control of preferment gave O'Connell an instrument for maintaining the

359

---

[71]Spellman to O'Connell, April 6, 1933, Spellman File, *ibid.*

[72]MacCormack to O'Connell, September 15, 1916, Priests' Correspondence Files, *ibid.*

cooperation of his priests. It served as a lever rather than a club, and his mastery of it was not complete. The variables of mortality and temperament determined its usefulness. A monopoly on appointments did not offer the cardinal the opportunity to achieve the maxiumum of unity and efficiency, much less quick and universl compliance. His increasing reliance on seniority as the basic criterion for creating parish priests implies that he enjoyed less discretion than had Williams. O'Connell could not have foreseen this consequence when he decided early in his regime to swell the number of diocesan clergy.

360 It is easier to discuss the social origins, beliefs, recruitment, training, assignment, and finances of Boston's priests than to describe their ministry, the most enduring part of their social history. Their spiritual and charitable labors, along with those of the religious, helped to realize Christianity for hundreds of thousands of people. Much of their work was private and hidden; it usually went unrecorded. These priests were not diarists, or they have been badly served by their heirs in the task of preservation. The richest available diary was kept by James Anthony Walsh for twelve months during 1898 and 1899, midway through his eleven-year-long first assignment to St. Patrick's, Roxbury. Walsh's young adulthood was less unusual than his origins or maturity. Born into an affluent family of Irish immigrants, he had briefly been an undergraduate at Harvard before entering St. John's Seminary and in 1911 began a distinguished career as the first superior-general of the Maryknoll missionary society. Yet nothing Walsh recorded while he was a curate in Roxbury seems extraordinary. His experiences there were probably representative of the labors of the dutiful priests who staffed the large urban parishes of the archdiocese between 1875 and 1944.

Walsh worked in a homogeneous environment in which people he knew personally took for granted both his authority as a priest and his responsiveness to their needs at their convenience. His ministry suggests the poverty of the attempt to explain face-to-face relations as specimens of one-sided social control. Although he shared a rectory with three or four colleagues, he seems to have lived in isolation from them. Only one is mentioned, and he because of an illness which required that his tasks be divided among the others. Walsh's private life centered around his own family—he faithfully spent his weekly night off at home—and a small group of clerical and lay friends. The laypeople were members of his own social class who resided outside of Roxbury. His work was seasonal, intense between early September and mid-June and leisurely during the summer.[73]

The sacrament of penance was central to Walsh's ministry, particularly during the seasons of Christmas and Easter and the annual parish mission. He was a counter and recorded that between November 1 and December 31 of 1898 alone he had heard 1,728 confessions, an average of over 28 a day. He sometimes spent continuous spells of up to five hours in the confessional. This sacrament was still integrally connected with the reception of the Eucharist, which was widespread but not yet as frequent as it would become during the twentieth century. St. Patrick's was the preserve of neither juveniles nor women, but Walsh was attentive to signs of adult male piety. He noted with pleasure on April 9, 1899, that 128 men had come to him as penitents that evening.[74]

The nonsacramental life of the parish revolved around a few large organizations whose gatherings drew crowds numbering in the hundreds. Sensitive to rising competition from secular entertainments, Walsh took pains to ensure a full house for the meetings of the groups for which he was responsible. He was also diligent in writing talks for such occasions, as that on "Immortality and How to Meet Death," which he delivered before 340 members of the ladies' sodality on February 28, 1899. His ordinary Sunday sermons lasted between ten and twenty-five minutes, and he was satisfied if he had two or three hours in which to prepare them. Pastoral work frequently entailed responsbilities that would later be assumed by social service agencies. Home visits to the sick sometimes required him to arrange for their hospitalization. He regularly had numerous callers, usually in the evening; some of them were touched by alcoholism, still more by poverty. Religious doubts do not seem to have troubled his parishioners. A passing reference to Robert Ingersoll, the stock freethinker of the age, suggests that Walsh was aware of unbelief merely as a set of arguments that demanded refutation, not as a human reality. In contrast, he was sensitive to the plight of a young Irish immigrant who was trying to liberate himself from what

361

[73]Diary of James A. Walsh, AABo: entries of February 16 and March 6, 1899; April 4 and November 12, 1899; February 11, 1899; January 4 and June 21, 1899; May 27, 1899; July 3, 1899.
[74]*Ibid.*: entries of December 31, 1898; December 16, 1898; April 9, 1899.

he saw as inherited superstition. It is difficult to reconstruct Walsh's average workday because he was constantly available when he was in the rectory and seldom the master of his own time. There were occasionally knocks on the door—the telephone was not yet generally used—rousing him from bed. He rushed out to attend someone who was near death around midnight, just as he assured a visitor at 5:30 A.M. that he would pray for her intention. Like those who summoned him, this priest saw it as his primary office to mediate the holy for the benefit of others.[75]

362   The changes that affected the archdiocese of Boston and its priests between 1875 and 1944 were not insubstantial. Walsh once wrote with pity of a Canadian prelate that he had been "tied to Ecclesiasticism from the age of four."[76] William Henry O'Connell never sought to create so encompassing a system. He succeeded, however, in exercising greater control over the public activities of his priests than his predecessors had sought. Once his rule was established it would have been impossible for Neagle to join the other clergymen of Malden in openly endorsing a candidate for the governor's council, as he had shortly before the death of Archbishop Williams. It would likewise have been unthinkable for Walsh to take the initiative and write a long letter to the *Evening Transcript* protesting the decision to bar a confrere from visiting patients in a public sanatorium, as he did in July 1899.[77] Although priests were unable to cooperate with Protestant ministers in civic causes or to express their opinions freely in print, they could still outspokenly address issues of the day from their pulpits.[78] As the names of a number of streets, highways, and squares in Boston and other towns testify, the influence of many pastors proved to be tenacious. Cardinal O'Connell's adhesion to the ecclesiastial policy of Pope Pius X long after Rome had modified it reinforced the position of his subordinates within their own parishes. In 1944 the organization of

[75]*Ibid.*: entries of April 18 and September 18, 1899; February 28, 1899; April 10, 1899, and December 24, 1898; December 12, 1898, and January 19, 1899; January 22 and April 11, 1899; March 9, 1899; January 2, 1899 (overleaf); January 17 and April 2, 1899.

[76]*Ibid.*: entry of February 6, 1899.

[77]Handbill dated [August ?] 23, 1907, Parish Files, *ibid.* 56:21; Diary of James A. Walsh, *ibid.*, July 12-15, 1899.

[78]St. Thomas Aquinas's parish, Jamaica Plain, pulpit announcement books, 1927–1935, *ibid.*, entry of August 27, 1933.

the church of Boston remained more decentralized than that of other major archdioceses. In Boston more than elsewhere the church was enduringly the concern of its priests.

Only in the 1960s would pervasive change begin to affect the Catholic community of Boston. The condition of its members changed. With suitable caution Stephan Thernstrom allowed more than a decade ago that Catholics born after 1930 may be experiencing "a distinct departure from the historic pattern manifested by previous generations of Catholic residents in the city." For the first time they seemed to be enjoying widespread upward social mobility and freedom from occupational slippage.[79] This development fostered a change in their perception of their own identity. The Catholics of Boston grasped the victory of John F. Kennedy in the presidential election of 1960 as a talisman of acceptance. Their sense of being a people set apart and viewed with suspicion by others had a painful basis in their history. It sustained the posture of tight defensiveness that was fundamental to O'Connell's ecclesiastical policies. Before 1960 this community had known many successes. Thereafter it started to relax in an environment in which it formed the majority. At the same time the changes in the worship and ethos of Catholicism that followed the Second Vatican Council hit a local church that had scarcely anticipated them. The tasks of understanding the present-day conjunction of social, cultural, and religious innovations and of weighing their consequences belong to the future. To contemporaries these deep transformations offer a standard by which to judge the relative influence of continuity and change in the past.

363

---

[79]Thernstrom, *Other Bostonians*, 157-158.

The Jesuits and Joe McCarthy

Donald F. Crosby, S.J.

The Jesuits frequently attract public attention, and one such occasion for notoriety occurred in the days of the Communist hunt commonly associated with the name of the junior Senator from Wisconsin, Joseph Raymond McCarthy (1908-1957). During the years from 1950 to 1957 there were repeated attempts to link McCarthy with the Jesuits, (or, paradoxically, to link him with the Senator's opponents). The national Jesuit weekly *America* became embroiled in one of the most bitter arguments which broke out in the controversy. The events illustrate not only the intensely divisive nature of the dispute over McCarthy, but the peculiar position of the order both in the Church and in the intellectual life of the nation as well.

The Jesuits and McCarthy first met at Marquette University in Milwaukee, Wisconsin. Following a strict Catholic upbringing in northern Wisconsin, young McCarthy entered the Jesuit university in the fall of 1930, registering in the engineering college. Changing later to law, he carved a wide path through Marquette, making a name for himself as a "big man on campus." The Jesuit Fathers at Marquette with memories of McCarthy describe him as fun-loving, possessed of a winning personality, faithful to his religious duties, and always deferential toward the clergy. They also remember that he was beginning to develop an "Irish wit" that tempered his personality.[1] His stay in the law school was neither distinguished nor poor, and he graduated on schedule in 1935, soon gaining admission to the Wisconsin bar.

Viewed in retrospect, his Marquette experience appears to be less an exercise in formation at the hands of the Jesuits than simply a stop on the way up the ladder to political success. Marquette University gave him the legal background he needed to advance in politics, but he does not seem to have undergone any kind of transformation as a result of his years there. As a student in the law school, he certainly would have learned the Church's position on Communism, but it seems to have made little impression on him. In sum, the Marquette Jesuits seem to have had little impact on either McCarthy's character, or his system of values.

1. Interviews with Rev. James Orford, S.J., November 15, 1971; Rev. Robert Sampon, November 17, 1971; Rev. Raphael Hamilton, S.J., November 16, 1971; Rev. Perry Roetz, S.J., November 13, 1971.

Mr. Crosby is assistant professor of history in the University of Santa Clara, Santa Clara, California.

McCarthy and the sons of Loyola would have little to do with each other for the next fifteen years, as he began his turbulent career. He started as an up-country lawyer, soon afterwards becoming an energetic (and highly controversial) judge, and when World War II broke out, he joined the Marines and fought in the South Pacific. The War over, he won election to the Senate in 1946, becoming the junior Senator from Wisconsin.

What happened next has become a standard chapter in the McCarthy legend, and since it involves the Jesuits, is of great interest here. The story goes that following a completely unremarkable three years in the Senate, McCarthy found himself in 1950 desperately in need of a winning issue. At precisely the right moment, Edmund Walsh, a Jesuit *365* priest from Georgetown University, intervened and convinced him that the Communists-in-government issue was the one for him. The conventional wisdom has it that on January 7, 1950, McCarthy met for dinner with Walsh and two others. When he told his dinner companions that he needed an "issue" to win re-election in 1952, Walsh told him to try the Communists-in-government topic, since it was a guaranteed political platform. McCarthy jumped at the idea, and he was off immediately on his famous Communist hunt. The story began with Drew Pearson's newspaper column and received embellishment from Jack Anderson and Ronald May in their popular biography of the Senator. It has since become a permanent fixture of the McCarthy legend, enduring to the present.[2]

The incident has an apparent plausibility. It made sense, after all, to say that a Jesuit priest had started McCarthy on his career as the paradigmatic anti-Communist because the Jesuits had educated him at Marquette, and Catholic priests were known to have a special argument with Communism. Unfortunately, the story's foundations are extremely shaky. First, Walsh bitterly denied having given McCarthy any ideas at all about Communism, and even challenged Pearson to prove his claim. Unfortunately, Walsh failed to make his objections public, probably because he wanted to avoid "getting into the gutter" with Pearson. Second, it was entirely out of character for Walsh to engage in public polemics about domestic Communism, since his political interests centered exclusively on the issue of international Communism. Third, neither Pearson, Anderson and May, nor anyone else has produced documentary evident to support the story. (The Walsh papers are silent

---

2. Pearson column in *Washington Post*, March 14, 1950; Jack Anderson and Ronald May, *McCarthy, the Man, the Senator, the Ism* (Boston, 1953), pp. 172-173; Richard Rovere, *Senator Joe McCarthy* (New York, 1959), pp. 122-123; Eric Goldman, *The Crucial Decade* (New York, 1959), pp. 139-140; Fred Cook, *The Nightmare Decade* (New York, 1971), pp. 139-141; David Halberstam, *The Best and the Brightest* (New York, 1972), pp. 117-118.

on the matter.) Fourth, McCarthy actually began using the subversion issue some two months *before* the Colony dinner.[3]

Since all of the participants in the event are either dead or unavailable for comment, it is impossible to acquire firsthand information about it. It is obvious, however, that the tale is extremely suspect, and future historians would do well to consign it the oblivion it has long deserved.

With or without the help of Edmund Walsh, Joseph Raymond McCarthy was soon off and running. On February 9, 1950, he told the Republican Women's Club of Wheeling, West Virginia, "I have here in my hand a list of 205—a list of names that were made known to the Secretary of State as being members of the Communist party and who nevertheless are still working and shaping policy in the State Department." A whirlwind of publicity greeted this pronouncement, beginning a flurry of headlines that would last for almost five years. The debates and oral violence that surrounded McCarthy have received abundant documentation, as has the divisive nature of its impact on the American Catholic community.[4] What about the Jesuits and McCarthy? Few of them chose to speak openly about America's newest and most sensational Communist-hunter, though the national Jesuit weekly *America* ventured an occasional mild criticism of the Senator's early forays. It concluded that McCarthy's charges of Communists in the State Department were "pretty irresponsible," yet the "ruinous collapse" of the nation's China policy more than warranted a careful investigation of the agency.[5] McCarthy himself, however, did not warrant a careful investigation, at least in the view of *America*. In the two years that followed, years marked by some of the most intense political warfare in American history, the magazine stood mostly aloof, occasionally criticizing McCarthy's sallies against Democrats and liberals, but more often avoiding the issue.[6]

366

3. Walsh's Jesuit confidants who insist that he denied Pearson's claim were: Rev. Louis Gallagher (letter of October 19, 1971, to author); Rev. Daniel Power (interviewed February 4, 1972); Rev. Brian McGrath (interviewed Feb. 8, 1972); Walsh Papers, Georgetown University; on McCarthy's earlier use of the subversion issue, see Michael O'Brien, "Senator Joseph McCarthy and Wisconsin," (Ph.D. diss., University of Wisconsin, 1971), p. 97.
4. For an exhaustive study of the speech, see Robert Griffith, *The Politics of Fear* (Lexington, Ky., 1970), pp. 48-51; Michael P. Rogin, *The Intellectuals and McCarthy: The Radical Specter* (Cambridge, Mass., 1967), pp. 238-39; David Oshinsky, "Senator Joseph McCarthy and the American Labor Movement," (Ph.D. diss., Brandeis University, 1971), pp. 253-257, 263; Donald F. Crosby, "The Angry Catholics: American Catholics and Senator Joseph R. McCarthy, 1950-1957," (Ph.D. diss., Brandeis University, 1973).
5. "Senator McCarthy's Charges," *America*, April 1, 1950, p. 737. See also, " . . . and the Search for Truth," *America*, April 1, 1950, p. 737; ". . . And the Power to Investigate," *America*, April 8, 1950, p. 3; "Is the Red Peril a Distraction?" *America*, May 27, 1950, p. 235.
6. See, for instance, "The Battle of the Files," *America*, April 22, 1950, pp. 78-79; "Communists in Washington," *America*, July 21, 1951, p. 391; "Wedemyer Versus McCarthy," *America*, June 30, 1951, p. 323; "Benton-McCarthy Showdown?" *America*, March 22, 1952, p. 660.

America's definitive break with the junior Senator did not come until
the Presidential campaign of 1952. What prompted *America's* sudden
move was McCarthy's violent attack of October 27, 1952, against the
Democratic candidate for President, Adlai Stevenson. Speaking before a
nationwide television audience, McCarthy insinuated that Stevenson had
betrayed his country, just as Alger Hiss had done some years before. To
the delight of his partisan listeners, McCarthy referred slyly to "Alger, I
mean Adlai, Stevenson." McCarthy's slippery tactic naturally angered
Democrats and liberals everywhere, but none more so than the
liberally-minded editor of *America*, Father Robert Hartnett. Long an
admirer of the Democratic party's social reform programs, Hartnett had
supported both the Truman Administration's Fair Deal legislation and
Stevenson's bid for the White House. An ardent Stevensonite with a
high-minded view of political ethics, Hartnett bristled at McCarthy's
abrasive slur. Hartnett became especially incensed when McCarthy
waved a photostatic copy of the Communist *Daily Worker* before his
audience, saying that the *Worker* had endorsed Stevenson's candidacy for
the Presidency. After a delay of several weeks during which he painstak-
ingly gathered together the copies of the *Worker* that he needed,
Hartnett published a broadside against McCarthy. With his copy of the
Worker for October 19 lying before him, Hartnett wrote, "Now this
writer holds in his hands, not a photostat but the actual complete copy of
the *Daily Worker* for October 19. It says just the opposite of what
McCarthy claimed it says . . . Governor Stevenson is not even mentioned
in this editorial." McCarthy's "cheap stunt" with the *Worker* was a good
example of "what are euphemistically called McCarthy's 'methods,' "
wrote Hartnett. Nothing could have been less convincing than McCarthy's photostats, because he made off with them immediately after the
address, in spite of "ostentatiously promising" during the speech to let
the reporters examine them as soon as he had finished speaking.[7]

McCarthy quickly replied to Hartnett's attack. In a long letter to the
editor, he accused Hartnett of carrying a "completely and viciously false"
article about his Chicago speech. The *Worker* editorial did indeed urge its
readers to vote for Stevenson, McCarthy said, and it was simply not true
that he had vanished with the documents after completing the speech.
The burden of McCarthy's letter was not what he had said in the
address, however, but how he felt about the Jesuits at *America*. Wrote the
Senator:

> I realize that your magazine has been extremely critical of my fight to
> expose Communists in government. Obviously that is your right. I am sure
> you will agree with me, however, that while you may owe no duty to me to
> correct the vicious smear job which you attempted to do on me, you do owe a

7. Robert Hartnett, "Pattern of GOP Victory," *America*, November 22, 1952, p. 209. For
McCarthy speech, see *New York Times*, October 28, 1954, pp. 1, 26, 30.

heavy duty to the vast number of good Catholic people who assume that at least in a Jesuit operated magazine they can read the truth.

Being an ardent Catholic myself, brought up with a great respect for the Priesthood, which I still hold, it is inconceivable to me that a Catholic Priest could indulge in such vicious falsehoods in order to discredit my fight to expose the greatest enemy of not only the Catholic Church, but our entire civilization.

If you do not see fit to correct the falsehoods in this article, then it would seem that common decency would demand that you publish not only the letter but also the Daily Worker editorial to which I referred at Chicago so that your readers may determine the truth.[8]

McCarthy's riposte failed to impress Hartnett. He immediately published McCarthy's long letter, as well as the disputed article from the *Worker*. Once again he plowed through the pages of the *Worker*, attempting to see if McCarthy's interpretation of it had any validity at all. He found, first of all, that McCarthy had confused different editions of the *Worker* for October 19, and in doing so had mixed up an editorial on Stevenson with an article on the same man. Far more serious, however, was Hartnett's pained discovery that the *Worker* for that date had positively disavowed Stevenson's candidacy, saying that he was as unacceptable a nominee for President as was Dwight Eisenhower. Lest McCarthy fail to get the point, the *Worker* on October 29 attacked him for saying that it had ever approved of a "slick warmonger like Stevenson." Hartnett concluded that the McCarthy version of what the *Daily Worker* had said was a "badly garbled and distorted account" of what really appeared in the newspaper.[9]

In the weeks that followed, Hartnett continued to attack McCarthy, calling his Stevenson address a "tissue of innuendoes."[10] McCarthy responded by reasserting his earlier claim that he was "an ardent Catholic" whose "very religious mother" had implanted in him "a deep and abiding respect for the priesthood." What could he say, now that those very Jesuits whose "religious zeal, high intelligence and complete integrity" he had come to know at Marquette University, were actually obstructing the fight against "atheistic Communism?"[11]

Unhappy with Hartnett's continued recalcitrance, McCarthy wrote to Hartnett's Jesuit superior in New York City, Father John McMahon. McMahon answered McCarthy politely, saying only that he had read the Senator's letter "with interest."[12] The McCarthy-McMahon correspon-

8. McCarthy to Hartnett, in *America*, December 13, 1952, p. 316.
9. Robert Hartnett, "Daily Worker on Stevenson," *America*, December 13, 1952, pp. 302-303.
10. Hartnett, "Documents and Innuendoes," *America*, December 20, 1952, pp. 327-328. See also, "Detecting Subversives," *America*, January 3, 1953, p. 370.
11. McCarthy to Hartnett, January 6, 1953. Stencilled copy in "McCarthy" file, Patrick McCarran Papers, College of the Holy Names (Oakland, California).
12. Ray Kiermas [for McCarthy] to John McMahon, January 13, 1953, in "America" file, Jesuit Archives, Fordham University (hereafter cited as JAFU). John McMahon to McCarthy, January 15, 1953, JAFU.

dence is important because it marked the first of a long list of attempts by persons outside the order to force Jesuit superiors to bring pressure on Hartnett. Meanwhile, public reaction to *America's* bout with McCarthy ran clearly in its favor, as the mail and the national press seemed to show.[13]

For Hartnett, the first debate had been a strictly political affair. He had paid no attention at all to McCarthy's repeated and insistent attempts to bring Catholicism into the argument. Looking at the Senator in exclusively political terms, he used the standard Democratic (and liberal) arguments against McCarthy: the Senator had misused his evidence, had imputed statements to the opposition that it had never made, had hinted falsely at insidious connections between liberals and Communists, and had defamed the reputations of honorable men. At the same time, however, Hartnett's personality and background gave a peculiar cast to the liberal thesis he was developing. He had researched the documents of the case with a dogged thoroughness that few editors would have shown, and he pursued McCarthy's false statements and innuendoes with immense rigor, checking even the most minute details. He would prove to be a stubborn and relentless foe of McCarthyism.

In the two years that followed, Hartnett further expanded his argument against McCarthy. He was convinced, first of all, that the problem of domestic Communism was largely a thing of the past, since previous investigations had routed most of the Communists out of the government. Hartnett believed himself exceptionally well informed on this subject, since he had highly-placed friends in Washington. Senator McCarthy, he concluded, was raising a false issue simply to gain publicity and to make a political career for himself. But the McCarthy investigations were not only unnecessary, they were truly harmful as well because they destroyed the democratic processes that Hartnett, as a civil libertarian and a scholar of political science, believed essential to the life of the nation. Thus the casualties in McCarthy's campaign were not the Communists, but rather "our historic procedures of 'due process of law,' our standards of honesty in the discussion of grave political issues," and "respect for public and professional authority."[14] Finally, like the *Commonweal* (as well as the many Catholic Democrats who opposed McCarthy), Hartnett grieved that McCarthy had distracted the public from the all-important social issues, from such problems as unemployment, education, health, and housing.[15]

13. Hartnett to John McMahon, October 28, 1952, "America" File, JAFU; *America*, January 10, 1953, p. 412; *Washington Post*, January 4, 1953.
14. Robert Hartnett, "Congress, Communists and the Common Good," *America*, March 27, 1954, p. 678; see also, "The Image and Echo of the Multitude," *America*, December 19, 1953, p. 311; "Campus Commies," *America*, February 14, 1953, p. 530; "'Fifth Amendment' College Teachers... Who Is to Judge?" *America*, January 2, 1954, p. 349.
15. Interview with Robert Hartnett, September 9, 1971.

For Hartnett, as for most Catholic editors of the postwar years, the burning question was the position of the Catholic citizen in American society. How did the American Catholic carve a place for himself in American life that was at once fully American and truly Catholic? For conservative Catholics such as Patrick Scanlan, the right wing editor of the *Brooklyn Tablet*, the answer lay in a return to red-blooded American patriotism, in hewing to a love of country so passionate that none could question it. For Hartnett, the answer was much more complex. Patriotism was good, yes, but what happened to the image of Catholicism when the patriotism it preached became strident, intolerant, conformist? Patriotism made no sense if it violated the "common good," that is, the welfare of all the nation's citizens. Patriotism became a menace if it drowned out the quiet, scholarly investigation of political questions that Hartnett like to conduct in the pages of *America*. Did the American Catholic find his place in American society by supporting the search for subversives in the government? Of course he did, but the Church had a long tradition of teachings both on the problem of Communism and on the nature of the political order as well: the Catholic anti-Communist ought to make this tradition part and parcel of his own thought, Hartnett believed.[16] For Hartnett, therefore, McCarthyism represented the essence of all that was wrong with American Catholicism.

The Eisenhower landslide of 1952 swept the Republican party into the White House and both houses of Congress, carrying Joseph McCarthy of Wisconsin with it. The victorious Republicans, anxious to press the charge of "softness on Communism" against the opposition party, gave McCarthy the chairmanship of the Permanent Subcommittee on Investigations, an arm of the Senate Committee on Government Appropriations. Armed with a mandate to smoke out Communists hidden in the federal government, McCarthy pressed his investigations into the Voice of America, the federal government's overseas information programs, and other federal agencies.[17] Though the targets were new, the arguments for and against McCarthy were not: to liberals like Hartnett, McCarthy's "methods" of investigation represented an intolerable assault on civil liberties, while to conservatives like Pat Scanlan he stood out as the only man in the government who was "doing something" about Communism.

McCarthy's quest for Communist spies reached a sensational climax in the first half of 1954, when he attacked the United States Army, accusing it of "coddling Communists" in its ranks. In several editorials discussing the McCarthy committee's work (popularly known as the "TV hearings"), *America* advanced a "constitutional" case against McCarthy, rebuking him for his assault on the rights of the President, his "insulting"

16. Hartnett interview.
17. Griffith, *The Politics of Fear*, pp. 212-220.

handling of witnesses, and his cavalier disregard for civil liberties.[18] Those were Hartnett's public worries over McCarthyism. In private he told his superiors that McCarthy had become a "national liability," since he distracted national attention from the real problems the country faced. To his friend Wilfred Parsons (*America's* Washington correspondent), he confided his growing concern over Catholic acceptance of McCarthy.[19]

In late March and April of 1954, *America* softened its McCarthy line slightly. It went out of its way to praise the "wholly admirable" instincts of McCarthy's Catholic adherents, insisting only that the "particular good" of rooting Communists out of the government ought not to interfere with the more important "common good," or the welfare of the whole nation.[20] What *America* said was not soft enough, however, to mollify its Catholic critics, who sent it an avalanche of violent protest mail. "The situation here is undoubtedly becoming awkward," Hartnett worried, noting especially the "emotionalism" of the Catholic McCarthyites.[21]

371

In mid-April, *America* published most of the mail it had received on McCarthy, and nothing gave a better illustration of the verbal mayhem that had crept into the Catholic argument over the Senator. A priest in upstate New York, for instance, wrote that he was not cancelling his subscription since he had been wise enough not to have one in the first place. Nevertheless, he believed that if enough subscribers dropped the magazine, "it might bring you to your senses. Please accept my prayers for your conversion." A reader in Toledo, Ohio, wrote curiously, "Senator McCarthy is a good Catholic. . . . Look at his enemies: the *Daily Worker*, Tito, and Stevenson—a divorced man and member of the ADA."[22]

Notwithstanding its Catholic critics, *America* still had its supporters among the Catholic faithful. A man in Connecticut wrote that he dreaded the "slowly developing but perceptible undercurrent of public opinion that whispers that the Church approves of Senator McCarthy because he is a Catholic." Others shared his viewpoint and took *America's* side in the dispute.[23]

18. "We Can Do Better Than This," *America*, March 6, 1954, p. 585; Robert Hartnett, "Presidential Leadership vs. Senate Hegemony," *America*, March 13, 1954, pp. 621, 623.
19. Hartnett to the Fathers Provincial, March 15, 1954, "America" file, JAFU. Hartnett to Wilfred Parsons, March 10, 1954, Parsons Papers, Georgetown University (hereafter cited as GU).
20. "Fighting Communism: The Scope of 'Opinion,'" *America*, April 10, 1954, p. 34; Robert Hartnett, "Congress, Communists, and the Common Good," *America*, March 27, 1954, pp. 677-679.
21. Hartnett to Parsons, April 7, 1954, Parsons Papers, GU.
22. "Feature X," *America*, April 17, 1954, p. 71.
23. Joseph T. Prentiss to *America*, in "Feature X," *America*, April 10, 1954, p. 44; "Feature X," *America*, April 17, 1954, p. 70.

America might well have been able to ride out the stormy seas of McCarthyism had it not been for a blistering attack that Hartnett administered to McCarthy in the issue of the journal for May 22, 1954. No Catholic essay on McCarthy, either for him or against him, ever attracted as much attention as Hartnett's vigorous editorial, " 'Peaceful Overthrow' of the U.S. Presidency." (The occasion of the piece was McCarthy's acceptance of highly classified information from an Army officer, in open defiance of the President's strict prohibition against making such documents public. McCarthy had praised the "courage" of the young officer, much to the consternation of the liberal press. and politicians, who now saw McCarthy becoming a menace even to the established legal order).[24] Hartnett's editorial warned of the "grave constitutional issue posed by Senator McCarthy's 'Methods.' " McCarthy's actions seriously threatened the "rule of law" which was the "hallmark of free government," Hartnett wrote. The President was the choice of all the people, and was responsible to all of them. Therefore it was the obligation of the whole country to decide whether the President was properly discharging his duties; McCarthy had no business arrogating the nation's duty to himself. Hartnett feared that McCarthy was bringing about a "peaceful" but nevertheless "piecemeal" overthrow of the Presidency, and one that might well do immense harm to the American system of government.[25]

372

Liberal newspapers across the country took note of Hartnett's editorial, some of them quoting long passages from it.[26] All of this was too much for the *Brooklyn Tablet,* which immediately assaulted *America.* It quoted "a number of prominent Jesuits" who said that the publication represented the thinking of only a "small number" within the order. One Jesuit even wrote the *Tablet,* "from the logic of the article it sounds as though Eleanor Roosevelt wrote it." The *Tablet* concluded that McCarthy was seeking "not to destroy the Presidency, but to save it from its enemies within the Government itself.[27] The national press also picked up the *Tablet's* rejoinder to *America,* thus making a national event out of a debate between two Catholic weeklies.[28] Never one to ignore an unfounded attack, Hartnett wrote an immediate reply to the *Tablet,* saying that there simply was no "official Jesuit position" on McCarthy, and that

---

24. *New York Times,* May 28, 1954, p. 1; and May 29, 1954, p. 1.
25. "'Peaceful Overthrow' of the U.S. Presidency," *America,* May 22, 1954, pp. 210-211.
26. The article went out over the Associated Press (AP) wires on May 18, 1954. (The May 22 issue of *America* appeared several days before the date shown on the magazine.) The AP article appeared in the *Boston Daily Globe,* May 18, 1954; in the *Washington Post,* May 18, 1954; in the *Baltimore Sun,* May 18, 1954, and in many other newspapers as well.
27. *Brooklyn Tablet,* May 21, 1954.
28. See for example, *Denver Post,* May 22, 1954; *Washington Post,* May 22, 1954; *New York Journal American,* May 22, 1954.

the Jesuit editors of the magazine were completely free to say whatever they believed was just and reasonable. Perhaps he grew defensive when he noted that the superiors of the order had chosen the editors because they believed them to have the "necessary qualifications" for this "difficult and specialized work."[29]

Hartnett's Jesuit enemies remained utterly unmoved by his arguments. Ready now to take the battle into the public arena, they wrote to both the *Brooklyn Tablet* and the *New York Journal-American* (a pro-McCarthy Hearst publication), expressing their bitter disagreement with *America*. The *Tablet* and the *Journal American* were only too happy to print the letters, since they were anxious to discredit the anti-McCarthy forces. One Jesuit from Wisconsin wrote that *America's* editors represented only a "minority opinion," and besides, only Jesuit superiors "speak officially for American Jesuits."[30]

While the battle of the Jesuits was appearing in the New York press, the Jesuit brethren were fighting it out in private as well. Some of the Jesuit communities in New York City disagreed so violently over *America* and McCarthy that they finally decided, quite on their own, not to discuss the subject any more. Meanwhile, the superior of the New York Jesuits, the Reverend John McMahon, was coming under increasing and severe pressure to discipline *America*. The most impassioned letters he received came, not surprisingly, from other New York Jesuits, who believed that the magazine's militant stand on McCarthy was bringing deep embarassment to the order.[31] McMahon replied noncommittally to their pleas, as he did to similar missives from lay Catholics. (One layman even hinted that donations to the Jesuits might dry up if *America* did not change its tune.)[32]

As it happened, neither donations to the order nor complaints to *America* showed signs of diminishing. So many objections against the magazine came into Saint Patrick's Cathedral that it cancelled its subscription.[33] More serious than the cancellation at Saint Patrick's, however, were the violent and abusive telephone calls that inundated *America's* switchboard. For the first few days after the May 22 editorial,

29. "Freedom of Catholic Opinion," *America*, June 5, 1954, p. 261.
30. Rev. Robert H. Millmann to *Brooklyn Tablet* in *Tablet*, May 29, 1954; Rev. Patrick F. Hurley to *Tablet* in *Tablet*, May 29, 1954; Rev. J. A. Lennon to *New York Journal American* in *Journal*, May 29, 1954.
31. On agreement not to discuss McCarthy issue: interview with Thurston N. Davis, Feb. 21, 1972. Jesuit McCarthyites complain to their superior: Joseph McGowan to John McMahon, May 25, 1954, "McCarthy Editorial" folder, JAFU; McMahon to McGowan, May 25, 1954, Ibid.; Joseph A. Lennon to McMahon, May 25, 1954, Ibid.; John F. Hurley to McMahon, May 25, 1954, Ibid.; McMahon to Hurley, May 26, 1954, Ibid.
32. Daniel K. Shanley to McMahon, May 26, 1954, Ibid.
33. Bishop Joseph F. Flannelly to Hartnett, May 19, 1954, Ibid. Flannelly to McMahon, May 20, 1954, Ibid.; McMahon to Flannelly, May 21, 1954, Ibid.

the McCarthyites bombarded *America* with angry calls, so many of them coming in that the editors had to take turns answering them. "The same Irish voices kept calling," one of the assistant editors recalls.[34] And as always, irate readers mailed their furious thoughts to the magazine, some seventy "shocked" and "outraged" missives arriving immediately after the publication of the now-famous editorial.[35]

At the height of the uproar, someone shot a bullet through the door of Saint Ignatius Church, the Jesuit parish on Park Avenue in New York City. No one knows who shot the gun, or for what reason, but it was widely assumed that the May 22 editorial caused the incident.[36] So anxious had the the New York Jesuits become over the McCarthy crisis that they were ready to attribute even acts of violence to the McCarthyites.

374

It seemed that the furor over Hartnett's essay had begun to abate slightly when on May 29, *America's* superiors suddenly silenced the magazine on the topic of Senator McCarthy. Nothing could have come as more of a shock to Hartnett, since he knew that his superiors had long resisted pressures to silence the journal. What had happened? Though the superiors had refused to yield to the power tactics of the Catholic McCarthyites, they were deeply concerned that the McCarthy dispute had divided the nation's Jesuits. The founder of the order, Ignatius of Loyola, had repeatedly inveighed against public arguments between Jesuits, believing that unity in thought and action would be the key to the order's future success. Clearly the Jesuit debate over McCarthy had violated this rule. Nevertheless, *America* seemed to be breaking a long-standing command not to engage in "disputes among Catholics," a directive that went back to the founding of the periodical some fifty years before and that was still in effect. Finally, *America's* superiors believed that in its zeal to pursue the McCarthy question, it had neglected other issues "which are hardly less important than the Army-McCarthy case." On May 29, 1954, the magazine's superiors directed it to drop the McCarthy issue, and to keep their directive strictly secret.[37]

Hartnett immediately protested the decision, as the Jesuit rule allowed

34. Interview with Thurston N. Davis, February 21, 1972.
35. Hartnett wrote that the magazine had received 70 letters for McCarthy and about six for *America*. See Hartnett to Parsons, May 21, 1954, Parsons Papers, GU.
36. Davis interview.
37. John McMahon, William E. Fitzgerald, and William F. Maloney to Hartnett, May 29, 1954, "McCarthy Editorial" folder, JAFU. In a covering letter, McMahon wrote Hartnett, "We do not wish you to interpret this Directive as a vote of no confidence. It is not that. You still have our support. But in the present heated state of public opinion, particularly among Catholics, we think silence for two months will be golden. . . . P.S. If some extraordinary and crucial situation should develop which you and the Staff think should warrant an editorial or comment, you may represent this to me and I shall take it up with the Committee." McMahon to Hartnett, May 29, 1954, Ibid.

him to do. He argued not only that it would be impossible to keep the order a secret for long, but that it violated the principle of freedom of expression, one which he believed to be of paramount importance both to the magazine and to the Roman Catholic Church in America. If *America* were allowed to continue speaking its mind on McCarthy, everyone would see that the Church believed in open debate and freedom of thought. If *America* had achieved any success at all, it was because of the large measure of editorial freedom that it had always enjoyed, a freedom that the directive might destroy entirely.[38]

Impressed by Hartnett's pleas, the superiors modified their earlier order. They would now allow *America*'s editors to write about McCarthy, provided that they acted as "censors" for each other, and that they avoided the subject unless the "good of the Church" clearly required it.[39] Hartnett agreed fully with the revised order, and accepted it "with gratitude."[40]

The problem would undoubtedly have ended at that point, if the Father General of the Jesuits in Rome had not intervened. Father John Baptist Janssens, S. J., had been following the *America*-McCarthy dispute with intense interest, and in June, 1954, he issued a series of commands to *America*'s superiors in the United States, ordering them to take a hard line on the magazine. He was "deeply grieved," he wrote, that Jesuits in the United States had taken to the "public press" to express their disagreement with *America,* and had done so with obvious bitterness. Yet if one examined the problem carefully, he said, one saw that the underlying cause of all the difficulty was the magazine itself, which plainly had violated the rule laid down in its charter not to engage in "bitter disputes among Catholics." Concluded Janssens emphatically: "I cannot fail to think that the Fathers Provincial [superiors], especially those assigned to the direction of the magazine, have failed somehow in their duty. Therefore let the Fathers Provincial see to it that the Editor withdraws himself from this dispute immediately."[41]

In a later communication he expanded further on what seemed to bother him most of all, namely Hartnett's belief that the magazine ought to have complete freedom of expression. To Janssens, this was errant nonsense: every Jesuit should understand that the order "gives no one a freedom to write which is not subject to strict censorship."[42] With the McCarthy question settled by Rome, the Jesuit superiors relayed Janssens' unyielding order to Hartnett, who accepted it quietly and with

38. Hartnett to Vincent McCormick, May 31, 1954, "America" box, JAFU; Hartnett to McMahon, June 2, 1954, Ibid.
39. McMahon, Maloney, Fitzgerald, to Editors of *America*, June 3, 1954, Ibid.
40. Hartnett to McMahon, June 4, 1954, Ibid.
41. John B. Janssens to John McMahon, June 2, 1954, "America" box, JAFU.
42. Janssens to McMahon, June 17, 1954, "America" box, JAFU.

grace.[43] *America* said nothing more about McCarthy until his death in 1957, when it noted the Senator's demise almost in passing.[44]

Drained from the long battle with the McCarthyites and thoroughly "sick of the thing," as he said of the McCarthy affair, Hartnett took a long vacation. In September of 1955 he retired from the editorship of *America*.[45] Rumors still persist that his superiors "fired" him from his post because of the McCarthy episode, but no documentary evidence exists to prove this. On the contrary, the voluminous evidence in the Jesuit archives of New York shows that Hartnett retired because he was worn out, tired of the job, and believed that the magazine needed a new man at the helm.[46]

376

In looking back at the episode (one so painful that the editors of *America* still wince when talking about it), it seems clear that Janssens overreacted. The furor over the editorial had begun to subside, Hartnett was ready to devote less space to the McCarthy issue, and local superiors clearly had the situation well under control. Janssens' intervention therefore was precipitous, blunt, and peremptory. Fearful both of innovations in the Church and of Jesuit involvement in controversy, he worked tirelessly to form a body of Jesuits who asked no questions and did what they were told. One of the casualties of this approach was *America*, whose anti-McCarthy policy came to an abrupt and highly mysterious end. By contrast to Janssens, the magazine's superiors in the United States had acted with flexibility, tolerance, and obvious respect for intellectual freedom. Under intense pressure to silence the magazine, they had merely asked for moderation in the face of an issue of immense dispute. The pity is that they did not get the chance to let *America* pursue it to the end.

The American Jesuits divided decisively over Joe McCarthy. Not only did they disagree over *America's* editorials on McCarthy, but Jesuits across the country took opposing viewpoints on the Senator. On the east coast, such venerable Jesuit institutions as Georgetown and Fordham Universities found Jesuits on both sides of the issue, while on the west coast the Universities of Santa Clara and San Francisco also numbered Jesuit adherents to both causes. The same was true of Marquette University, the Senator's alma mater. Quite plainly Joe McCarthy and his "ism" represented two different political commitments, which, when taken to extremes, amounted to a contradiction. The McCarthy phalanx

43. Fitzgerald, Maloney, and McMahon to Hartnett, June 23, 1954, Ibid.; Hartnett to Thomas E. Henneberry, June 27, 1954, Ibid.; Henneberry to Hartnett, July 3, 1954, Ibid.
44. "The Passing of Senator McCarthy," *America*, May 18, 1957, p. 223.
45. Hartnett to Wilfred Parsons, September, 30, 1954, Parsons Papers, GU. On September 17, 1955, Thurston N. Davis took over as the new editor of *America*.
46. On Hartnett's personal reasons for leaving: author's interview with Hartnett, September 9, 1971. For documentary evidence, see "America" boxes, JAFU.

adhered to public displays of patriotism, took a dim view of the liberal legislation that had characterized the Truman and Roosevelt Administrations, and supported an all-out hunt for Communist subversives (while worrying little about possible incursions into civil liberties). The Jesuit McCarthyites, in sum, subscribed to the principles of conservative Republicanism, a political philosophy they found exemplified not only in Joe McCarthy, but in William F. Knowland, John Foster Dulles, and Robert A. Taft as well. All this had little to do with religion, though the conservative Jesuits would occasionally cite the Church's anti-Communist teachings for support, or they would sometimes point to the "sufferings of the Church behind the Iron Curtain" as an example of the consequences of Communism. On the issue of domestic Communism, however, they more often invoked the rhetoric of conservative American politics than the Church's teachings against Marxism.

377

In the case of the liberal American Jesuits who opposed McCarthy, the story was the same: their political views formed their positions on McCarthy. The anti-McCarthy forces adhered to the Roosevelt-Truman-Stevenson social programs, and to the Democratic party's theory on the problem of Communist subversion. That is to say, they favored a rigorous search for spies, but emphasized the need for preserving civil liberties as well. Strident displays of patriotism left them cold, as did the conservative notion that intellectuals and academics were somehow "eggheads," unpatriotic, and given to "softness on Communism." The Jesuits who subscribed to these tenets read not only the *Commonweal* and *America,* but the *New York Times* and the *Washington Post* as well. Though sympathetic to the editorial policies of the *Nation,* they tended to give that liberal journal a wide berth, since it supported Paul Blanshard (in their view a notorious Catholic-baiter) and in addition, opposed government assistance to parochial schools.

The Jesuit view of McCarthy differed little from that of other American Catholics, or even of the nation as a whole. The country's bitter split over McCarthy followed roughly political lines, in which liberals were ranged against McCarthy and conservatives took his side, and this division was reflected among lay Catholics as well.[47]

What was peculiar about Jesuit participation in the controversy was the *public* position of the order within the Church. Americans seemed to think that Jesuits "spoke for" or somehow "officially represented" the views of the whole Church. Perhaps they thought this because the order was the largest one in the Church, or because it was the one that received the most publicity, or the one that seemed closest to the Pope. Dubbed by slick journalists "the Pope's Marines" or "the Church's finest," the Jesuits in America found themselves in a tight spot: they were expected to say

47. Crosby, "The Angry Catholics."

whatever people wanted to hear them say. Thus the McCarthyites (and McCarthy himself) expected them to uphold the Senator, while political liberals demanded precisely the opposite. Catholic conservatives (symbolized by the Jesuit general in Rome) assumed that they would adhere willingly to rigid canons of censorship, while civil liberations such as Robert Hartnett favored the contrary doctrine of editorial freedom. American conservatives of every shade expected them to give unquestioning support to any kind of Communist hunt at all, while American liberals insisted that they choose carefully between authentic and bogus spy probes. With such contradictory demands placed upon them, it is no wonder that so few disappointed so many.

378   In fact America's Jesuits, like America's Catholic in general, had arrived at an advanced state of pluralism. They seemed light years removed from the Church of colonial times, or even from the era of religious strife that had marked the decade of the twenties. If the Catholic ghetto had not disappeared, it had at least weakened its hold on Catholics as they fled the city for the suburbs, seeking respectability, affluence, and higher status.

The comforting assurance that they were well on the way to full Americanization came to them not only from the Rotary Club and the Elks, but from such leading oracles of American civil religion as Dwight David Eisenhower, who seemed to think that one religion was as good as another, provided only that it supported America.[48]

With the march to the suburbs came the development of an all-pervasive national creed, the "American Way of Life," to which Jesuits were expected to conform along with the rest of the nation. To some Jesuits, the American Way of Life undoubtedly looked like the golden path to the Promised Land, offering as it did a new certificate of acceptance, a sure guarantee that Catholics were no different from anyone else. To others, however, the American Way of Life was something much less alluring: what if accepting the creed meant accepting Joe McCarthy, and all his pomps and works? Or what if it implied just the opposite, for instance the endorsement of Adlai Stevenson? America's Jesuits, in sum, found themselves on the horns of a dilemma: if full Americanization meant abandonment of one's freedom as well as capitulation to a mindless nationalism, was Americanization really a benefit? The McCarthy debate did nothing to solve the dilemma, but only made it more intense.

48. *New York Times*, December 23, 1952.

A Jesuit Runs for Congress: The Rev. Robert F. Drinan, S.J. and His 1970 Campaign

VINCENT A. LAPOMARDA

In his book, *People*, Richard T. Stout expressed the hope that the people involved in the antiwar campaign of United States Senator Eugene J. McCarthy in 1968 would not lose their enthusiasm.[1] The Vietnam Moratorium Day of 15 October 1969 was evidence that the people still wanted to be heard. With the 1970 mid-term elections approaching, two writers, James David Barber and David R. Mayhew, in an article published in the *New Republic,* suggested that the antiwar people concentrate on removing hawkish congressmen through the American political system. Among those mentioned as targets was Democrat Philip J. Philbin (1898-1972) of the Third Congressional District of Massachusetts, the twelfth ranking member of the United States House of Representatives and the vice chairman of the House Committee on Armed Services.[2] To oppose Philbin, an independent group of antiwar Democrats backed the Reverend Robert F. Drinan, S.J., a vigorous critic of the Vietnam War. It is the object of this study to examine the Drinan campaign and to determine its significance not only for politics in the Bay State but also for politics in the United States.

379

I

A lawyer and educator as well as a Roman Catholic priest, Father Drinan was a distinguished person for many liberals. As Dean of the Boston College School of Law for twelve years, Drinan had served as past Vice President of the Massachusetts

VINCENT A. LAPOMARDA (A.B., A.M., S.T.L., Boston College; Ph.D., Boston University), a Jesuit priest, is Assistant Professor of History at the College of the Holy Cross, Worcester, Massachusetts. The recipient of a Coe Fellowship in American Studies (Summer 1959) and two Batchelor Humanities Faculty Fellowships (Fall 1969 and 1970), he has written a number of articles on priests and politics, including a regular column, "Priests and Public Affairs," in the Jesuit newspaper, *SJNEws.*

1. Richard T. Stout, *People* (New York: Harper & Row, 1970).
2. See James David Barber and David R. Mahew, "From the Streets to the Polls," *New Republic,* 161 (6 December 1969): 9-11; and the obituary on Philbin, *Boston Globe,* 15 June 1972. In 1972, the Third Congressional District was redistricted so that it became the Fourth Congressional District in the 1972 elections.

Bar Association, Chairman of the Massachusetts Advisory Committee to the United States Commission on Civil Rights, and
Editor-in-Chief of *Family Law Quarterly*. Moreover, he was
known as a member of the bar association in Massachusetts and
the District of Columbia, Professor of Family Law and Constitutional Law at Boston College, and a respected spokesman of
American Catholicism on such abrasive issues as war and peace,
birth control, church and state, and abortion. At the same time
he had first-hand knowledge of the nation's problems through his
involvement in legal questions and his travels to the Middle East
in 1964 and Southeast Asia in 1969.[3]

380

With the growing unrest over his country's continued military
expansion and his own church's concern to help reform social
structures, Drinan soon realized that the role of a priest-educator
was quited limited. "I've written books, and I'm a professor,"
he once said. "But who reads books, who listens to professors?
It's Congress that turns it around, and I should be there."[4] Other
priests like James E. Groppi of Milwaukee and Daniel J. Berrigan, a classmate with Drinan at the Jesuit seminary in Weston,
Massachusetts, during the early 1950s, had taken to the streets
to protest against injustice. "By temperament, experience and
professional training," Drinan wrote, "I am not inclined to
engage in well-intentioned activities by clergymen such as Fr.
Daniel Berrigan, Fr. James Groppi and Rev. William Sloane
Coffin."[5]

Thus, when Drinan was approached in January 1970 by a
group of interested antiwar people to run for Philbin's seat, the
priest realized that it was an opportunity to revitalize the nation
by becoming "a new moral and spiritual voice" in a period of
violence.[6] "I don't burn draft records or take to the streets,"

3. The "Drinan for Congress Committee" provided comprehensive coverage of the
candidate's background and qualifications. Robert Frederick Drinan was born on
15 November 1920, entered the Society of Jesus on 29 June 1942, and was ordained
a priest by the Most Reverend Richard J. Cushing, Archbishop of Boston, on 20 June
1953.
4. Quotation from William Kennedy, "Father Runs for Congress," *Look*, 34 (22
September 1970) : 18.
5. Quotation from Robert F. Drinan to the Editor of *America*, "To Have a Voice
and Vote," *America*, 122 (6 June 1970). Also, see interview by Charles E. Fager,
"Priest, Law School Dean, Candidate for Congress," *Christian Century*, 87 (9 September 1970) : 1069-1072.
6. Quotation from mimeographed document, "Address of Robert F. Drinan at Convention of the Caucus of the Third Congressional District Held at Concord High
School, Concord, Massachusetts on Saturday, 21 February, 1970." According to Liz
Mest, *Waltham News-Tribune*, 31 October 1972, it was Christmas 1969 when the
Jesuit informed his brother, Dr. Francis W. Drinan, of his decision to run for
Congress.

Drinan said. "I believe in working within the law for change."[7] And, when the campaign was ending, he recalled: "I entered this campaign just so I could show the younger generation that you can work through the system."[8]

The next step, after Drinan expressed his willingness to take on Philbin in the September 15th primary, was for the priest to win the backing of the Citizens Caucus of Independent Democrats. On Saturday, 21 February 1970, about 1500 voters gathered at the Concord-Carlisle Regional High School in Concord, Massachusetts, to select a peace candidate. In addition to the 49-year old Drinan, there was the 26-year old John F. Kerry, a Yale graduate and a Vietnam naval hero; Gordon A. Martin, Jr., a 35-year old professor at Northeastern University; and Chandler H. Stevens, the 35-year old Concord native who had been defeated by Philbin when he ran as an Independent in the 1968 general election. While there were other interested candidates prior to the actual balloting, only Charles Ohanian, a state representative from Watertown, who withdrew because of his ideological disagreement with the Citizens Caucus, is noteworthy because of his later role in the campaign.[9]

Each candidate was permitted to address the group, but the touchstone of his qualifications was his position on the Vietnam War. "I suggest and submit to you that, if the incumbent in the Third Congressional District can be defeated by anyone in 1970," Drinan told the delegates, "that person is myself."[10] No candidate, the priest warned, could pass over the problems arising from inflation, the obsession with Communism, and the crisis in the Middle East. "A state which has sent the first Catholic to the White House, and the first Negro to the United States Senate," Drinan noted in anticipating the opposition to his candidacy, "would have no problem in demonstrating its independence by sending the first Jesuit to the Congress of the United States."[11]

7. Quotation from *Time*, 8 June 1970.
8. Quotation from Michael Widmer, *Clinton Item*, 30 October 1970. Also, see John W. Gardner's work, *The Recovery of Confidence* (New York: Harper & Row), on working within the system.
9. See Howard S. Knowles, *Worcester Telegram*, 22 February 1970; John H. Fenton, *New York Times*, 23 February 1970; and *Concord Journal*, 26 February 1970. Kerry made national news the following year in leading the Vietnam veterans against the war in Indochina, as "Man in the News," *New York Times*, 23 April 1971.
10. Quotation from Drinan's address, 21 February 1970. According to Thomas M. Cannon, "Reverend Father Congressman," *America*, 123 (21 November 1970); 424, it was a member of the military-industrial complex, Newton, Massachusetts, industrialist Arthur Obermayer, who had approached Drinan about running for Congress.
11. Quotation from Drinan's address, 21 February 1970.

Drinan was engaging in a "new politics." Compared to the "old politics," which characterizes the actions of party politicians, Drinan's candidacy would have a different basis. As he told the delegates, "my supporters would realize that they would be participating in a campaign created and implemented by the people themselves on behalf of a candidate whom they themselves have chosen because of his personal and professional qualifications."[12] Drinan was not interested in making himself the spokesman of the major ethnic or economic groups in the district. While bread-and-butter issues were important, the "new politics" would, as William V. Shannon later indicated, transcend such loyalties and avoid such favors, precisely because its area of concern are issues that are social and stimulate the consciences of individuals more than the economic issues that appeal to voters by aiming at the pocketbooks and wallets of Americans.[13]

382

Speaking in accents that recalled John Fitzgerald Kennedy, Drinan wanted a new foreign policy for the United States. The current policy was ruining American society. "I advocate, therefore, not merely the cessation of all hostilities in Vietnam," he told his audience, "but an imaginative and massive program to bring about disarmament."[14] "The only way to obtain a peace Congress in the United States," the priest said as he came to the end of his address, "is to fight at the local level against the solidly entrenched incumbents in primary struggles throughout the nation."[15]

Clearly the reaction of the Citizens Caucus was favorable to Drinan from the start of the balloting. To secure the nomination, it was necessary to win a two-thirds majority. Martin, in the interest of such an objective, withdrew from the race after attacking the records of both President Nixon and Congressman Philbin. Stevens withdrew after the second ballot. From a total of 45% of the vote on the first ballot, Drinan's support increased to 63.4% on the fourth ballot. Kerry, who had been Drinan's strongest contender throughout the balloting, urged the delegates to endorse Drinan by acclamation before they could take a fifth ballot. Thus, Father Drinan emerged as the peace candidate and the peace movement would not be thwarted as it had been in the

12. Ibid.
13. William V. Shannon, *New York Times* (iv), 20 September 1970. Also, see James A. Burkhart and Frank J. Kendrick (editors), *The New Politics: Mood or Movement?* (Englewood Cliffs: Prentice-Hall, Inc., 1971), for various views of the "new politics."
14. Quotation from Drinan's address, 21 February 1970.
15. Ibid.

1968 primary when Philbin won the Democratic nomination by capturing 48% of the vote against three peace candidates.[16]

II

Although there have been as many clergymen in Congress as there have been sessions of Congress, no Roman Catholic priest had ever been elected from any state to serve in that national body except the Sulpician priest, Gabriel Richard (1767-1832). Father Richard, however, was sent to Congress as a nonvoting delegate when Michigan was a territory of the United States. Previous to his election in 1822, this noted priest of the frontier had an interesting career as the editor of the territory's first Catholic newspaper, *The Michigan Catholic* (1809), and as a founder of the University of Michigan (1817).[17]

383

Yet, for a Roman Catholic priest to run for any public office was a radical idea not only for Roman Catholics to accept but also for members of other religious persuasions. This was quite evident in the Third Congressional District of Massachusetts where the population was about 75% Roman Catholic. Polls conducted early in the campaign and late in the campaign indicated that, while about half of the Catholics and the Protestants in the district could accept the idea, there was still a strong one third that could not. Perhaps much of this reaction, at least as far as Catholics were concerned, was due not only to the misunderstanding that Father Drinan was not a parish priest, but also to the relatively conservative Catholicism of voters unfamiliar with the Second Vatican Council's emphasis on the need of the church to become more deeply involved in social problems.[18]

Actually, as another Jesuit priest, John J. McLaughlin, pointed out in his own campaign as the Republican nominee for the office of United States Senator from Rhode Island, history and theory had settled the question. For, not only had clergymen served in the United States Congress, but Chief Justice Warren E. Burger and the American Civil Liberties Union saw no conflict between the idea and the constitutional requirement for the separation of church and state. Furthermore, as Drinan himself

16. See Knowles, *Worcester Telegram*, 22 February 1970; and Paul Driscoll, *Worcester Gazette*, 17 September 1968.
17. See Frank B. Woodford and Albert Hyma, *Gabriel Richard: Frontier Ambassador* (Detroit: Wayne University Press, 1958).
18. See *Boston Pilot*, 14 March 1970; polls conducted by the Becker Research Corporation, *Boston Globe*, 3 May 1970 and 29 October 1970; and Jules Witcover, *Los Angeles Times*, 20 July 1970.

emphasized, Roman Catholic priests did hold political office at various levels of the American government. This was true of Notre Dame's Theodore H. Hesburgh, Chairman of the United States Commission on Civil Rights, and of Francis J. Lally, Chairman of the Boston Redevelopment Authority. "Is it different," Drinan rightly asked, "if it's by election rather than by appointment?"[19]

With Drinan's example before them, a number of priests began to seek public office at various levels of government during and after the 1970 campaign.[20] This was particularly disturbing to the American Bishops because the Canon Law of the Roman Catholic Church prevented priests from campaigning for public office without preclearance from their ecclesiastical superiors. Such a requirement, as demanded by section 4 of Canon 139, raised eyebrows in a country that was so heavily Protestant and suspicious of Roman Catholics seeking public office before John Fitzgerald Kennedy demonstrated his own independence from his church on public matters. It was no wonder, then, that some ecclesiastical superiors judged it wiser to avoid making an issue of the canonical requirement. Fortunately, this was the policy that both the New England Jesuit Provincial and the Archbishop of Boston followed in Massachusetts where some 270 years previously Jesuits had been outlawed by the General Court, i.e., the state legislature.[21]

Moreover, both the secular and the religious press helped to break down the opposition to the idea of a priest running for public office. "Priests are American citizens," the *Worcester Gazette* editoralized a month before the Citizens Caucus, "and have all the rights that anyone else has."[22] "Whatever else might be said about the qualifications of either Congressman Philbin or

384

19. Quotation from *Clinton Item*, 2 May 1970. Also see John P. Hackett, *Providence Journal*, 13 September 1970.
20. In 1970, the following priests ran for the United States Congress: Robert J. Cornell of De Pere, Wisconsin; Robert F. Drinan of Newton, Massachusetts; Louis R. Gigante of the Bronx, New York; Joseph R. Lucas of Youngstown, Ohio; John J. McLaughlin of Providence, Rhode Island; and Stephen E. Vesbit of Grand Rapids, Michigan. See the articles in the *National Catholic Reporter* by Joe O'Sullivan (19 June 1970), James W. McCulla (21 August and 30 October 1970), Philip Nobile (21 August 1970), and Charles E. Fager (30 October 1970). Also, see the article by Sue Cribari, *Springfield Catholic Observer*, 30 October 1970.
21. See Kingsbury Smith, *Boston Record American*, 13 January 1971; James Stack, *Boston Globe*, 4 February 1972, for the position of Drinan's ecclesiastical superior(s). Also, see Robert H. Lord, John E. Sexton, Edward T. Harrington, *History of the Archdiocese of Boston in the Various Stages of its Development 1604-1943*, 3 vols. (New York: Sheed & Ward, 1944), 1:72-75. The position of the American Bishops in 1970 on priests in politics was explained in the *Worcester Catholic Free Press*, 1 May 1970.
22. Quotation from *Worcester Gazette*, 21 January 1970.

Fr. Drinan or any other candidate in the current campaigning across America," the *Worcester Catholic Free Press* warned its audience, "it should be admitted that any Catholic priest—as any other minister of religion—has a basic, inalienable right as an American citizen to make himself available for election to public office."[23] And, noting the irrelevance of the canonical requirement in the American context, the Jesuit weekly, *America*, said: "Indeed, in the United States at least, Canon 139 succeeds only in embarrassing the Church, not in furthering its ministry."[24]

Still the "non-issue," as the *Boston Pilot* called it,[25] remained constantly throughout the 1970 Drinan campaign. It was so much of an unknown quantity that the Drinan staff even considered confronting the problem in a public forum much as Kennedy had done before the Protestant ministers gathered in Houston, Texas, during the 1960 campaign. "Our own polls tell us that if we turn the corner on the Catholic issue," said one Drinan strategist, "we're in good shape. The main issue is the war and Drinan is on target with that."[26] Although the "non-issue" persisted, the Drinan strategy was to concentrate on the real issues in the campaign.[27]

385

III

Exactly what the issues were in 1970 varied from district to district throughout the nation. But no district, especially the Third Congressional District of Massachusetts, could escape the Vietnam War, campus unrest, civil rights, inflation, and law and

23. Quotation from *Worcester Catholic Free Press*, 5 June 1970.
24. Quotation from editorial, *America*, 123 (5 September 1970) : 104. *America* had taken this position following the attempt by the Most Reverend Russell J. McVinney, Bishop of Providence, to undermine the candidacy of Father McLaughlin. For more on the McLaughlin campaign, see Vincent A. Lapomarda, "John McLaughlin in Politics: The Development of a Presidential Advisor," *SJNEws* (supplement), September 1971.
25. Quotation from Boston *Pilot*, 23 May 1970.
26. Quotation from Kennedy, "Father Runs for Congress," p. 22. Although the strategy worked, it should be noted that there was strong opposition to his candidacy evident in such writings as that of James P. Drummey, *Twin Circle*, 19 July 1970, and the articles by Thomas C. Gallagher in the *Boston Herald Traveler*, especially 28 October 1970. After the election, the secretary of John Cardinal Wright of the Congregation for the Clergy, Reverend Donald W. Wuerl, published two articles in the English edition of *L'Osservatore Romano*, 19 November 1970 and 3 February 1972, critical of the involvement of priests in politics. I have disagreed with his views in my letters to the editors published in the *Worcester Gazette*, 15 December 1970; *Boston Globe*, 10 January 1971; and *Boston Pilot*, 19 February 1972. Also, see my article, "Priests and Politics: Two Valid Approaches," *Holy Cross Quarterly*, 4 (Spring-Summer 1971) : 46-49.
27. The literature of the "Drinan for Congress Committee" indicated a broad concern with both domestic and foreign affairs.

order. "What are these problems? asked the *New York Times.*
"They are the conduct of foreign policy, the management of the
Government's relationship with the economy, and the promotion
of social justice under law."[28] Clearly, the Drinan supporters
were not at all happy with what was going on in Southeast Asia
and the Middle East. And, they wanted to make the American
political system more directly responsive to the problems confronting Americans.

Yet, despite their idealism, the Drinan forces had to defeat
a powerful incumbent in Philip J. Philbin. A graduate of Harvard College, where he had played center in the school's only
Rose Bowl game, and of Columbia University Law School, the
Clinton Democrat had been an aide of the popular Senator
David I. Walsh (1872-1947), and, since 1942, the successor of
former Congressman Joseph E. Casey. During the fourteen terms
of devoted service to the people of his district, Philbin had moved
upward in seniority so that he ranked next to L. Mendell Rivers
(1905-1970) on the House Committee on Armed Services. A
constant supporter of the Johnson and Nixon policies in Southeast Asia, Philbin had also been a staunch advocate of the
Pentagon's interests. More concerned about bread-and-butter
issues than with those that trouble the consciences of Americans,
the congressman played a lethargic role in House debates and
was irreverently regarded as a "party hack."[29]

Following the reapportionment of his district in 1967, Philbin
was able to defeat the followers of Senator Eugene J. McCarthy
in the primary and win the general election in 1968. The district,
however, in 1970 numbered close to half a million people and was
very liberal in the eastern end because of the Harvard-MIT-BC-
BU-UMass-Northeastern-Brandeis educational complex. Stretch-
ing from the suburb communities of the state's largest city, the
district embraced thirty-one cities and towns that were located
between Boston and Worcester and ran on a northwesterly
direction to the New Hampshire border. Philbin was better
known in the western part, which actually was more conservative
and included more blue collar workers, than in the strongholds
of student power adjacent to Boston. While Philbin's influence
over military installations and defense contracts might impress
the people in the industrial areas of Fitchburg, Gardner, and

28. Editorial, *New York Times,* 12 October 1970. Also, see Warren Weaver, Jr.,
same newspaper, 15 October 1970.
29. Quotation from Norman C. Miller, *Wall Street Journal,* 8 September 1970.

386

Leominster, the students in Newton, Watertown, and Waltham could only be enraged at him.[30]

It was clear that, if Drinan faced Philbin in a two-way race, the priest would have a difficult time winning. However, if he were to face another candidate in the primary in a two-way race, namely, Charles Ohanian, the state representative from Watertown, Drinan could win by a two-to-one margin. Ohanian was a Democrat who had the typical record of liberalism in moderation during his service in the General Court. Although he voted in favor of protecting the right of Massachusetts servicemen to challenge the constitutionality of an undeclared war like Vietnam, the Watertown Democrat supported Nixon's policy in Southeast Asia, especially since he felt that the President should have enough time to test it before any one opposed him on it. "He is," as Clifford Gaucher of Maynard, a Philbin aide, put it, "a place to go for those who think the good father is a little kookie, or for those who think Cong. Philbin is too old."[31]

The incursions into Cambodia and the killings at Kent State in mid-spring 1970 further strengthened the resolve of the peace movement to unseat hawkish congressmen like Philbin. Moreover, with the publication of Father Drinan's new book, *Vietnam and Armageddon* coming in the wake of these developments, the priest emerged more and more as a strong contender for the Democratic nomination. Support flowed into his campaign from the Congressional Action Fund, a bipartisan group supporting progressive policies; the Movement for a New Congress, the Princeton University-centered organization aimed at assisting peace candidates; the National Committee for an Effective Congress, an independent organization; the Universities Antiwar Fund, a group of college and university teachers supporting antiwar candidates; and the Youth Caucus, an assembly concerned with helping peace candidates in Massachusetts. Furthermore, Drinan had the endorsement of such distinguished liberals as former United States Attorney General, Ramsey Clark; former United States Ambassador to India, John Kenneth Galbraith; and former United States Supreme Court Justice, Arthur J. Goldberg.[32]

387

---

30. See the two articles by James Higgins, "Drinan's Bay State Volunteers," *Nation*, 211 (21 December 1970): 648-652, and "Pray for Father Drinan," *Boston*, 63 (January 1971): 52-57, 61.
31. Quotation from Carol Liston, *Boston Globe*, 30 August 1970. Also, see *Clinton Item*, 6 March 1970, on Ohanian.
32. Drinan's book, *Vietnam and Armageddon: Peace, War and the Christian Conscience* (New York: Sheed & Ward, 1970), was published on 6 May. His other

At the same time, Philbin was not without his own backers. Members of both parties in the Massachusetts Delegation, Republican Margaret M. Heckler and Democrat James A. Burke, endorsed their colleague. Unlike the *Boston Globe,* which took a sympathetic view of the Drinan candidacy, the *Boston Herald Traveler* opposed the priest. So did the labor unions whose members would be affected by the reordering of the nation's priorities and the cutting down on defense contracts and military installations, namely, the International Brotherhood of Electrical Workers, the United Steel Workers of America, and the Central Labor Council of North Worcester County. Obviously, Philbin's 100% rating from COPE, the political arm of the AFL-CIO, gave the congressman widespread support in the district's industrial areas.[33]

Both Senator George S. McGovern, a Democrat from South Dakota, and Senator Mark O. Hatfield, a Republican from Oregon, sponsored an amendment to end the Vietnam War and have American forces out of Southeast Asia by July 1971. Father Drinan favored this amendment. He sought to reorder the nation's priorities by diverting federal funds from the expanding military-industrial complex to control pollution, assist the poor, improve education, and advance medical research. Philbin, who had distinguished himself as a superhawk, could not be expected to advocate such a drastic reordering of priorities. Neither could Ohanian who was upholding the Nixon policy in Southeast Asia.[34]

In addition to the strong backing of the peace movement, Drinan had an effective organization. Jerome Grossman, whose Vietnam Moratorium Day had attracted national attention, was the priest's financial chairman, and John Marttila, a 29-year old former Republican National Committeeman from Detroit, was Drinan's campaign manager. Grossman, a stationary manufacturer from Newton, had the task of raising more than $100,000 for the primary. Marttila, who employed his experience in some ten previous campaigns, was assisted by some 3,500 volunteers, including students as well as people over thirty, in canvassing

---

works include *Religion, the Courts, and Public Policy* (New York: McGraw-Hill, 1963), and *Democracy, Dissent and Disorder: The Issues and the Law* (New York: Seabury Press, 1969). For a list of backers of Drinan, McGlennon, and Philbin, see *Boston Globe,* 29 October 1970.

33. See Cornelius Dalton and Thomas C. Gallagher, *Boston Herald Traveler,* 24 February 1970; *Clinton Item,* 25 March 1970, and 9 and 12 September 1970; and Miller, *Wall Street Journal,* 8 September 1970.

34. See *New York Times,* 20 May 1970, and *Boston Globe,* 30 August 1970. The two senators introduced amendments to cut funds after 31 December 1970 and to have the troops out of Vietnam by 30 June 1971.

some 40,000 households. Armed with a five-point scale from positive to negative, these workers were able to reach a substantial block of voters. Employing computer cards and tapes, the Drinan organization was able to correlate the information and determine its strategy in selling the candidate. Thus, by primary day, Drinan headquarters, employing the best techniques of the old politics and taking advantage of television and technology, had a strong organization behind its candidate of the new politics.[35]

A poll taken around first of May 1970 indicated that Philbin would take 40% of the vote, Drinan 21%, and Ohanian 8%.[36] Understandably, as the election neared, there were few who were willing to predict a Drinan victory. However, once the ballots were in for that rainy Tuesday primary, the work of the Drinan camp showed its effectiveness. Working down to the last day in getting voters to the polls, the Drinan forces won 48% of the vote. Predictably, Congressman Philbin had done well in the western part of the district, but Father Drinan carried Newton by a margin of five to one, Concord by four to one, and Waltham by two to one. As one writer put it, it was "Tuesday's most notable victory of all."[37]

389

IV

With both the Citizens Caucus and the September primary behind him, Father Drinan had to undertake the fight for the November election, and State Representative John A. S. McGlennon, who had beaten Dr. Vahe A. Serafian, a native of Newton and a professor at Suffolk University, was Drinan's opponent. A native of Concord and a graduate of Bowdoin College, the 35-year old attorney had fashioned a liberal record for himself in the General Court. Unlike Serafian,, whom he had beaten by a five to one margin, McGlennon had criticized the incursions into Cambodia and the SST. At the same time, he supported Nixon's Vietnamization policy and had taken a position for the Shea-Wells Bill. A poll taken early in the campaign indicated that Drinan could beat the young Republican in a

35. See *Boston Globe,* 17 (Liston) September and 18 (Elliot Friedman, magazine) October 1970. Also, see the endorsement, *Watertown Press,* 10 September 1970.
36. *Clinton Item,* 6 May 1970.
37. Quotation from Howard S. Knowles, *Worcester Telegram,* 17 September 1970. Also, see *Boston Globe,* 3 (Liston), 13 (Robert Healy), and 17 September 1970; and *Boston Herald Traveler,* 17 September 1970. Healy, *Boston Globe,* 16 September 1970, said: "It was the major upset of the election."

two-way race by a margin of almost two to one.[38]

While McGlennon had been confident of his chances to win the nomination against Serafian, the young Republican had run a campaign with the expectation of facing Philbin in the November election. Yet Drinan's victory had upset McGlennon's strategy. While the representative was less dovish than Drinan, still he was much more liberal than Philbin. Further, the voting record that he had fashioned before the September primary would appeal more to Philbin supporters than the Drinan stand on the Vietnam War. Still, with only Drinan opposing him, McGlennon could pitch his campaign for the November election so that it would at least split the votes with Drinan in the eastern end of the district and sweep through the western parts. This, of course, was the reverse of his original strategy. For, if he had to face Philbin alone, then McGlennon would have been forced to divide the votes in the western section with the congressman and take those in the eastern towns.[39]

But neither Drinan nor McGlennon expected what actually developed. The tip came when the *Marlboro Enterprise* said that Philbin might run as an Independent in the November election. Within two weeks, it was clear that the Clinton Democrat would not surrender his seat too easily. His polls indicated that he could take 51% of the vote, Drinan 30%, and McGlennon 18% in a three-way fight. Determined to run a sticker campaign, Philbin struck out against the peace movement and criticized "ultra-liberal extremists and outsiders" as the veteran congressman prepared for another round against Drinan.[40] McGlennon, who had been trying to woo the Philbin supporters, was bewildered. "Virtually every political pundit I have talked to said," the young Republican declared, "it is impossible to win on a sticker campaign."[41]

Philbin's reentry, then, changed the whole outlook of the campaign. "About all that Mr. Philbin can reasonably expect

38. See *Boston Globe*, 6 May 1970, for the poll; and *Clinton Item*, 19 March 1970, on McGlennon, and 1 August 1970, on Serafian. For McGlennon's record on the Vietnam War, see mimeographed sheet, "House Roll Call on Shea-Wells Bill," prepared by the Citizens for Participation Politics. Also, compare the editorials on the Drinan victory in both the *Boston Herald Traveler* and the *Boston Globe* on 17 September 1970.
39. See Tony Mastro, *Worcester Telegram*, 17 September 1970; and Dick Gist, *Clinton Item*, 19 September 1970.
40. Quotation from *Clinton Item*, 6 October 1970. Also, see *Marlboro Enterprise*, 24 September 1970; *Clinton Item*, 29 September 1970; and John H. Hastings, *Worcester Telegram*, 6 October 1970.
41. Quotation from *Worcester Gazette*, 7 October 1970.

to accomplish," editorialized the *Providence Journal,* "is to play the role of a spoiler."[42] As Cornelius Dalton stated: "Now the crucial question is: Will Philbin take more votes away from Drinan or McGlennon?"[43] It was a tight fight before Philbin's announcement and it became an even more tight contest as the last month of the campaign developed. The White House was interested in the campaign because it was one of the forty possibilities for a Republican gain in the House. Moreover, both Philbin and McGlennon were determined to raise the funds to beat Drinan.[44]

With Drinan strong in the eastern part of the district and Philbin dominating the western section, McGlennon had to revise his strategy to meet the new situation. For he needed to be liberal enough to split the vote with Drinan and conservative enough to woo Philbin's supporters. However, since the Concord Representative had more of a chance among the blue collar workers than among the antiwar voters, he moved more directly to the right. Since a sticker candidate had not traditionally done very well in the state, McGlennon presented himself as the one realistic choice against Drinan. He was careful not to attack Philbin lest he alienate the possible votes among the congressman's supporters. At the same time, McGlennon moved against Drinan.[45]

391

Meanwhile the right had mounted its own attack on the antiwar movement. William F. Buckley, Jr., the conservative editor of the *National Review,* called the liberal priest, "the greatest threat to orderly thought since Eleanor Roosevelt left this vale of tears." Moreover, Buckley attacked the priest's ideas on disarmament as reflected in Drinan's *Vietnam and Armageddon.* In Buckley's view, Drinan was, "The Elmer Gantry of disarmament" because the priest advocated that the United States consider a policy of pacifism, rather than militarism, in its foreign policy and that it stand by its commitment to the preservation of the State of Israel.[46]

While Buckley's criticism was strong enough, it was not as vicious as either Philbin's or McGlennon's. At times they appeared to have taken their cues from Vice President Spiro T. Agnew, who had been campaigning against antiwar candidates

42.   Quotation from *Providence Journal,* 10 October 1970.
43.   Quotation from Dalton, *Boston Herald Traveler,* 8 October 1970.
44.   *Clinton Item,* 19 September (Gist) and 9 October 1970, on McGlennon's interest in spending as much as $130,000 and Philbin's in spending as much as $200,000.
45.   See *Clinton Item,* 25 September 1970, for McGlennon's praise of Philbin.
46.   Quotations from William F. Buckley, Jr., *Providence Journal,* 25 September 1970.

across the country. At one point in the 1970 campaign, Agnew went so far as to attack another clergyman, Joseph Duffey, a Congregationalist and the Democratic nominee for the office of United States Senator from Connecticut, as a "Marxist revisionist."[47] McGlennon, in an attempt to set himself off from Drinan's ideology, attacked the priest as "a person of extreme points of view."[48]

Perhaps the source of both Philbin's and McGlennon's strategy against Drinan was Charles Ohanian, the Watertown Democrat whom Drinan had defeated in the September primary. Ohanian, who came close to coming out for McGlennon before the Watertown Democrat himself helped persuade Philbin that he should continue the fight for his seat, came out quite strongly against Drinan as he placed himself firmly behind Philbin. "I can tell you," Ohanian said in speaking against Drinan, "I am frightened of this man. I am frightened of his position on the issues. I'm frightened of some of the people who are backing his candidacy."[49] Ohanian's opposition to Drinan was such that the Watertown Democrat was even thinking of opposing the priest in 1972 if Philbin's sticker campaign were to fail.[50]

Philbin, who had attributed his loss to Drinan in the primary as due to the poor weather, the complacency of his constituents, and the lack of Republican participation, conducted a campaign that indicated how important the Clinton Democrat was to Massachusetts. Compared to Drinan, Philbin had a long and distinguished service in the cause of peace. He was not at all for those ideas of disarmament and civil disobedience that the priest was advocating. Moreover, if Drinan should win, such a victory might cost the state some 50,000 jobs. Also, the congressman's opposition to free trade would protect the jobs threatened by the priest's desire to increase free trade.[51]

Despite Philbin's insistence on his own importance, it was dubious that the Democrat was so powerful. For, with the winding down of the Vietnam War, it had already been projected by the Arthur D. Little Company that Massachusetts would lose about 20% of its jobs. Furthermore, while it was true that

47. Quotation from *Providence Journal*, 10 October 1970.
48. Quotation from *Worcester Telegram*, 22 October 1970.
49. Quotation from *Clinton Item*, 14 October 1970.
50. As the *Clinton Item*, 29 September 1970, pointed out, Drinan blamed Ohanian for distorting his views. Also, see Rowland Evans and Robert Novak, *Boston Globe*, 14 October 1970.
51. See *Clinton Item*, 9, 19-20 (letters) October 1970; and Gallagher, *Boston Herald Traveler*, 16 October 1970.

Philbin had been influential in the state retaining Fort Devens, Veterans Hospitals, and Hanscom Field, it was also true that he was losing his effectiveness. There was not only an indication of this in the primary vote of such towns as Gardner, but also in the refusal of the Democratic Town Committee in that town and Fitchburg to endorse the congressman for the November election. Philbin's own campaign rhetoric, with its attacks on Drinan's views of the law and the sources of the priest's support, indicated that the congressman was desperate and that much of his influence had already vanished.[52]

But, it was McGlennon, more than Philbin, who lowered the level of political dialogue. Careful not to alienate any of Philbin's supporters, the Concord Republican, in attacking Drinan, changed his views to suit his audience. McGlennon sought to discredit Drinan by deplicting him as an extremist on various issues. This was evident in one radio commercial which had excerpted a quotation from the 6 April 1970 issue of the *Worcester Gazette* declaring that the priest advocated disobedience to an unjust law. Another had distorted quotations from Drinan's *Vietnam and Armageddon* to indicate how dangerous were the Jesuit's views on disarmament and conscientious objectors.[53]

The Drinan camp was bewildered by the attacks. "We stayed away from answering the charges," Marttila later recalled, "until the last week of the campaign and that almost cost us the election."[54] Fortunately, at least for the Drinan camp, the newspapers of the various cities and towns in the district came out in defense of the priest.[55] Moreover, Drinan defended himself against Philbin's allegations that the priest's campaign was being financed substantially by "outsiders" and against McGlennon's "distortions" of the ideas in *Vietnam and Armageddon*. The truth of the matter was that Philbin had received a larger percentage of his funds from outside of the district and the state than Drinan. Likewise, anyone reading the priest's book would realize that he had advocated disobedience to the law in the context

393

---

52. Ibidem. Also, see *Clinton Item*, 19 and 31 October 1970; and David E. Lynch, *Worcester Telegram*, 15 November 1970.
53. See Evans and Novak, *Boston Globe*, 14 October 1970; and Richard S. Kline, *Worcester Telegram*, 15 November 1970.
54. Quotation from *Worcester Gazette*, 9 November 1970.
55. See, for example, editorials in *Weston Town Crier*, 24 September 1970, *Leominster Enterprise*, 27 October 1970, and *Watertown Press*, 29 October 1970. Also, see *Boston Globe*, 14 (Healy) and Liston, 22 October and 2 November 1970; and Kline, *Worcester Telegram*, 15 November 1970.

of the Germans in Nazi Germany.[56]

As the campaign neared the November election, it became clear that Drinan had taken the lead. Philbin, it is true, continued to enjoy the support of the labor movement. The Building and Construction Trades and the International Association of Machinists were also among the unions supporting the congressman. McGlennon, who was backed by such liberal Massachusetts Republicans as John A. Volpe, Elliot L. Richardson, and Edward W. Brooke, was not at all happy with his campaign strategy. And, Father Drinan, endorsed by such national leaders of the Democratic Party as Edward M. Kennedy, Eugene J. McCarthy, Edmund S. Muskie, and Lawrence F. O'Brien, was advocating reconciliation in a compassionate society as the campaign came to an end.[57]

Drinan had climbed from a recognition factor of 16% to one of 90% during the 1970 campaign. Philbin, who had run a strong sticker campaign, carried Fitchburg, Leominster, Clinton, Hudson, Maynard, and Marlboro, as he piled up 45,734 votes. McGlennon, who won the endorsement of both the *Hudson Son* and *Marlboro Enterprise*, carried Weston, Concord, Lincoln, and Acton, as he finished with 61,129 votes. And, Drinan won the election with 64,129 votes as he took such towns as Gardner, Newton, Waltham, Watertown, and Westford. Thus, Robert F. Drinan became the first Roman Catholic priest ever elected to vote in the Congress of the United States.[58]

V

The significance of the Drinan victory for both the state and the nation is open to considerable dispute. This is clear with respect to the ideology of the Democratic party in Massachusetts, which, as one columnist pointed out shortly after the election, covered the spectrum in the congressional delegation with Louise

56 See *Worcester Telegram*, 22 October and 15 (Kline) November 1970. As Gannon, "Reverend Father Congressman," pointed out (427), one Drinan aide regretted the failure of the organization in not reading Drinan's book more carefully.
57. See *Clinton Item*, 29 September, 2 and 9 October, and 2 and 3 November 1970, for Drinan's backers; 31 October and 2 November 1970, for Philbin's support; and 16, 23, 31 October and 2 November 1970, for McGlennon's. Also, see *Worcester Telegram*, 6-7 October 1970, and *Boston Globe*, 22 and 29 October 1970.
58. See *Hudson Sun* and *Marlboro Enterprise* for endorsements in editions of 29 October 1970. Totals are taken from *Newton News-Tribune*, 5 November 1970. Also, see Bill Kovach, *New York Times*, 5 November 1970. According to the *Washington Post*, 19 September 1970, Drinan, commenting on his September primary win, had said: "We made a model for new politics candidates across the nation." Certainly, this was even more true with his November victory.

Day Hicks from the Ninth District dominating the right and Robert F. Drinan from the Third District dominating the left. This is even more evident when one tries to determine where the majority of Bay Staters stood in the 1970 election.[59]

The difficulty becomes even more acute when one considers whether or not the priest would have won if Philbin had not entered the contest. For, if one considers the totals, it is clear that the district was more center and right than it was center and left. Perhaps, if Philbin had endorsed Drinan, the election might have been more decisively liberal in its results. Yet, given the defections of Philbin supporters to the McGlennon camp after the September primary, it is doubtful that Philbin would have done much more than keep public silence. The congressman's subsequent injection of himself as an Independent would seem to confirm this view of the 1970 campaign.[60]

395

Refreshing as it was for the frustrated antiwar movement, the 1970 Drinan campaign indicated how difficult it was to unseat a hawkish incumbent. If the Drinan effort was just able to do it with the best in the technology of politics at its command, then it was a clear example to the antiwar movement that it would be quite difficult to bring about change. The antiwar movement could have no rest so long as there were hawkish incumbents who disagreed with its objectives. Yet, it should be a source of encouragement to those who feel frustrated with the American political system that it is quite possible to bring about changes by working within the system. However, it should be emphasized that the Drinan victory was not so much a victory for his ideas as it was a victory for organization. For, as the state referendum indicated, the majority of the people in both his district and outside his district did not favor the priest's stand on an immediate withdrawal from the war in Indochina.[61]

Finally, the most refreshing aspect of the Drinan victory is

59. See *Boston Globe*, 20 September (Richard H. Stewart), and 8 November (S. J. Micciche) 1970. Richard M. Scammon and Ben J. Wattenberg, *The Real Majority* (New York: Coward-McCann, 1970), emphasized "the Social Issue," that umbrella under which one gathers all those concerns of the majority of Americans in a divided society. As the advertisement in the *New York Times*, 20 November 1970, described it: "The book that called the shots in the '70 elections. . . ."
60. See *Newton News-Tribune*, 5 November 1970; and *Clinton Item*, 9 November 1970.
61. Of the three choices in the fifth referendum on the 1970 Massachusetts ballot: "Win a military victory" (A), "Withdraw our armed forces in accordance with a planned schedule" (B), and "Withdraw all our armed forces immediately" (C), most people voted for B. See *Worcester Telegram*, 1 November 1970; *Newton News-Tribune*, 5 November 1970; and *Clinton Item*, 9 November 1970.
During his first term in Congress, Father Drinan fought vigorously to help end

that it was a landmark in the ecumenical movement. For Massachusetts, which one time had driven Jesuits out of its territory by laws enacted some 270 years ago, in 1970 welcomed leading the way in politics once more. It had given the nation its first Roman Catholic President, its first Negro Senator in the twentieth century, and in that year its first Roman Catholic clergyman in the United States House of Representatives.[62]

the war in Southeast Asia. His stature had increased to such an extent that he was chosen as the keynote speaker at the Massachusetts Citizens Presidential Caucus that endorsed Senator George S. McGovern (Drinan himself was one of some twenty candidates whose names were placed in nomination on that day, 15 January 1972). At a press conference in Washington, 21 January 1972, the priest publicly endorsed McGovern for the presidency. He led the state pledged to the Senator from South Dakota, in the Massachusetts presidential primary on 25 April 1972, and, after that victory, Drinan was chosen to lead the Massachusetts Delegation to the Democratic National Convention at Miami Beach. Subsequently, he devoted his attention to his own re-election for Congress and won by defeating his chief rival, Martin A. Linsky of the Republican Party, and the weak candidate of the Conservative Party, John T. Collins. See Richard M. Weintraub, *Boston Globe,* 16 January, 22 May, 10 and 12 July, and 31 October 1972. Also, see the same newspaper 27 April, 20 September, and 8 November 1972 for results of various elections in which Drinan was a candidate.

Father Drinan had fashioned an impressive record during his first term in Congress. This was emphasized by the *Ralph Nader Congress Report* both in its study, *Who Runs Congress?* (edited by Mark J. Green, James M. Fallows, and David R. Zwick; New York: Bantom Books, 1972), pp. 218-219, and in its profile, *Robert Drinan* (Washington, D. C.: Grossman, 1972), written by Marcie Hemmelstein.

Finally, it should be noted that, despite the accords signed at Paris on 27 January 1973, terminating the American involvement in Vietnam, Drinan continues to criticize American foreign policy with respect to Indochina. This was evident as recent as his newsletter of 1 May 1973.

62. See editorial, *Boston Globe,* 5 November 1970. In its document on "The Ministerial Priesthood," the Third Synod of Bishops declared (Part 2, Section 2, Paragraph b) its position on priests and elective office:

> Leadership or active militancy on behalf of any political party is to be excluded by every priest unless, *in concrete and exceptional circumstances, this is truly required by the good of the community,* and receives the consent of the bishop after consultation with the priests' council and, if circumstances call for it, with the espisopal conference. [Emphasis added]

While the 1971 statement does not absolutely exclude the priest-politician, it does discourage the idea. This was evident when John Cardinal Krol of Philadelphia sought to discourage Drinan's involvement in politics before the 1972 campaign was launched. That the Jesuit Provincial of New England, William G. Guindon, came out in defense of Father Drinan indicates the differences of interpretation within American Catholicism. See *Boston Gobe,* 10 January 1972, and *National Catholic Reporter,* 4 February 1972.

It is doubtful that Americans will witness any more than a very few qualified priests running for public office. For example, compared to the hundreds of elective offices available throughout the United States on the local, state, and national levels, only a very small number holding elective office in 1972 were priests (Mimie B. Pitaro, the first priest to serve as a Massachusetts representative; Lawrence W. Voelker, the first priest to serve as an Indiana assemblyman; Francis X. Lawlor, the first priest to serve as a Chicago alderman; Wilfred Illies, the first priest to serve as Mayor of Clear Lake, Minnesota; and Roland H. St. Pierre, the first priest to serve as Mayor of Plattsburgh, New York, to single out the more prominent examples). Certainly, such involvement by priests underlines the evolving concept of the priest since the Second Vatican Council. In this connection, the recent cover story, "The Jesuits' Search For a New Identity," *Time,* 23 April 1973, was quite relevant.

The Heritage of
American Catholicisim

1. EDWARD R. KANTOWICZ, EDITOR
   MODERN AMERICAN CATHOLICISM, 1900-1965:
   SELECTED HISTORICAL ESSAYS
   New York 1988

2. DOLORES LIPTAK, R.S.M., EDITOR
   A CHURCH OF MANY CULTURES:
   SELECTED HISTORICAL ESSAYS ON ETHNIC AMERICAN CATHOLICISIM
   New York 1988

3. TIMOTHY J. MEAGHER, EDITOR
   URBAN AMERICAN CATHOLICISM:
   THE CULTURE AND IDENTITY OF THE AMERICAN CATHOLIC PEOPLE
   New York 1988

4. BRIAN MITCHELL, EDITOR
   BUILDING THE AMERICAN CATHOLIC CITY:
   PARISHES AND INSTITUTIONS
   New York 1988

5. MICHAEL J. PERKO, S.J., EDITOR
   ENLIGHTENING THE NEXT GENERATION:
   CATHOLICS AND THEIR SCHOOLS, 1830-1980
   New York 1988

6. WILLIAM PORTIER, EDITOR
   THE ENCULTURATION OF AMERICAN CATHOLICISM, 1820-1900:
   SELECTED HISTORICAL ESSAYS
   New York 1988